VICHY FRANCE

VICHY FRANCE

Old Guard and New Order
1940–1944

ROBERT O. PAXTON

Columbia University Press / New York

Library of Congress Cataloging in Publication Data

Paxton, Robert O.
    Vichy France : old guard and new order, 1940–1944.

    Reprint. Originally published: New York : Knopf, 1972.
    Bibliography: pp. 392–7
    Includes index.
    1. France—Politics and government—1940–1945.
2. France—History—German occupation, 1940–1945.
I. Title.
[DC397.P37   1982]   944.081′6   81-15221
ISBN 0-231-05426-2   AACR2
ISBN 0-231-05427-0 (pbk.)

Columbia University Press   New York
Columbia University Press Morningside Edition 1982
Manufactured in the United States of America

p 10 9 8
c 10 9 8 7 6 5 4 3 2

TO

Henry W. Bragdon

William A. Jenks

James G. Leyburn

Teachers, scholars, exemplars

CONTENTS

ACKNOWLEDGMENTS

More people and institutions have helped with this work than I can readily acknowledge or ever hope to repay. Research in France on several occasions was made possible by the University of California Summer Faculty Fellowship program, the American Philosophical Society, and the Research Council of the State University of New York. The Institute of Social Sciences at the University of California at Berkeley purchased microfilm for me, and the Institute of International Study at Berkeley supported a summer of work in the captured German archives in Washington.

The staffs of several institutions helped me far beyond mere performance of duty: the U.S. National Archives (especially Dr. Robert Wolf), the Hoover Institution (especially Mrs. Agnes Peterson, curator of the Western and Central European Collections), the Centre de Documentation Juive Contemporaine in Paris, and the Bibliothèque de Documentation Internationale et Contemporaine, also in Paris.

Research assistance by Janis Trapans in the German archives, Claudio Segrè in captured Italian archives, and Mrs. Mary Lynn McDougall in social statistics was invaluable. Others whose help was indispensable are M. Henri Noguères of Paris, Warden F. W.

Deakin of Saint Antony's College, Oxford, Professor René Rémond of the Institut d'études politiques in Paris, and Professor Stanley Hoffmann of Harvard. Stanley Hoffmann's perceptions have crept into the very language in which modern France is discussed, on both sides of the Atlantic, to the point where my intellectual debt to him is too pervasive to calculate. More concretely, he read this work in manuscript form and saved me from several *gaffes*. So did Konrad Bieber, Richard F. Kuisel, Arno J. Mayer, and Judith H. Wishnia. I thank them all.

Arlene Jacobs typed a complicated manuscript in record time, and Carol Brown Janeway was a knowledgeable, wise, and sympathetic editor. I am indebted to Enrique Ucelay Da Cal for preparing the index.

These friends and helpers are in no way responsible, of course, for whatever errors, perversities of judgment, or downright idiosyncrasies may appear in this book. Those belong altogether to the author.

INTRODUCTION TO
THE MORNINGSIDE EDITION

By the time I had finished writing an earlier book on the German occupation of France during 1940–44,[1] I had come to feel that most general works about Marshal Pétain and his armistice regime at Vichy were wrong-headed. They regarded all the impetus as coming from victorious Germany, in a way that made Vichy French responses to defeat and occupation appear misleadingly passive—whether as a culpable defeatism (as the Resistance viewed it) or as a prudent caution (as collaborators claimed in justification after the war).

Even a look at Vichy French newspapers belied that perspective. The press of the unoccupied southern zone after June 1940 bubbled with projects for remaking France, some of which were even retained after the liberation of 1944. Study of the archives of the German occupation forces in France rounded out my perspective. As Eberhard Jäckel was showing at about the same time,[2] the German authorities were not much interested in what went on in the southern unoccupied third of France as long as German military security and supplies were assured in the occupied northern zone. It became clear to me that military

---

[1] *Parades and Politics at Vichy* (Princeton, 1966).
[2] *Frankreich in Hitlers Europa* (Stuttgart, 1966).

occupations tell us at least as much about the occupied as about the occupier.

It was not that I had unearthed some great cache of secret documents, although some readers suppose that a new historical interpretation must resemble a treasure hunt. •In fact, French government archives for 1940–44 were not open when I wrote this book. Simply perceiving the Vichy regime as another act in the long French drama of internal conflict opened in 1789 and still raging with the Popular Front election of 1936 allowed much information that was in no way secret to become intelligible. Vichy's internal project—replacing the cosmopolitan and libertarian Republic by an authoritarian, homogeneous, corporatist state—was revenge against the Popular Front more than accommodation to some Nazi blueprint. Vichy's external project—keeping France and the French Empire out of the fighting—was reaction against France's futile bloodletting of 1914–18 and the feared post-war revolution more than obedience to some Hitlerian demand for collaboration. It was Pétain who wanted collaboration; Hitler wanted only booty.

Reactions in France to this book have helped me understand the place of those bitterly divisive years in French self-awareness today. The Vichy regime has been met since the war mostly by embarrassed silence. After the immediate post-war round of trials, purges, and self-justifying memoirs, no major political grouping had any interest in exploring the internal roots of Pétain's policies. The Resisters who controlled the Fourth and early Fifth Republics cherished the image of massive support for de Gaulle from the first hour; the Communist Left wanted to divert attention from its neutralism from 1939 to 1941; conservatives saw Pétain's noble passivity as sabotaged by his prime minister Laval; technocrats rejected any suggestion of Vichy legacy in post-war economic planning and social corporatism. Robert Aron's moderate synthesis of 1954[3] satisfied almost everyone: a point of view largely limited to high politics, all initiatives from the German side, well-meaning but inadequate responses from the aged Marshal Pétain, self-seeking maneuvers

[3] *Histoire de Vichy* (Paris, 1954).

from Laval and a handful of opportunists, and massive resistance from the French people.

In 1973, when my book was translated into French, a new curiosity about Vichy was awakening. In 1966, for the first time in over twenty years, the face of Marshal Pétain had appeared on French newsstands, on the cover of a conservative illustrated monthly, *Le Monde et la vie*. That issue had quickly sold out. It had been followed by a stream of books and articles, quickening as the rebellious young of 1968 seized upon Vichy to belabor their elders.

The new approach to Vichy was more personal and less political than the immediate post-war one. The struggles of ordinary daily lives were the focus of Henri Amouroux' many best-selling volumes of *La Grande Histoire des français sous l'occupation*. It was the sons this time who wrote their memoirs. Pascal Jardin repeatedly evoked his happy childhood at Vichy where his father had served as Laval's chief of staff. Above all, the new generation's curiosity expressed itself in the highly personal medium of film, beginning with Marcel Ophuls' multiple interviews of real people, *The Sorrow and the Pity*. Made for West German television in 1970 but not shown on French television until 1981, it drew crowds to Paris movie houses in 1972.

At their best, the films rejected traditional stereotypes of heroic resisters and evil collaborators to explore the bewilderment of ordinary people and the ambiguity of their various fates after 1940. Ophuls aroused not only sorrow but pity for the manicurist, drawn into collaboration by a love affair with a German soldier and then ostracized when the world turned, and a half-guilty fascination for the well-born adventurer Christian de la Mazière who had volunteered in adolescent enthusiasm for the Waffen-SS. Louis Malle's *Lacombe, Lucien* rejected post-war assumptions about the easy clarity of wartime choices in its tale of an average young rustic who winds up in the French auxiliary to the Gestapo, the Milice, mainly because the local Resistance leader has rejected him as too young.

Other 1970s films, however, recreated Vichy retrospectively as mere spectacle, in what the French call the "mode retro," mere "fragments in the here and now"[4] suggesting that the mixture of humiliation and national powerlessness with recovered opulence in the French experience since 1940 have left many French people without any integrative conception of the recent past. One of the handsomest and most engaging of the Vichy films, Michel Drach's *Les Violons du bal,* managed to clothe the most sordid episode of all, the deportation of Jews, in a pretty nostalgic haze by viewing it through his own eyes as a child.

Arriving in France at a moment of renewed curiosity about Vichy, this book aroused controversy. It offended conservatives who wanted to believe in a double game at Vichy, in which Marshal Pétain's moral order was pitted against Laval's collaborationist deals. Former Vichy Navy Minister Admiral Auphan declared that I could not have understood something that occurred when I was only eight years old. Even some who approved the book fitted it selectively into earlier orthodoxies. *L'Humanité,* for example, praised it as if it were a quite different book, one that attributed Vichy to the pro-Nazi views of a reactionary minority. It has remained normal in France to continue to think of Vichy as something imposed from outside. Even though such films as *Mister Klein* and *Black Thursday* accurately showed French police rounding up Jews for the Germans to deport, for example, they never referred to the Vichy government's own earlier initiatives in anti-Jewish measures. Emotionally, the Vichy regime has not yet been reintegrated into any consistent sense of past.

One reason for this is the telescoping of time. The French public remembers Vichy as it had become by 1944: the last die-hards, clinging to German shelter against the overwhelming condemnation of their fellow citizens. I tried to peel back the successive layers of that fast-evolving epoch to uncover the summer of 1940 in all its raw confusion. An American reader who honestly recreates the way the world looked from France then can not assume that he or she would easily have found the path to a 1944 hero's role. The feckless Republic was discred-

---

[4] Stanley Hoffmann, "Fragments in the Here and Now," *Daedalus,* Winter 1979, pp. 1–26.

ited, and all its values. France's greatest living World War I hero was in charge, and was guiding bold experiments to build a stronger, more united France on the ruins of the 1930s. Flags and ceremonies were beginning to revive national spirits. The handful in London around General de Gaulle looked like accomplices to a British scheme to seize parts of the French Empire, while few could imagine a day when faltering Britain and distant America would set foot on the continent again. Pétain's regime had not yet revealed its exclusive, vindictive side that would by 1942 drive half of France—trade unionists, schoolteachers, civil libertarians, free-thinkers, Masons, and Jews—out of the spontaneous unity of 1940.[5] By 1942, the course of the war was beginning to make Hitler's failure plausible. But even in 1944 it was not always easy for even the most passionately anti-Nazi French man or woman to share Americans' simpler and more optimistic faith that the coming invasion of France was going to bring Europe inevitably to better days through the sheer weight of American weaponry and good will.

It is indeed hard for the two peoples to comprehend each other across the chasm of two such different experiences: recent America, with its "good war" against Hitler and its casual acceptance as normal of its extraordinary post-1945 privileges, and millennial and sceptical France with its long history of ups and downs. Some of the most sobering letters I received from French readers asked me how someone who had known only the facile progress of recent America could presume to judge French responses to a calamity on the scale of that of 1940. Those letters did not change my interpretation of Vichy, but they made me want to make it clearer that this book was not written in a mood of easy moral superiority. Indeed it was written under the shadow of the Vietnam War, which sharpened my animosity to nationalist conformities of all sorts. The comparisons that haunted me when I wrote in the late 1960s were not with the defeated French but with the smugly confident Germans of the summer of 1940.

During the decade since this book appeared the French gov-

---

[5] H. R. Kedward, *Resistance in Vichy France* (Oxford, 1979), explains the beginnings of resistance in the unoccupied zone convincingly in these terms.

ernment has opened some of its archives for the occupation period. Much important new detail unavailable to me then may now be found in such works as Claude Bellanger, Henri Michel, and Claude Lévy, *Histoire générale de la presse française de 1940 à 1958* (Paris, 1975), Isabelle Bouchard, *La Corporation paysanne* (Paris, 1980), W. D. Hall, *The Youth of Vichy France* (Oxford, 1981), Richard Kuisel, *Capitalism and the State in Modern France* (Cambridge, 1981), Michael Marrus and Robert O. Paxton, *Vichy France and the Jews* (New York, 1981), and the forthcoming work by John Sweets on the occupation years in Clermont-Ferrand. There have been penetrating discussion and revealing testimony about the Vichy experience in Stanley Hoffmann, *Decline or Renewal? France Since the 1930s* (New York, 1974) and in the proceedings of two conferences, *Le Gouvernement de Vichy, 1940–44* (Institut d'Etudes Politiques, Paris, 1972), and *Eglises et chrétiens dans la deuxième guerre mondiale,* edited by Xavier de Montclos (Lyon, 1978). While I might alter a detail here and there, I have not been shaken in my main conclusions of a decade ago. At Vichy, a coalition of the losers and victims of the Third French Republic seized the opportunity offered by defeat in 1940 to try to impose their vision of France on a population that was, at least at first, willing if not enthusiastic partners in a "national revolution." These efforts left legacies in post-war French politics, society, economy, and even foreign policy. My view of Marshal Pétain and his regime remains fundamentally critical. But an American who looks honestly at collaborationist France must judge not only with sorrow and pity, but with fear of what his own countrymen might do under equivalent stress.

Gilgo, New York
November 1981

VICHY FRANCE

In the space of several days, we have lost all certainty. We are on a terrifying and irresistible slope. Nothing that we could fear is impossible; we can fear and imagine absolutely anything.

—*Paul Valéry, 18 June 1940*

Prologue: Summer 1940

NO ONE WHO LIVED THROUGH THE FRENCH DEBACLE of May–June 1940 ever quite got over the shock. For Frenchmen, confident of a special role in the world, the six weeks' defeat by German armies was a shattering trauma. For France's allies, her shocking collapse raised doubts about further resistance to Nazism's spread. Even Hitler, whom General Ludwig Beck, chief of the General Staff, had earnestly warned in 1938 that the French Army was "still the strongest in Europe," [1] found himself casting about, after that much-photographed jig of triumph at the armistice-signing ceremony at Rethondes on June 25, for further plans. No one had imagined that German armies could reach the Pyrenees in a mere six weeks. The shock of this feat was all the more devastating.

This is not another book about why France fell. It is about what Frenchmen decided to do next. The two questions are hard to separate, of course. One of the first things they had to do was

---

[1] Wolfgang Förster, *Ein General Kämpft gegen den Krieg* (Munich, 1949), 84, 86, 92. A *New York Times* editorial expressed a similar opinion on 7 May 1938.

to find someone to blame for the fall. Frenchmen of the Liberation charged Vichy Frenchmen with having wanted or even
helped a German victory in order to further their reactionary
schemes. Vichy Frenchmen charged the Popular Front, "mon-
strous alliance of Muscovite Communism, Masonic radicalism,
and Jewish finance," with having "precipitated France into an
ideological war, after having weakened her." [2] The Left's mental
image of the defeat was profascist officers fleeing to the rear in
staff cars and profascist politicians stepping forward to take
over the government. The Right's mental image of the defeat was
the fatal panic on May 13 of the 55th and 71st Infantry Divisions
which allowed the German panzers to cross the Meuse near
Sedan, Paris-based divisions thought to contain large numbers of
Communist troops. Punishing the guilty—two sets of them—was
a large part of what Frenchmen wanted to do next, in 1940 and
again in 1944–46.

But it is no longer very enlightening to treat the defeat and
the subsequent Vichy regime as treason or cabal. As for the
defeat, the most convincing studies of the campaign on both sides
make it clear that the outcome is explicable in classical military
terms: troops stretched too thinly along the Meuse facing the
Ardennes, where the main German attack actually fell; slow
communications, which hampered French realization of where
the main German thrust lay; obsolete tactics which wasted excellent tanks and artillery in static line defense; and sagging
morale. Indirectly, that flabby descendant of the French Army
of 1918 was the product of French politics and society, of course,
but direct political or conspiratorial causes—treason, Fifth
Columns, insufficient or poor matériel, Communist or Fascist
refusal to fight—were peripheral influences or, at any rate, were
unnecessary to explain the outcome. [3]

[2] Jean Berthelot, speech to railroad workers, 21 August 1941. *Ministère
public c/ Berthelot,* 140.
[3] The most authoritative study of German campaign records, Hans-
Adolf Jacobsen, *Fall Gelb* (Wiesbaden, 1957), recalls how risky the German plan was and how nervous the leaders were. The most convincing
French study, Colonel A. Goutard, *1940: La Guerre des occasions perdues*
(Paris, 1955), makes the possibilities of another Marne more genuine than
used to be thought. The latest account of the good numbers and superior
quality of French tanks is R. H. S. Stolfi, "Equipment for Victory in

Nor was the new regime a mere cabal. I shall try to show that it enjoyed mass support and elite participation. Its programs drew less from German and Italian models than from long-festering French internal conflicts. It is easy to show, of course, that some Frenchmen had received German and especially Italian secret funds in the late 1930's: impecunious journalists like Frédéric Le Grix, league leaders like Jacques Doriot, hired assassins like Jean Filliol and his accomplices who killed the Rosselli brothers for Mussolini in 1937. There were outspoken fascist sympathizers, like the young novelists Robert Brasillach and Pierre Drieu la Rochelle. But those were not the men who made the decisions of 1940. Although it has been dramatic as well as expedient to treat the new regime of 1940 as an alien cabal,[4] twenty years of access to the Axis archives have turned up little to substantiate a conspiratorial thesis. Even the prosecution in Pétain's trial in 1945 quietly toned down the initial charge of "a plot formed long in advance against the Republic" to the more anodyne final accusation that he did nothing to stop the speculations around his name in the late 1930's.[5] Similar elements existed in England in the late 1930's as well, and if the Battle of Britain had been fought with the same effect as the British land campaign in Flanders in 1940, no doubt these elements would be the subject of an equally popular conspiratorial history of the fall of England. The Third Republic background is vital to understanding the decisions of 1940, but that background has to do with more fundamental social, economic, and political matters than a few disgruntled novelists and foreign agents.

France in 1940," *History,* vol. 55, no. 183 (February 1970), 1–20. The old clichés about French material inferiority still apply to only one sector, albeit a crucial one: aviation. Even here the vulnerable Stuka played a diminishing role, and new Allied planes were coming on the line at the end. France was more vulnerable in 1940 than she had been in 1914, but defeat was by no means a foregone conclusion.

[4] Fifth column literature is an apparently irresistible genre. It runs from Albert Bayet, *Pétain et la 5e colonne* (Paris, 1944), to Max Gallo, *La Cinquième colonne* (Paris, 1970). Louis de Jong, *The German Fifth Column in the Second World War* (Chicago, 1956), disposes of most of these legends.

[5] *Le Procès du maréchal Pétain,* Albin Michel edition (Paris, 1945), 31–33, 117 ff.

I have chosen to begin, then, with military defeat an accomplished fact in metropolitan France. The last government of the Third Republic was formed constitutionally, but not calmly, at Bordeaux around midnight of the night of June 16–17 for the purpose of asking what German peace terms would be. The Third Republic forms were observed, but once that threshold had been crossed, everything was bathed in a new light. Outgoing Premier Paul Reynaud proposed Marshal Pétain as his successor and prepared to serve the new government as ambassador to the United States. President Albert Lebrun gave Marshal Pétain his charge to form a cabinet. The new government's composition was a recognizable example of Third Republic *union nationale*. It ranged from conservatives through socialists, with SFIO deputies Albert Rivière and André-Louis Février officially participating. Only those adamantly opposed to an armistice feeler were excluded, from conservative Georges Mandel to Radical Pierre Cot. The Pétain government's formation on June 17 was a big step out of the war but a hardly perceptible step out of republican legality. By such modest steps, and not by conspiracy, a major part of the French masses and elite came to participate in an unforeseen new political world.

Defeat is a state of mind, however. To the last moment and beyond, some members of the Reynaud government had grappled with finding ways to continue fighting. The British and French troops brought off the beach at Dunkirk at the beginning of June had been brought back to man a "Breton redoubt," but when General Alan Brooke arrived at Rennes on June 13 to oversee the deployment of British troops with the French command, German forces had already crossed the Seine between Paris and the sea, and the plans had been submerged by the torrent of events.

Far more promising was the project to continue the war from French North Africa. There, on soil reckoned an integral part of France, General Noguès' forces were "burning" to fight, as he wired the commander in chief, General Weygand, on June 18. They expected powerful reinforcement from an intact French Navy, the new Dewoitine D520 fighter planes just coming into service, other planes and equipment already en route from the

United States, and whatever could be brought away from metro-politan France to create a vast Mediterranean Dunkirk. Even with Spanish and Italian help, and despite North Africa's poverty as a supply base, it is hard to imagine the German Navy, ill-equipped for amphibious operations, transporting an army to Africa against the combined British and French fleets.[6]

The transfer actually began. Even after Pétain had been named premier to make a peace feeler, the cabinet voted on June 19 for part of the government and all the assemblies to go to Morocco, as Bordeaux was threatened with German capture even before the negotiations could begin. Then the climate shifted and the epithet "émigré" began to be heard. Eventually a diehard remnant of twenty-nine deputies and one senator sailed from Bordeaux aboard a chartered liner, the *Massilia,* on June 21. The Mediterranean squadron was at Mers-el-Kebir, on the Algerian coast, and nearly a thousand pilots flew their planes across in the last days.

There were valid alternatives to an armistice, therefore, and they were Hitler's nightmare. A belligerent French Army in North Africa would have dangerously dispersed Axis military efforts in the summer of 1940, offsetting the advantages of total occupation of the continent. Indeed, Hitler saw that total occu-pation as a liability. His lenient armistice proposals, he told Mussolini on June 17, were intended to forestall "the situation in which the French government might reject the German pro-posals, then flee abroad to London to continue the war from there, quite apart from the unpleasant responsibility which the occupying powers would have to assume, among others, in the administrative sphere."[7]

Hitler was spared those pains. The alternatives to an armistice

---

[6] Gen. André Truchet, *L'Armistice de 1940 et l'Afrique du Nord* (Paris, 1955), makes the most thorough case for fighting on from North Africa. General Weygand argued to the end of his life that such a course was suicidal. See his *En lisant les mémoires du général de Gaulle* (Paris, 1955), 91. The Noguès telegrams are in *Ministère public c/ General Noguès,* 26.)

[7] *Documents on German Foreign Policy* [*DGFP*] Series D, vol. IX, no. 479, p. 608. Berlin was also kept informed through the German ambas-sador at Madrid of French plans to move the government to North Africa.

were not so much decided against as they became unthinkable. The Reynaud government never voted formally on the choice between armistice and a fight to the finish. The hawks probably feared putting things to a vote. The proposal around which a consensus formed at Bordeaux, Vice-Premier Camille Chautemps' suggestion on June 16 that they inquire about German terms in order to have more information, was in fact a decision not to decide. The heart was out of it, and it would have taken a miracle of inspiration or coercion for Reynaud or anyone else to have led a fight to the finish. In the absence of any clear decision, the deepest priorities came into play. At bottom, a fight to the finish was unthinkable in terms of those priorities, and they formed the general climate in which the new regime could germinate.

> *Or what king, going to encounter another king in war, will not sit down first and take counsel whether he is able with ten thousand to meet him who comes against him with twenty thousand? And if not, while the other is yet a great way off, he sends an embassy and asks terms of peace.*
>
> —*Luke 14:31–2 (the Gospel for Sunday, 23 June 1940)* [8]

FOR THERE IS SIMPLY NO MISTAKING THE JOY AND relief which came flooding after the anguish when Marshal Pétain announced over the radio, shortly after noon on June 17, that the government he had formed the night before was seeking an armistice. "With a heavy heart, I tell you today that it is necessary to stop the fighting." Without waiting for the actual negotiations, soldiers and civilians simply made peace themselves. General Erwin Rommel, plunging toward Brittany almost unopposed that day, found French soldiers standing along the road thinking that the armistice had taken immediate effect (the negotiators didn't even set out from Bordeaux until June 20; the armistice took effect on June 25). Those who wanted to fight on suddenly seemed to threaten awakened hopes of survival. When all cities over twenty thousand were declared "open" on

[8] Robert Brasillach, *Journal d'un homme occupé* (Paris, 1955), chap. 1.

June 18 to avoid useless destruction, smaller towns and their mayors eagerly followed suit. The soldiers and civilians in Sartre's novel *La Mort dans l'âme* who tried to keep Mathieu from his last-ditch resistance had plenty of historical counterparts. At Vierzon, at the crossing of the Cher River, the populace killed a tank officer who wanted to try to hold the bridges. A Colonel Charly, who ordered his troops to fight their way out of an encirclement near the Maginot Line on June 20, was shot by his men, who feared that "he's going to have us all massacred."[9] As for opponents of the armistice at the top, Reynaud (if he still opposed the armistice at all) had been in an automobile accident on his way to Spain, and Georges Mandel was in Morocco trying to get in touch with the British. Charles de Gaulle recalled bitterly in his memoirs that "not a single public figure raised his voice to condemn the armistice."[10] These painful memories are worth reviving only to emphasize that the armistice was no minority plot.

It is easy, of course, to contemplate the sterner alternative of last-ditch resistance years later in the safety of an academic study. In retrospect, it was almost certainly the correct policy to fight on. Those who would have paid the cost had been scorched by Blitzkrieg, however, and wanted no more of the fire. War to the finish seemed to make no strategic sense at the time. It was easy to believe that the German forces that had smashed the proud French Army were not likely to be stopped by the British, whose army had contributed far less in 1940 than in 1914. Most of the leading figures in France were convinced that the final peace conference was a matter of weeks or months away,[11] what-

[9] *The Rommel Papers*, ed. B. H. Liddell Hart (New York, 1953), 69–73. The Vierzon case is recounted in Gen. André Beaufre, *Le Drame de quarante* (Paris, 1965), 265; contemporary press coverage of the trial of Colonel Charly's killers in 1949 may be found in William L. Shirer, *The Collapse of the Third Republic* (New York, 1969), 875–6. The parliamentary committee investigating the war and prewar years looked into a number of such cases. *Evénements survenus en France de 1933 à 1940*, II, 384–404.

[10] Charles de Gaulle, *War Memoirs*, I, 73.

[11] *Foreign Relations of the United States* [*FRUS*], 1940, II, *passim*, and especially William C. Bullitt's telegram of 1 July 1940 in which various French leaders predicted a speedy British collapse, 462 ff.

ever the remnants of French forces did. The Germans had rediscovered the short war of movement so sought after in World War I, and the war was over. French actions spoke even louder than words about their expectation of an early peace. After all, Pétain's government had inquired about peace terms, not just armistice terms, when Foreign Minister Paul Baudouin relayed his message through Spanish Ambassador Lequerica shortly after midnight on the night of June 16–17.[12] A mere armistice was second best, but it in no way changed expectations of a peace conference later that summer in which France would receive somewhat more lenient terms than if she had fought to the finish. As Pétain was to tell Hitler on October 24, he hoped the peace would "favor those who had tried to make a new start."[13] Texts of French armistice legislation also obviously anticipated a brief armistice and an early peace. The pension arrangements for officers who could not serve in a small temporary "Armistice Army," for example, were scheduled to last only three months. Wladimir d'Ormesson, French ambassador to the Vatican, was trying to interest the Papacy in a peace plan based upon a Catholic Latin bloc, including France, Italy, Spain, and Portugal. On their side, German Foreign Office officials were at work on quite different Franco-German peace terms.[14] Despite postwar claims that the armistice was intended as a brief respite before

---

[12] Paul Baudouin's postwar denials are contradicted by the contemporary texts. See Col. A. Goutard, "Comment et pourquoi l'armistice a-t-il été 'accordé' par les allemands," *Revue de Paris,* vol. 67 (October 1960), and Baudouin and Goutard letters in the subsequent two issues. The text of Baudouin's inquiry as relayed from Madrid to Berlin may be consulted in the archives of the German Foreign Office, Büro des Staatssekretärs, "Beziehungen zwischen Frankreich und Deutschland," vol. 2, (T-120/121/119600). Material from microfilmed German archives will hereafter be cited in this form: U.S. National Archives Series (e.g. T-120)/serial (e.g. 121)/frame (e.g. 119600).

[13] *DGFP,* Series D, XI, no. 227, 385 ff. Camille Chautemps told William C. Bullitt on July 1 that Pétain, Laval, and Weygand thought France would get easier peace terms if she set up some kind of dictatorship. *FRUS,* 1940, II, 468.

[14] Ministère de la guerre, *Bulletin officiel* (1940), 1100, 1112; *Actes et documents du Saint-Siège relatifs à la seconde guerre mondiale* (Vatican City, 1967), IV, 97; Büro des Staatssekretärs, "Friedensverhandlungen mit Frankreich" (T-120/365,368,378).

returning to war against Germany,[15] every contemporary sign points to overwhelming acceptance of two strategic assumptions: the war was over, and Germany had won.

Fighting to the finish was worse than militarily futile, moreover; it seemed socially suicidal. Frenchmen had gone to war in the first place, in September 1939, with anything but enthusiasm. Since the German menace had first taken clear form, with the denunciation in March 1935 of the arms limitations provisions of the Versailles Treaty and the remilitarization of the Rhineland in March 1936, the possibility of war against Hitler aroused mixed emotions. To several groups in French opinion, the putative cure seemed worse than the disease. Broad groups of conservatives whom Charles Micaud has called "resigned nationalists"[16] believed that war against Germany could only serve Stalin, by destroying his main enemy in the West and by undermining the European social structure. After the strike wave of May–June 1936 and the electoral victory of the Popular Front had raised fear of Communist revolution in France to hysteria, fighting Hitler came to seem "a war where the interests of France are not at stake but only those of International Communism."[17] The "resigned nationalists" were supplemented by two marginal groups with little else in common: a few outright Nazi sympathizers (a very small group indeed, and not necessarily part of the traditional Right), and some traditional pacifists on the Left who had not swung with Blum and Thorez from antimilitarism to armed antinazism. Still others felt a non-ideological dread of war spurred by new weapons and the frightening dynamism of the new Germany. War meant poison gas and the bombing of cities. Paris would be worse than Guernica.

Further, any Frenchman over thirty remembered the blind wastage of young men in 1914–18, which had made France a

[15] E.g., General Weygand, *Mémoires*, III. *Rappelé au service* (Paris, 1957).

[16] Charles A. Micaud, *The French Right and Nazi Germany* (Durham, N.C., 1943), 97–9.

[17] Video, "L'Armée et la politique," *Action française*, 25 August 1936. I owe this reference to Mr. Lawrence Abrams.

nation of old people and cripples. That stark fact was brought home daily by the sight of mutilated veterans in the street. It took on particular urgency in the middle 1930's with the advent of the "hollow years," the moment when, as demographers had predicted, the annual draft contingent dropped in half because so few boys had been born in 1915–19. One more bloodbath, and would there be a France at all? Céline simply put it more crudely than the others. He predicted twenty-five million casualties and the "end of the breed."

> We'll disappear body and soul from this place like the Gauls. . . .
> They left us hardly twenty words of their own language. We'll be
> lucky if anything more than the word "merde" survives us.[18]

That was why France did not declare war on Germany until several hours after the British, on 3 September 1939. There were two negative votes on the Conseil supérieur de guerre (Generals Condé and Prételat) and massive gloom among civilians. The declaration of war came only after agonizing days of negotiation, in which Foreign Minister Georges Bonnet and his supporters clung passionately to the hope of another Munich through the good offices of Mussolini. The nagging suspicion remained that the war was not necessary.[19]

No doubt, if Hitler had been defeated in his daring and over-exposed tank thrust across northern France, those doubts would have been dispersed as quickly as they were in England. But with France defeated, doubts came flooding back magnified into a vengeful "I told you so." The prewar fear that Stalin's war would spawn revolution took on terrifying concreteness. French society began to come apart at the seams.

In the north and east of France, half the country turned nomad. "All Belgium and Artois are on the road," wrote Paul Valéry, who left Paris for Dinard ahead of the Germans around

[18] Louis-Ferdinand Céline, *L'Ecole des cadavres* (Paris, 1938), 78–79. P. E. Flandin predicted a million casualties in his campaign against war over Czechoslovakia in September 1938.

[19] A. J. P. Taylor's controversial *Origins of the Second World War* (London, 1961), was the first postwar attempt to place scholarly support behind a popular attitude that has been much more widespread in France since 1940 than it ever was in England or the United States.

June 10. "The impression of living, poignant disorder. Every possible conveyance, carts stuffed with blond children in the straw. They don't know, nobody knows, where they are going." [20] Perhaps the most familiar image of that hellish June was the millions of refugees, Belgian and French, military and civilian, who clogged the roads in the last days, strafed by Italian fighter planes, harassed by each other's desperation. Their lemminglike swarm for survival reduced them to a Hobbesian war of all against all. Sartre's description in *La Mort dans l'âme* of Sarah and her child, browbeaten and cheated by their taxi driver who has run out of gas on the jammed road, was not contrived. The Norman town of Evreux scattered before the invader, leaving only 172 persons out of a normal 20,000 there on June 11. A week later there were only 218, and on June 30, still only 6,800. Even on July 15, nearly three weeks after the armistice, the population was about half of what it had been before the "exodus." This example could be repeated many times over, except that refugees from Alsace-Lorraine and from the "forbidden zone" adjacent to those provinces were not allowed to go home at all.[21]

While some public officials clung to their posts as the German tide rolled over them, others joined the exodus. René Bousquet, second-ranking official in the Prefecture of the Marne at Reims, recalled that his whole office had "fallen back" to Albi, within sight of the Pyrenees, by the end of June 1940 [22]—one example among many. Essential services ground to a halt.

As soon as the French government itself vacated Paris on June 10, rumors of a Paris Soviet began to spread. No one knows today for certain whether General Weygand's report to the cabinet meeting on June 13 at the Loire chateau of Cangé that the Communists had seized Paris and installed Jacques Duclos in the Elysée Palace was a ruse or a "genuine" rumor. It is clear enough that the desire to save the French Army as a guarantee of order had a lot to do with Weygand's pressing arguments for

[20] Paul Valéry, *Cahiers,* vol. 233 (Paris, 1960), 307.

[21] For Evreux, see Marcel Baudot, *L'Opinion publique sous l'occupation* (Paris, 1960), which, despite its title, studies a single department, the Eure. Jean Vidalenc, *L'Exode de mai–juin 1940* (Paris, 1947), estimates a total of ten million refugees.

[22] *Ministère public c/ Bousquet.*

an armistice. But it was not merely officers who expected a repeat of 1871. "Shall we escape revolution?" wrote Father Teilhard de Chardin on 18 June. "Everything is possible after such a shock." [23]

The German occupation of Paris on June 14 was not altogether reassuring on this point. After all, Hitler and Stalin were allies, and there were national socialist ideologues like Dr. Friedrich Grimm among the first German occupation authorities who dabbled with winning over the French Communist party by stressing their shared enmities: priests, Jews, and the upper middle class.[24] German Ambassador Otto Abetz himself seems to have encouraged these contacts. In Berlin, however, the rumors of good Nazi-Communist relations at Paris were as scandalous as they were at Vichy, and the Germans soon rejected the party's efforts to resume publication of *Humanité* and to continue its neutralist propaganda of 1939. But not until June 1941 did Vichy really abandon a vague uneasiness about some strange Nazi-Soviet combine in Paris.[25]

It was Marshal Pétain who won fervent gratitude as "the leader who saved us from the abyss." [26] In truth, there was rather an instinctive shrinking from chaos that made war to the end against Germany simply unthinkable. The final weapon of a people whose conventional army has disintegrated is chaos. Fighting on from abroad would mean not only the agonies of

[23] P. C. F. Bankwitz, "Maxime Weygand and the Fall of France," *Journal of Modern History* 31:3 (September 1959). U.S. Ambassador William C. Bullitt also expected a Communist rising in Paris; see Gordon Wright, "Ambassador Bullitt and the Fall of France," *World Politics* 10:1 (October 1957), 63–90. Pierre Teilhard de Chardin, *Letters to Two Friends, 1926–1952* (New York, 1968), 145.

[24] Memorandum by Dr. Friedrich Grimm, 19 June 1940 (Centre de Documentation Juive Contemporaine, Paris, document no. LXXV-253.) The Centre is abbreviated hereafter as CDJC.

[25] For Abetz, see Dr. Best memorandum, 17 August 1940 (CDJC, document no. LXXV-152); *The Halder Diaries,* 10, 11, 15, 26 August 1940, report with alarm Abetz' reputed deals with French Communists. The party's efforts to resume activity in Paris in the summer of 1940 are very widely reported, in hostile sources. See A. Rossi, *Physiologie du parti communiste français* (Paris, 1948), 395–410, for the fullest account.

[26] The phrase is Jean Berthelot's, from his May Day speech, 1941. *Ministère public c/ Jean Berthelot.*

total occupation for mainland France (and every Frenchman was nurtured on stories of German atrocities in Belgium during World War I). It also meant accepting reprisals upon mainland Frenchmen for acts of war committed by other Frenchmen overseas. It meant guerrilla warfare on the mainland, the conscious provocation of disorder, the replacement of established administration by vigilantes, and a deliberate policy of making the occupation costlier for everyone. It was probably the right choice. But it would be a hard choice for any comfortable people. It was an unthinkable choice for a people fighting its second war in less than a quarter century, haunted by the specter of revolution behind every crisis: 1871, 1917, 1936.

To use chaos itself as the ultimate weapon, a people must have been stripped of the comforts of property and the solace of routine irrevocably enough to have renounced them, but not quite to the point of passivity. When the United States Air Force studied the effectiveness of its World War II bombing of civilian populations in Germany, it discovered that after Hamburg had been reduced to rubble, its productivity actually increased—unessential, labor-wasting frivolities had been burned away. France, by contrast, had been stunned and demoralized but not spartanized by the quickest but least destructive of her twentieth-century home wars. French cities had not been systematically bombed, as London was about to be, nor had wide areas of her soil been reduced to a no-man's-land, as in 1914–18. As a complacent German officer remarked to Jacques Benoist-Méchin in July 1940, "The offensive was so rapid that it killed the war." [27] Like householders after an earthquake, Frenchmen turned to salvaging their shaken affairs and keeping thieves out.

The men who made the armistice were quite explicit about the dangers of disorder if the war went on. Chaos was something to be prevented, not exploited as the ultimate weapon against Hitler. The danger of moving the government overseas, Marshal Pétain told the cabinet at Cangé on June 13, when he was still

[27] U.S. Strategic Bombing Survey, as quoted in J. K. Galbraith, *The Affluent Society* (New York: Mentor, 1963), 131–3; Jacques Benoist-Méchin, *La Moisson de quarante* (Paris, 1941), 67.

minister without portfolio in Reynaud's government, was that an émigré government "might not be recognized as such." What might fill the vacuum in mainland France?

> To deprive France of her natural defenders in a period of general disorder is to deliver her to the enemy, it is to kill the soul of France —it is, consequently, to make her revival impossible. . . . We must expect French revival much more from the soul of our country, which we will preserve by staying in place, than by the reconquest of our territory by allied cannon, under conditions and after a delay impossible to foresee.[28]

By "natural defenders" of French society, Marshal Pétain meant the administrative carapace of France, from ministry down through prefect to village mayor, buttressed by police and army. The personnel of these agencies made it a matter of professional honor to serve. The new regime was the lawful successor of the old, and there was work to be done. Moreover, according to a Hobbesian-Napoleonic view deeply rooted in French public service, the state was no mere instrument of a sovereign general will nor an arbiter among people but a positive good in itself, the bearer of values greater than the sum of individuals who made it up. It had to be kept running. To what horrors would Frenchmen be exposed by the eclipse of the state? Loyal service to the state was a frequent Vichy alibi at the postwar trials, of course, but it permeates Vichy participants' arguments so disingenuously that it is obviously an unfeigned reflection of priorities at work in 1940.

At his trial, René Bousquet, prefect of the Marne in 1940 and later Laval's chief of police, defended his efforts to restore France's "armature" in the summer of 1940. He didn't touch politics, he asserted in a typical civil servant's denial that administration is support of a policy. Insisting that it was "not heroic to flee," he argued that it was necessary to work with the Germans to restore the necessary order for survival. His pride was evident when he claimed to have "restored normal functions" in the Marne by July 17. Pierre Angéli, prefect of the Finistère in 1940 and later regional prefect at Lyon, praised the

---

[28] General Emile Laure, *Pétain* (Paris, 1941), 432.

loyalty of the prefects of 1940, not one of whom resigned. They understood, he said in his final defense in the trial at Lyon in November 1944, that prefects have a sort of "cure of souls" [*charge d'âmes*]. The "pride of the prefectoral corps" was their constancy in safeguarding the essential elements of national sovereignty and easing the physical rigors of the occupation.[29] Yves Bouthillier, senior treasury official whom Paul Reynaud brought into his war cabinet in May 1940 and who went on to be Pétain's finance minister for the first two years, put the civil servants' case succinctly in his postwar memoirs. "Orderly activity in the presence of the occupying authority was the best kind of civic spirit." [30]

Civil servants' sense of the state was reinforced by a general thirst for normalcy in the summer of 1940. Many who would later become the very antithesis of Vichy supporters were still sorting out the wreckage of their lives in the summer of 1940. Simone de Beauvoir, for example, describes vividly the emotional daze in which she hitchhiked back to Paris in July. She achieved some feeling of control over her life only by going back to teaching in a girls' *lycée* in Paris, even though that meant eventually taking the teachers' oath to Pétain.

> For three weeks now I have been in a sort of limbo: vast public events brought their own individual, physiological agony, but I wanted to become a *person* again, with a past and a future of my own. Perhaps here in Paris I shall achieve this aim. If I can draw my salary, I shall stay for a long time.[31]

Jean Guéhenno, for whom the regime's values were anathema, found solace in his lycée professorate in Paris, even submitting to taking the oath to Pétain, until Education Minister Abel Bonnard demoted him to other duties in September 1943.[32]

Nearly everyone tried to get normal life going again. Refugees

[29] Haute Cour de Justice, *Ministère public c/ Bousquet*, 38–58; Cour de Justice de Lyon, *Ministère public c/ Angéli*, 100.

[30] Yves Bouthillier, *Le Drame de l'armistice* (Paris, 1950), II. *Les Finances sous la contrainte*, 245–47.

[31] Simone de Beauvoir, *La Force de l'âge* (Paris, 1960), 459–72.

[32] Jean Guéhenno, *Journal des années noires* (Paris, 1947), 11 September 1943.

made their way home or sought shelter in a safer place. Families tried to get in touch. Around two million young Frenchmen in prisoner-of-war camps on French soil anxiously awaited release. A flood of job applicants wrote to Marshal Pétain. Alarmed at the level of unemployment, French economic officials worked to revive the economy. Businessmen turned to German Army contracts. Gaston Bruneton, for example, went to the German military headquarters in Paris in July and got an advance for making airfield matting for the Luftwaffe.[33] *Le Temps* and *Le Figaro* made temporary arrangements to use printing presses in Lyons and Clermont-Ferrand, while *Action française* borrowed the presses of the *Courrier du Centre* at Limoges.

The government itself struggled to get out of provisional quarters and back to Paris. It never expected to be stuck permanently in the southern mountain spa of Vichy. Having remained one jump ahead of the German armies through the chateaux of the Loire to Bordeaux, the government had to move again. Bordeaux was threatened by the German advance guard by June 18 and was bombed on the 20th. When the armistice was signed, Bordeaux was in the Occupied Zone. More suitable temporary quarters had to be found. Something was wrong with all the major southern cities. Some, like Marseilles and Perpignan, were too close to the temptations of emigration. Others were the fiefs of powerful Third Republic figures. Lyons had been under the thumb of its mayor, Radical leader Édouard Herriot, since 1905, as was Toulouse under the Radical Sarraut dynasty. Pierre Laval owned the newspaper and radio station of Clermont-Ferrand. Vichy was a negative choice: the most hotel rooms in the center of France and no dominant political fiefdom. It was to this rococo cure center for liverish bourgeois, then, that the ministers, deputies, and senators straggled after the armistice took effect on June 25.

At Vichy, government offices commandeered the hotels,

---

[33] See the German police report of 23 August 1940 (Nuremberg document NG-5418); for Bruneton—only one example out of many, but made public in a postwar trial because he later served as commissioner for French labor in Germany—see Haute Cour de Justice, *Ministère public c/ Bruneton,* 4.

packed filing cabinets into baths and dressing rooms, and replaced beds with desks. There was no need to arrange central heating, however, for the government was sure to be back in Paris before the frost. The armistice agreement said so (Article 3), and in any event the armistice arrangements would soon give way to peace negotiations. American representatives following the government were told on July 14 that the government would move to Paris around the 20th.[34] The government, no less than its citizens, itched to get back into some settled routine.

So there was a kind of tacit accord between Hitler's hopes for an economical armistice and French longing for a quick return to orderly life. The armistice rested upon that shared interest. "Collaboration," the word and the thing, already appears in the armistice document. Article 3 provides that the French government assist the German authorities in exercising the "rights of an occupying power" in the Occupied Zone. In particular, it orders French officials and public services to "conform to the decisions of the German authorities and collaborate faithfully with them." Fateful word. *Collaboration,* a banal term for working together, was to become a synonym for high treason after the occupation had run on for four years. The most elementary promptings of normalcy in the summer of 1940, the urge to return to home and job, started many Frenchmen down a path of everyday complicity that led gradually and eventually to active assistance to German measures undreamed of in 1940. Delivering the mail, repairing bridges, teaching school, relocating refugees—everything that restored France to tranquillity and order fulfilled the tacit Franco-German bargain to withdraw France from the war, socially intact, and to turn her energies inward.

The month of June 1940 marked in our country's history a crisis in the face of which each person today must rethink his position. . . .

[34] U.S. Department of State Serial File 851.01/82. Heating was hurriedly patched up in late October. See *ibid.,* 740.0011 Eur War 1939/552.

We are among the few who have been proclaiming since 1932 the necessity of a total revolution. That was not for us just another opinion among many; it was the very meaning and vocation of our twenties.

—*Emmanuel Mounier, November 1940* [35]

BUT VICHY WAS MORE THAN A REPAIR JOB. YVES Bouthillier's eloquent postwar defense of the policy of "presence" in the summer of 1940, the administrator's dutiful serving of his suffering people's most elementary needs, conflicts with what he told Otto Abetz in September 1940. When he first crossed the Demarcation Line to Paris to meet the German ambassador, he eagerly forecast "a new economic and social order." [36] Vichy was not a Band-Aid. It was deep surgery. To an extent unique among the occupied nations of Western Europe, France went beyond mere administration during the occupation to carry out a domestic revolution in institutions and values.

For it was unthinkable simply to put things back the way they had been. In losing the war, the Third Republic had lost its legitimacy. No modern French regime has survived a military defeat, and even the *ancien régime* was mortally wounded by defeat in the Seven Years' War. Since war had become total, defeat was felt as a reproach to every man. That self-reproach was abnormally bitter in 1940—far bitterer, say, than the recriminations that followed the Prussian defeat of the Second Empire in 1870. For it mingled with a mood of national self-doubt that had been brewing since the 1890's, and it followed twenty years of disappointment with the fruits of the victory of 1918. The moral and psychic wounds were even more tender than the material ones in France in the summer of 1940.

France had been the most powerful and most populous western kingdom under Louis XIV, the greatest nation in Europe under Napoleon, one great power among several under Na-

---

[35] *Esprit,* 8e année, no. 94 (November 1940).
[36] Der Vertreter des Auswärtiges Amts beim Oberbefehlshaber des Heeres, "Frankreich." "Aufzeichnungen über politische Besprechungen in der Zeit vom 6. bis 15. September 1940." (T-120/364/206021 ff).

poleon III and Clemenceau, and now—what? It was easy to link this decline to social and moral decadence, for it was the census in 1891 and 1896 that first called attention to the low French birthrate while other peoples, notably Germans, were increasing rapidly. Alarm over the French birthrate and other expressions of national vitality had never really abated since the time of Maurice Barrès' "novel of national energy" of 1897 and Gabriel Hanotaux's *L'Energie nationale* of 1902. That sense of decay returned, magnified tenfold by the defeat of 1940 and ripened by sixty years of habit. With morbid fascination, Frenchmen of 1940 turned over the stones of their national life and contemplated the crawling things, real or imaginary, that they believed festered there.

In this mood of self-flagellation, as in Jacques Benoist-Méchin's description of German soldiers amazed at French farms in which "everything seemed to have stopped fifty years ago," [37] the myth of the German stroll through nonexistent French defenses became established. And with it, a repudiation of the Third Republic and a thirst for something different.

"Too few allies, too few weapons, too few babies." Pétain's lapidary formula for defeat in his June 20 speech carried the debate deftly from the realms of foreign policy and military doctrine to the realm of social decadence. A wide range of other Frenchmen followed in his train of thought. It was only to be expected that the antiparliamentarians of the Right, having long identified electoral politics with decay, would cry vindication in such works as Charles Maurras' *La Seule France* (1941) or Henri Massis' *Les Idées restent* (1941). Nor was it surprising that younger and angrier rebels should exult in the wreckage of the tired, old, boring middle-class France which they had been mocking since their student days in the 1930's. The two angriest novels to appear under the occupation, Lucien Rebatet's *Les Décombres* and Céline's *Les Beaux draps,* took a ferocious joy in destruction that was an extension of the antibourgeois hatred of the 1930's younger right. What is notable is how vigorously

[37] *La Moisson de quarante* (Paris, 1941), 105.

others, who stood far outside the 1930's far right, joined in the exposure of decadence. Even after the regime's anti-Semitic bent was clear, the Jewish essayist Daniel Halévy, long troubled by the replacement of organic rural societies by faceless urban masses, hailed the new regime's return to "verities . . . under the ashes and wreckage of defeat." [38] Paul Valéry, soon to lose his job as director of the University Center at Nice, was already using the words "old regime" for the Third Republic in his notebooks at the end of June. "The war was lost during the peace," he wrote. André Gide, who had taken up rereading Zola's novel about the Franco-Prussian War, *La débâcle,* on June 26, filled his diary with reflections on French "decomposition," the "excessive freedom," the "sorry reign of indulgence" that was being brought to an end. "All my love for France could not keep me from being aware of our country's state of decay." [39] François Mauriac bridled in the columns of *Figaro* at those who dared speak of hope at such a time. France must recognize her humiliation and accept the "repose of the bottom of the abyss." The Germans deserved to win, wrote Teilhard de Chardin on 3 August, for no matter how bad or mixed their spirit, they had more spirit than the France which had been stuck in the old routines since 1919. [40]

Each had his own diagnosis of the rot. Some looked to superficial signs, like jazz, alcohol, Paris night life, short skirts, moral depravity among the young, birth control. Enjoyment itself was blamed for softening the nation: the "spirit of facility," the "cult of ease." Intellectuals had mocked sacred institutions: Léon Blum had written a youthful work ridiculing marriage. Jean Cocteau's play *Les parents terribles* had undermined the authority of fathers. Most of all, André Gide had opened the way to libertine

[38] Daniel Halévy, "Le réformateur inconnu," *Le Temps,* 18 August 1940. See also Alain Silvera, *Daniel Halévy and His Times* (Ithaca, N.Y., 1966), 204–6.

[39] Paul Valéry, *Cahiers,* vol. 23 (Paris, 1960), 386, 505; *The Journals of André Gide,* translated and edited by Justin O'Brien, vol. IV (New York, 1957), 26, 31, 39, 47.

[40] *Le Figaro,* 19 June and 15 July 1940; Pierre Teilhard de Chardin, *Letters,* 147.

self-fulfillment in "gratuitous acts."[41] How it reveals the depth of the 1940 shock, therefore, to find Lafcadio's own creator, whose fascination with free spirits always warred with a deepseated Puritan austerity, echoing the same sense of freedom gone too far.

> Indulgence, indulgences. . . . That sort of puritan rigor by which the Protestants, those spoilsports, often made themselves so hateful, those scruples of conscience, that integrity, that unshakable punctuality, these are the things we have most lacked. Softness, surrender, relaxation in grace and ease, so many charming qualities that were to lead us, blindfolded, to defeat.[42]

The irony seemed strongest in that those very features which had made France so delightful and artistically creative had illfitted her for the new harsh age. Paul Valéry wrote in his notebooks some time in late June 1940,

> The abuse of things good in themselves has brought France to grief: among them, the bounty of the soil, liberty of the spirit, insouciance of individuals, all of which degenerates into facility, negligence, improvisation. . . . We are victims of what we are, and France, in particular, [is a victim] of her advantages.[43]

More fundamental critics found more basic faults in the whole development of modern moral values. Like those historians of national socialism who sought its roots in Luther and Tacitus, some thought the crash of 1940 revealed wrong turnings taken at the very beginning of the modern era. The diagnosis of Maurrassian writers was the "regime of palaver," the unbridled individualism inherited from Descartes and Rousseau, which had led to the dismantling of hierarchy and authority in 1789 and their replacement by flaccid parliamentarism. Forgetting Valmy, Jemappes, the Marne, and Verdun, they argued that the postrevolutionary regime was too spineless and too indulgent to

---

[41] René Gillouin, "Responsabilités des écrivains," in *Journal de Genève,* no. 33, 7–8 February 1942, attacks these three. See Emmanuel Mounier's attack on the "Intelligentzia folâtre et décadente" in *Esprit,* no. 97 (February 1941).

[42] *The Journals of André Gide,* translated and edited by Justin O'Brien, vol. IV (New York, 1957), 39 (28 July 1940).

[43] Paul Valéry, *Cahiers,* vol. 23 (Paris, 1960), 384, 421.

narrow individual self-interest ever to rise to greatness. It had been imported from the Anglo-Saxons, along with every other assault on French grandeur. They rejoiced in "the end of 'la France babillarde.' " [44]

Young Catholic radicals around Emmanuel Mounier traced the wrong turning to the Renaissance, which "failed to achieve the personalist renaissance and neglected the communitarian renaissance. Against individualism, we have to take up the first again. But we won't succeed without the help of the second." For such thorough critics of modernity, 1940 was a "judgment of history" not merely upon the Third Republic, which was beneath contempt, but upon a whole liberal, secular, individualist world view. [45]

In the summer of 1940, it was not yet clear what kind of new government would create what kinds of new institutions, but it was clear that the old ways had vanished irretrievably. June 1940 seemed, at the time, a clean break. "There is no more France in yesterday's meaning of the term," wrote Paul Valéry in his notebooks. [46]

> You would think—such was the impact of the last elections—
> that in France in 1936 there were 38 million republicans.
> What has become of them?
>
> —Jean Guéhenno, 1942 [47]

WE CAN SEE NOW HOW MISLEADING IT WAS AFTER the war to cloak the Third Republic's self-immolation at Vichy on July 9–10 as a "coup" by Pierre Laval. It became expedient

[44] Charles Maurras, *La Seule France* (Paris, 1941); Henri Massis, *Les Idées restent* (Paris, 1941); Jacques Benoist-Méchin, *La Moisson de quarante* (Paris, 1941), 50, 175, seeks "counterpoisons" to Descartes and Rousseau. The last phrase is from Jacques Chardonne, *Chronique privée de l'an 1940* (Paris, 1940), 90. René Gillouin and Maurras, drawing on Le Play, both insisted that the values of the French Revolution were "Anglo-Saxon."

[45] Emmanuel Mounier, "D'Une France à l'autre," *Esprit,* 8e année (November 1940), 1–40. *Esprit's* first editorial in 1932, some of which is quoted here, was called "Refaire la renaissance."

[46] *Cahiers,* vol. 23 (Paris, 1960), 429 ff.

[47] *Journal des années noires* (Paris, 1947), 25 July 1942.

to load everything on those stooped shoulders, especially after Laval was shot in the courtyard of Fresnes Prison in Paris on the morning of 15 October 1945. In postwar memoirs and recollections of those first days at Vichy, Laval is everywhere, cajoling, promising, threatening that Weygand and General de Lattre de Tassigny's army division waiting nearby at Clermont-Ferrand would sweep the Assembly away if it did not do its job, warning that Britain would make a favorable peace first at French expense if the French did not hurry, and so on. How convenient to have a pariah available on whom to blame those lopsided votes at Vichy on July 9–10. Laval was an ideal scapegoat, a man plausibly reputed to have invincible lobbying prowess, a symbol of evil incarnate by 1944, a man who was dead and could not cry "tu quoque." Black Peter, the only French politician whose name spelled the same whether one moved from Left to Right or Right to Left, a cartoonist's godsend with his swarthy round face, his inevitable cigarette, and his white necktie.

The Laval conspiracy theory, as legends go, is an unusually incoherent one. While seeming to vilify the man, it elevates him to political wizardry. That reputation for skill in smoke-filled rooms was handy to exculpate the others of any say in the matter. The legend also draws upon contradictory currents. Old conservatives deplore Laval as the epitome of Third Republic chicanery; the republican Left abhors him as a renegade. Looked at more dispassionately, Laval was considerably less than the legend. He was neither an invincible cajoler nor an unscrupulous turncoat. None of his bold forays into summit diplomacy succeeded: neither with Brüning nor Hoover in 1931, with Mussolini or Stalin in 1935, nor with Hitler after 1940. Moreover, it is hard to dismiss as rank opportunist the headstrong Laval who was pacifist in World War I, voted against the Versailles Treaty in 1919, opposed war in 1939, and held on to neutrality at Vichy until the bitter end, long after the more ordinary careerists had slipped away into one belligerent camp or another.[48]

The son of a village entrepreneur, the innkeeper-butcher-

[48] The essential study of Laval in any language is now Geoffrey Warner, *Pierre Laval and the Eclipse of France* (London, 1968).

mailman of the Auvergnat hill town of Châteldon, Pierre Laval had ascended the steps that the Third Republic offered an ambitious poor provincial. Success in school led to a period of teaching (biology) and then to a scholarship to study law in Paris. After entering law practice in Paris, Laval won early notoriety by winning the acquittal of a workman accused of anarchism. He became a specialist in labor cases and an attorney for the Confédération générale du travail. It was as a socialist that he was elected to the Chamber of Deputies in May 1914 for the Paris working-class suburb of Aubervilliers.

Laval had never been a doctrinaire socialist, however. His power base in Aubervilliers rested far more on the deputy's bonhomie and service to constituents than on ideological purity. Although Laval belonged to the moderate pacifist tendency of the SFIO (Jean Longuet's followers) and made a sensation in June 1917 by accusing the government of using Vietnamese troops to crush peace demonstrations, he was strongly tempted by office. He felt that call first in late 1917 when Clemenceau was looking for a socialist to round out his cabinet, though Laval does not seem to have been seriously considered. His links with the Left were further snapped when he lost his parliamentary seat in the elections of 1919.

Laval's comeback in 1924, as both deputy and mayor of Aubervilliers, required defeating a strong Communist party local. That campaign began the Laval-Communist feud that eventually became a dominant feature of Laval's political career. He sat in Parliament now as an independent. No longer kept from office by socialist scruples, Laval first became a minister (Public Works) at the age of 31 in the Painlevé government of 1925. He was to be eleven times minister and four times prime minister in the next ten years.

Laval was now an eminence in Third Republic politics. The combination of law practice and politics having proven lucrative, he built a modest press and radio empire around Lyon and Clermont-Ferrand. Geoffrey Warner reminds us that Laval was "one of the wealthiest men in French politics between the wars." [49]

[49] Warner, 21.

He bought the run-down chateau of Châteldon, becoming the first citizen of his birthplace. Laval always insisted that his fortune was built by buying marginal enterprises on credit, managing them well, selling them off at a profit, and living frugally; and the postwar trial investigation in 1944 was unable to prove any of the rumors about graft. Be that as it may, Laval was now tied by business and personal links to another world. When he ran for the Senate in 1927, it was in opposition to the Cartel des gauches. Nevertheless, Laval can be understood only if one remembers that his political base in working-class Aubervilliers remained intact, nurtured by Laval's plebeian manner and his effectiveness in helping constituents. A nonparty man, pragmatic, nurturing ties with both Left and Right, basing everything upon personal contacts—that had become Laval's political style.

When Laval reached his political summit in the early 1930's, he was thrust into crises for which he was ill-prepared: world financial collapse and the rise of fascism. Laval was prime minister for all of 1931 and foreign minister under successive governments from October 1934 until early 1936. He was also simultaneously prime minister from June 1935 to February 1936. Politically, he filled the vacuum left by Poincaré, Tardieu, and Briand. From Briand, who had been his foreign minister in 1931, Laval drew a language of Franco-German conciliation already familiar to him. His conservative majority, however, that of Poincaré and Tardieu, precluded any meaningful concessions. Personally, Laval brought to foreign and financial affairs the supreme self-confidence of a self-made man, contempt for the cautious upper-class rituals of professional diplomats and international bankers, techniques of direct bluff talk, and the inveterate fixer's enjoyment of knot-cutting, which had worked so well at Châteldon and Aubervilliers. This political and personal mixture was disastrous. Laval rushed into delicate affairs with inexperienced directness. In 1931 his personal negotiations with German Chancellor Brüning and President Hoover did nothing to stem the world financial crisis or to ease Franco-German relations. In 1935 he seemed to give Mussolini a free hand in Abyssinia, was unable to prevent the storm that followed in French and British public opinion, and managed to antagonize everyone.

It is not clear to this day what he told Mussolini. After negotiating a mutual security agreement with Stalin in 1935, he made no effort to have it ratified at home.

The Popular Front elections of 1936 sent Laval into the political wilderness. He was almost silent for four years. The resentments he expressed in 1940 against the parliament elected, as he told Dr. Friedrich Grimm in August, on the slogan "Hang Laval" added one more ingredient to Laval's political character. The parliament "vomited me up," Paul Baudouin claimed Laval said on 26 June 1940; "now I shall vomit it up." [50]

When the Pétain government, having signed the armistice and awaiting the imminent opening of a peace conference, also decided to summon the National Assembly for the purpose of abolishing the Third Republic Constitution of 1875 and empowering Pétain to draft a new one, Laval seems to have been eager to help. He had been excluded from the June 17 cabinet as too typical of the old "republic of pals" (as Weygand claimed at the time) or as too anti-British (as Weygand claimed after the war).[51] A government led by nonparliamentarians needed a major Third Republic leader, however, if it planned to deal with the Chamber and Senate. Major Third Republic leaders were in short supply in the summer of 1940. Most of the recent prime ministers were out of the question, either as too Left (Léon Blum) or too compromised by the defeat (Daladier, Reynaud), even if they had been willing. Among conservatives, Poincaré was dead, Tardieu had withdrawn as the "hermit of Menton," and Caillaux, whose notoriety as a proponent of Franco-German conciliation might have won him a major role at Vichy, was too old. Pierre-Etienne Flandin showed up late at Vichy and seemed to wish to go no further than making Pétain president of the Third Republic. It was Laval, therefore, who became deputy prime minister (*vice-président du conseil*) on 27 June. Pétain

[50] T-120/2624/D525934-37; Paul Baudouin, *Neuf mois au gouvernement* (Paris, 1948), 219.

[51] For Weygand's wish to exclude all parliamentarians from the government in 1940, see his 28 June note to Pétain published in Paul Baudouin, *Neuf mois au gouvernement* (Paris, 1948). Weygand's postwar version may be found in *Mémoires,* III, *Rappelé au service* (Paris, 1950), 298.

wrote him on 7 July, "as it is difficult for me to participate in the meetings [of the National Assembly] I ask you to represent me." We do not know what role Laval had in originating the government's constitutional plans, except to observe that projects for new French institutions swarmed around Vichy in July 1940.[52] What is clear is that Laval was charged with submitting the government's bill to the National Assembly and steering it through. Hence his starring role on those two days. Laval's front-bench role was made even more conspicuous by the personal qualities he brought to the job: his ambition, his penchant for blunt language, his self-confident directness.

Laval, of course, did not create the mood of national self-recrimination in which the senators and deputies gathered, physically and emotionally exhausted, in Vichy on July 9. Or at least most of them. Twenty-nine deputies and one senator had persisted in the earlier plan to move the government to North Africa and had sailed on the *Massilia* on June 21, only to find themselves detained and identified as cowardly émigrés three weeks later; the seventy-odd Communists had been unseated by the Daladier government in January 1940. Those present at Vichy did not have to be persuaded by Laval to ditch the Constitution of 1875. There was almost total unanimity on its faults. Even Léon Blum's *A l'échelle humaine,* written in prison in 1942–43, stresses the old republic's inadequacies in his plans for the new. The main rival project of July 1940, offered by Senate war veterans around Senator Taurines and sidetracked by Laval, according to conventional wisdom, proposed to "suspend" the Constitution of 1875 and to grant Pétain full powers to establish, in collaboration with the Chamber and Senate, "the bases of a new constitution." Even the republican diehards who signed Socialist deputy Vin-

---

[52] The period between the armistice of June 25 and the National Assembly of July 9–10 is even more obscure, if possible, than the prearmistice days and the Vichy days, which get the lion's share of attention in the postwar memoirs and most accounts. Two famous examples of projects for the reconstruction of France are Weygand's note of 28 June (see previous footnote) and Gaston Bergery's Declaration of 7 July, signed by some seventy parliamentarians and published by one of them, Jean Montigny, *Toute la vérité sur un mois dramatique de notre histoire* (Clermont-Ferrand, 1940), 139 ff. This work helps magnify Laval's role in the July days.

cent Badie's handwritten proposal, who "refused to vote for a bill which would lead ineluctably to the disappearance of the republican regime," affirmed that they "know the imperious necessity of carrying out urgently the moral and economic revival of our unfortunate country and of pursuing the negotiations envisaging a lasting and honorable peace." Pierre Laval did not have to coerce the Assembly into voting 624 to 4 on July 9 that "the constitutional laws should be revised." [53] Indeed, the French electorate voted in 1945, twenty-five to one not to return to the Constitution of 1875. The Assembly's stand of July 9, 1940, was no revolution from above. It reflected almost unanimous French public opinion.

Let there be no mistaking the gravity of the next day's work, however. Although the armistice of 25 June had made a diplomatic revolution, nothing obliged France to make a constitutional one. An armistice regime administering France just to keep essential services functioning during this interim period, as in Belgium and Holland, was a valid alternative. Even the July 9 vote jettisoning the Constitution of 1875 left open the nature of the future regime. Above all, when should the new constitution be drafted, and by whom? Before or after the end of the occupation and signature of peace with Germany? By an elected assembly or by an authoritarian wartime emergency regime? The government's bill of July 10 answered both questions in the way most hostile to Third Republic traditions. It gave Marshal Pétain full powers, not merely the *pleins pouvoirs* by which many 1930's prime ministers had legislated by decree during crises, but explicit authorization to draft a new constitution. That document was to be "ratified by the nation and applied by the assemblies which it shall have created."

Although timing is not specified here, this bill appealed to the country's massive urge for instant change. One doesn't em-

---

[53] The Taurines and Badie proposals had only about fifty supporters between them. They are printed in full, among other places, in Louis Noguères, *Le Véritable procès du maréchal Pétain* (Paris, 1955), 157, 160–61. One Socialist deputy (Biondi), two Radical deputies (Roche, Margaine), and one senator (the Marquis de Chambrun, not to be confused with Laval's son-in-law, the Comte René de Chambrun) voted "no" on 9 July.

power an eighty-four-year-old man to draft a new constitution unless work is expected to begin at once. That impatience determined other things. Authoritarian predilections aside, it would be impossible to hold elections or assemble a garrulous and quarrelsome constituent assembly while German troops occupied two-thirds of the country. The republican practice of elected constitutional conventions had to give way to a Bonapartist executive constitution-making. Furthermore, major changes would be wrought in French public life at the moment of maximum rebound from the defeated regime, in the presence of an occupying army, while awaiting peace negotiations with a victorious Hitler. It was a formula for the most blatant possible partisanship in the new regime.

Revolution from above? Perhaps, but it is a serious distortion to represent it as a "coup" by a handful of conspirators. What survives of genuine contemporary language suggests something very like massive assent to the idea of building a new regime at once, even under German eyes. There were not merely monarchists like Weygand out for revenge. There were those who believed, as Pétain was to tell Hitler the following October 24, that France could hope for a more lenient peace because she had "made a new start."[54] There was Gaston Bergery, that frustrated young Jacobin who wanted a pure, strong republic capable of fighting both fascism and communism and who had invented the term *Popular Front* in 1934, calling now for France to "rebuild today from top to bottom on the ruins which they [the Third Republic leaders] have piled up." And there were simply the weary, like Chamber President Edouard Herriot, urging placidity upon the deputies on July 9. "Around the Marshal, in the veneration which his name inspires in us all, our nation has rallied in its distress. Let us be careful not to trouble the accord which has been established under his authority."[55]

In this climate, Laval did not really have to work very hard

---

[54] See footnote 13, above.

[55] The Bergery Declaration is published in Jean Montigny, *Toute la vérité sur un mois dramatique de notre histoire* (Clermont-Ferrand, 1940), 139 ff. The full Herriot speech may be consulted in the *Journal officiel, débats, Chambre,* 11 July 1940.

to get the Popular Front parliament, elected in May 1936, to approve the government's plan. The deputies and senators voted 569 to 80 (the famous 80 who later boasted of fathering the Resistance), with 17 abstentions, to give Pétain constitutional powers.[56] The opposition, which seems in the postwar memoirs to have been railroaded into silence, was never very strong. The Taurines proposal, which differed from Laval's not in advocating any delay in drafting a new constitution but in providing that Pétain "consult" with the National Assembly while drafting it, had some 25 backers. Twenty-seven members signed Vincent Badie's handwritten last-ditch defense of the republic (which also called for change). As one reads the stenographic transcript of the morning session on July 10,[57] the members' mounting impatience at plodding parliamentary procedures is evident. It was the rank and file, not Laval's claque, that howled for an immediate vote. Pierre-Etienne Flandin, whose words about clinging to French traditions of liberty are often quoted, ended his speech by advocating a vote for the government's project. Laval had no serious opposition.

The Popular Front parliament did not quite "crucify itself," as Léon Blum's virulently disillusioned ex-colleague Charles Spinasse urged on July 6. Neither had it been coerced into voting against its true feelings. It had, rather, in Anatole de Monzie's phrase, left the scene as "penitents" who "consented to the abandonment of power and the sacrifice of liberty in the conviction that the new regime would assure order.[58] That is why no outcry arose the next day, July 11, when Marshal Pétain formally assumed the new office of "Head of the French State." Constitutional Acts One, Two, and Three gave him authority to carry

[56] The names of the 80 are printed conveniently in Robert Aron, *Histoire de Vichy* (Paris, 1954), 153 n., for those without access to the *Journal officiel* for 11 July 1940. They included 36 SFIO, 13 Radicals, and a scattering from other groups. A majority of both Socialists and Radicals voted "yes." Five Socialists and two Radicals (including Herriot) abstained.

[57] The morning session of July 10 does not appear in the *Journal officiel*. See Commission parlementaire d'enquête, *Evénements survenus en France de 1934 jusqu'en 1945*, vol. II, 479–97.

[58] Noguères, 158; Anatole de Monzie, *La saison des juges* (Paris, 1943), 8.

out all executive and legislative acts except declarations of war without referring to the Assembly. The gravity of these widely accepted steps cannot be exaggerated. Collaboration no longer meant merely accomplishing one's daily round under enemy occupation. Collaboration now meant taking advantage of a foreign army to carry out major changes in the way Frenchmen were governed, schooled, and employed.

AN OLD WORLD WAS ENDED. SOME FEATURES OF THE new were already apparent. Never had so many Frenchmen been ready to accept discipline and authority. A kind of jack-booted toughness had been part of the Fascist Leagues' appeal to the young in the 1930's, and a cult of outdoorsy muscularity was already a form of youthful rebellion against the Third Republic. "Thanks to us, the France of camping, of sports, of dances, of voyages, of collective hiking will sweep away the France of aperitifs, of tobacco dens, of party congresses, and long digestions." [59] Cultists of virility like Henry de Montherlant renewed the call for spartan values. "What we need most is a cure of purity," wrote Jacques Benoist-Méchin.[60]

The discipline theme penetrated even into the Third Republic's elite. Edouard Herriot, president of the Chamber of Deputies and the soul of the Third Republic's accommodation politics, appealed to his colleagues at the National Assembly at Vichy on 9 July to accept "a hard discipline." Gide found Pétain's 17 June speech "simply admirable." Pétain claimed that "the spirit of enjoyment has won out over the spirit of sacrifice. People claimed more than they served." Gide's response was to accept limitation on excesses of freedom. "I should rather gladly put up with restraints, it seems to me, and would accept a dictatorship, which is the only thing, I fear, which might save us from de-

[59] Marcel Marion, of the PPF, as quoted in Robert J. Soucy, "The Nature of Fascism in France," *Journal of Contemporary History* I:1 (1966), 55.
[60] Jacques Benoist-Méchin, *La Moisson de quarante* (Paris, 1941), 51. See also Henry de Montherlant, *Le Solstice de juin* (Paris, 1941).

composition. Let me hasten to add that I am speaking here only of a French dictatorship." [61]

Suffering itself was supposed to burn away the dirty dross of interwar France, to purify and strengthen the national fiber. Of course Frenchmen knew they would have to suffer in June 1940, whether they liked it or not, but seeing some merit in suffering helped reconcile them to the armistice position. Spokesmen for the regime liked to proclaim that "suffering purifies." Camus satirized them in Father Paneloux' sermon at the end of the first month of the plague:

> If today the plague is in your midst, that is because the hour has struck for taking thought. . . . For the plague is the flail of God and the world his threshing floor." [62]

But men much farther from Vichy circles also talked about the redemption in suffering. There would be some benefit in the war, Gide thought, for those who suffered directly and learned.

> Yes, long before the war, France stank of defeat. She was already falling to pieces to such a degree that perhaps the only thing that could save her was, is perhaps, this very disaster in which to re-temper her energies. Is it fanciful to hope that she will issue from this nightmare strengthened? [63]

This yearning for discipline's chastising hand led directly to a father figure. The upwelling of feeling around Marshal Pétain among this skeptical people would be hard to imagine under less cataclysmic circumstances. In 1940 any victorious World War leader would have been balm to wounded pride. Pétain fitted the moment even more perfectly. Here was a genuine national hero without visible ties to the politics of the sorry 1930's. By sheer age he had outlived the animosities of his military car-

[61] *The Journals of André Gide,* 23, 31. Gide accepted authority only as a choice among evils. "If tomorrow, as is to be feared, freedom of thought or at least of the expression of that thought is refused us, I shall try to convince myself that art, that thought itself will lose less thereby than in excessive freedom." See pp. 38, 49.

[62] General Léon Huntziger, quoted in *Le Temps,* 17 August 1941; Albert Camus, *The Plague* (New York, 1954), 87 ff.

[63] *The Journals of André Gide,* translated and edited by Justin O'Brien, vol. IV (New York, 1957), 34, 186 (17 July 1940, 7 March 1943).

eer; by taciturnity he had not acquired new ones. His public political roles since retirement, as minister of war in the Doumergue government following the riots of February 1934 and as first ambassador to Franco Spain in 1939, were seen merely as an old soldier's civic duty in an emergency; for the rest, he said little in public on national issues beyond the officer's traditional disdain for politics. He had become a blank image, ready to be stamped with each Frenchman's conception of savior.

For some, Pétain was simply "le drapeau," a personification of abiding Old France: an erect old soldier of austere tastes, of Catholic peasant stock, marshal of France, member of the French Academy, returning from his modest country estate once more to rescue his country from the rabble. On the other side, Pétain seemed less threatening to republicans than many another senior officer. No "booted Jesuit" like Foch or Currières de Castelnau, Pétain was a mere nominal Catholic. Although he had allowed Colonel de la Rocque's newspaper, *Le Flambeau,* to publish an "apolitical" interview endorsing the Popular Front's opponents in May 1936, Pétain was less suspect of links with far right movements than Marshal Franchet d'Esperey. Although he had commanded the most costly defense of the whole 1914–18 war— Verdun—his rejection of the doctrine of attack made him seem a hoarder of French blood. His settlement of the mutinies in 1917 seemed fair as well as firm. Even Léon Blum called Pétain France's "noblest and most humane soldier," while deploring his appointment as ambassador to Franco. Reynaud named him to the cabinet on 18 May 1940 as a kind of flag. Only the irreverent young right had mocked Pétain without compunction in the 1930's.[64] In the summer of 1940, therefore, Pétain fitted the national mood to perfection: internally, a substitute for politics and a barrier to revolution; externally, a victorious general who would make no more war. Honor plus safety.

Inside the icon, however, dwelled a Philippe Pétain of flesh

[64] Emanuel d'Astier de la Vigerie, in *Sept fois sept jours,* refers throughout to Pétain simply as "le drapeau." For the interview in *Le Flambeau,* see issue of 9 May 1936. Léon Blum's remarks on Pétain appeared in *Le Populaire,* 3 March 1939. Céline ridiculed Pétain as "le maréchal Prétartarin" in *L'École des cadavres* (Paris, 1938), 84–96.

and blood. What sorts of decisions could one expect from this man to whom millions of Frenchmen had entrusted their public destinies?

Contrary to a common postwar assumption, Pétain was not senile in 1940. Other doctors at Vichy believed that Dr. Bertrand Ménétrel, Pétain's personal physician, secretary, and son of an old friend, heightened the marshal's morning spirits with shots of Benzedrine or Ephedrine. That may be. In any event, visitors as late as 1943 recorded their surprise at the health, alertness, and vigor of the still-erect old man of eighty-seven. Contemporary reporters of Pétain's conversations in 1943 with German visitors, at unspecified hours of the day, had no apparent motive to invent the forceful expressions, wide curiosity, and command of detail his words displayed.[65] Pétain's acts were conscious and deliberate choices.

Age, however, had unquestionably deepened a lifelong caution. As a colonel destined for early retirement in 1914, he had already won some notoriety for an acid skepticism about the prevailing tactical doctrines of attack. He reached supreme command in World War I when the partisans of attack had been discredited. As commander in chief of the French Armies in 1917–18, Pétain attacked only when careful preparation had assured a clear advantage, in a manner more reminiscent of an Eisenhower than a Patton or Montgomery in 1944. Poincaré's memoirs suggest that Pétain expected French defeat in February–March 1918. Paul Valéry, welcoming the marshal to the Académie française in 1934, recalled even in the midst of eulogy his "cold and almost severe attitude" and his reputation for pessimism. By 1940 these qualities had hardened into "morose skepticism."[66]

Pétain had also learned a quarter century earlier about revolu-

---

[65] Janet Flanner [Genêt], *Pétain: Old Man of France* (New York, 1944), 47, is the only biographer to mention drugs. For transcripts of Pétain's conversations in 1943, see the references in chap. 4, note 63. When interviewed by the parliamentary investigating commission in 1947 in his prison on the Ile d'Yeu, however, Pétain was clearly senile.

[66] Poincaré, *Mémoires,* X, 63–64, 85–86, 88. Paul Valéry, *Oeuvres* (Pléiade edition, 1957), I, 1098 ff. The last words of this paragraph are from de Gaulle's radio speech of 26 June 1940.

tion. At the moment when he replaced the discredited General Robert Nivelle at the head of the French Armies in May 1917, half the front-line divisions were in mutiny. Pétain understood better than most other officers that futile sallies "over the top" for a few yards of terrain at the cost of thousands of lives had been the mutinies' root cause. Like most other officers, however, he attributed almost mythic powers to "outside agitators" and Bolshevik influences.[67]

The 1917 alarms left their mark on Pétain's lifelong concern for patriotic morale. When Pétain claimed in the 1930's that education had become his main interest, he meant morale, not knowledge. In 1940 he was convinced, as he told U.S. Ambassador Bullitt, that unpatriotic schoolteachers had been responsible for French defeat.[68]

All this meant that Pétain saw his mission in 1940 less in terms of finding the right policy than of instilling the right attitudes. He put immense effort and care into his role as moral tutor to the French people. That terse manner, once used for irony as well as for military reports (Pétain's military nickname was "Précis-le-sec"), was now applied to homilies composed of brief, simple phrases which turned more often to platitude then to epigram. The schoolmaster began to lecture his pupils on the values of social stability: *travail, famille, patrie.*

It was not that Pétain had plotted in advance for power or had seized it illegally. His grip on office, released only when the Germans dragged him protesting out of the Hôtel du Parc at Vichy in August 1944, ahead of the advancing Allied armies, rested upon a subtler vanity. Having grown accustomed to being listened to on every subject as his country's savior for a quarter century, Pétain thought he was indispensable. He had given France, he said in his radio message of 25 June 1940, "the gift of my person." He clung to office with the embrace of conscience, far more dangerous than ambition. A merely ambitious man

---

[67] Guy Pedroncini, *Les Mutineries de 1917* (Paris, 1967), has significant contemporary material on officers' evaluation of the mutinies.

[68] Admiral Fernet, *Aux côtés du maréchal Pétain* (Paris, 1953), 150, reports that Pétain wanted to be minister of education in 1934. For his remark to Bullitt, *FRUS*, 1940, II, 384.

would have trimmed to the tide later on, rather than carry down with him all those who worshipped the icon.

WHERE, ONE WILL ASK, WERE THE "RESISTERS OF THE first hour," as numerous by 1944 as Mayflower descendants at a DAR convention? Nothing said here should diminish the honor due those who recognized, even in 1940, that Frenchmen could not recover their freedom without force. Their number, however, was minuscule, and it was to grow smaller still during the first year. There was silent dissent, of course, on the model of the old man and his daughter in the first major novel published underground during the occupation—Vercors' *Le Silence de la mer* (Editions de minuit, 1942)—who refuse to speak to a quite decent young German officer billeted in their home. The subject here is active resistance of the sort that troubles regimes, from gathering intelligence for the Allies or publishing underground newspapers, to acts of violence. Very good contemporary sources are now available: some French police records and many German ones. They reveal no serious problems of dissent for the regime until well into 1941.

A number of obstacles stood in the way of an active French Resistance movement in the early days of the occupation. It was hard to believe in late 1940 that the war was not over. Only British tenacity and the endless expanses of Russia were to show that Hitler's French campaign had not been as decisive as it seemed at the time. Resistance needs some modicum of hope, and this was absent in late 1940.

The very existence of the Pétain regime further confused the issue. While the direct German presence in the northern two-thirds of France left no doubt where the enemy lay, it was not clear in the south whether anti-Germanism meant opposing Vichy or rejoicing in its simulacrum of independence and its nationalist rhetoric. One of the first clandestine newspapers, Captain Henri Frenay's *Combat,* carried quotations from both Pétain and Foch on its masthead until early 1942. This was not an isolated case.

The disarray of the French Left further obstructed a vigorous early resistance. One would have expected the Popular Front alliance of 1936, once the main proponent of strong action against Hitler and now the regime's chief whipping boy, to form a natural focus for an anti-Hitler underground. It was not, and the main reason lies less in governmental repression—although the Pétain regime arrested Léon Blum and five of his ministers in September 1940 and although the Communist party had remained illegal since September 1939—than in ideological confusion. The Popular Front partners had all renounced their 1936 position. The Radicals, that anachronistically misnamed party of laissez-faire middle-class Frenchmen, had been the first to grow lukewarm as their majority slipped behind the rising Marxist parties in the 1936 elections. The Socialists, with Léon Blum in eclipse, reverted in 1940 to a traditional pacifism around people like Paul Faure, once Blum's deputy party leader, a lifelong pacifist, and a doubter about national defense even in the late 1930's. The Communists executed their about-face of 23 August 1939 with the loss of only a few intellectuals, so that the party for which one Frenchman in six had voted in 1936 denounced the war against Hitler in 1939 as imperialist fratricide whose victor, be it the City of London or the Nazis, was of no concern to workers. In the summer of 1940, from underground, the Communist newspaper *Humanité* urged a peace of reconciliation between French and German workers. To be sure, it attacked Pétain as the lackey of French capitalists, permitting the party to claim after the war to have launched the Resistance. In the same breath, however, it attacked the Allies as fomenters of imperialist war and asserted that France could remain free only by avoiding becoming a British Dominion. "Ni Pétain, ni de Gaulle" read a Communist poster in Paris in January 1941. "France wants neither cholera nor the plague." [69]

Without clear signals from the organized Left, and with every expectation of rich rewards for the Right at Vichy, the

[69] See the ex-Communist A. Rossi [Angelo Tasca], *La Guerre des papillons* (Paris, 1954), Appendix X, for clandestine Communist posters from 1940 and early 1941. Jacques Fauvet, *Histoire du parti communiste français,* vol. 2 (Paris, 1965), quotes extensively from the party press in this period. Even the official party histories now play down the spurious "appeal of 10 July."

early Resistance in 1940 was the work of exceptional individuals, usually already outside the social fabric in some way, or of such amorphous effervescence as student demonstrations. The first major public display of opposition was an illegal student parade up the Champs-Elysées on Armistice Day 1940, focused, it should be noted, upon a traditional patriotic rather than revolutionary symbol: the tomb of the unknown soldier under the Arch of Triumph. On 6 September 1940, retired Air Force General Cochet imprudently circulated a signed appeal for civil disobedience. The first clandestine newspapers, other than the pacifist *Humanité,* appeared only at the very end of 1940. Captain Henri Frenay left the army in November to found *Combat. Libération* (the future *Libération-nord*), the work of two moderate trade union leaders, Christian Pineau of the Catholic bank clerks' union and Robert Lacoste of the civil servants' union, appeared on 1 December in seven mimeographed copies. At year's end, a group of Catholic law professors, François de Menthon, Pierre-Henri Teitgen, and René Capitant, were preparing the first *Liberté* in the unoccupied zone. The first intelligence-gathering network was being formed in late 1940 among anthropologists at the Paris Musée de L'Homme, led by two Russian émigré ethnologists, Boris Vildé and Anatole Levitsky. These tentative individual gropings, more often ideologically conservative than Left, were only the germs of what the Resistance was to become.

At the time, they posed no real problem for the regime. Some of them—Frenay, Major Loustenau-Lacau, army officers hiding weapons—claimed to be acting in Pétain's name. Even the Catholic trade union leaders around *Libération-nord* urged a complete transformation of past institutions and a variant of current corporatist theory: "a free union in an organized profession in a sovereign state." [70] No Resistance groups in France supported de Gaulle at first; the Left found him too Maurrassian, the Right too disloyal. Their most daring expression was a handful of mimeographed broadsides. The best measure, perhaps, of the

[70] Christian Pineau, *La Simple vérité* (Paris, 1960), 593, publishes this curious text.

early Resistance was the authorities' calm. The Germans carried out no "grand operations of repression" in the first months except against Communists, whose honeymoon period in occupied Paris ended with mass arrests on the night of 4–5 October 1940. The first signs of official alarm appeared in the spring of 1941. The Musée de L'Homme group was swept up in the first major wave of Resistance arrests in March 1941; the prefect of the Seine-et-Oise required householders on 2 April 1941 to efface troubling slogans from their property, the first indubitable sign of the ubiquitous "V" for victory advocated by Radio London.[71] There was simply no significant organized domestic alternative to Pétain for most of 1940.

The real threat to Pétain in the summer and fall of 1940 came from an elite movement abroad rather than a mass movement at home. The men in command of France's overseas empire found the armistice of June 1940 very hard to swallow. Spared the direct impression of blitzkrieg and schooled to the concept of saving France with imperial resources, the governors-general and army commanders overseas were the most bellicose Frenchmen left in the summer of 1940. The two most important overseas commanders, General Auguste Noguès in North Africa and General Mittelhauser in the Near East, raised strenuous objections in the days before the armistice took effect. General de-Gaulle's first strategy, it appears, was to contribute his London group to this larger effort. In the end, however, General Noguès swallowed his anguish and obeyed the firm orders of the commander in chief, General Weygand, who sent General Koeltz to explain to him that since the navy would not come to North Africa, further resistance was futile. General Mittelhauser could only follow suit. The only overseas commanders or governors to join de Gaulle—Generals Le Gentilhomme in Djibouti and Catroux in Indochina—did so as individuals without bringing their men and territories with them. Rebuffed at Dakar in September 1940, de Gaulle was able to win the allegiance of only

[71] Henri Noguères, *Histoire de la résistance en France* (Paris, 1967), I, 208, shows the absence of German "grand operations" against the Resistance at first. See *DFCAA*, IV, 454, for the beginning of German executions for resistance in the Occupied Zone in May 1941.

parts of French Equatorial Africa and a few Pacific Islands by the end of 1940. Vichy's legitimacy and the chain of command, exploited vigorously by General Weygand, who toured French Africa in person in the fall of 1940, kept almost the entire empire in line.[72]

That left Charles de Gaulle high and dry in London, unexpectedly nearly alone, having burned his bridges by the radio appeal of 18 June. A look at the first Gaullists makes perhaps the best case for the marginal nature of Pétain's early opponents. Their number was small and their status mostly obscure. Prominent prewar figures were virtually absent. The only deputy who joined de Gaulle was Pierre-Olivier Lapie, who happened to be in London anyway as a reserve officer with the returning Narvik force. There was only one admiral, Muselier, who had quarreled with Darlan in the late 1930's. The only senior army officers were from the colonies. In addition to the two generals (Catroux and Le Gentilhomme) there was only one colonel, de Larminat, who left Syria after failing to bring his unit over to rejecting the armistice. The only high civil servants were men already in trouble with the new regime. Gaston Palewski and Maurice Dejean, who had been Paul Reynaud's administrative aides, reached London in August 1940. The only inspector of finance was André Diethelm, who had been Georges Mandel's administrative aide and whose fate was sealed when Mandel was arrested in Morocco in June and charged with trying to set up a rival antiarmistice regime with British support. Paris law professor René Cassin was the only leading academic, and the senior journalist was probably Maurice Schumann, former religion editor with the Havas news agency and future Fifth Republic foreign minister.

De Gaulle's recruits came mainly from the outcasts of the new regime and from those already overseas. The outcasts were not automatically Gaullist, however. Many on the Left found de Gaulle's following far too clerical, military, and nationalist for comfort. Warm relations between de Gaulle and the internal

---

[72] I have followed this process much more fully in *Parades and Politics at Vichy* (Princeton, N.J., 1966), chap. 3.

Left resistance were a good two years in the future. So eminent an outcast as Léon Blum expected to settle quietly in the south of France. Few of those purged from government service joined de Gaulle, at least at first. Jean Moulin was the only dismissed prefect among the 1940 recruits. The only ambassador removed from his post at German insistence—Ambassador to Turkey René Massigli (de Gaulle's eventual commissioner for foreign affairs), who was implicated when the Germans discovered a set of war plans for a Balkan operation—remained in France until early 1943.

Having to leave French soil was a serious obstacle. Vichy's successful control of most of the empire was a major victory, for it meant that one could join de Gaulle only through the total rupture of normal life, through flight and exile. Only the soldiers and civil servants of colonies that swung integrally into the Gaullist camp, such as most of French Equatorial Africa in October–November 1940, had the luxury of becoming Free French while staying put. For the rest, one had to face criminal charges, physical danger, and the obloquy of emigration. Was not going abroad a kind of shameful escape? "I would be ashamed to leave my fellow countrymen when everything goes wrong," wrote Jean Renoir to the American filmmaker Robert Flaherty on 8 August 1940.[73] More particularly, going to London came to seem changing one enemy for another. On July 3–4, the British Navy carried out a preemptive raid on the French fleet at Mers-el-Kebir (Algeria) and seized French ships in British harbors, on the assumption that Vichy's verbal assurances were insufficient guarantee that the Germans might not seize the French fleet whenever they wished. Over 1,200 French sailors died in that painful act of Realpolitik. Thereafter, de Gaulle had to struggle against charges that his movement was a stalking horse for British imperial interests.

Not all of those already outside France were Gaullists, either. Many who were physically in a position to join him did not. Colonel Antoine Béthouart, de Gaulle's military school class-

[73] Jean Renoir to Robert Flaherty, 8 August 1940, in Robert Flaherty MS, Columbia University.

mate and a man later arrested for helping the Allied landing in Morocco in November 1942, was in England in June 1940 on his way home from the Norway campaign. While giving his officers and men a free choice, Béthouart felt that duty required him to return to serve where his government assigned him. Naval recruitment was even smaller after the Mers-el-Kebir tragedy. Of some 500 officers and 18,000 sailors already in England in June 1940, all but 50 French naval officers and 200 sailors chose to go home rather than stay with de Gaulle.[74] The one prominent businessman opposed to the regime, brandy merchant Jean Monnet, who had served as French purchasing agent for war matériel in Washington and London, preferred to remain in the United States, as did the ex-Secretary General of the Foreign Office, Alexis Léger. They were joined by a stream of refugees, from Popular Front Air Minister Pierre Cot through the Rothschilds to the Curies, journalist Henri de Kérillis and novelists Jules Romains and André Maurois. Anthropologist Jacques Soustelle, en route from Central America to London via the United States in the late summer of 1940, could well feel that he was swimming against the tide.[75]

The total Gaullist movement, then, amounted to only 7,000 in July 1940 and approximately 35,000 by the end of 1940, a figure around which it hovered until November 1942.[76] The bulk of these numbers came from more or less "automatic" Gaullists among soldiers and government officials from Equatorial Africa, filled out by Gaullists of genuine decision such as whole villages of Breton fishermen. The leaders were mostly new men thrust into unanticipated prominence. The prewar obscurity of the Companions of the Liberation is a good measure of how few leading Frenchmen joined de Gaulle in 1940.

Most future Gaullists were still years away from making that commitment. A few future Gaullists had the misfortune to publish their thoughts white-hot in the summer of 1940. Those re-

---

[74] *Mitteilungen über die Arbeiten der WaKo,* no. 46, 19 August 1940 (T-120/353/206537-40).

[75] Jacques Soustelle, *Envers et contre tout* (Paris, 1947), I, 29.

[76] Charles de Gaulle, *Mémoires de Guerre,* vol. I, *L'Appel* (Paris, 1954), 100; Marcel Vigneras, *Rearming the French* (Washington, D.C., 1957), 10.

minders of the confused and intense emotions of that dreadful summer were a not inconsiderable embarrassment to them later. The quietist editorials of François Mauriac are one famous case. Another was Paul Claudel's effulgent ode to Pétain, which cynics enjoy comparing to his equally breathless 1944 tribute to de Gaulle. Jean Maze amused the French reading public in 1948 with a collection of such awkward quotations entitled "A New Dictionary of Weathervanes," named for a famous Restoration pamphlet exposing the tergiversations of celebrated turncoats during the Hundred Days of 1815.[77] M. Maze had to use a pseudonym himself, however, for he had been assistant editor of the newspaper of Gaston Bergery, militant for the new regime in 1940 and its ambassador to the Soviet Union. Genuine "resisters of the first hour" were a rare breed indeed in 1940.

It TAKES MORE THAN THE USUAL LEAP OF HISTORICAL thought to recapture the elusive moods of the summer of 1940. The stunning shock of defeat, which turned a proud and skeptical people briefly into self-flagellants craving the healing hand of suffering and discipline, passed as quickly as the daze of an automobile accident victim. The scraps of contemporary conversation and writing that survive are mostly the views of special people—writers, diplomats, propagandists—as the reader will have noticed in this prologue. Most misleading of all, one sees 1940 through the changed lenses of the Liberation, through the postwar trials and memoirs that have placed the stamp of their perspectives on a basically fictitious image of 1940. By 1944 the universe had so completely turned on its axis that the main strategic assumptions of 1940—short war, British defeat, danger of revolution, imminent peace—seemed nonsense. Vichy veterans had every incentive to produce a flood of selective, self-justifying prose designed to show that in 1940 they had already seen the world in 1944 terms. Their very lives depended on doing so.

Recapturing the moods of 1940 requires stripping away en-

[77] Orion [Jean Maze], *Nouveau dictionnaire des girouettes* (Paris, 1948).

crusted layers of postwar perspectives. These have so permeated consciousness that fragments of new information tend simply to be assimilated into old patterns. This happens, for example, to the occasional stray German documents that appeared in French periodicals from time to time after the Liberation. In this book I have attempted the painful business of breaking up these old patterns and suggesting another way of looking at a controversial time. Wherever possible, I have relied upon contemporary materials rather than postwar trial testimony or memoirs where the two conflict.

One notion to strip away is the "double game." It was tempting to claim in 1944 that one had foreseen the Liberation all along and had only apparently gone along with the Vichy solution in order to gain time. Hitler believed this, at first, and decided only in October 1940 after talking face-to-face with Pétain that the marshal and his former protégé de Gaulle had no secret connection. Indeed many Frenchmen who had supported Vichy for a time came to work heroically for Liberation, and thus they passed from a 1940 perspective to a 1944 one. But it will not do to telescope those successive stands into a simultaneous "double game." The German and American diplomatic conversations with French leaders are all now available, and it seems quite clear that Vichy cabinet members said very much the same things to both. There was no official "double game." The first and fourth chapters of this book try to show how earnestly Vichy sought neutrality, an early peace, and a final settlement on gentle terms with Germany.

An even more tenacious Liberation perspective is Vichy's passivity. After the war, Vichy was treated by both friend and foe as a mere reactor to German initiatives. To sympathizers, Vichy was a brake, an obstacle, a device for delaying or mitigating limitless German demands and preventing total occupation (as if the Germans wanted that!). "Après nous, la Polonisation." To opponents, Vichy seems a capitulation, either craven or corrupt, to insatiable German desires. From either perspective, motor energy was believed to come from Berlin. "Collaboration" seemed mere response.

We can now see almost exactly when this perspective was

skillfully planted, as an element of Marshal Pétain's postwar trial defense. When the retreating German armies carried Pétain off in August 1944 to the old Hohenzollern castle of Sigmaringen, where the upper Danube comes out of the Black Forest, the marshal's final proclamation set the tone of passive defense. "If I could not be your sword, I tried to be your shield." He elaborated on this idea in his one statement at the trial in 1945. "Day after day, a dagger at my throat, I struggled against German demands."[78] This was not so much a lie as a half-truth. It obscured all the things Vichy had done without German pressure and all the things Vichy had begged and implored the Germans to do. Marshal Pétain's prosecution, ill prepared and looking for conspiratorial gossip rather than calm historical judgment, let the trial slip away from what Vichy struggled *for* to what Vichy struggled *against*. Unable to prove that Pétain had conspired actively before the war for a German victory, the prosecution shifted its focus from sins of commission to sins of omission.

Subsequent defendants gladly followed the emphasis upon German initiative and Vichy passivity. When Laval was asked about the laws against Freemasonry, for example, he replied that the Germans had forced it upon him—an outright lie.[79] Other defendants simply claimed that their role had been a subordinate or technical one, which left them ignorant of high policy. Among the makers of high policy, Darlan had been assassinated, and Laval's trial was too hasty and too impassioned to reach substantive issues. Among the trials of subordinates before the High Court of Justice, only those of Jacques Benoist-Méchin and Fernand de Brinon, Vichy representatives at Paris, allow some glimpse of Vichy initiatives. Subtly but thoroughly, the trials helped implant the general assumption that public affairs under the occupation were a simple matter of German demand and Vichy response (wise or cowardly, according to one's preference). Maître Isorni, Pétain's lawyer, won his case with public opinion, if not with the court.

The principal act of historical re-creation, then, is to restore

[78] Georges Blond, *Pétain* (Paris, 1966), attributes the August 1944 message to Henri Massis. See also *Le Procès du maréchal Pétain* (Paris, 1945), 9.
[79] *Le Procès du maréchal Pétain* (Paris, 1945), 191.

Vichy's initiatives to view. France, in fact, enjoyed a quite extraordinary range of freedom for a defeated and half-occupied state. German control of the Vichy zone was light for some time, for reasons both calculated and uncalculated. The calculated reasons were the economy and political astuteness of letting France keep herself out of the war and docile, as long as she seemed inclined to do so. This calculation meant that France was the only defeated nation allowed to treat state-to-state for an armistice [80] and the only defeated nation divided into occupied and unoccupied zones. For uncalculated reasons, German political direction in Paris took time to form. At first, the real German authority in France was the Militärbefehlshaber in Frankreich, located in Paris, and all dealings with French authorities were conducted through the Armistice Commission at Wiesbaden. It was expected in those early days that Franco-German relations would be limited during the brief period before peace negotiations to technical questions of French demobilization and German security. Otto Abetz was at first a mere foreign office representative on the Militärbefehlshaber's staff. For the first month after the armistice was signed, he saw only one member of the French government, Pierre Laval, on July 19. On August 8 Hitler made him ambassador, and gradually an independent German political office in Paris established its own identity outside the more pragmatic military men in Paris and Wiesbaden. [81]

Vichy's first hundred days, then, took place without close, direct German political supervision. Long afterward, that influence remained essentially negative—vetoing things rather than imposing things—until the summer of 1941, when the assassina-

---

[80] Spaak and other leading Belgian ministers wanted an armistice, but the Germans refused. Thomas J. Knight, "Belgium Leaves the War, 1940," *Journal of Modern History* 41:1 (March 1969), 62–63.

[81] See Délégation française auprès de la commission allemande d'armistice, *Recueil de documents publié par le gouvernement français,* 5 vols. (Paris, 1947–59). With the exception of a few major documents omitted, this provides the best day-to-day account of technical negotiations between the German military and the French government at Vichy. It is cited hereafter as *DFCAA.*

tion of Germans began, and the summer of 1942, when forced labor and the deportation of Jews to the east started. Some of the most earnest Vichy concerns never interested the Germans very much. One of this book's main intentions, therefore, is to restore Vichy's initiatives to view. I want to restore Vichy to its rightful place in indigenous French history, a link between the incipient civil war of the 1930's and the social transformations of the postwar years.

This means emphasizing Vichy at the expense of the Paris collaborators. All too often the two are lumped together indiscriminately. Some of the most notorious figures of the occupation were the Frenchmen who led political groups or published newspapers at Paris in return for the high life of the occupied capital and, in many cases, direct subsidies from the German embassy.[82] Although these personages were conspicuous, their direct effect on Vichy policy is doubtful and their vassalage to Abetz is certain. They enjoyed neither the independence nor the broad following that make Vichy interesting. Their attitude to Vichy was hostile; they criticized it for being too lukewarm and too old-fashioned in the face of the fascist revolution. Only in January 1944, with Déat and Darnand, did important figures from the Paris circle gain influence in an eclipsing Vichy. The most able of the Paris crowd—Doriot, for example—never did. So the Paris collaborators occupy the wings rather than center stage in this book.

This book also emphasizes social history. Some of the more poignant and dramatic aspects of life under Marshal Pétain have not received as much attention here as some readers would no doubt like. The internal politics of the regime is still much shrouded in mystery, and as for a dramatic sense of the squalor and heroism of occupied France, one must still turn to novels such as Jean Dutourd's *The Best Butter* or Jean-Louis Curtis' *The Forests of the Night*. I thought that some other questions, whose answers are already less obscure, could also arouse a reader's

---

[82] Some information on Abetz' subsidies to the press may be found in *Pariser Botschaft*, Ordner 1134, "S 8 Geheim, 1940–44" (T-120/3112).

curiosity and engage his convictions. What did the Vichy regime do with its share of independence? What groups benefited? Who were its supporters? We shall begin, then, with the first French external use of that independence: the French campaign for a Franco-German settlement.

Why have you [Germans] never supported us?

　　—*Laval to General von Neubronn, June 1943*

*We know the immense difficulties which await us to assure
the vital needs of the country and, moreover, we know nothing
of the intentions of the Reich, which up to now hasn't shown
the slightest sign of a desire for collaboration.*

　　—*Yves Bouthillier to Gen. Doyen, 23 October 1940* [1]

I / The French Quest for Collaboration, 1940–1942

COLLABORATION WAS NOT A GERMAN DEMAND TO
which some Frenchmen acceded, through sympathy or guile.
Collaboration was a French proposal that Hitler ultimately rejected. Put so baldly, of course, the statement needs qualification.
Hitler was not passive either. He insisted upon a docile and
amenable France, a secure base for his assault upon England
and the richest source of supplies in occupied Western Europe.
It was from the Pétain regime, however, that a stream of overtures came for a genuine working together: for a broad Franco-
German settlement, for voluntary association as a neutral with
Hitler's efforts to keep the Allies out of Europe and the empire,
and eventually for full partnership in the new European order.
Briefly, in October–December 1940 and again in May 1941
when a free and willing associated France seemed useful for
German aims in the Mediterranean, Hitler was tempted. Other
senior German advisers, particularly military men like Admiral

---

[1] Deutscher General Vichy, "*Akte 7a*" (T-501/120/412–16); *Ministère
public c/Bouthillier,* 52.

Raeder and General Walther Warlimont and some high Foreign Office people like Ambassador Ritter (but never Ribbentrop), were enthusiastic about the idea. In the end, Hitler rejected the proffered hand. In the end, "Kollaboration" meant only booty, a cheap way to get the French to keep their own people. quiet, and an eventual peace of revenge.

The armistice was presumed by both sides to be a temporary arrangement, removing France from the war and maintaining order there during the final battle for Britain. The ink was hardly dry on the signatures, however, when the situation began to evolve in ways neither party had foreseen. The war did not end. Churchill did not sue for peace in Pétain's wake. Nor was Germany capable of launching a cross-channel invasion until she achieved air superiority, which was eluding her grasp in the fall of 1940. Northern France remained a war zone. The armistice was transformed from an instrument for overseeing an orderly French disarmament into an instrument for continuing active war against Britain from French soil. The letter of the armistice began to matter less to German authorities than the spirit of the preamble, that statement by General Keitel which had not been part of the document itself: France was expected to do anything required for Germany's prosecution of the war against Britain.[2]

"Germany could have thought, even as recently as two weeks ago, that negotiations with England would be possible," General von Stülpnagel told General Huntziger at Wiesbaden on August 1. "That hope has been disappointed, and the Reich has been obliged to take security measures which are dictated by circumstances and by the need to continue the war." Thus, with the blame placed squarely upon recalcitrant England (General Huntziger said on August 7 that "we are once more victims of the continuation of the war"), the Germans began interpreting the armistice with the utmost rigor.[3] During the first week of

---

[2] For the preamble, see *DGFP,* IX, no. 512, p. 644. For its subsequent use to justify German demands beyond the armistice, see, for example, forced French delivery of gasoline to the Italians in January 1941. (T-120/378/209359–60).

[3] The August 1, 1940, conversation is omitted from *DFCAA.* See Délégation française auprès de la Commission allemande d'armistice pour

August, French military equipment, originally stockpiled in France under Article 5 of the armistice, began to be taken to Germany.[4] On 26 August, after weeks of fruitless negotiations, the French government acceded to a figure of 20 million marks a day for the occupation costs payable under Article 18. This meant 400 million francs a day under the exaggerated exchange rate of twenty to one. Then the prisoners of war, whose liberation "even before the peace talks begin" had been requested by General Huntziger, began to be moved in early August from temporary encampments in France to German Stalags.[5] The first French plans for the armistice army were sent back for further pruning.

Most ominous of all, the Demarcation Line between occupied and unoccupied zones became a virtual sealed frontier. Only three hundred letters a day were allowed to cross at a moment when millions of Frenchmen were trying to relocate their families; in August Laval and Abetz worked out a bland postcard on which the correspondent crossed out the messages which did not apply ("I am well"; "I am not well"), the sole fragile contact across the line. Frenchmen authorized to cross the line were allowed after September 13 to carry no more than two hundred francs.[6] And very few Frenchmen could cross it. Government officials, in particular, found their travels impeded. At the moment when Vichy was trying desperately to establish its authority, local administrations in the Occupied Zone hardly had word of its existence. Although Article 3 of the armistice recognized

---

l'économie, "Comptes-rendus des réunions du 1er juillet 1940 au 5 août 1944" (consulted at the Bibliothèque de documentation internationale et contemporaine, Paris). For August 7, see *DFCAA*, I, 110.

[4] "Mitteilungen über die Arbeiten der WaKo," nos. 35 and 38, 2 and 6 August 1940 (T-120/365/206457, 206473). The French tried to have some of the matériel sent to the colonies instead (T-120/368/206878). By February 1941, 7,500 railroad carloads of French armaments had been removed to Germany (T-120/1067/313181).

[5] Hemmen (Wiesbaden) no. 81 to Berlin, 23 August 1940 (T-120/365/206573–74); *DFCAA*, I, 167–74; "Mitteilungen über die Arbeiten der WaKo," no. 35, 2 August 1940 (T-120/365/206457–58).

[6] *DFCAA*, I, 137, 140, 190–91; U.S. Department of State Serial File 851.00/2094. Gilbert Renaud ("Rémy"), *La Ligne de démarcation,* is a long collection of anecdotes about crossings. Jean-Louis Curtis, *Les Forêts de la nuit,* gives a most moving fictional account of clandestine crossing.

French sovereignty over the whole of France except for "the rights of the occupying power" and explicitly recognized the right of the French government to return to Paris, French requests to return the government to Paris, starting with Paul Baudouin's proposal of July 7, were all denied.[7] The Demarcation Line was becoming a garrote.

German authorities were also beginning to explore longer-range possibilities of exploitation going beyond the armistice arrangements. Already at the end of July a group of German officers and industrialists had insisted upon visiting French aluminum plants in the unoccupied zone (France was, before the German conquest of Yugoslavia, the richest European source of bauxite available to the Axis).[8] It seemed probable that they planned to demand the supply of bauxite or aluminum to Germany. At the same time, German industrial representatives began approaching French industrialists directly in the Occupied Zone about accepting German war contracts. At first, Minister of Industrial Production René Belin and Léon Noël, the French government representative in Paris, seem to have urged French industrialists not to accept. On July 27, however, the French government, perceiving that French industrialists were accepting anyway and hoping to negotiate the issue, agreed provided that German contracts with French industry in the Occupied Zone were funneled through a central French office and that French manufacture were limited to "passive," not "aggressive," matériel. In the end, General von Stülpnagel simply asserted in a letter on 2 September that "the German High Command has the right to call upon French industry [in the Occupied Zone] in the form and to the extent that the continued war against Britain makes necessary."[9]

Next, on 4 September, the German economic delegate to the Armistice Commission at Wiesbaden first proposed that French aircraft and airplane engine plants in the unoccupied zone also

[7] Paul Baudouin, *Neuf mois au gouvernement* (Paris, 1948), 227, 238, 270; T-120/121/119692.

[8] For French reluctance and then acquiescence, see *DFCAA*, I, 73–75, 84.

[9] The issue of German contracts with French industry in the occupied zone may be followed in *DFCAA*, I, 118–20, 155–56, 206–24.

work for German account.[10] It was clear that the German economic authorities were pressing far beyond the letter of the armistice for concrete material gains in France. Control over industry in the Occupied Zone had escaped French government hands, but, as General Huntziger observed on 6 September, "the situation appears much more favorable as concerns the industrialists of the free zone." [11] All the more reason to try to win some striking concessions for these new German proposals outside the armistice.

Even more frightening German acts exceeding the armistice pointed to their intention to annex Alsace-Lorraine. The French learned on July 15 that customs control had been set up on the old frontiers of 1871. On October 19 the Armistice Commission demanded that all natives of Alsace and Lorraine be freed from the Armistice Army and the Chantiers de la jeunesse. Then, on November 18, over the objections of Abetz and in conflict with the new era of good relations opened at Montoire three weeks before, Gauleiter Bürckel of Lorraine expelled some 100,000 Lorrainers who wanted to keep French citizenship. Gauleiter Wagner of Alsace did the same with some 4,000 refugees in early December. Until mid-December trainloads of refugees with little more than the clothes they were wearing were dumped into an already impoverished France. Many of them gathered around Clermont-Ferrand with part of the faculty and the archbishop of Strasbourg, where they made the Germans nervous with recollections of Sainte-Odile, the patron saint of Alsace, and her prophecies of the evils to come from "The Antichrist from the Danube." Reacting more sharply than to any other incident except perhaps the shooting of hostages in August 1941, Marshal Pétain issued a public statement denying that the current Franco-German negotiations had anything to do with "a measure of this kind." The communiqué was censored in the Occupied Zone.

Other territorial worries were raised by the closed zone of the northeast, on the frontiers of Alsace and Lorraine, where no French refugees were permitted to return, by the administration

[10] *DFCAA*, I, 194, 206–24.
[11] *DFCAA*, I, 207.

from Brussels of the departments of the Nord and Pas-de-Calais, and by local German hints of favor to Breton and Flemish separatists.[12] As a provisional arrangement, the armistice was galling; as a permanent one, it was unbearable. As General Huntziger told General von Stülpnagel at Wiesbaden on August 21, it was "leading France to ruin."[13]

A parallel evolution brought France and Britain almost to the brink of war with each other in the days following the armistice. Franco-British relations had already been strained to snapping by discordant priorities during the battle in northern France.[14] A struggle for control of the French Navy shattered them. Article 8 of the armistice provided that French warships, the second most powerful fleet of Europe, return to home ports, most of them in the Occupied Zone. Unmollified by promises that Admiral Darlan might be unable to keep even if he were willing, Churchill reckoned that the French fleet was about to fall into Hitler's hands. Early on July 4, after a British ultimatum to the French Mediterranean squadron either to join the British, go to distant French colonial ports, or scuttle itself had been rejected, British ships opened fire on the French ships in the harbor of Mers-el-Kebir, Algeria, killing 1,267 sailors and sending a hot spasm of anger through France. On the same day the British seized French ships in British ports. Marshal Pétain's government considered a joint Franco-Italian naval operation against Alexandria and issued orders on July 8 for preparation of an

---

[12] T-120/365/206284; *DFCAA*, II, 380–89. Marshal Pétain's protest note of 19 November 1940 and its German rejection are published in *DGFP*, XI, nos. 331 and 354, pp. 570, 610. André Lavagne, in *Procès Pétain*, 310, claimed that ninety-nine protests on Alsace-Lorraine were eventually issued. German intelligence reports on opinion among the refugees are in OKW. Abteilung für Wehrmacht-Propaganda. "Geheime-Akten über fremde Staaten: Frankreich" (T-77/OKW-1605). The best brief treatment of German policy toward Brittany is Eberhard Jäckel, *La France dans l'Europe de Hitler* (Paris, 1968), 74–78. For the Flemish movement, see E. Dejonghe, "Un mouvement séparatiste dans le Nord et le Pas-de-Calais sous l'occupation, 1940–44," *Revue d'histoire moderne et contemporaine* XVII:1 (January–March 1970).

[13] *DFCAA*, I, 170.

[14] John Cairns, "Great Britain and the Fall of France. A Study in Allied Disunity," *Journal of Modern History* XXVII:4 (December 1955).

attack from Dakar upon Freetown, Sierra Leone, but in the end contented itself with a minor air raid upon Gibraltar on July 5.[15] A de facto Franco-British war had begun that was to pit French forces against Anglo-Gaullist forces at Dakar in September 1940, in French Equatorial Africa in September–November 1940, and in Syria in May–July 1941.

The prospect of a break with England was not necessarily a bleak one. In the colonial realm, after all, Britain had been a more serious rival than Germany. In a world in which Germany seemed to be rising and Britain declining, France might be compensated overseas for what she was losing on the continent. Fertile minds at Vichy, drawing bold geopolitical conclusions from the wave of Anglophobia that swept France after Mers-el-Kebir, even glimpsed opportunities for expanding overseas at British expense.

The imperial visions unfolding at Vichy in the summer of 1940 were built, like so many Vichy positions, upon a current of late Third Republic opinion. After Munich, a *repli impérial*— falling back on the colonies—seemed to many the only way for French policy to be both active and safe. On the mainland, France stood athwart German ambitions without any real prospect of help from Italy, sharing a common anti-German interest only with dangerous Soviet Russia. After the war scare of September 1938, the empire was the only direction in which a Frenchman could brandish the flag without appearing to advocate war alongside Stalin against Hitler. "Once and for all," wrote the nationalist Radical Pierre Dominique in October 1938, "let us look out towards the sea and turn our back on the

[15] P. M. H. Bell, "Prologue à Mers-el-Kebir," *Revue d'histoire de la deuxième querre mondiale,* no. 33 (January 1959). French fury was increased by Admiral Gensoul's failure to send the full text of the British ultimatum, which included the option of sending the French fleet to French bases in the Caribbean. It was another Ems telegram. Contemporary sources for the planned attack on Alexandria are published in *DFCAA,* V, 440–44; orders for the attack on Sierra Leone are found in *Ministère public c/Weygand,* 25, and *Ministère public c/Rivière.* I. S. O. Playfair, *The War in the Mediterranean* (London, 1954), I, 142–43, describes the Gibraltar air raid, which a reader of Baudouin, *Neuf mois,* would assume had been put off indefinitely.

continent." Jean Piot, in the Radical newspaper *L'Oeuvre,* urged France to replace the *revanche* policy of Clemenceau with the colonialist policy of Jules Ferry.[16]

After the defeat of 1940, such ideas came even more naturally. France was hemmed in altogether on the continent. The colonies had become simultaneously even more precious and even more vulnerable. The colonial realm was also more fluid than it had been for fifty years, holding out the possibility of imperial gains at British expense. Those heady possibilities, however, were over-balanced by the probability that Germany would reclaim her former African colonies (France held part of the former German Cameroons) and the possibility of intensified colonial rivalry with Italy, Spain, and Japan. Vichy faced the dual challenge of keeping a colonial empire intact after military defeat and of using her colonial leeway to compensate for the losses of 1940.

Vichy went about the first of these two tasks with the ut-most urgency. General Weygand brought the governors-general into line for the armistice and then, after September 1940 as delegate-general for French Africa, personally oversaw the check-mating of Gaullist infiltration in all of French Africa except part of the Congo basin by the end of 1940. Conversely, Vichy also tried to keep German inspection teams in the colonies to a minimum and, except for Syria in May 1941, denied direct Axis use of bases in the French Empire. The aim was to seal the empire against encroachments by both Allies and Axis lest the two belligerent sides split it between them.

Vichy colonial aims were not purely defensive, however. Both Laval and Darlan, as we shall see, tried to interest the Germans in making France the colonial and maritime link to an African

---

[16] *La République,* 17 October 1938; *L'Oeuvre,* 15 December 1938. Pierre Dominique subsequently directed the Vichy press service, the Office fran-çais d'information (OFI), from 1941 to 1943. Advocates of the *repli im-périal* seem to have been strongest in the right wing of the Radical party and among far-right journalists. See also P.-A. Cousteau in *Je Suis Partout,* 11 November 1938, and Paul Marion in Doriot's *La Liberté,* 10 November 1938. Prime Minister Daladier's son Jean organized a "Youth for the French Empire" group in this period. I am indebted to Dr. Benton Stark for these references.

"hinterland" for the New Europe. The first sounding in this direction came almost at once, in July 1940. A staff study found by German intelligence on the desk of General Huntziger, French representative to the Armistice Commission at Wiesbaden, dated 10 July 1940, proposed that the French Middle Eastern Army seize the Iraqi oil fields of Mosul and Kirkuk, together with the pipelines leading to Syria and the Mediterranean coast, "for the account of France, Germany, and Italy at the same time, and with the agreement of these latter two." Germany and Italy would then join France among the stockholders of the Iraqi Petroleum Company, which would then be required to increase its oil output substantially for the benefit of continental Europe. "This program presents probably the greatest advantage 'Fortress Europe' can draw from the present war." Since oil production would henceforth be governed by "business needs" rather than by the rules of the "Anglo-Saxon trusts," "that will be the revenge of the consumers upon the producers." For France in particular, "all of these services rendered to Germany and Italy would permit us counterservices in the drawing up of the Peace Treaty." [17]

Was this curious document meant to fall into German hands? Perhaps so. In any event, all the ingredients of a positive imperial policy are there: the expectation of early peace, the hope for easier terms for France, the lure of British spoils, all clothed in demagogic jargon attacking the "Anglo-Saxon trusts" on behalf of continental consumers.

These multiple evolutions after June 1940 gave the Pétain government both the incentive and the opportunity to try to buy its way out of the harsh armistice into some less restrictive, more normal arrangement. It is only half true to argue, as General Weygand did after the war, that Vichy policy in the fall of 1940 had been strict interpretation of the armistice, no more, no less. [18]

---

[17] Deutsche Waffenstillstandskommission, Wiesbaden/Chefgruppe Ia, Nr. 21/40 g.Kdos. to OKW/Abt. L., 17 July 1940 (T-77/OKW-1347/5, 573, 576–80) forwards a German translation to Berlin.

[18] General Weygand, *Mémoires,* III, *Rappelé au service* (Paris, 1950), 317 ff. repeats the arguments Weygand used at his trial. Guy Raïssac,

The French delegation to the Armistice Commission at Wiesbaden did indeed employ arguments of strict construction in 1940–41 to oppose details like the rate of occupation costs, transport to Germany of prisoners of war and matériel, and the tightening of the Demarcation Line. In those early months, it was the Germans who used the loosely worded preamble to the armistice and Article 10, in which France agreed "not to undertake any hostile action whatsoever against the Reich" and to prevent her citizens from going abroad to do so, to justify going beyond the armistice where war needs demanded it. It was France that had something to gain by strict construction of such armistice provisions as Article 3, which acknowledged French "administration from Paris of occupied and unoccupied territory." It was French spokesmen who repeatedly affirmed their loyalty to the armistice, and it was German officials who had to admit that France was obeying the armistice more scrupulously than they had anticipated.[19]

At the same time, however, Marshal Pétain's government began asking to go beyond the armistice. If a peace treaty was impossible, summit talks might at least establish more normal, comfortable relations in anticipation of a final settlement. In the white heat of anger that followed Mers-el-Kebir, and even before the National Assembly had convened at Vichy to vote full powers to Marshal Pétain, General Huntziger proposed at Wiesbaden on July 7 that France and Germany step beyond the armistice relationship.

Normally, an armistice is an intermediate stage between war and peace. . . . but our armistice is irregular, for defeated France finds

---

Combat sans merci (Paris, 1966), and Philip Bankwitz, *Maxime Weygand and Civil-Military Relations in Modern France* (Cambridge, Mass., 1967), essentially accept this perspective.

[19] The German Armistice Commission reported to Berlin on 10 July 1940 that French policy appeared to be "strict literal interpretation of the armistice" (T-120/365/206231–34). General Halder observed that the French had turned in more guns than the Germans knew they had (Halder, "Diary," 10 October 1940). The rather legalistic negotiations over application of the terms at Wiesbaden may be followed in *DFCAA* or in T-120, Serials 365, 368, and 378, Büro des Staatssekretärs, "Akten betreffend Friedensverhandlungen mit Frankreich," 1–111.

herself almost at war with the same enemy as her victorious adversary.

The regular procedures are no longer sufficient. They ought to be supplemented by additional contacts between persons not belonging to the Armistice Commissions. For new situations, new measures! [20]

This was no bizarre personal initiative on General Huntziger's part. Two days later, Foreign Minister Paul Baudouin, stating that he spoke with Marshal Pétain's authorization, relayed word through Madrid (the same channel used three weeks earlier for the French armistice message) that he wanted to come to Germany to meet Ribbentrop. France, he said, wanted to become an "associated power." [21] Hardly two weeks after the armistice, the last government of the Third Republic was already asking for a Franco-German summit meeting.

Hitler responded to the new situation arising out of Mers-el-Kebir not by grasping the profferred French hand but by asking on July 15 for German base rights in North Africa. Pétain's letter of refusal tends to be cited as Vichy's first "resistance" to German demands. Indeed Pétain wrote Hitler that he was "painfully surprised," after France had shown its loyalty to the armistice above older loyalties (a reference to Mers-el-Kebir), to receive "new demands" in "flagrant contradiction" to the armistice signed a mere three weeks before. But Pétain went on to say that the bases demand created "an entirely new situation" going beyond the Armistice Commission's competence. He then made a frank bid for wider negotiations.

I believe that only a new negotiation can solve these problems. In expressing this opinion, I think that my country can usefully make

[20] This capital document is omitted from *DFCAA.* See Délégation française auprès de la Commission allemande de l'armistice pour l'économie, "Comptes rendus," 7 July 1940, at the Bibliothèque de documentation internationale et contemporaine, Paris.

[21] Stohrer (Madrid) 2295 to Berlin, 9 July 1940 (T-120/121/119698–99). Gaston Bergery said at his trial that Pétain had asked him in July 1940 to establish contact with Germany. Alfred Mallet, *Pierre Laval* (Paris, 1954), I, 217 n.

its voice heard. . . . I have a sincere desire that after so many quarrels our countries grow to understand each other better.[22]

Pétain was clearly understood in Berlin to be asking for a new Franco-German relationship. Otto Abetz, newly attached to the German occupation forces as Foreign Office representative, thought that the French were ready for a "renversement des alliances" in the aftermath of Mers-el-Kebir,[23] But then Abetz always fell victim to optimistic exaggerations about Franco-German conciliation. Cooler heads at the Foreign Office, however, like Otto Grote and Unterstaatssekretär Ernst Woermann, understood that Pétain was trying to set the bases issue in a new context of "free negotiation among equal partners." [24]

Pétain's hint was followed up in early August. On August 7 General Huntziger told his opposite number at Wiesbaden, General von Stülpnagel, that he wanted to meet the German chief of staff, General Keitel. The following day, Ernest Lagarde, director of political affairs at the Quai d'Orsay and a member of the French diplomatic delegation to the Armistice Commission, told the German Foreign Office representative Hencke that the French government wanted to discuss broad European and colonial questions "outside the narrow realm of the armistice." France had great experience in the Mediterranean and colonial areas, he said, and she could play a useful role in solving problems there in the interest of both nations. It was nothing less than a French bid to be the Mediterranean and colonial partner of the New Europe.[25]

[22] DFCAA, V, 463, 469. The text of Pétain's reply is also printed in Yves Bouthillier, Le Drame de Vichy, vol. I, 289–91. Georges Blond, Pétain (Paris, 1966), errs in saying that the appeal for wider negotiations, present in Jacques Guérard's draft of July 17, was omitted in the final draft.

[23] Pétain et les allemands. Mémorandum d'Abetz sur les rapports franco-allemands (Paris, 1948), 13. The telegrams published in this book may all be verified in the German archives, but Abetz' own observations date from 1943.

[24] T-120/F1/0366–67; Woermann (1147) to Madrid, 26 July 1940 (T-120/121/119759). See also DGFP, X, no. 208, 274–75.

[25] DFCAA, I, 139; Hencke (Wiesbaden) no. 119 to Berlin, 8 August 1940 (T-120/363/206498). A letter of 4 August 1940 from Baudouin to Ribbentrop requesting an "audience" and regular contacts between the two foreign ministers was perhaps not sent, as Baudouin claimed in his trial (Ministère Public c/Baudouin, 107), but it is certainly in the spirit of his government's policy at that time.

From the first days after Mers-el-Kebir, therefore, both French and German authorities were groping for some new arrangement beyond the armistice. German authorities wanted tighter security, French economic spoils, and base rights in the French Empire. Vichy wanted normalcy, a promise of territorial integrity, and a chance to start making the New France. Every French official with some access to a German ear was lobbying for a broader Franco-German settlement in July–August 1940. But it was Pierre Laval who won the race to good German contacts.

Pierre Laval and the Paris Connection

WHILE PÉTAIN AND FOREIGN MINISTER BAUDOUIN were trying to reach Ribbentrop via Madrid, and while General Huntziger was trying to reach General Keitel through Wiesbaden, Pierre Laval turned his eyes to Paris. It was for domestic utility that Laval had been brought into the cabinet in late June. It was the Ministry of Foreign Affairs he had wanted, however, and it was in diplomacy that he now proceeded to make himself indispensable. Laval had, after all, been foreign minister in the early 1930's longer than any Frenchman since Briand, and it was with an interpellation against Daladier's wartime alliance system in March 1940 that he had broken his long silence in the Senate and begun his political comeback. Laval, like most conservatives, wanted to build a "Latin bloc" with Italy and Spain; unlike most conservatives, he could actually claim some personal contact with Mussolini.[26] By July 1940, however, it was too late to work for Italian neutrality, and Laval's main challenge was to break the wall of silence in Berlin.

Laval decided to cultivate Otto Abetz. He sent three unofficial messengers to Paris to work for "the resumption of normal

---

[26] Geoffrey Warner, *Pierre Laval and the Eclipse of France* (London, 1968), 148, 156, shows that Laval exaggerated the credit he enjoyed with Mussolini by spring 1940.

relations with Germany": Fernand de Brinon, an old companion of Abetz in the 1930's Comité France-Allemagne; Jean Luchaire, editor before the war of the proappeasement weekly *Notre temps,* whose secretary had become Mme. Abetz; and Jean Fontenoy, a journalist of fortune who had fought the Soviets in the Finnish campaign of 1939–40. On July 14 Abetz reported to Berlin that Laval wanted to come to Paris and that he wanted to meet Goering. The necessary passes were provided, and on July 19 Laval became the first French minister to return to the capital, and for several months the only one with a working relationship there. Foreign minister Baudouin didn't get to Paris for the first time until September 13. Laval was full of optimism when he discussed his visit to Paris with the American diplomat, Robert Murphy, on July 29.[27]

Laval's efforts to meet Goering differed in no way, of course, from the efforts of Pétain and his other colleagues to meet their German opposite numbers. Furthermore Paris could hardly seem a very fruitful channel at that stage. Laval was vice-president of the Council, but he was not foreign minister and he had no authority in foreign relations. Otto Abetz, a former drawing teacher and then Ribbentrop's agent in Paris in the 1930's, was still merely the German Foreign Ministry's representative to the German military authority in Paris, the Militärbefehlshaber in Frankreich, General von Brauchitsch. Abetz did not become ambassador and acquire some independent authority until August. The real German authority in France was military, and all negotiations were supposed to pass through military channels at the Armistice Commission at Wiesbaden.

In time, however, Laval's Paris connection was to become the chief avenue of Franco-German relations, partly because Paris was the capital, partly because intergovernmental relations slipped from the Vichy-Wiesbaden military channel to the Paris-Berlin civilian channel as the war went on beyond anyone's an-

[27] Schleier (Paris) 270 to Berlin, 25 July 1940 (T-120/121/119751); Abetz (Paris) 128 to Ribbentrop, 14 July 1940 (T-120/121/119723); *Les Procès de la collaboration: Brinon, Darnand, Luchaire* (Paris, 1948), 87–89, 370–73. Pierre Cathala, *Face aux realités* (Paris, 1948), 113 ff, is diametrically wrong in saying that the Germans sought out Laval. For the Laval-Murphy conversation, *FRUS,* 1940, II, 377–79.

ticipation, and partly because Abetz and Laval found each other useful to expand their respective roles.

Abetz and Laval found much in common. Laval's socialist origins and his earthy contempt for the clerical, traditionalist circles at Vichy appealed to Abetz' vestigial early-Nazi radicalism.[28] Tactically, both men wanted to establish civilian channels of authority outside the military channels of the Armistice Commission at Wiesbaden, whose competence was limited to applying the armistice and which, by definition, was forbidden to rise to the new occasions offered by Mers-el-Kebir and the French efforts to achieve a wider settlement. Ribbentrop, too, was eager to assert a Foreign Office role in Franco-German relations. Thus Abetz returned from his first trip home on August 5 as ambassador (though not officially accredited to a French government, since the two states were still officially at war). Laval followed up his July 19 visit with another on August 10, and in the interval Brinon and Luchaire shuttled back and forth with messages. Laval also met General von Brauchitsch and Dr. Friedrich Grimm, an international lawyer on Abetz' staff, on August 28. The most serviceable contacts outside the Armistice Commission were falling into Laval's hands.[29]

Laval's August 1940 conversations in Paris, especially his two-and-a-half hour talk with Dr. Friedrich Grimm, unfolded a reasoned argument why Germany should reach a generous final settlement with France on the basis of shared interests. France, he told Dr. Grimm, now had more interests in common with Germany than with Britain. He recognized that France had been defeated and must pay a penalty. The final peace, however, could not be arranged until Britain had been defeated too. The more totally Britain was defeated, the less France would have to bear the brunt alone. For example, the French loss of Alsace (Laval conceded Alsace to Germany, but not Lorraine) could be compensated with parts of British Africa. While

---

[28] *DGFP*, XI, no. 531.

[29] Abetz (Paris) 356 to Ribbentrop, 10 August 1940 (T-120/121/119795-96); *Les Procès de la collaboration*, 87–89, 370–73; Abetz (Paris) 475 to Ribbentrop of 30 August 1940 (T-120/121/119833), also published in *DGFP*, X, no. 411, p. 580. Laval-Grimm conversation, T-120/2624/D525934–47.

Germany had it in her power to impose a harsh victor's peace on France, a peace of reconciliation would end the era of "revanche" and usher in the age of Franco-German cooperation for which Laval said he had been working since he voted against the Treaty of Versailles in 1919. He foresaw chances of "beautiful Franco-German collaboration in British Africa."

In the meantime, Frenchmen must be given something to hope for. The peace must not offend French pride, or Europe would fall back into a renewed cycle of war. The most "pressing problem," he told Dr. Grimm, was the Demarcation Line's choking grip between occupied and unoccupied France, which obstructed a unified administration. Laval was particularly eager to obtain a German guarantee of French territorial integrity, so that Frenchmen would know they had everything to gain by an early settlement with Germany. Simultaneously, the French delegates at Wiesbaden were working to reach endurable levels of occupation costs, the early release of prisoners of war, and the return of the government to Paris. The point, Laval was to tell Luftwaffe General Hanesse at a breakfast in Paris in early December 1940, was that "with the fruits of collaboration in hand" he could "bring the French people with him" to "Germany's side." [30]

Laval had something more immediate to offer in August 1940 than long-range goodwill. At the end of July he sent a colonial ministry official, Paul Devinat, to Wiesbaden to offer Germany a share of French colonial products in exchange for German help in getting French colonial trade started again, in the face of British and Japanese threats to the empire. Laval, Devinat said, needed German support in order to dampen internal opposition to his policy of reconciliation with Germany. He was very eager to meet the German leaders.[31] He also stressed Vichy's plans for anti-Masonic, antiparliamentary, anti-Jewish legislation. Laval began to offer "volunteers" against England. He told Abetz on August 10 that Colonel René Fonck, the World War I ace, had

[30] T-120/3485H/E019467–68.
[31] Hemmen memorandum of 2 August 1940 (T-120/3527H/E021556).

assembled two hundred French pilots who were ready to participate in the war against England.[32]

Laval's August conversations in Paris raise several vital questions about Vichy's overtures. The postwar memoirs tried to depict Laval as a lone wolf, spending long periods in Paris and keeping his colleagues in ignorance of promises which "overcommitted" the regime to Germany.[33] Contemporary German archives, however, suggest a much more broadly shared and concerted Vichy policy of preparing to step beyond the armistice to an accommodation within Hitler's Europe. We have already seen the July–August efforts for a Franco-German summit meeting. The military relaxations in the armistice to permit French defense against Britain were the work of Weygand and Huntziger. Finance Minister Yves Bouthillier, whose postwar memoirs try to establish his distance from Laval, got to Paris himself on September 30 and proposed that instead of stripping French industries, Germany give war contracts to French industry, even in the unoccupied zone. This policy would revive the French economy and end unemployment. At the same time, Bouthillier promised, France was ready to embark on a new social and economic order.[34] Laval struck a somewhat more aggressive note than the others about military aid against Britain, but in September, as we shall see, others, including Baudouin and Admiral Darlan, supported active reconquest of French Equatorial African holdings from the Gaullists. Laval was exceptional in August 1940 more for his success in meeting German officials and his growing link with Abetz than for the substance of his overtures.

The other notable point is the lack of German interest in July

[32] Abetz (Paris) 356 to Ribbentrop, 10 August 1940 (T-120/121/119795–96). German archives do not, however, support Baudouin's contention (*Neuf mois,* 325) that Laval promised General von Brauchitsch on August 28 that France would go to war against England. Abetz (Paris) 475 to Ribbentrop 30 August 1940 (T-120/121/119833).

[33] Paul Baudouin, *Neuf mois au gouvernement* (Paris, 1948), 258, 325; Yves Bouthillier, *Le Drame de l'armistice* (Paris, 1951), I, 171, 196.

[34] Abetz memorandum, "Aufzeichnung über politische Besprechungen in der Zeit vom. 6. bis 15. September 1940" (T-120/364/206021–30).

and August 1940 in voluntary association with France. German peace treaty preparations during this period were strikingly punitive.[35] Even Laval's most startling offers of French pilots for the British campaign seem to have aroused no interest in German circles. The French resistance to Britain at Mers-el-Kebir had, to be sure, resulted in some temporary suspensions of the military armistice provisions so that French forces in the colonies could defend themselves, but these were not yet expected to be permanent.[36] General von Stülpnagel observed at Wiesbaden that despite the armistice "we are still at war with France."[37] The Armistice Commission continued to rule by Diktat. By September, Laval's constant probings for a summit meeting had got nowhere. He told an American diplomat, with discouragement, that the Germans apparently held him in low esteem and didn't want to negotiate. Yves Bouthillier lamented on 23 October that "up to now the Germans haven't shown the slightest sign of a desire for collaboration."[38]

The Archimedian Point from which Vichy finally interested Berlin in collaboration was the issue of how to defend the French Empire against British-Gaullist encroachment. The Gaullist takeover of French Equatorial Africa, which was first reported in Berlin on August 28 and which threatened to spread to West Africa with the British-Gaullist naval expedition that reached Dakar on 20 September, suddenly made Vichy's authority and independence seem vitally useful to Germany.

[35] For German designs on French Equatorial Africa, see *DGFP,* XI, no. 298, p. 483. France was not intended to belong to the "Greater European Economic Sphere," according to the plans for a "weakened" France outlined in a Foreign Office dossier on the *Grosswirtschaftsraum* (T-120, Serial 830). German intentions toward France are discussed most fully in Eberhard Jäckel, *La France dans l'Europe de Hitler* (Paris, 1968).

[36] Robert O. Paxton, *Parades and Politics at Vichy* (Princeton, New Jersey, 1966), 75, describes the German concessions after Mers-el-Kebir.

[37] T-120/365/206229.

[38] U.S. Dept. of State Serial File 851.00/2068, 2069, 2073. See also Baudouin, *Neuf mois,* 363; Bouthillier letter to General Doyen, 23 October 1940, *Ministère public c/Bouthillier,* 52.

The "New Policy," September–December 1940

HITLER HAD LONG SUSPECTED SOME SECRET PÉTAIN-de Gaulle deal, he told Mussolini at Florence on October 28, 1940. After hearing details of the French defense against Anglo-Gaullist forces at Dakar on September 23–24 and hearing Pétain tell him at Montoire on October 24 that de Gaulle was a "blot on the honor of the French officer corps," and having recently seen films of the French defense at Mers-el-Kebir, back in July, he had now come to the view that Vichy was sincerely hostile to the British and the Gaullists. The best policy, Hitler told Mussolini, was for Vichy France to defend French Africa herself.[39] It was a decisive turning point in French-German relations. Dakar had brought Hitler himself around to seeing some utility in voluntary assistance from an autonomous France.

The Anglo-Gaullist raid on Dakar was the climax of de Gaulle's second attempt to bring the French Empire back into the war. The first attempt after the armistice had brought away a few individual officers—Colonel Edgard de Larminat from Syria, General Catroux from Indochina, General Paul Le Gentilhomme from Djibouti—but had left the colonies intact under Vichy control. It is well to remember how hard Vichy had worked to assert its sovereignty in July and August in order to win its right to speak for France under the armistice. Vichy feared losing both the metropole to Germany and the empire to England if it did not do so.

At the end of August, the handful of Gaullists in London tried again. With the support of the black Governor-General Félix Eboué in the Chad and a few local officers, Colonel de Larminat, René Pleven, and a few others visited the capitals of French Equatorial Africa during August 24–28 and tipped most of the area into the Gaullist camp by a bloodless coup. Simul-

---

[39] *DGFP*, Series D, XI, no. 246, pp. 411 ff.

taneously, a sea-born Anglo-Gaullist force with de Gaulle himself aboard sailed on August 31 for Dakar in an effort to swing the balance in West Africa too. With the first news, Vichy had obtained German and Italian permission to send three cruisers and three destroyers out of Toulon to reassert her shaking authority in tropical Africa, and with these reinforcements, Governor-General Pierre Boisson at Dakar stood off the Gaullists on September 23–24 with a vigorous show of force. British and French ships exchanged fire again, as in July, and once again the French armed forces fought off the Allied "aggressor."

De Gaulle's discomfiture ("The following days were cruel," he wrote in his memoirs [I, 137]) was Vichy's opportunity. French spokesmen redoubled their efforts to gain a general settlement from Germany with a unity of language that argues once again for the basic accord between Laval and the rest of the government.

At Wiesbaden, where he had been keeping General von Stülpnagel informed of the fighting, General Doyen (the new French chief delegate) wrote on September 25:

> We find ourselves in a situation without precedent in history. You are making war on England, but we are too, and we are in a state of war with you.

The striking proof at Dakar of French loyalty to the armistice, Doyen said, "demands in all equity an equivalent gesture on your part." He asked that Germany come to French aid materially, by allowing the French military a free hand to defend the empire and master the "dissidence," and morally, by guaranteeing that in the peace treaty to come, the French Empire would remain French.[40] General Huntziger, now minister of war, tried to make the same point to General von Brauchitsch on September 26.

> It is a fact that France and Germany have an armistice, but it is also a fact that France is fighting with Germany against Britain. This anomalous situation must be settled.

[40] *DFCAA*, I, 389–90. See also "Mitteilungen über die Arbeiten der WaKo," no. 76, 23 September 1940 (T-120/368/207014–16), for similar language on September 21.

Stressing France's determination to resist the attacks of Britain and the Gaullists on the empire, Huntziger said that France must be given the means to do so—not only the military means, but some clear promise that the empire would remain French in the peace, some easing of the Demarcation Line, and improved economic conditions.[41]

French planes dropped some six hundred tons of bombs on British installations at Gibraltar in three raids on September 24 and 25, lending some weight to the two generals' assertions that France was virtually at war with Britain.

Laval had already rushed to Paris on September 24 to see Abetz. "He wished and hoped that France could make her modest contribution to the final overthrow of Britain." That language goes further than that of his colleagues, but his main point was the same. France was determined to resist the British attack on West Africa, but only a German declaration that West Africa would remain French in the peace treaty would refute de Gaulle's propaganda that the only way to save the empire lay through Allied victory.[42]

Yves Bréart de Boisanger, governor of the Bank of France and chief French economic negotiator at Wiesbaden, also struck the new note in his daily struggles with the chief German economic delegate, Richard Hemmen. France was ready to cooperate economically "to a greater extent than previously," he said on 23 September, provided some political concessions were made. France wanted to get out of the present "state of suspense under the armistice" and "into settled conditions." The following day, arguing with Hemmen about the new risks to which German war contracts would expose French industries in the unoccupied zone, he insisted that German concessions must be political, not merely economic. "Now I understand your position," Hemmen said finally. "It is an altogether new question which is before us." [43]

---

[41] Memorandum Pol. IM 1358g of 1 October 1940 (T-120/121/120017–23). Baudouin, *Neuf mois,* 362, implies that mainly internal matters were discussed.

[42] Abetz (Paris) 684 to Berlin, 25 September 1940 (T-120/121/119917).

[43] *DGFP,* XI, no. 98, p. 174; *DFCAA,* I, 413.

Pétain took part himself in this urgent Vichy campaign of late September. He had already told a German industrialist on September 22 that if he still had military means and were not limited by the armistice, he would not refuse, "before my conscience and before history," to order active operations against England. With the news of Dakar, he sent the blind conservative deputy and war veterans' leader Georges Scapini, a man who had been received by Hitler in the 1930's and who had been a co-founder of the Comité France-Allemagne with Brinon and Abetz in 1935, to Berlin as his personal emissary. Scapini spent September 27–30 visiting top German officials: Ernst von Weizsäcker, the permanent secretary-general of the Foreign Office, and two diplomats, Emil von Rintelen, and Roland Krug von Nidda. We do not know what Scapini's instructions were, but after painting a black picture of economic hardship in France and Vichy's fear of revolution, he told his German auditors that France wanted to swing sharply around ("um-wälzen") to the European sphere. France, he said, was "ready to enter the continental front." He foresaw a valuable role for France as the leading colonial power of the New Europe, provided, of course, that she kept those colonies. As for continental peace terms, he proposed a plebiscite in Lorraine. He led his hearers to believe that he, Scapini, would be ambassador when relations were normalized.[44] Then, on 11 October, Pétain broadcast a major policy address containing a foreign policy section. The new regime must "liberate itself from traditional friendships and intimacies." Although France was prepared for good relations with all her neighbors, Franco-German relations dominated her future. The victor, Pétain said, could choose "a new peace of collaboration" or a "traditional peace of oppression." If Germany knows how to "rise above her victory, we will know how to rise above our defeat."[45]

[44] Reports of Scapini's various talks may be found in T-120/121/119929-37 and T-120/587/243341, 243347-48. Scapini's postwar memoirs, *Mission sans gloire* (Paris, 1966), treat his role as a purely technical matter of overseeing the condition of French prisoners of war in Germany. He says nothing of these September–October 1940 missions.

[45] *Le Temps,* 12 October 1940. According to Baudoin, *Neuf mois,*

Whatever different nuances were contained in this flood of Vichy overtures, Berlin could hardly fail to receive the essential signal. The Vichy regime wanted to negotiate a general settlement with French territory intact in exchange for active defense of the French Empire against the British. Set us free, and we will cooperate with you. The German archives of late September and early October 1940 are preoccupied with debates about a "new policy" toward France. Halder's diary, for example, changes tone strikingly. On September 16, he observes that Abetz' function is to install a cabinet in France that will accept a harsh peace. By September 28 he is talking about the "new policy." In the afternoon of September 24, Hitler decided to reverse an earlier distrustful decision to deny further reinforcements to the French forces in Africa, by releasing French air forces in Africa from armistice restraints.[46] On September 26 Hitler told top military advisors that he wanted to try to "hook France to the German wagon" and mentioned a possible meeting with Pétain.[47] While Ribbentrop remained skeptical as always, some top German military agencies seized the "new policy" as a major new strategic alternative to the increasingly dubious cross-channel invasion of England. Admiral Raeder was a permanent supporter of an active Mediterranean strategy. The German Armistice Commission at Wiesbaden forwarded a plan to Berlin on October 4 for the "active inclusion of France in the war against England." In closer touch with French spokesmen than with other German officials, the Germans at Wiesbaden were sure that the French would defend their empire against the British and even expand it (for example, by helping to take Gibraltar), contributing economically as well as militarily to the German war effort, if they were given "assurances of favorable peace terms."[48]

---

366 ff, preparation of this statement of social and foreign policy went back to October 1.

[46] Weizsäcker memoranda nos. St. S. 726, 727, 728, all of September 24, 1940 (T-120/368/207021–42), trace the change of mind. Also see Greiner war diary, Section L, 25 September 1940, quoted in Walter Warlimont, *Inside Hitler's Headquarters* (London, 1964), 122.

[47] Jäckel, 158. Halder mentions Hitler's desire to meet Pétain on 11 October and says on 16 October that the date has been set.

[48] "Aufzeichnung zur aktiven Einschaltung Frankreichs in die Kriegsführung gegen England." D.W.St.K. 8/40 g.Kdo Chefsache, 4 October

A new Mediterranean-naval-colonial strategy pointing south-ward opened up a Pandora's box of rival claims, however; Spain wanted Morocco and Italy wanted not only Tunisia but the Constantine area of Algeria. Laval, General Doyen, and Yves Bréart de Boisanger had all insisted that Vichy couldn't fight French "dissidence" if the Axis was going to take the French Empire away anyway. Hitler's efforts to reconcile these con-flicting aims took him on a tour of Latin Europe, starting with a meeting with Mussolini at the Brenner Pass on October 4. There he admitted that the attack on England had been "post-poned," proposed the seizure of Gibraltar, promised Mussolini Tunisia, Corsica, and Nice, and tried to balance out the various claims to North Africa by compensating France from conquered British colonies. The main thing was to postpone this redistri-bution of spoils to the peace, for if French officers found out, instead of defending the empire from the British, they would turn Morocco over to the British and join the other side. Fortu-nately, Hitler thought, the Pétain government could be in-fluenced, which would not be the case if the French government fled abroad.[49] Then on October 20 Hitler set out in his special train "Amerika" to Hendaye to try to bring Spain into an attack on Gibraltar. Stops were planned in France going and coming: October 22 and October 24. An obscure village railroad station near Tours, Montoire-sur-Loir, with a convenient tunnel nearby for air raid protection, was hastily embellished with potted palms, red carpets, and antiaircraft batteries. It was there that Pierre Laval, expecting he was about to get his long-requested meeting with Ribbentrop, was brought to Hitler on October 22, 1940. Two days later, returning from a frustrating meeting with a stubbornly neutral Franco, Hitler met Pétain at the same spot.

The Montoire meetings came as such a total surprise to the French government that they usually intrude brusquely, as a pure German invention, into the history of Vichy. Indeed, there had been little diplomatic homework even on the German side. Even so, the Montoire meetings were the culmination of months

---

1940 (T-77/OKW/1347). The Germans began to use the loan-word *Kollaboration* at about this time in discussing Franco-German relations.
[49] *DGFP*, Series D, XI, no. 149, pp. 245–59.

of French entreaty. The July–August appeals already mentioned did not abate in September. Pétain told a German industrialist on September 22 that he wanted to meet Hitler. He sent Colonel René Fonck to Abetz in mid-September to make the same request. Scapini had taken the same message to Weizsäcker in Berlin on September 30, and Professor Burckhardt and the ex-Khedive Abbas Hilmi reported to Abetz on October 11 that Pétain had repeated this wish to them.[50] What had changed by October 22 was German receptivity.

The two Montoire talks were more remarkable for public effect than for anything said there. Hitler, Laval, and Pétain agreed that the war had been a French blunder and that France and Germany must now work together. Pétain said he was in no position to define the exact limits of the cooperation he hoped for, and Laval pointed out that Pétain could not declare war without a parliamentary vote. Hitler did not ask for a formal French alliance or war against Britain, nor did he advance any of the concrete proposals to be found in German Foreign Office working documents prepared just before the trip. No joint document was signed at the end.[51]

Embryonic divergences of aim were already apparent at Montoire, however. Already on October 4, talking over the "new policy" with a reluctant Mussolini at the Brenner Pass, Hitler had promised Italy colonial satisfactions that could come only at the expense of France and promised that France should never again become a great power capable of another war of *revanche*. Hitler went to Montoire explicitly planning to conceal the harsh future from the French.[52] Even at Montoire, he warned Laval that France had been the first Ally conquered and so "an enemy held primarily liable." Moreover, nothing about the peace could be decided until the war was over. France could soften the blow only to the extent that she "mobilized everything against England." Pétain, by contrast, asked for a

[50] Abetz reported all these démarches to Berlin. See T-120/364/206021–30; T-120/121/119936–37, 120059–60; and T-120/3681H/E035166–74.

[51] Jäckel (pp. 162–67) shows that the "protocols" published in *DGFP*, X, nos. 207–8, were not actually brought up at the meetings.

[52] *DGFP*, Series D, vol. XI, no. 149, pp. 245–59.

peace that "favored those who had tried to make a new start" and said that he anticipated as a result of cooperation "a more advantageous outcome of the war for France." [53] These divergent statements should have been an ominous warning to Vichy of the futility of the "new policy."

Nonetheless the Vichy government tried earnestly in the days following Montoire to give concrete form to these new signs of German interest. Domestically, the most vital need was to reopen all those issues of internal order on which the Armistice Commission had overruled them in the discouraging days in August: Demarcation Line, occupation costs, return to Paris, liberation of prisoners of war. Externally, the possibility arose of using a well-disposed Germany to block the chief threats to French territorial integrity: Italy and Spain in North Africa, Japan in Indochina, and Britain in tropical Africa.

The Vichy government lost no time in prodding the Germans forward in both these areas. Five days after Montoire, on October 29, Laval returned to Paris with Minister of War General Huntziger and Minister of Finance Yves Bouthillier in tow. He told Abetz that Huntziger would plan the military follow-up with General von Stülpnagel at Wiesbaden, while Bouthillier would negotiate the domestic alleviations with Hemmen. By now Laval was foreign minister as well as vice-premier, the initiative in foreign affairs having clearly fallen from Paul Baudouin to the Laval-Abetz connection. [54]

Marshal Pétain demonstrated his solidarity with these efforts by sending Scapini off to Berlin again on October 29 to negotiate the early release of the prisoners of war. [55]

[53] German Foreign Office interpreter Paul Schmidt's version of the Montoire talks is printed in *DGFP*, Series D, XI, nos. 212, 227, pp. 354 ff., 385 ff.

[54] Baudouin, *Neuf mois*, 379 ff., repeated the claim made at his trial that he had resigned in protest on October 29. One must observe, however, that Baudouin remained Secrétaire d'état à la présidence du conseil, with the rank of minister, even after the public announcement that the cabinet had unanimously approved the Montoire policy at its October 26 meeting.

[55] Abetz (Paris) 1044 of 30 October 1940 (T-120/121/120100–1), and Pétain letter to Scapini, 18 December 1940 (T-77/OKW-999/5, 632, 934). The letter was actually signed by Baudouin as secretary to the cabinet council.

The crucial thing for Vichy was to get results. Public statements of the week after Montoire put the government far out on a limb of promises. Installed in the Matignon Palace for the first time (Abetz let him fly the French flag), Laval publicly announced on October 31 his "first contacts" with German officials since Montoire.

In all domains, and especially in the economic and colonial spheres, we have discussed and we will continue to examine in what practical form our collaboration can serve the interests of France, Germany, and Europe.

Pétain's famous speech of the same day in which he announced that "I enter into the way of collaboration" included even more golden prospects. He assured his listeners that

In the near future, the weight of suffering of our country could be lightened, the fate of our prisoners ameliorated, occupation costs reduced, the demarcation line made more flexible, and the administration and supply of our territory easier.[56]

French officials kept up the pressure for results in private conversations as well. Over lunch with Abetz on October 31, Laval predicted that when they saw the results of collaboration, the French people would soon come around to accepting the new policy. They would, like Laval, desire the victory of Germany. But for this to happen, Vichy needed results that "strike people in the eye" ("die ins Auge fallen"), he told Marshal Goering during a two-hour conversation in Paris on November 9. If conspicuous benefits flowed from collaboration, he told Luftwaffe General Hanesse at a breakfast on December 3, he could "bring the French people with him" to the "German side." There was a subtle blackmail in the pressure of other prominent Frenchmen for results. Passing through Paris on 30 October on his way to Berlin for the second time, Scapini discussed the early release of French prisoners of war with Abetz. Although he admitted it was not possible, or even desirable in a period of unemployment, for all the prisoners to

[56] Laval's Matignon Declaration of 31 October 1940 is published in Jean Thouvenin, *Avec Pétain* (Paris, 1940), 33; Pétain's speech of 31 October 1940 is published in *ibid.*, 30.

come home at once before the peace conference, he warned Abetz that some results from Montoire were essential for stability in France. Agriculture Minister Caziot and Finance Minister Bouthillier observed to a German official over lunch on November 9 that post-Montoire propaganda was building up fantastic hopes that might give way to dangerous despair. From outside the government, Pierre-Etienne Flandin, the conservative Third Republic premier who had publicly congratulated Hitler for "saving the peace" at Munich in September 1938, told an unidentified informant for the German embassy on November 19 that he hoped for a new Franco-German relationship growing out of Montoire, but there was danger of "backfire" in public opinion if French hopes for the release of prisoners, economic revival, moving the government to Paris, and easing passage between the two zones grew too high.[57] No wonder Abetz and the officials of the Armistice Commission at Wiesbaden who were closest to this French barrage were more eager for results and concessions after Montoire than anyone in Berlin.

Results were to be denied, at least in the domestic sphere. Considering his eager remarks to General Hanesse about his forthcoming trip to meet Ribbentrop, Laval would have been devastated by Ribbentrop's own plans for that meeting. Ribbentrop intended to "open French eyes." Germany was not going to make any one-sided concessions, as Laval seemed to think.[58]

Nevertheless, the Vichy government went ahead at the end of November in a curious unilateral effort to act as if these domestic concessions had been granted. The French government

[57] Abetz (Paris) 1059 of 31 October 1940 (T-120/121/120111–12); German minutes of the Laval-Goering talks of 9 November 1940, the Laval-Hanesse conversation of 3 December 1940, and Caziot's and Bouthillier's remarks in a letter from Dr. Karl Heinz Gerstner to Roland Krug von Nidda, 6 November 1940, are all to be found in Pariser Botschaft: Geheime Akten der Politischen Registratur, Binder, 98–101, "Beziehungen Frankreichs zu Deutschland," microfilmed as T-120/3485H. The talk with Flandin of 19 November 1940 is found in Sicherheitsdienst, Abteilung Deutschland, Referat D11, "Akten betreffend Frankreich," Band 1, microfilmed as T-120/686.

[58] Ritter (Berlin) 1777 to Abetz, 4 November 1940 (T-120/3485H/E019439). This is a reply to Abetz' account of his lunch with Laval on October 31, cited in footnote 57.

declined to make the occupation costs payment due December 1, alleging that continued payment at the rate imposed in August would prejudice the upcoming negotiations.[59] In the continuing negotiation on replacing the Demarcation Line with some gentler security arrangement, the French were suddenly no longer willing to accept German customs inspection on the national frontiers as a substitute, except in return for satisfying a number of French requests overridden the previous July, such as abolishing the closed zone in the northeast and returning the Nord and Pas-de-Calais department from German military administration in Brussels to Paris. General Doyen explained that Pétain's government was now stronger, that French needs in Africa were greater, and that Vichy could not afford to compromise her sovereignty in the face of Gaullist propaganda.[60] Most dramatically of all, the Pétain government cut short the negotiations on the move to Paris that had been reopened fruitlessly on 30 October. On November 27 General Doyen notified the German Armistice Commission that "Marshal Pétain had decided to move the seat of government to Versailles" around December 10–15. German authorities were asked to vacate the palaces at Versailles so that Pétain could live in the Trianon. Fifteen hundred French Mobile Guards were supposed to accompany him. Public announcement of this move on December 2 cut off all retreat. The Americans were reassured that the permanent diplomatic services would remain at Vichy, free of direct German surveillance, and that Pétain would be back in a couple of weeks. In a "flutter of excitement," plans were made to move Labor, Finance, Agriculture, Trade, and Public Works to Versailles, to

---

[59] Doyen to Stülpnagel, Nr. 8517/EM, 27 November 1940 (T-120/3699/E036200). This whole file (Pariser Botschaft, Geheim-Akten der Politischen Registratur, Ordner 123, "Pol. 3, no. 1. Französische Regierung, Ministerien, Zusammensetzung der Kabinette. Ubersiedlung nach Versailles—21. Juni 1940–30. Dezember 1940") contains mostly the negotiations on moving to Paris that were renewed on 30 October. For occupation costs see "Mitteilungen über die Arbeiten der WaKo," no. 129, 7 Dec. 1940 (T-120/368/207375–77), *Ministère public c/Bouthillier*, fascicule 2, 74 ff, and Bouthillier, *Le Drame de l'armistice*, II, *Finances sous la contrainte* (Paris, 1951).

[60] T-120/368/207378–79, 207384, 207435–37.

divide Justice, Education, Interior, and Colonies between Versailles and Vichy, and to leave the main staffs of the military
ministries and Foreign Affairs in the unoccupied zone.[61]
    What had come over Vichy? Had Abetz misled them on the
likelihood of a German change of heart about the way the
armistice was being applied? Had Vichy decided to present
Berlin with a daring *fait accompli*? We still do not know, but
it is clear that the German authorities firmly rejected all these
unilateral Vichy actions. Internally, the French would have to
be satisfied with a spectacle: the return of the ashes of Napoleon's son, the Duc de Reichstadt, from Vienna to the Invalides, suddenly announced for the hundredth anniversary of
Napoleon I's burial there, 15 December 1940.

THE MILITARY HALF OF THE POST-MONTOIRE FOLLOW-
up went much more smoothly. Here German and Vichy interests
overlapped. Germany wanted to keep the French Empire out
of Allied hands. Vichy wanted to keep it intact, neutral, and
out of both Allied and Axis hands. Vichy gained some ground
when German policy evolved from envisaging direct Axis intervention in the French Empire (as in the bases demand of July 15)
to Hitler's statement to a skeptical Mussolini at Florence on October 28 that the best solution was for France to defend French
Africa herself.[62] This evolution gave some substance to the Vichy
gamble that order was best maintained in the empire with Germany rather than against her.
    Threats to the status quo in the French Empire in the fall

[61] Doyen to Stülpnagel, Nr. 8517/EM, 27 November 1940 (T-120/
3699/E036200), and the rest of the same file: Pariser Botschaft. Geheim-
Akten der politischen Registratur, Ordner 123, "Pol. 3, no. 1. Französische
Regierung, Ministerien, Zusammensetzung der Kabinette. Ubersiedlung
nach Versailles—21. Juni 1940–30. Dezember 1940." See also *DFCAA*, II.
United States and Swiss objections to moving the foreign embassies into
the Occupied Zone may be found in U.S. Dept. of State Serial Files 740.0011
Eur War 1939/6827 and 851.0/181. Pétain's personal explanation to Robert
Murphy on December 9 is published in *FRUS* 1940, II, 414.
    [62] *DGFP*, Series D, XI, no. 246, pp. 411–12. OKW planners were even
more emphatic on this point. North Africa "could only be defended by
French troops," General Warlimont wrote on December 3 (T-78-OKW-
117).

of 1940 came, in ascending order, from Spain, Italy, Japan, and the Anglo-Gaullists. Vichy sought the aid of Germany as the ally of the first three and as the enemy of the fourth. From the beginning, Laval tried to persuade Abetz of the joint Franco-German interest in the empire by proposing the sharing of tropical products in return for German help in getting colonial shipping going again.[63] As for the risk of colonial aspirations on the part of Germany herself, the former German Cameroons seemed little enough to sacrifice in exchange for German help with more vital areas.[64]

The threat to French Morocco and the Oranais from Spain was never to materialize, thanks to Franco's neutrality. Although Foreign Minister Serrano Suñer kept up a running drumfire of reports to Germany about the danger of French duplicity in North Africa and offered to have Spain replace France as the force of order there, in the end Spain abandoned the expansionist policy that her takeover of Tangiers on 14 June 1940 seemed to forebode.[65] The French delegation at Wiesbaden was quite explicit in telling the Germans that it wanted French troops left intact in Morocco in order to guard the border with Spanish Morocco, and the Germans knew that French troops were moved to the Spanish Moroccan border in August 1940.[66] The "new policy," by allowing the French the forces to defend Morocco themselves against the British, amounted also to a tacit choice of France over Spain after the disappointing Hitler Franco talks at Hendaye on October 23.

Vichy also played off Germany against Italy with some success under the "new policy." Italian claims to Tunisia and eastern

[63] Cf. the Devinat mission to Wiesbaden in July, p. 66.

[64] Laval told General Warlimont on December 10, 1940, that he had told Pétain that France "did not have to concern herself with the Cameroons." *DFCAA,* V, 456, and T-78/OKW-132/5,508,978 ff.

[65] See T-120/121/passim and T-120/365/206504, 206597–98 for alarmist Spanish reports about French North Africa. On the general question of the French-Spanish-German triangle, see Donald S. Detwiler, *Hitler, Franco, und Gibraltar: Die Frage des spanischen Eintritts in den Zweiten Weltkrieg* (Wiesbaden, 1962).

[66] T-120/365/206541–43, 206552–53; T-120/831/280465. Laval protested strongly to Schleier, on 16 November 1940, against the 150,000 Spanish troops on the border of French Morocco and warned that they could have a "disastrous" effect on the native population.

Algeria were far more overtly expressed than Spain's claims farther west, and they were now backed by two weeks of war. To be sure, Italian arms had been able to conquer only a few high Alpine valleys, and the Germans had contemptuously dismissed General Roatta's plan to have Italian troops ferried into the Lyons region through German-occupied territory.[67] The Pétain government had been forced to sign an armistice with Italy as the only way to bring the German armistice into effect, but General Huntziger carefully explained that France did not consider Italy a victor. In the fall of 1940, French delegates went out of their way to demonstrate in the Armistice Commission their contempt for Italy, to the point where the Italian government complained about hostility in Tunisia and rudeness at meetings. The Italian threat was real, however, and the French government used the "new policy" to postpone and then annul Italian demands to disarm the French in North Africa. French force levels in North Africa were raised from 30,000 to 125,000, the total French evacuation of Bizerte and Constantine was never achieved, and the French Navy and Air Force had more freedom of action in Africa than Italy wanted. The Italian government went along with the "new policy" only reluctantly—and under German pressure. This small Vichy success had its price, of course, in the expansion of German rather than Italian control inspection teams in the Mediterranean and Africa, such as the German team sent to Morocco under French protest in the spring of 1941. When Laval asked, as on December 10, for German support against Italian territorial claims, he tacitly accepted the replacement of Italy by Germany as the dominant Axis partner in French Mediterranean areas.[68]

The Vichy regime was less successful in getting German help against Japanese expansion into Indochina. Neither General Catroux nor his successor as governor-general, Admiral Decoux, had the power to oppose Japanese demands for bases by any

[67] The Halder Diaries, 24 June 1940.
[68] The December 10 conversations may be consulted in *DFCAA*, V, 446–62, or T-78/OKW-132/5,508,978 ff. The military aspects of German vs. Italian policy in the Mediterranean are more fully explored in Robert O. Paxton, *Parades and Politics at Vichy*, (Princeton, 1966).

means other than diplomatic. A base rights agreement in exchange for Japanese recognition of French sovereignty was concluded on 22 September 1940, after Japanese troops had already violated the frontier. Germany, however, refused repeated French requests to permit arms shipments from France or the empire to Indochina in the fall of 1940 and after, although she later got a share of French rubber shipments from Indochina and hence had some interest in its remaining French.[69] The Germans had no objections to France's diverting to Indochina some of the arms bought in the United States before the armistice, however. Although Cordell Hull objected formally to the Franco-Japanese agreement of 22 September, he also forbade the shipment of any military equipment from the United States to the French in Indochina.[70] The "new policy" won nothing in French Asia, therefore, and the French were left alone to slip steadily beneath Japanese influence in Indochina until the outright Japanese takeover of March 9, 1945.

It was against the Anglo-Gaullists in Africa that the "new policy" built most firmly upon shared Vichy-German interests. The Germans now allowed the French to unstock more weapons and even tanks in Africa, overriding Italian preferences for French disarmament there; they also freed specially trained French colonial officers from German prison camps to serve in Africa. Not lukewarm in this case, the German authorities twice sent a special representative, General Walther Warlimont of the OKW staff, to Paris to confer with Laval and the French service chiefs, on November 29 and on December 10. His assignment was to find out about French plans for reconquest of segments of French Equatorial Africa that had fallen under Gaullist influence and, beyond that, for attacks upon British Africa. France was not supposed to declare war on Britain, but it was "important that the French be brought into a clear confrontation [Frontstellung] against England by an attack (even if it were only against Gambia)." Or, as Abetz put it at the 29 November meeting, in his characteristically more ambitious fashion, it was

---

[69] T-120/315/206541–206552; T-120/368/207878–79; 2069-19; Baudouin, *Neuf mois,* 233–361. For rubber, T-120/1680H *passim.*

[70] For U.S. objections, see U.S. Dept. of State Serial File 851.00/2121.

a step toward "the unification of the continent against England." [71]

War Minister Huntziger launched the military follow-up on 31 October by presenting Colonel Speidel, the Militärbefehlshaber in Frankreich's chief of staff, with an ambitious request for bigger and more independent French Army, Navy, and Air Forces. Vichy would then put these to work in "military collaboration" with Germany to keep and even extend Vichy control over French Africa.

The frank and unswerving conception of Marshal Pétain and his associates is not only to resist the English in Africa but also, where it is necessary, to attack them in order to get back lost territory. "Il faut chasser les anglais." [72]

Germans like General Warlimont had every reason to take Huntziger's bellicose promises seriously. While the African situation remained fluid in August–September 1940, Vichy had done its conspicuous best to throw the Anglo-Gaullists out of Africa. The three cruisers and three destroyers they sent down the African coast on September 6 acted decisively to thwart the Gaullist mission to Dakar. They got General Têtu released from a prisoner-of-war camp to command loyal French forces in the Gabon, and General Falvy to command the planned operation into the Chad. They bombed Gibraltar on September 24 and 25. They proposed to convoy French merchant shipping with warships through the straits of Gibraltar, which the Germans denied. They appealed repeatedly for release from armistice restrictions on the French Army in Africa. No doubt it was German and Italian reluctance more than French hesitancy that kept them from doing even more.

When Franco-German joint planning actually began a month

[71] For General Warlimont's views, see Abteilung Landesverteidigung Nr. 33 388/40 g.K. chefs. Abt. L (1), "Beurteilung der Lage im Mittelseeraum und in Afrika im Hinblick auf die Zusammenarbeit mit Frankreich," 3 December 1940 (T-77/OKW-117). For Abetz, T-77/OKW-132.

[72] Militärbefehlshaber in Frankreich, Der Chef des Kommandostabes, Chef. Nr. 113, Paris, 31 October 1940 (T-78/OKW-132). Huntziger's requests for releasing more arms and men under the armistice are also here. The phrase "Il faut chasser les anglais" is in French in the German original —almost certainly General Huntziger's exact words.

later on November 29, however, the French military ministers had become much more cautious. Conditions by then had stabilized in Africa. The Gaullists had won the Gabon in October, rounding out French Equatorial Africa, but they were unable to make any headway in West Africa. A rollback operation seemed much more hazardous, too, after Sir Samuel Hoare had warned Ambassador de la Baume at Madrid that French action against the Gaullists in Africa would lead to war with Britain.[73] Abetz was bitterly disappointed to hear General Huntziger explain to General Warlimont a future French plan for a march east across the desert from Niamey to Zinder and Lake Chad that could not take place for another year—that is, not until November 1941.[74]

The following day, agreeing with Abetz that the 29 November session had been a disappointment, Laval promised to bring pressure upon Marshal Pétain to support more aggressive plans in Africa.[75] Did he mean it, or was he simply trying to blame his own caution upon others while talking to Abetz? We know that he returned to Vichy to reassure the cabinet on December 9 that these operations would not lead to war with Britain. The following day, contradictorily, he told General Warlimont that he expected the British to fight back, exposing France to even greater risks—perhaps merely in an effort to impress Warlimont with the urgency of greater concessions to France. Just before leaving for Paris, he told American representative Robert Murphy that he "hoped" for a German victory, for then "Britain will pay the bill and not France."[76]

Reassured by Laval that action in Africa would not produce a war with England, while it would persuade Germany to make

[73] This was Laval's account to General Warlimont on November 29, at any rate. See OKW/132.

[74] The November 29 talks between the French service chiefs and General Walther Warlimont of the Wehrmachtführungsstab are recorded in OKW/132. No French text appears to have survived. See DFCAA, V, 447 n. The only French participant to leave memoirs, Gen. Stehlin, *Témoignage pour l'histoire* (Paris, 1964), 284–85, says he wasn't even at this meeting, which conflicts with the German minutes.

[75] Abetz (Paris) 1361 to Ribbentrop, 1 December 1940 (T-120/121/120211-13).

[76] *DFCCA*, V, 445; *FRUS*, 1940, II, 414.

Italy less demanding in Africa, leaders of the French cabinet decided in an "armistice meeting" on December 9 that a plan for retaking Fort-Lamy and Lake Chad should be prepared. The following day, December 10, General Warlimont was back in Paris to discuss military plans.[77] It was a much more positive occasion than two weeks earlier. General Huntziger now thought a spring 1941 operation was possible. He asked for the liberation of three thousand selected colonial officers and NCOs from prisoner-of-war camps, along with release of the motorized equipment necessary for offensive operations.

Warlimont wanted to know about operations even beyond Equatorial Africa, in British colonial territory. Huntziger made it clear that the air raids on Gibraltar had been reprisals for previous British attacks, but he outlined further reprisals that "France is willing to undertake if there were new British destruction attempts." If, for example, Britain opposed French efforts to retake French Equatorial Africa, France contemplated air attacks on Northern Nigeria, the conquest of Bathurst, or some action against Freetown. Admiral Darlan, who had said on November 29 that Freetown was not important, now thought a joint air-submarine attack was feasible. Major Stehlin thought that a "general air war" was possible in Africa, growing out of these reprisals, provided that Germany permitted the free movement of French planes, the resumption of French plane and bomb production, petroleum imports from Italy, the liberation of air force prisoners of war, and the reopening of pilot schools. The French, for example, could bomb Takoradi (now in Ghana), where U.S. planes were being assembled. Laval wound up with an impassioned plea for the cooperation agreed to at Montoire. The Italians, he complained, were the main obstacle in Africa, and they weren't doing very well in Greece anyway. The question was political. If Germany could issue a clarifying statement promising that the French Empire would remain

[77] *DFCAA*, V, 445. Present were Laval, Huntziger, Darlan, Bergeret, Bouthillier, Belin, and Régnier. German minutes of the 10 December meeting are published in *DFCAA*, V, 446–62, and microfilmed in T-78/OKW-132.

French at the peace, then Vichy could expose de Gaulle as no defender of the French Empire against Axis annexation, but a mere British agent. For results, however, Germany must help France, especially against Italy. Laval had denied the American Robert Murphy's contentions that Germany wanted to take Dakar and the French fleet and had told him that "it is in our own interest that we desire a German victory. . . . If you help us, we are ready to negotiate. France is ready to bargain, to bargain now."

Abetz and General Warlimont concluded that French readiness to act in Equatorial Africa had been "buoyed up since their first meeting" with the French on November 29 and that there could be "no doubt of the sincerity of the military plans of the Pétain government." In mid-December 1940, it looked from Berlin as if the French were about to go on the march in Anglo-Gaullist Africa.[78]

The "new policy" did not preclude simultaneous Vichy efforts to reach some understanding with the Allies as well. Vichy wanted normalcy more than expansion, and a prime ingredient of normalcy was in British hands: the revival of trade and colonial shipping across the British blockade. Vichy could neither feed France nor keep in contact with the empire without at least the acquiescence of Britain. Although diplomatic relations with Britain were broken after the Mers-el-Kebir raid and never restored, civilian proposals for war against Britain were rejected by the military men in the cabinet, according to what American observers could learn at the time. Laval told Hitler on October 22 that Pétain could not declare war on Britain without the assent of the National Assembly, and Pétain told the French public in a speech on April 7, 1941, that it was "against French honor" to attack "former allies."[79] Instead, it was imperative to

[78] Chef Abt. Landesverteidigung Nr. 001132/40 g.K., 12 December 1940 (T-78/OKW-132).

[79] U.S. Dept. of State Serial File 851.00/2085, 6 August 1940, contradicts Baudouin, Neuf mois, 232, on who opposed and supported a declaration of war against Britain on July 4. Article 9 of Constitutional Act No. 2 of 11 July 1940 explicitly denies to Pétain the power to declare war without the assent of the National Assembly.

seek some peaceful solution to the two burning issues between France and Britain: the blockade and British support for the "dissidence."

Even before the Churchill-de Gaulle agreement of 7 August 1940 had made British aid to anti-Vichy Frenchmen public, Foreign Minister Paul Baudouin, whose frantic Anglophobia seemed diminished to U.S. observers, began making proposals to Britain around August 1 about the blockade.[80] There developed a three-sided negotiation, in which Washington urged the British to relax restrictions on essential supplies going into unoccupied France in exchange for assurances that such supplies would not be transshipped to the German-occupied zone, while informal Franco-British contacts were resumed through the embassies in Madrid.

The Franco-British negotiations at Madrid from September 1940 to February 1941 between the two ambassadors—M. Robert de la Baume followed by François Piétri, facing Sir Samuel Hoare—were the real link between Vichy and London. Few aspects of Vichy policy have been more subject to postwar mystification than this. Two unofficial links, Professor Louis Rougier of the University of Besançon and Jacques Chevalier, Vichy minister of education and then of health in 1940–41, claimed after the war to have negotiated secret Churchill-Pétain "accords." Although Professor Rougier did go to London in November 1940, the notations on his document are not in the handwriting of Winston Churchill, as he claimed.[81]

Jacques Chevalier did indeed receive a note for Marshal Pétain through the Canadian ambassador, Jean Dupuy, from his old Oxford classmate Lord Halifax. But that note, contrary to M. Chevalier's postwar claims, simply revealed the chasm between the two. Churchill offered to send six divisions if the French government moved to North Africa. Pétain read the note and said, "We have not received it." There was no agree-

[80] U.S. Dept. of State Serial File 740.00. Eur War 1939/1674; *FRUS*, 1940, II, p. 382.
[81] Professor Rougier's memoirs became almost an industry. See *Les Accords Pétain-Churchill* (Montréal, 1945, and subsequent editions to 1954). I am indebted to Mr. F. W. Deakin, former warden of Saint Antony's College, Oxford, for assistance on this problem.

ment.[82] Neither Rougier nor Chevalier affected Vichy-British relations substantially.

The Germans were not ignorant of the Madrid contacts for long. Fernand de Brinon, still an unofficial Laval contact man in Paris at that point, told Abetz about them on November 11. Laval, on November 16, promised to keep the Germans informed of every such negotiation in order to prove French loyalty to the armistice.[83]

Vichy achieved neither of her aims at Madrid—loosening the British blockade and ending British support for the Gaullist "dissidence." The British blockade was indeed loosened in September 1940. For several months French merchant ships were able to use the Mediterranean and even the Straits of Gibraltar until, by the end of November, French shipping at Marseilles was estimated as 80 percent of normal, although French shipping was still blocked south of Dakar. The real reason for this, however, was British naval shortages rather than any agreement, as the tightened blockade of 1941 was to show. Eventually, foodstuffs and oil were brought from the U.S.A. to North Africa through the British blockade under the Murphy-Weygand agreement of 10 March 1941, which the British accepted only reluctantly. The British never by choice relaxed their efforts to keep war supplies out of France.[84]

As for the "dissidence" issue, it was settled by stalemate rather than agreement. After some fighting in the Gabon in October 1940 that rounded out Gaullist holdings in French equatorial Africa but kept them out of all French West Africa, the Vichy-Gaullist balance was set in Africa. That Vichy would fight the Anglo-Gaullists against any further encroachment was proven in the war over Syria in June–July 1941. That the Allies

[82] The text of the note and Freeman Matthews' account of its delivery (*FRUS*, 1940, II, 432–36) are to be preferred over Jacques Chevalier's account in *Procès Pétain*, 694 ff, repeated in his own and other trials and in later works such as Georges Blond, *Pétain* (1966).

[83] Schleier (Paris) 1157 and 1216 to Ribbentrop, 11 Nov. and 16 Nov. 1940 (T-120/587/243349–52, 243357–59).

[84] For shipping reports, see T-120/368/206915–16, 207331. W. N. Medlicott, *The Economic Blockade*, 3 vol. (London, 1952–59). W. L. Langer, *Our Vichy Gamble* (New York, 1947).

would try not to tar their efforts to liberate France with the brush of dissidence was shown by the exclusion of Gaullists and all but a few British from the Allied landing in French North Africa in November 1942 and by the exclusion of the Gaullists from any share in the Normandy invasion of June 1944. But, of course, the Allies did not withdraw support from de Gaulle. The "dissidence" issue was settled by a tacit armed truce.

The Vichy government, including Laval, seems to have wanted above all to keep good relations with the neutral United States, despite the "new policy." The United States was useful as a source of supply. Diplomatic recognition by the United States was a precious reinforcement to Vichy legitimacy. And the United States was a potential arbiter for the early compromise settlement of a war whose prolongation could only damage European social structure irremediably. The United States could not only arbitrate with the British, whose "brutal selfishness" [85] kept a fruitless war grinding along, but could also counterbalance the Germans and Japanese. Not only men like General Doyen, French representative to the German Armistice Commission at Wiesbaden and eventually an active participant in the Liberation, spoke of the United States as the only power capable of restoring France to her full extent, the "great arbiter of today and to-morrow" whose good relations France must not forfeit. Laval, too, even while telling Robert Murphy that he "hoped" for German victory, said that the United States was the only counter-weight to Japan in Indochina.[86]

Vichy spokesmen tried hard, therefore, to reassure the United States of the French will to autonomy under the armistice. Montoire produced some exaggerated rumors abroad about major French cessions of bases to Germany, and both President Roosevelt and King George VI wrote personally to Pétain. While King George VI's letter received a curt reply, Vichy went out of its

---

[85] Pétain quoted by Robert Murphy (Vichy), No. 227 to Washington, 7 August 1940 (*FRUS*, 1940, II, 380). Even after the Liberation, Yves Bouthillier wrote of the "blind egoism" and "implacable fanaticism" of Britain for continuing the war. *Le Drame de l'armistice*, I, 164, II, 451.

[86] General Doyen's remark is in "Enseignement de dix mois à Wiesbaden," written as he left his post on 16 July 1941. *DFCAA* IV, 650. Laval-Murphy conversation, 9 December 1940, *FRUS*, 1940, II, 414.

way to convince the United States that France meant to remain autonomous and neutral under the armistice. General Réquin, who had been French delegate to disarmament conferences between the wars, came to tell Murphy on October 25 that "those who understood the position of France and her powerlessness before the Germans and consequently the necessity for reaching some agreement should explain this position to the United States." Georges Bonnet, former foreign minister, argued on November 1 that Europe couldn't afford a war every twenty-five years. Britain must be brought to accept a "reasonable peace." Laval himself, while saying that he was sure of a German victory and annoyed with Cordell Hull's suspicions of French policy, told the American Press Association on November 15 that a break with the United States would be "horrible." The written reply to Roosevelt's letter about Montoire was just formally cool enough to be described as "sharp" by Laval to Abetz on 16 November, but the main effort was to reassure.[87]

The military meetings in Paris on November 29 and December 10 had to be most carefully explained to the Americans. Admiral William D. Leahy was expected in January, the most important ambassador to be accredited to Vichy. Pétain told Robert Murphy on December 12 how pleased he was, although he claimed to the Germans that Leahy had been forced upon him.[88] Then Pétain went on to observe that General Weygand was organizing an expeditionary force to Lake Chad to "defend" the area against any British or Gaullist expedition, though both must have known that the Gaullists were already there. Ex-Foreign Minister Paul Baudouin explained the same plan as a ruse to obtain more French arms in Africa.[89]

As mid-December 1940 approached, the Americans, too, were being prepared for a more vigorous French presence in Equatorial Africa. Despite the alarm in Washington over Montoire, Admiral Leahy was on his way to France, and it looked as if

[87] *FRUS*, 1940, II, 394–99; 403–11; T-120/587/243357–59.

[88] *FRUS*, 1940, II, 418; *DGPF*, Series D, XI, no. 645, pp. 1077–78. Contradictory statements to German and American representatives were uncommon with Pétain, who played no "double game."

[89] *FRUS*, 1940, II, 418; U.S. Dept. of State Serial File 740.01 Eur. War 1939/8369.

the "new policy" had been squared with good relations with pro-Allied neutrals like the United States. Was there one Vichy policy or several? Did Vichy seek an autonomous, neutral middle way, or the "renversement des alliances" that Abetz thought he foresaw? The evening of December 13, when Marshal Pétain dismissed Pierre Laval from the government, raised these questions to the headlines.

The Meaning of December 13

ON THE AFTERNOON OF FRIDAY, DECEMBER 13, 1940, Pierre Laval, home from the second round of military talks on Africa with General Warlimont, presided over a routine cabinet meeting. A few hours later, a surprise meeting of the whole Council of Ministers was called by Marshal Pétain. The Marshal asked each member of the government to write out a letter of resignation. Then he accepted those of Pierre Laval and Georges Ripert, minister of education. In the meantime, Laval's floors of the Hôtel du Parc were occupied by special security forces responsible to Marcel Peyrouton's Ministry of the Interior. Laval was taken to his country home at Châteldon, a few miles away, and placed under house arrest. Communications with Paris were cut off. This was the most Byzantine of all the many Vichy changes of cabinet, the only one accompanied by the threat of force. It was also the only Vichy cabinet change to arouse the passionate hostility of German Ambassador Otto Abetz and to cause the near rupture of Franco-German relations. It has naturally become a focus for judgments about intentions at Vichy in December 1940.

Laval's removal from office on December 13 has been so overlaid with self-serving explanations since the Liberation that it has become almost impossible to uncover the contemporary play of issues and interests. Participants in that palace coup and those who subsequently took office under Laval's successor Darlan took pride in "our audacious initiative" and took credit for "the turning point of the war." They described it as a set-back for Germany "as serious as the loss of a battle," the "end of military collaboration," and a "decisive turning" in Franco-German relations.[90]

Partisans of Laval argue, with equal but contrary self-interest, that so far from ending active collaboration, it was Laval's successors and principally Darlan who went on after December 13 to preside over the high point of Franco-German collaboration.[91] Nor are the rich German and United States diplomatic reports for December 1940 directly helpful here, for foreign observers were as surprised by these events as Laval himself.

A few general points are now clear, however, if one limits oneself to contemporary sources of information. Laval's removal did not end Vichy efforts to reach a comfortable working arrangement within Hitler's Europe. Quite the contrary; if anything, his successors pressed even more eagerly for the negotiation of a sweeping general settlement and came even closer to direct military collaboration than Laval had done. Furthermore, relations with Britain grew worse in 1941 than they had been even in the fall of 1940. On the other side of the coin, it is also true that in fact French forces did not move actively against Gaullists or British in Africa after some fighting in the Gabon in October–November 1940, which stabilized the lines fairly neatly between Gaullist Equatorial Africa and Vichy West Africa. Moreover, a period of cordial relations with the neutral United States opened with the arrival of Ambassador Leahy in January 1941. If one looks for decisive changes accompanying Laval's removal, the most genuine turnabout took place in German attitudes toward France. December 13 brought the "new policy" to an abrupt end.

Hitler's support for the "new policy" had always been grudg-

---

[90] Yves Bouthillier, *Le Drame de Vichy*, I, *Face à l'ennemi, face à l'allié* (Paris, 1950), 10, 260, 283. In April 1941, however, Bouthillier "deplored" the events of December 13 and told Abetz that he wanted closer cooperation with Germany. (T-120/121/149248). Marcel Peyrouton, *Du service public à la prison commune, Souvenirs* (Paris, 1950), 183; *Le Procès Flandin* (Paris, 1946), 175.

[91] Pierre Cathala, *Face aux réalités, Les finances françaises sous l'occupation* (Paris, 1948), 115.

ing and opportunistic. Furthermore, it rested upon deception. It was useful for the French to keep the Allies out of Africa themselves, but they would do so only if the losses in store for them in a German peace were concealed by postponing all substantive negotiation indefinitely. In any event, nothing could deflect Hitler from savoring revenge for 1918. His suspicions of French revanchism, always sharper than the reality,[92] seemed confirmed by Pétain's dismissal of the man he had dealt with at Montoire and by the spoiling of the Duc de Reichstadt's reburial in the Invalides on December 15. Abetz, whose link with Laval was an integral part of his own rise to prominence, replacing the military channel at Wiesbaden with the diplomatic one at Paris, reacted most violently of all. After going through sullenly with the macabre torchlight ceremony at the Invalides on December 15, he erupted into the Free Zone on December 16 with an armed escort, brandished a pistol about the Hôtel du Parc, pronounced an ultimatum for the restoration of a government acceptable to the German embassy, and took Laval back to Paris with him. The Demarcation Line was sealed, even to French officials. The German policy toward France, wrote General Halder, was "a cold shoulder." It was almost with relief that he noted that "we are no longer bound by any obligation toward France."[93] Even before December 13, Hitler had already ordered plans drawn up for the next step after abandoning the direct invasion of England. It was not to be a Mediterranean strategy, in which French help would be vital, but an eastern strategy: Operation Barbarossa against the Soviet Union. Except for Abetz, the German reaction was more loss of interest in France than anger.

It is much less clear that the basic intentions of Vichy foreign policy changed on December 13. The main problem is to discover what those intentions had been on the eve of Laval's departure.

[92] At the very climax of the post-Montoire negotiations, Hitler approved the draft plan "Attila" on 10 December 1940 for the speedy occupation of the rest of France in case General Weygand or other colonial leaders resorted to "dissidence." (T-77/OKW-117).

[93] The Halder Diaries, 16 January 1941.

A whole gamut of responses to the Anglo-Gaullist spread in Africa was possible. At the most pro-Allied extreme was a possible stratagem of pretending to fight the Anglo-Gaullists in order to trick the Germans out of more arms which the French could eventually use for their own liberation. This is the interpretation of the Chad preparations in General Weygand's memoirs, and indeed Paul Baudouin explained to Robert Murphy in 1940 that the aim was to secure the release of more French colonial officers from prison.[94] A more realistic position is that Vichy meant to repel vigorously any attempt to swing parts of the empire into Gaullist (and thereby British) hands. Nobody at Vichy disagreed with this position. There is no mistaking the hard anger at Churchill and de Gaulle and the conviction with which Vichy French troops fought the Anglo-Gaullists at Dakar in September 1940, in Syria in June–July 1941, and in North Africa in November 1942.

At the other extreme of belligerency was the possibility of full-scale French participation alongside Germany in the war against Britain. There may have been figures in Paris who longed for such a commitment, but it would be difficult to find anyone at Vichy who agreed. Laval told Hitler at Montoire that Pétain did not have constitutional authority to declare war on England without the support of the Assembly. He told Marshal Goering on 9 November that there was no question of French and German troops fighting side by side in Africa. With both Abetz on 31 October and Goering a week later, he took care to re-emphasize Hitler's not having asked France to enter the war, in the fashion of a skilled negotiator who singles out the acceptable part of the other side's statement. In any event, the matter is academic, for Hitler never wanted France as a co-belligerent. Mussolini always complained to him about any hint of special favors to France. In pragmatic terms, Germany had more to gain by the cheap neutralization of the French Empire than by an uncontrolled spread of the war to additional fronts. France must be ready to defend her empire by force, as at Dakar,

[94] General Weygand, *Mémoires,* III, *Rappelé au service* (Paris, 1950), 462–63. Admiral d'Harcourt said approximately the same thing to an American representative in Morocco, *FRUS,* 1940, II, 627.

but German policy papers after Montoire all refer to France as a "nichtkriegführende Macht." [95] December 13 did not block a war upon Britain at Germany's side. Nobody wanted one.

It is the intermediate possible courses of action dicussed in November–December 1940 that make December 13 a fascinating puzzle. There were two possibilities: an offensive course—French attack upon Gaullist Equatorial Africa and even upon exposed British colonies such as Sierra Leone; and a course of active defense—French action in Africa only as reprisals in case of further Anglo-Gaullist advance. The Vichy military planners of late fall 1940, after the spasms of anger over Mers-el-Kebir and Dakar had cooled and Britain had still not been invaded by Germany, clearly preferred the less ambitious course. Not only to Americans, to whom General Huntziger said in October that he opposed military operations in Africa except defensive ones,[96] but even in the military conversations with General Warlimont on November 29, the French service chiefs emphasized that no action was planned against British territory in Africa unless the British attacked further. It is hard to find anyone on the French side working very hard for aggressive French attack on British colonies; even Laval thought that wider conflict, if it came, would emerge from a British attack which would then free France from her "difficulty" (i.e., inhibitions) respecting operations against England.[97]

Were the plans to recapture the Gaullist areas of French Equatorial Africa serious? Although General Huntziger's plans sounded lukewarm at the meeting with General Warlimont on November 29, Abetz and Warlimont had no doubt of Vichy's resolution after the December 10 meeting. Much later, around the first of November 1942, Laval told a group of leaders of the Chantiers de la Jeunesse that he had really meant to take the

---

[95] See General Warlimont's preliminary working paper of 2 November 1940 (T-77/OKW-117) and Hitler's General Order No. 18 of 12 November 1940 (T-77/OKW-141). German minutes of the Laval-Goering conversation of 9 November 1940 are on microfilm as T-120/3485H/EO19424 ff.

[96] U.S. Dept. of State Serial File 741.51/430.

[97] (T-120/587/24335709) Abetz (Paris) 1216 to Berlin, 16 November 1940, and in November 29 talks. See also *DGPF*, X, no. 234, p. 401.

Gaullist colonies back in December 1940 and that that was why "the British" had forced him out. He had gone out of his way to assure the cabinet on December 9 that the operation would not lead to war with Britain, while assuring Abetz and Warlimont that it would, though he may only have been magnifying France's risk in order to get more concessions. The curious thing is that Pétain himself told Robert Murphy on December 12 about the planned operation to "defend" the Chad as if he supported it. Governor-General Boisson read parts of his instructions from Pétain and Weygand to the American diplomat Thomas C. Wasson at Dakar on December 10. "I gathered the impression that the British colonies may be invaded should de Gaulle make any further moves in these parts." [98]

The whole French cabinet seems to have agreed on retaliating with force against any further Anglo-Gaullist encroachment. Vigorous defensive force in the empire against the Allies was Vichy policy both before Laval's removal, as at Dakar, and after, as in Syria in June 1941.

The fact that an offensive Chad operation was never actually carried out has usually been taken to prove that Laval's removal stopped it. That may be. Or possibly the hostile German reaction to Laval's removal, which interrupted the release of additional French forces for Africa, did more to stop it than Laval's removal itself. The important point is that the larger commitment to the "new policy" was never called into question. December 13 was not meant to end the quest for good relations with Germany and for normalcy under the armistice.

The Montoire meetings had followed months of effort by the whole French government to establish good working relations with Berlin. The follow-up after Montoire had also been the work of the whole government. From Vichy's point of view, this policy was not Pierre Laval's private reserve. It could go on without him. Furthermore, the Chad operation was only a small part of the "new policy." Collaboration could develop in a more

[98] Laval's 1 November 1942 speech is contained in the unpublished diary of General Bridoux. *DFCAA*, V, 445, 446–62; *FRUS*, 1940, II, 418, 630. See p. 91 above.

neutral fashion, based on a vigorous defense of the status quo against any further Anglo-Gaullist attacks (as in Syria in June 1941), but avoiding any inflammatory effort at rollback. Even if one accepts the thesis that Laval's removal meant blocking an aggressive Chad expedition (and the evidence is not all in), it was most certainly not intended to be the end of the "new policy." It is pure postwar invention to suggest, as do the memoirs of Bouthillier, Peyrouton, and others, that Laval was removed in order to reverse the post-Montoire negotiations.

So we must look again at the internal interpretation of Laval's fall. Not only the Germans but the Americans (who might have preferred to hear an anticollaboration explanation) were assured that Laval's dismissal was a purely internal affair.

One point to notice is that Laval's quest for domestic concessions had been an abysmal failure. Flandin later claimed he could get more results than Laval by being more independent. Not one of the major domestic issues had been settled in Vichy's favor, despite the Bor Mines, the gold, and other striking French concessions. Vichy's refusal to pay the occupation costs bill of December 1 had simply evoked a German ultimatum. Pétain told American officials on November 16 that he had been promised the liberation of at least some prisoners of war, but the Reinecke-Scapini agreement of November 20 won the release only of fathers of more than four children who were in need.[99] Pétain's regime was left out on the limb of those October 31 promises, following Montoire, that France would soon enjoy a less uncomfortable existence. He needed more collaboration, not less.

At the heart of Laval's failure to achieve post-Montoire domestic concessions was the move to Paris. Although Article 3 of the armistice had acknowledged that Paris was the seat of the French government, Foreign Minister Baudouin's official request of July 7 for a return to Paris was answered by secret Ribbentrop instructions on August 19 for German services to treat this

---

[99] Abetz (Paris) 1595 to Ribbentrop, 26 December 1940 (T-120/587/243398–403); *FRUS*, 1940, II, 411; T-120/368/207282–85. Maurice Catoire, *La Direction des Services de l'armistice*, 44, says only 120,000 prisoners of war were ever liberated, mostly after the Syrian fighting in 1941.

question "in a dilatory fashion."[100] Furthermore, major neutral powers with embassies accredited to Marshal Pétain's government, chiefly the United States and Switzerland, objected to a "Vatican City" arrangement at Versailles that would subject their diplomatic communications to passage across a German military zone of occupation.[101] In the eager days of the "new policy," however, the Vichy government came up with a two-capitals compromise that they proceeded to put into effect unilaterally at the end of November, without admitting any need to negotiate with the Germans. They were simply told on November 27 that Pétain would be moving to Versailles.

Laval was opposed to Pétain's move. On November 29, when he was in Paris to meet with General Warlimont, Laval privately told Abetz' deputy, Rudolph Schleier, that Pétain would probably be satisfied with a temporary trip into the Occupied Zone. In Berlin, Vichy's "sudden" announcement aroused prompt counterorders. Hitler ordered the Armistice Commission to drag out the matter on technicalities, and then on December 3 Ribbentrop vetoed the move on the ground that the whole Occupied Zone was an operations area. Was Laval trying to keep the Paris connection to himself? Otto Abetz, reporting Laval's opposition to Vichy plans, saw some advantage for Germany in establishing Pétain at Versailles, away from his entourage and under German influence.[102]

This humiliating veto of Pétain's publicly announced visit to Paris on December 3 was followed by Flandin's summons to Vichy and Pétain's first letter to Hitler announcing Laval's removal from office. That letter was countermanded, but the issue

[100] Hencke (Wiesbaden) No. 36 to Berlin of 7 July 1940 (T-120/121/119692); Ribbentrop (Berlin) to Abetz No. 480 of 16 August 1940 (T-120/121/119810).

[101] United States and Swiss protests may be found in U.S. Dept. of State Serial Files 740.0011 Eur War 1939/6827 and 851.0./181.

[102] T-120/3699H/*passim;* Abetz (Paris) 1392 to Rintelen of 4 December 1940 (T-120/587/243360–61). Laval was supposed to try again at his forthcoming meeting with Ribbentrop. See *DFCAA*, V, 445. The United States wasn't told about German pressures, but only that Pétain's visit had been postponed. (740–0011 Eur War 1939/7043). M. Martin du Gard, *Chronique de Vichy* (Paris, 1948), 94, like so many postwar French memoirs, is diametrically wrong on the Paris visit.

came up again when it was learned suddenly on December 12 that Pétain was supposed to go to Paris on German conditions, to participate in the reburial of Napoleon's son at the Invalides.

Otto Abetz always believed that the Paris trip dispute was a mere pretext and that Laval's removal was a gesture of defiance at Germany—and at his own growing share in Franco-German relations through Laval's special position at Paris.[103] Beginning with Abetz, the story has circulated that Pétain thought Laval was trying to get him to Paris where he would be powerless. It seems rather the reverse: that Pétain was trying to get to Versailles and that Laval was failing to win this concession, as well as all the other post-Montoire domestic concessions. Darlan stressed the Paris visit issue in his explanations to Hitler at Beauvais on December 24.[104]

Pétain had other reasons to dislike Laval. Their personal styles and manners were antithetical. The marshal's complaint that Laval blew smoke in his face stands for a host of grating minor irritations. But most of all, Laval was arrogating to himself the whole post-Montoire negotiation.

The leaders of the anti-Laval movement also had personal or internal reasons for opposing him. After all, men like Alibert and Peyrouton were hardly partisans of the Allied cause. Peyrouton suspected, rightfully, that Laval wanted his strategic position of minister of the interior, with its control over the national police network. Bouthillier also seems to have suspected that he was going to lose office.[105] Authoritarians like Alibert may have noticed that Laval was the only Third Republic parliamentarian left after the new government of 6 September. Without accepting Abetz' ideological view that the reactionaries of army, church, and high capitalism were out to get Laval, one can find plenty of domestic rivals and opponents in the cabinet.[106]

Vichy policy afterward was an attempt to undo the damage.

[103] Abetz (Paris) 1556 to Ribbentrop of 18 December 1940 (T-120/587/243366 ff.; also printed in *Mémorandum d'Abetz*, 44–54).

[104] T-120/587/243383 ff.

[105] Bouthillier, I, 177 ff.

[106] For Laval's designs on Peyrouton's office, see *DGFP*, XI, no. 234, p. 491; Abetz' view is in Abetz (Paris) 1392 of 18 December (T-120/587/243360–61 or *Memorandum d'Abetz*, 44–55).

The urgent first priority was to salvage the "new policy." Flandin tried and failed during January–February 1941. Darlan tried and, for a time, succeeded. Vichy policy after December 13, therefore, was not an expression of the motives that had led to Laval's removal but the expression of efforts to undo the damage that his removal had unexpectedly created. The major point remains. Vichy policy in the fall of 1940 had been an effort to win autonomy, to cooperate as an equal within the European status quo. December 13 did nothing to change that. December 13 made a change most clearly in German policy. The harsh German reaction only made it more urgent for Vichy to win back the "new policy" that had seemed so promising in October.

The Cold Shoulder: Flandin and Darlan

GERMANY, WROTE GENERAL HALDER IN HIS DIARY IN January 1941, was now maintaining a "cold shoulder" toward France.[107] That had not been Marshal Pétain's intention. Whatever the motives for removing Laval, every Vichy effort was devoted now to trying to appease the tantrums and to open up good relations again.

Pierre-Etienne Flandin, the new foreign minister, was a good choice to develop normal and cordial relations with Berlin —or would have been, if Abetz had not identified his own growing role with Laval's primacy. Flandin was a leading prewar conservative deputy of a rather imposing patrician mien— Peyrouton said he would have made an excellent Victorian statesman—who had reacted to the Popular Front and the dread of war with an active campaign for accommodation with Hitler. He had split his party, the Alliance Démocratique, in September 1938 by writing a public letter of congratulation to Hitler over Munich. He had opposed the declaration of war in 1939 and

---

[107] General Keitel also used the term "kalte Schulter." It was no longer German intent "to bring about collaboration" with Vichy, he wrote General Thomas on 10 January 1941. T-77/OKW-2012/5, 596, 112–13.

was known in Berlin during the phony war as an opponent of the Reynaud war government. After the defeat, he lived quietly in the Yonne, carefully maintaining good contacts with the German embassy in Paris. To his German contacts he denounced the "war party" in London as the tool of international Jewry, attributed French decline to Freemasons and Jews, and "dropped his political reserve" on August 30 to accuse the Vichy government of holding back on necessary reforms. On December 6, when Marshal Pétain summoned him to Vichy, Flandin sent a message to Abetz promising loyal support to Laval and to the policy of collaboration. Flandin, Abetz reported to Berlin on December 18, had a procollaboration reputation and had been chosen as the new foreign minister in an attempt to appease German feelings.[108]

Flandin did indeed make restoring normal relations with Germany his main business after December 13. He sent messengers to Abetz and to the Armistice Commission asking to reschedule the interrupted summit conference with Ribbentrop that had been planned for Laval. He let the word spread that he was in touch with Hitler and that he would get much more effective results than Laval. He formed a governing triumvirate with Admiral Darlan and General Huntziger, who had been leaders of the post-Montoire military negotiations.[109]

As before, the whole government joined in these overtures. Pétain sent Admiral Darlan to Hitler at Beauvais on Christmas Eve with a handwritten note insisting that Laval's dismissal was a purely domestic affair that made no change in Vichy's relations with Germany. Scapini, who had been sent to Berlin at the end of October to negotiate the release of some prisoners of war, was instructed on December 18 to work for a general settlement ("Vertrag"). As the quarantine of Vichy spread to the Armistice Commission and showed no signs of abating in the new year, General Doyen managed to meet General von Stülpnagel on January 6. In Marshal Pétain's name, he explained that Laval's removal had not "the slightest" effect on the fullest French

---

[108] T-120/1540/372456–58; T-120/587/243362; T-120/121/119713.
[109] All these gestures were reported to Berlin and may best be followed in the files of Ernst von Weizsäcker, T-120/221.

loyalty to the "agreements" of Montoire. He urged the renewal of contact between ministers and, above all, a meeting between Flandin and Ribbentrop. Collaboration could continue if the Germans wanted it.[110] War Minister Huntziger was supposed to deliver the same message on the same day to Richard Hemmen, chief German economic delegate at the Armistice Commission. Finally reaching him on January 16, Huntziger asked Hemmen to tell Ribbentrop that Pétain would cooperate as in the past and regretted that "practical relations did not exist any longer." Meeting General Studt of the Armistice Commission inspection team on February 5, Huntziger assured him that France would obey the armistice. The Germans should strengthen Pétain, he said, by making the necessary concessions. He volunteered that France was ready to manufacture war matériel for Germany as a gesture of loyalty.[111] Vichy's first priority was clearly the restoration of normal relations with Germany.

Washington and London wanted to believe that Flandin, as a leading 1930's republican statesman, was more friendly to them than Laval had been, and from those hopes was born the legend that Flandin's arrival signaled a Vichy return to "attentisme," awaiting the favorable moment to rejoin the Allied war effort. Churchill wrote Flandin on 14 November 1945 that "I was delighted when you came to power in 1940."[112] His accession to the Foreign Ministry coincided with the arrival of Admiral Leahy as U.S. ambassador. Furthermore, the long-stalled Franco-British negotiations at Madrid over the blockade now seemed to move forward. The British government, which had been urged all fall by Washington to let consumer goods into the Vichy zone, was ready to take up the matter at Madrid. The talks were scheduled to open on January 8. The French had long agreed to the Allied

---

[110] Hencke (Wiesbaden) nos. 4 and 6, 6 January 1941 (T-120/378/209347/50). These two telegrams are somewhat more effusive than Doyen's own texts as published in *DFCAA*, III, 403. A German account of the Darlan-Hitler meeting at Beauvais is published in *DGFP*, XI, no. 564, pp. 950–55.

[111] Hencke to Wiehl, 6 January 1941 (*DGFP*, XI, no. 654, pp. 1096–99); Hencke HWIX no. 3982 of 6 February 1941 (T-120/378/209443, 209451–52).

[112] *Le Procès Flandin*, 200.

condition that foodstuffs imported in this way must not be transshipped to the Occupied Zone, and the British government now appeared to accept these assurances.

Flandin, keeping Laval's promise of 16 November 1940 to inform the Germans of developments in its Madrid contacts with the British, notified the Armistice Commission on January 6 that the food crisis had forced France to enter into negotiations with the British at Madrid over the blockade. Then, as Sir Llewellyn Woodward found in the British records of these talks, they broke off unaccountably at the end of January. When the Germans ordered these talks stopped on February 13, after Flandin's resignation, Darlan could truthfully answer that the Madrid negotiations had already ceased.[113]

On the other side, Flandin seems to have suspended or canceled none of the pending projects for economic collaboration. For example, the plan for joint construction of fighter aircraft for both Germany and France in the unoccupied zone, first proposed by General Huntziger on 30 October 1940, was pressed forward by Flandin, Darlan, and Air Minister General Bergeret at an "armistice meeting" on January 29, as a means of refloating the French economy, keeping control of French industrial production for the Germans, and obtaining more planes for France. There are no striking signs of redirecting French policy back toward clandestine aid to the Allied war effort, nor should that have been expected of a man who had opposed the war altogether in September 1939 and who now, like Pétain, clung even more tightly to neutrality and social safety.

Much of the contemporary evidence for secret pro-Allied leanings on the part of Flandin comes from friends of Laval and Darlan who were trying to damage Flandin's reputation with Abetz. The writer Alphonse de Chateaubriant and two deputies, Spinasse (SFIO) and Montagnon (Neosocialist, close personally to Laval), all told Abetz in January 1941 that Flandin was the

[113] U.S. Dept. of State Serial File 851.5018/95; Hencke (Wiesbaden) nos. 4 and 6 to Berlin, 6 January 1941 (T-120/378/209347–50; 209467–72); E. L. Woodward, *British Foreign Policy in the Second World War* (London, 1962), 100; *DFCAA*, IV, 52, 73, 112. François Piétri, *Mes Années d'Espagne* (Paris, 1954), is not helpful for Piétri's service as French ambassador in Madrid during this period.

main barrier to Laval's return and that he was working closely with Allied agents. Darlan proposed in February that the Germans allow Flandin to go home to the Yonne so they could trace his Allied contacts in the Occupied Zone. Abetz refused altogether to deal with the man who had replaced Laval. These kinds of German hostility, Allied wishful thinking, and the letters of intercession that Churchill, Roosevelt, and Leahy wrote in December 1943 when Flandin was imprisoned in Gaullist North Africa all helped acquit him of the charges leveled against him in the High Court of Justice in 1946. Flandin was able to convince the court that he had resigned in February 1941 rather than assent to renewed contacts with the Germans.[114]

In fact, it seems to have been the other way around. Flandin resigned on February 9 because he failed to reopen the German contacts upon which Laval's preeminence had rested. We do not know what Flandin would have done with such contacts, but he did his best to raise the quarantine imposed on Vichy after December 13. It would be tiresome to describe all the Byzantine transactions of January–February 1941 over whether Laval should return. On the one hand, Abetz insisted upon a Vichy "investigation" of what had happened, the removal of those responsible for the affront to Hitler, and the formation of no new cabinet until Hitler had replied to Pétain's explanations. On the other hand, Flandin tried to go ahead unilaterally with forming a new cabinet. In a note countersigned by Pétain on January 8, he announced that Vichy would announce the composition of the new cabinet on January 10, without awaiting further German response. Abetz threatened to cut off Radio Vichy from the Occupied Zone and seal hermetically the already closed Demarcation Line. From that moment on, Flandin functioned in a kind of vacuum: a foreign minister unable to talk to the representatives of the chief foreign power. Informally, there were various proposals for Laval's return in various cabinet positions and, on January 18, a meeting between Laval and Pétain in the Randan Forest near Vichy that solved nothing. If

[114] T-120/221/149019–20, 149070, 149107, 149113; *Le Procès Flandin*, 191–200. Minutes of the "armistice meeting" on airplane construction of 29 January 1941: *DFCAA*, IV, 68–72.

Fernand de Brinon can be believed, there were strong partisans of Laval's return at Vichy, including General Huntziger, who grew so unnerved at the diplomatic blackout that he urged on January 31 "in the name of the army" that Laval be recalled immediately.[115]

The impasse was broken by two developments. Navy Minister Admiral Darlan became the leader most acceptable to both sides, and Hitler decided he would rather have Laval in Paris than as a member of the Vichy government. Darlan, who had been Pétain's mollifying emissary to Hitler at Beauvais on Christmas Eve, now began to emerge as the figure most likely to restore collaboration.

One may follow in Abetz' correspondence with Berlin the gradual acceptance of Darlan as a valid interlocutor. Abetz gradually subsided from pistol-brandishing fury on December 16 to support of the Darlan regime by late February 1941. After the January 10 veto of Flandin's new government, it was Darlan who made himself the chief spokesman for concessions to German anger, devising formulas by which Laval might be brought back into the government without humiliating Marshal Pétain. An exploratory handwritten note of January 12 asked whether Laval's return was an irreducible German requirement for restoring relations. If so, Pétain would take Laval back into the Directorate if Laval wrote a letter affirming his loyalty. Pétain would then get his sojourn at Versailles and would publicly reaffirm the policies of Montoire. As late as March 5 Darlan was still proposing to Abetz formulas for Laval's return.[116]

This amenability was not the only thing that recommended Darlan to the Germans. He had been active in plans for French military operations against the Anglo-Gaullists in the summer of 1940. The sound anti-Gaullist record of Darlan's navy was also reassuring: only 200 of the 18,000 sailors and 50 of the 500

---

[115] The best contemporary source for these developments is the "France" file of Ernst von Weizsäcker, T-120/221. General Huntziger's statement will be found in T-120/587/243437; also published in *DGFP*, Series D, XI, no. 736.

[116] Abetz (Paris) 94 to Ribbentrop, 12 January 1941 (T-120/221/149022–24), also printed in *Mémorandum d'Abetz*, 68–71; Abetz (Paris) 763 to Ribbentrop, 6 March 1941 (T-120/221/149146–47).

naval officers in Britain at the moment of the armistice had remained there. General Halder thought that Darlan was so "flattered" by his growing authority that the Germans should support him. Abetz was sure that Darlan opposed a French government move to North Africa and thought he supported the plan for a French military operation against the Gaullists in French Equatorial Africa.[117] By his special combination of assiduity, guile, and good credentials, therefore, Darlan managed to be the first French minister to get out of quarantine after December 13 and be received by a high German official. Abetz agreed to see him in Paris on February 3.[118]

With Flandin's quiet withdrawal on February 9 and Darlan's assumption of his positions the next day, the "triumvirate" or "Directorate" scheme of January at last gave way to a regular government. Ribbentrop sent Abetz a personal letter of inquiry on February 11 about conditions in France. Abetz replied that he thought the restoration of Laval was still possible and that Darlan agreed with Laval on reconquering Lake Chad from the Gaullists without actually declaring war on England (which, Abetz pointed out, had the same effect). Ribbentrop had suggested that Darlan would use the fleet against England and permit German use of bases in the empire "in exchange for peace with us." Abetz seemed to agree. In fact this hypothetical deal discussed by Ribbentrop and Abetz on February 11 went further than the Germans were ever willing to go and so counted on concessions that Darlan was never willing to grant. But it suggests Darlan's growing acceptability to Germans in high places.[119] By February 27 Abetz declared that the government in which Darlan was vice-premier and held simultaneously four other ministries had lost its "provisional" character. He pronounced the French political situation "stabilized" again.[120]

[117] T-120/365/20637–40; The Halder Diaries, 28 January 1941; Abetz (Paris) 1 to Berlin, 1 January 1941 (T-120/221/148994); Abetz (Paris) 697 to Berlin, 28 February 1941 (T-120/221/149138–39).

[118] Abetz (Paris) 379 to Ribbentrop, 4 February 1941 (T-120/221/149088–90). Also published in *DGFP*, XI, no. 645.

[119] Ribbentrop's letter and Abetz' reply are in T-120/F10/142–43. They are also Nuremberg document NG-5471.

[120] Abetz (Paris) 674 to Berlin of 27 February 1941 (T-120/221/149131–34).

At working levels in the Foreign Office, there had been regrets all along at the rupture. Staatssekretär Ernst von Weizsäcker feared as early as January 8 that the "nearly complete" German reserve (Zurückhaltung) was leaving a vacuum into which the Anglo-Saxons could enter, and Richard Hemmen, the head of the economic branch of the Armistice Commission, grieved that his vital negotiations for German arms and aircraft manufacture in the unoccupied zone had been interrupted.[121]

Eventually even Abetz, who had made the post-December 13 crisis something of a personal vendetta not always in step with Berlin, came to feel that Darlan, like Laval, was sufficiently "socialistic" in his bluff, anticlerical saltiness to satisfy those early national socialist atavisms that still moved him.[122]

The clinching argument, both in Berlin and in Paris, was the recognition that Laval could be more useful as a sword of Damocles in Paris than as a member of the Vichy government. If Vichy needed coercing, Abetz could always threaten to set up a rival Laval regime in Paris. This argument appealed to Hitler's mood of rebound from the "new policy." Hitler, who still ordered as late as the third week of January that there should be no direct contact with prominent Frenchmen, no longer wanted Laval in the government but in Paris as a threat. Abetz came to accept that argument as if it had been his own.[123] Laval, at Abetz' urging, set his terms for return so high he knew they could not be accepted: prime minister (i.e., kicking Pétain upstairs to the office of head of state alone).[124]

By February 9, when Flandin withdrew (and there had been no specific German order that he do so), he had never seen a German official except the enraged, pistol-waving Abetz on December 16. Abetz' sense of personal affront and the diminishing interest in France at Berlin made Flandin useless for Marshal

---

[121] Weizsäcker memorandum of 8 January to Ribbentrop (T-120/221/ 149010); *DGFP*, XI, no. 654, pp. 1096–99.

[122] *DGFP*, XI, no. 531.

[123] *The Halder Diaries*, 28 January 1941; *Memorandum d' Abetz*, 79, 93; Hitler's order of no contact is reported on January 22 in T-120/221/149066.

[124] Laval set this condition when he met Darlan in Paris on 3 February 1941. Abetz (Paris) 379 to Ribbentrop, 4 February 1941 (T-120/221/ 149088 ff.). He obtained these terms in April 1942.

Pétain's major goal: the establishment of good relations with the occupier and the insulation of France from the conflict. Darlan turned out to be better able to renew those German contacts that had been the source of Laval's power.

The "new policy," however, was dead. Even upon acquiescing in the new Darlan regime, Abetz pointed out that France had "forfeited" all possibility of good relations with Germany by the exclusion of Laval.[125]

Darlan's Grand Design

THE GOVERNMENT THAT HAD EMERGED BY LATE FEBruary 1941 was dominated by one man to a far greater extent than any of the several governments of late 1940. Already navy minister, Darlan assumed the posts of vice-president of the Council, foreign minister, and minister of information on February 10, minister of the interior on February 17, and minister of defense the following August 11. Compared to Laval's two ministries in late 1940 and four in 1942–44, it was the greatest accumulation of offices during the Vichy regime. Much of what was to follow was shaped by Darlan's world view and by his bargaining position, as well as by German pressures and the evolution of the war.

Like Laval, Admiral François Darlan had been a Third Republic eminence. Contrary to strong royalist and Breton traditions in the French Navy, Darlan came from an old republican family in the southwest. His father had been a small-town lawyer (Nérac, Lot-et-Garonne) and political figure, an *opportuniste* deputy, and minister of justice in the Méline cabinet, 1896–98; he had also been a close friend of Georges Leygues. When Georges Leygues served several times as minister of the navy in the late 1920's and early 1930's, Darlan enjoyed a succession of assignments as head of the minister's staff. In effect, except for brief

[125] Abetz (Paris) 692, 28 February 1941 (T-120/221/149137).

interruptions, Darlan was "permanent Minister of the Navy" from 1926 to 1939.[126] As rear admiral, he had also begun acquiring diplomatic experience in 1930 as a member of the French delegation to the London Naval Conference. In 1937, the Popular Front government named Darlan chief of staff of the navy and commander-designate in case of war. Although the famous witticisms about Darlan's never having been to sea were erroneous, it is true that after midcareer he enjoyed far more political and diplomatic experience than any of his colleagues.

The main result of that career was Darlan's considerable success in winning funds from a parsimonious Third Republic for naval construction between the wars. The French Navy was, in 1939, at its strongest point in history. Darlan's navy played a limited role in the 1939–40 war, however. Darlan was a very active proponent of a northern operation against Russia in the Russo-Finnish war, ostensibly to seize the Scandinavian "iron ore route," and after that war's end in March 1940 cut short his plans, he threw his energies into the Norway campaign. When the German western offensive began in 10 May, however, none of the great European navies risked a sea battle. Against Italy after June 10, Darlan carried out only one hurried sea bombardment of Genoa.[127] At the armistice, therefore, the French Navy was intact and relatively unbeaten. The fleet, France's last major military resource, made Darlan inevitably a central figure in any future regime. More than any other individual except perhaps Pétain himself, Darlan could make or break the armistice. In June 1940, he committed the French Navy to the armistice position, while reassuring the British that the fleet would not be used against them and issuing secret orders to scuttle the ships if the Germans attempted to seize them.

The armistice released latent antagonisms toward Britain that had probably always simmered in Darlan. The frictions of the interwar naval conferences in which Britain tried to set French and Italian naval limits at the same level, the famous

[126] Jules Moch, *Rencontres avec Darlan et Eisenhower* (Paris, 1968), 22. In the absence of any scholarly study of Darlan, Moch is a useful corrective to Alain Darlan, *L'Amiral Darlan parle* (Paris, 1952).
[127] Moch, 71 ff.

"snub" at George VI's coronation in 1936 when Darlan came, in his own words, "behind Siam and Ecuador" because the French did not use the rank of Admiral of the Fleet [128]—all these accumulated irritations were magnified a thousandfold by the British shelling of the French squadron at Mers-el-Kebir on 4 July 1940. Darlan became the chief proponent of active military operations against Gibraltar and British Africa. Perhaps because Darlan had always been more a technician than an ideologue, the metamorphoses of 1940 carried him further into bold initiatives than even Laval. Whereas it is usually Laval who is treated as turncoat and opportunist, it was Darlan who actually was to move France closest to outright military cooperation with Germany in 1941 and then to find himself, perhaps accidentally, on the Allied side in November 1942. His opponents have called Darlan "l'amiral Courbette." [129] It was not the admiral's spinelessness that explains his emergence in 1941, however, but his vigorous initiatives.

Darlan had assumed office as the man best suited to reopen the German connections snapped in the December 13 crisis. Furthermore, he came to power as the figure most closely identified with Laval's policies, at least as seen by Abetz and Ribbentrop. He was the personification of the message he had taken to Hitler at Beauvais on Christmas Eve 1940: that nothing was changed in France's external relations. Finally, Darlan took power under the constant menace of a rival Laval government in Paris. Despite these negotiating liabilities, Darlan was determined to make the most of France's assets in order to make a place for her as a neutral member of the New Europe.

There were varying expectations about Darlan in the most interested capitals as he took office. As seen from Washington, good relations with Darlan were possible only if Vichy kept autonomous French resources, the empire and the fleet, out of Axis hands. Darlan began at least with the favorable impressions created in Washington by Laval's removal, and even when Darlan's tirades against Britain shocked U.S. Ambassador Leahy,

---

[128] Alain Darlan, 39.
[129] Alexander Werth, *France 1940–55* (New York, 1956), 112.

as at their first meeting on January 21, 1941, the two admirals found a certain professional common ground. Leahy found Darlan a "well-informed, aggressive, courageous naval officer" even at that first meeting. Darlan was categorical in his assurances that fleet and empire would remain neutral.[130]

As seen from Berlin, Darlan's role after February 1941 was to keep Britain and France apart. The British blockade, whose tightening in the early spring of 1941 raised the question of French armed convoys, was admirably suited for this policy. German officials in France were explicitly instructed to use it to sharpen and aggravate the Franco-British conflict. In more general terms, Darlan was supposed to keep the Allies from using French resources anywhere in the world and to keep order on the German flank and rear in Western Europe. He was expected to use force if necessary to do this, but France was still not to be allowed to become a full co-belligerent against England.[131] Having France perform these services was far cheaper than occupying all of French territory and performing them themselves. But there were to be no concessions until the war was over, and France was not to buy her way out of a harsh peace. Hitler was relieved that his brief interest in a "new policy" in the fall of 1940 had led nowhere. He wanted docility, loot, and perhaps bases, not cooperation among equals.

Darlan's own expectations differed from those of both Washington and Berlin. Darlan had visions of a French naval and imperial power within a new continental system. This role fitted into a German victory with less competition than into a British victory. If the British won, Darlan told a radio audience· on 2 May 1941, France, stripped of her navy and empire, would become a "second-class Dominion, a continental Ireland." The vic-

---

[130] Leahy (Vichy) to Department of State, no. 89, 21 January 1941 (U.S. Dept. of State Serial File 740.0011 Eur War 1939/7820). See also William L. Langer, *Our Vichy Gamble* (New York, 1947), 123.

[131] For instruction to sharpen Franco-British conflict over the blockade, see Deutsche Waffenstillstandskommission, Gruppe Wehrmacht—1a Nr. 370/41, 15 March 1941, to OKW/Abt. Ausland (T-77/OKW-999/5,632, 956). Keitel instructed the Armistice Commission on 6 June "not to work for war between France and Britain or the United States." OKW/W.F.St./ Abt. L (IV/k Nr. 001082/41 g.Kdos of 6 June 1941 (T-77/OKW-1444/ 5,594,731).

torious Germans would probably take less. But by the turning of the year 1940–41, Darlan saw victory by either side less likely. Although he no longer believed by the end of December 1940 that Germany could invade Britain, Britain on the other hand was "finished on the continent." Her overseas empire was gravitating into American hands. The ensuing stalemate permitted France to realize the colonial and maritime role that the uncomprehending Third Republic and British jealousy had blocked for her before 1940.[132] Darlan went out of his way to explain to Germans the advantages of his plans. When Brinon reported to Abetz on the Pétain-Franco meeting of February 1941, Darlan instructed him to observe that all of Africa should be reserved for continental Europe, making possible a friendly settlement between French and Spanish claims. In this perspective, it was in France's interest to "cleanse" the Mediterranean of British influence. A policy paper submitted to Abetz in the spring of 1941 by some of the young technocrats and activists in Darlan's cabinet (Pucheu, Lehideux, Marion) referred to France as Europe's "Atlantic bridgehead." [133]

An early peace would help France realize this maritime-colonial potential. Darlan shared fervently in the Vichy longing for a quick compromise peace within the status quo of 1941. A weakened Britain would be welcome. Furthermore, continued war threatened the French potential for recovery in two ways. It increased domestic disorder, as Darlan was finding to his pain in 1941. Darlan warned both the Americans and the Germans that continuing the war would spread communism. It also heightened the instability of the French empire. The longer the war lasted, the greater the occasions for both Allies and Axis to

---

[132] *Le Temps,* 2 June 1941 (also T-120/221/149379–88). Murphy (Vichy) 1140 to Secretary of State, 14 December 1940 (FRUS, 1940, II, 490). See also *FRUS,* 1941, II, 189, for similar views. Darlan still believed in November 1941 that Britain would have to seek a compromise peace (U.S. Dept. of State Serial File 851.00/2503). For Darlan's blame of the Third Republic and Britain for thwarting France's rightful overseas role, see his preface to Espagnac du Ravay, *Vingt ans de politique navale* (Grenoble, 1941), published on luxurious paper in that year of penury.

[133] Abetz (Paris) 548, 15 February 1941 (T-120/221/149106); *Pétain et les allemands: Mémorandum d'Abetz sur les rapports franco-allemands* (Paris, 1948), 79–84.

seize parts of the empire for their own use. And if either belligerent set foot in the empire, the other was sure to follow. So Darlan not only committed Vichy troops vigorously to keeping the British out of Syria in June–July 1941; he also fought a losing two-month diplomatic battle in the spring of 1941 to keep German armistice inspection teams out of Morocco. Once there, they were kept under surveillance and required to remain in civilian clothes. Their Arab contacts were arrested and even shot by French police. The natives must not be allowed to see the victors in uniform.[134] German bases were never permitted in the empire. Darlan's program, then, was a revival of France through maritime and colonial resources, alongside a great continental Germany. All he needed to begin was a speedy and generous peace settlement with Germany.

Darlan made no progress with his program in the spring of 1941. The German "cold shoulder" resisted Vichy efforts to thaw it. Darlan's own first meetings with Abetz, on March 5 and 31, after his government had been recognized on 27 February as more than merely temporary, were limited to current business. The other ministers were still forbidden until late in the spring even to cross the Demarcation Line. When they finally got to Paris, however, they had some propositions based on the notion of Franco-German economic complementarity in a technically advanced, united Europe. Finance Minister Yves Bouthillier finally reached Paris on April 24 for the first time since December 13, profuse in apologies for the Laval fiasco and brimming with assurances of the French will for collaboration and with hopes for the revival of the sweeping negotiations envisaged before Laval's dismissal. Thirty thousand tons of copper were ceded to Germany on April 29 by Pierre Pucheu, minister of industrial production. Jacques Barnaud, the chief economic negotiator for Vichy, came to an agreement on May 8 with German aluminum interests for a vast mutual production venture ap-

---

[134] For Darlan's warnings about the social risks of continued war, see *FRUS,* 1941, II, 185, 189; Leahy (Vichy) 89 to Dept. of State (U.S. Dept. of State Serial File 740.0011 Eur War 1939/7820); there is a fuller account of the Morocco armistice inspection struggle in my *Parades and Politics at Vichy* (Princeton, 1966), 113, 221–26.

proximately doubling French output in this vital commodity in which France and Yugoslavia could dominate Europe. Communications Minister Jean Berthelot finally reached Paris for the first time on May 7, with plans for joint European construction of roads and railroads. At Wiesbaden, the French delegation still refused the German proposal of substituting German supervision of France's external borders for the galling Demarcation Line, and although it had to give in about inspection of Morocco when German insistence reached "its sharpest phase," France never agreed to sack General Noguès for his close police restrictions upon the German inspectors. But stubborn negotiations at Wiesbaden could not cancel out the general impression of longing for a broad settlement, especially in such documents as the plan for French participation in a European economic community, which was submitted to Abetz in February by Jacques Benoist-Méchin in the name of the young technocrats and Europeanists, Pucheu, Lehideux, and Marion.[135]

For his part, Darlan took the stiffer position against Britain that was expected of him. The blockade negotiations with the British at Madrid seem to have been abandoned already, even before the Germans ordered them halted on February 13. Following this rupture at Madrid, positions hardened on both sides of the blockade. Having more ships available than they had in the fall of 1940, the British tightened their surveillance of French shipping. Fewer ships passed than in 1940, and Franco-British incidents increased.[136] As for Darlan, he resorted to armed convoying. On March 10, he formally notified the British government through U.S. Ambassador Leahy that if the British did not stop seizing French merchant ships, Darlan would use the French fleet to stop them. Darlan asked German permission on

---

[135] For the Bouthillier visit, see Schleier (Paris) 1291 to Schwarzmann, 25 April 1941 (T-120/221/149248 or T-120/3485H/019450). *Ministère public c/Lehideux*, 5. *Ministère public c/Jacques Barnaud*, 10. Berthelot's letter of 8 May 1941 to Richard Hemmen, in *Ministère public c/Berthelot*, and Hemmen's report of 7 May of Berthelot's initiatives, T-120/221/149289. *Mémorandum d'Abetz*, 79–84.

[136] I. S. O. Playfair, *The Mediterranean and Middle East,* 4 vols. (London, 1954–59), and W. N. Medlicott, *The Economic Blockade* (London, 1952–59), I, 557–66.

March 15 to use French naval vessels for convoying, and the German Armistice Commission supported it enthusiastically on the ground that Franco-British relations would be further aggravated.[137] A virtual Franco-British undeclared naval war was taking shape in the spring of 1941. British torpedo boats pursued a freighter right into Port-Etienne, Mauretania, on March 24, and a week later an armed French convoy fought a pitched battle off Nemours, Algeria, with a British cruiser and five torpedo boats. On March 26 and 29 British planes bombed French merchant shipping at Sfax, Tunisia, after the Italians had used the port. French armed escorts prevented British seizure of several French ships in the Atlantic, and there seem to have been British orders not to use force in such cases. On May 31, 1941, Darlan published a passionate diatribe against the British, summarizing their acts of "piracy" and claiming that 167 ships, or a total tonnage of 790,000, had been seized by the British. Relations were at their worst, despite United States efforts to moderate them.[138]

It was neither Darlan's economic proposals nor his anti-British ardor but German desert visions that thawed the cold shoulder finally in late April 1941. When the Iraqi nationalist Rashid Ali-al-Gailani revolted against British forces in April 1941, French Syria became a vital link for German exploitation of this new colonial crisis. Having in April 1941 conquered the western Balkans and Greece, Hitler was ready temporarily to exploit Mediterranean possibilities if they offered themselves cheaply. Once again, therefore, France briefly came to seem more a useful partner than an object of revenge.

Darlan, in turn, like much of French public opinion, had been forcibly struck by German successes in Yugoslavia that April. He was all the more ready, therefore, when Abetz told him on April 26 that Hitler himself would receive Darlan at

---

[137] Serial 221, frames 149159–60. *FRUS.* T-77/OKW-999, 5, 632, 956; T-120/378/209364–66. At the same time, on March 10, Darlan approved the Murphy-Weygand agreements for the shipment of supplies from the United States to North Africa. Langer, 135–36.

[138] The declaration is published in *Le Temps* for 2 June 1941. Langer, 155 ff.

Berchtesgaden in early May. Darlan was going to have his own Montoire.[139]

This time, even before meeting Hitler, Darlan and his fellow cabinet members were busy drafting a Grand Design. The Hitler-Darlan meeting would become the occasion for the major settlement of Franco-German relations that had eluded Laval. Darlan learned and accepted the German requests for use of Syrian equipment and airfields for clandestine aid to Rashid Ali, in meetings at the German embassy in Paris on May 3 and May 6.[140] In return, the Germans had reopened the occupation costs negotiations with a new proposal and had offered military concessions. Darlan wanted to go much further. He asked for easing of the Demarcation Line between the two zones, and he stressed the necessity of maximum publicity for these concessions. On May 11 Darlan went to see Hitler at Berchtesgaden. On May 20 General Walther Warlimont of the Wehrmachtführungsstab arrived in Paris for talks on German use of French bases in north and west Africa. A major agreement on German base rights in the French Empire, the Protocols of Paris, was signed on May 28.[141]

The protocols granted three major French military concessions to Germany: the use of Syrian airfields and military supplies stocked in Syria to help Rashid Ali's rebellion in Iraq; the use of the Tunisian port of Bizerte as a supply route for Rommel's Afrika Korps; and eventually, a German submarine base at

---

[139] Abetz (Paris) 323 to Berlin, 26 April 1941 (T-120/221/149149). Keitel thought that Darlan had been influenced by the German success in Yugoslavia (T-77/OKW-1444/5,594,751 ff.), but he had wanted such a chance all along. For the profound effect of German success in the Balkans upon French public opinion in the spring of 1941, see German intelligence reports, May 1941 (T-120/221/149371–72), and the new doubts about the possibility of Allied victory in Jean Guéhenno, *Journal des années noires*, 11 April 1941. "For the first time I tell myself that the defeat may be definitive."

[140] Woermann memorandum no. 366 of 3 May 1941 (T-120/221/149271); Abetz (Paris) 1376 to Ribbentrop, 5 May 1941 (T-120/221/149272–74); Abetz (Paris) to Ritter, 6 May 1941 (T-120/221/149277–79).

[141] For the Berchtesgaden meeting, the best contemporary account is the notes of the translator, Schmitt. The Protocols of Paris are published in *DFCAA*, IV, 472–80. A German text may be found in OKW/2012, frames 3, 596, 066 ff.

Dakar. In return for the Syrian part of this bargain, there were German concessions: a small reduction in occupation costs, easier passage of the Demarcation Line, release of World War I veterans (70,000–80,000) in German POW camps, and some small improvements in Vichy military posture. Further concessions would be worked out when Parts II and III of the protocols were implemented. Like Laval in 1940, Darlan insisted that these concessions have maximum publicity.[142]

As at Montoire, the Protocols of Paris were eagerly grasped by Darlan and his cabinet as the entering wedge for a broad negotiated agreement by which France could escape from the armistice constraints into a voluntary neutral role in the New Europe. What unfolded in the next few months was nothing less than Darlan's Grand Design: a peace treaty, or at least a broad preparatory agreement, that would restore normal economic and administrative life to a France willing to be associated in a German-dominated continental system, willing even to defend that continent against British counterattacks.

As after Montoire, German agencies began to talk about a "new era."[143] It was the OKW, the military, and Ambassador Abetz who were most interested in the prospects, Ribbentrop (as before) who was most reluctant, and Hitler who was only slightly less cautious.

At the heart of the protocol negotiations, however, lay profound differences of goal. On the German side, there was interest only in "getting the use of French facilities and bases for German campaigns."[144] Darlan wanted "first steps toward a happier future for our two lands" and toward "European cooperation," as he wrote to Hitler on 14 May 1941 after returning from Berchtesgaden. Or, as he explained it more propagandistically to the French people in a message of 14 June 1941, he wanted to prepare for the coming peace treaty by creating "a favorable climate

[142] Details of these negotiations may be found in T-120/221/149271–89.

[143] E.g., OKW guidelines in OKW/1444, frame 5,594,751. Richtlinien für die Verhandlungen der Waffenstillstandskommission. OKW WFSt/Abt L (IV, 1082), 6 June.

[144] Keitel order of mission to General Warlimont, OKW WFSt/Abt. L 111/M. Nr. 00929/41 g.Kdos. of 19 May 1941 (T-77/OKW-1444/5,594,767–78).

for honorable treatment" and, beyond that, to prepare a "new Europe" which can survive "only if France has her honorable place." [145] He also went out on the familiar limb by making public promises in a 19 May press communiqué and a 23 May speech suggesting that the peace terms could be softened by collaboration.

The priority of economic and political concessions to France was the crucial difference. The OKW's "new guidelines" for the German Armistice Commission gave first priority to military concessions that would enable the French to withstand the new pressures the planned German bases in Africa would be likely to generate; after that were to be considered "political concessions" to enable the French government to fulfill its policy of collaboration—to buy off domestic opposition. As Hitler himself, always suspicious of French attempts to euchre him out of the delights of vengeance, put it to Darlan at Berchtesgaden, concessions to France would be meted out to pay for each specific French military aid, "donnant-donnant." [146] Darlan, by contrast, like Laval before him, desperately needed conspicuous improvements in French living conditions. Laval had told Goering on 9 November 1940 that a French government friendly to Germany needed conspicuous concessions, "die ins Auge fallen," in order to survive. Darlan followed the same reasoning. The concessions must deal first with the major French preoccupations (prisoners, Demarcation Line, etc.), and they must be given maximum publicity. Then, in the ensuing climate of mutual confidence, closer cooperation would become possible. The need was even more urgent when the Syrian affair led to more fighting with Britain. [147]

[145] The Darlan telegram of 14 May 1941 to Hitler may be found in Generalstab des Heeres, Operationsabteilung, T-78/H2/184/6,428,758 ff.). The Darlan message is printed in *La France militaire,* 14 June 1941.

[146] The phrase is Darlan's own account of Berchtesgaden. *DFCAA,* IV, 415 ff., 459 ff., 560 ff.

[147] The Laval-Goering meeting may be found in Pariser Botschaft, Geheime Akten der Politischen Registratur, "Beziehungen Frankreichs zu Deutschland," Binder 98–100 (T-120/3485/E019424–29). For Darlan's urgent efforts to obtain some major concession to release in a communiqué after the British bombardment of Palmyra and Aleppo, during May 15–19, see Unterstaatssekretär Woermann file (T-120/589/243494 ff.).

This latent misunderstanding was ripped into the open by two developments, one near and one distant, which shifted all the presuppositions on which the "new policy" of May 1941 had been built. First, the discreet use of Syrian airfields and matériel by the Germans did not escape British notice, and following the British bombing of Palmyra and Aleppo airfields on May 14, British and Gaullist forces actually moved into Syria on June 8. As heavy fighting developed, Darlan declined *Luftwaffe* assistance. Hasty reinforcements from North Africa could not prevent the surrender of Vichy forces, however, at Acre, on July 14. France had reached the high point of military aid to Germany, only to lose Syria for her pains. Second, the German invasion of the Soviet Union on June 22, 1941, definitively turned Hitler's interest away from the Mediterranean and from French voluntary assistance. He had lost Iraq anyway by that time. He was later to want much more support from France but not "collaboration" between equals in the way Darlan and Pétain meant.

War in Syria aroused opposition to Darlan's Grand Design, most strongly among military and colonial figures. The French delegate to the Armistice Commission at Wiesbaden, General Paul Doyen, took the position that France had far more to lose than to gain when she allowed Germany to drag her into colonial wars. General Weygand, French delegate-general in North Africa, hurried to Vichy to attend a heated cabinet meeting on June 3 and 4.[148]

It has been accepted history since the Liberation that Weygand and the others blocked the Protocols of Paris on June 3-4. There is even some contemporary evidence for this view, for Emmanuel Monick told an American diplomat at Rabat after Weygand's return that Weygand had "succeeded in calling a halt to the proposed adoption of a new policy."[149] The turning point

---

[148] *DFCAA,* IV, 642–50. Even Admiral Darlan accused Germany on July 9 of leaving France "in the lurch" in Syria. Furthermore, the recent United States occupation of Iceland was a further warning of possible Allied counteraction if the Germans used Dakar. Vogl-Darlan conversation, 9 July 1941 (T-77/OKW-1444/5,594,826).

[149] Maxime Weygand, *Rappelé au service* (Paris, 1947), 428–40. *FRUS,* 1941, II, 368.

was rather July 8–12, and the cause was Syria. Darlan did modify —and enlarge—his Grand Design after the Syrian fiasco, but it was toward more dramatic proposals for settling Franco-German relations. The Germans did not in fact use Bizerte or Dakar as promised in Parts II and III of the protocols, but it was as much by their own decision as by French reluctance. And the opponents to Darlan's policy were removed from power before the end of 1941.

Indeed, from the beginning Darlan had tried to subordinate fulfillment of Parts II and III of the protocols to prior political preparation: those conspicuous concessions that would sweeten the pill and mollify the opposition.[150] In July, as the loss of Syria increased French costs, Darlan raised his price considerably for the fulfillment of Parts II and III. The protocol was not abandoned; it was submerged in a vast Darlan bid for French voluntary association on equal terms. German rejection, more than Weygand or any other Frenchman, blocked the Grand Design.

On July 12 Darlan notified the Germans that Part II of the protocols (supplying Rommel through the Tunisian port of Bizerte) could only be fulfilled after extensive political and economic concessions had prepared public opinion and after extensive military autonomy had prepared France for the inevitable Allied reprisals. The Bizerte accord was, Darlan pointed out, just one part of a broader reorientation of Franco-German relations. Until the whole basis of collaboration had been changed into voluntary associations between equals, Part II of the protocols could not go into effect by itself.[151]

The Germans abandoned Part III for themselves. The French negotiations had already watered it down in the pre-protocol negotiations, suggesting on May 26 that it be carried out in two stages: in the first, German merchant ships could use Dakar and then supply German submarines at sea; only later would German submarines use Dakar directly. General Warlimont described this as "a step backward." Late in June, however, Hitler

---

[150] See the Supplementary Protocol of 28 May 1941, printed in *DFCAA*, IV, 479–80.

[151] *DFCAA*, IV, 589. Darlan handwritten note, T-120/3485H/E019480; T-120/368/211199.

himself abandoned the use of Dakar "on political grounds." Ribbentrop, always a hard-liner on French matters, proposed that a German air base be set up at Dakar since some British effort to seize the port seemed to him inevitable, and once it was lost to the French, the Germans would never get the use of its naval facilities. General Keitel opposed this scheme on July 8, arguing that the safest course was to keep Dakar neutral and avoid provoking Allied ripostes. In effect, let the French guard it.[152] Keitel had come around to the French view, and the German center of interest had shifted to the east.

Darlan revealed on July 14, 1941, what he meant by the basic reorientation of Franco-German relations, the price of executing Part II of the protocols. That day his representative in Paris, Jacques Benoist-Méchin, handed the German embassy a *note verbale* containing the most ambitious French proposal of the Vichy period. (Note that it follows the supposed blockage of Darlan's policy by Weygand and the cabinet on June 3–4.) The deal had ended with the military aid to Rashid Ali in Iraq, as far as Hitler was concerned. The deal had hardly begun, as Darlan saw it. The *note verbale* of 14 July 1941 asserted that the armistice of 1940 was no longer adequate to the new situation. France had gone to war and lost in Syria, British threats to the rest of the empire had increased, and French populations saw no concomitant political reward. Under these conditions, carrying out the rest of the protocols would expose France to further imperial wars and losses that must be compensated for by other means. So far, he seemed to respond to Weygand's alleged pressures. Then Darlan proposed nothing less than releasing France from the restraints of the armistice and restoring normal relations with Germany. Furthermore, if French defense of her empire led to war with Britain and the United States, Germany must assure the integrity of France's prewar borders (including Alsace, which Laval had given up, as well as Lorraine) and her African Empire, perhaps with compensation for necessary adjustments. After these concessions, in a "changed political cli-

---

[152] OKW/2012, frames 5,596,029–034, contains the Ribbentrop-Keitel letters.

mate," Darlan expected to be able to carry out the protocols.[153]

Officials in Berlin, unlike later historians, made no mistake about the scope of these proposals. The Army General Staff (OKH) tersely summarized it as "replacing the armistice with a new treaty providing for French sovereignty and cooperation." Some German officials were tempted. Ambassador Karl Ritter had been saying since late June that France should be treated as a "budding ally." Abetz had been rushing ahead with timetables for graduated concessions through late June, his usual enthusiasm heightened still further by a great project that would enhance the scope of his office. When Darlan began backwatering on Bizerte after July 8, however, he felt that any German concession before France had fulfilled Part II of the protocols was "extortion." Ribbentrop saw the *note verbale* quite simply as "a naive French blackmail attempt." He chose to see Darlan's July 12 harder bargaining position on Bizerte as a rupture of negotiations rather than an attempt to broaden the negotiations.[154]

Ribbentrop's hard line prevailed. The *note verbale* received no direct response, though Abetz told Benoist-Méchin on July 31 that the French government's record was insufficient for the demands made. The real reasons for the rebuff appear in a briefing by Ambassador Karl Ritter for army staff on the 26th of July. Germany did not envisage "turning the Armistice into collaboration." She did not wish to "influence or commit herself to the

---

[153] Because Darlan was assassinated in December 1942 and therefore not tried after the war, this climactic French offer has been lost from view. DFCAA, IV, 564, reports the delivery of the *note verbale* without any text, which the French editors were apparently unable to locate. A damaged German photocopy of the text is filmed in T-120/F10/462–78, and the text as wired to Abetz (then in Berlin) is contained in Achenbach (Paris) 2101 to Abetz, 15 July 1941 (T-120/386/211214–28). It is also published in *DGFP,* Series D, XIII 142–49, along with a footnote reference to additional documents found in Abetz' papers: a draft revision of the Armistice terms, a draft Franco-German treaty, and a draft French declaration of adherence to the Tripartite (Anti-Comintern) Pact. I have not seen these additional documents.

[154] OKH. Abt. Fremde Heere West, 5296/41, 16 July 1941 (T-120/855/285093); *Mémorandum d'Abetz,* 107–10; Abetz (Paris) 2274 to Ribbentrop, 31 July 1941 (T-120/386/211278–80); Ribbentrop note to Hitler, 16 July 1941, forwarding the *note verbale* (T-120/F10/460–61).

future," i.e., to a generous peace. Abetz was ordered to show more reserve to the French. Such low-level technical negotiations as occupation costs and the new plan by Paris collaborators for French volunteers for the Soviet front were to be handled in a "dilatory fashion." On August 13 Ribbentrop told Abetz to engage in no "concrete negotiations" with the French. The threads of negotiation should not be broken, but if Frenchmen made proposals, they were to be told that Germany was completely involved in the Russian campaign. At about the same time, Unterstaatssekretär Woermann prepared a circular telegram on Franco-German relations for mission chiefs abroad. The French, he said, had asked for release from the armistice. They had not acted properly. The request was all the more impossible since all German strength was now turned against bolshevism. Germany held to the armistice. There was now a "stillstand" in Vichy-Berlin relations.[155]

Darlan was in an awkward position. His "new era" had lasted a shorter time than Laval's new policy. France had gone to war against the Anglo-Gaullists, lost Syria, and come close to outright military collaboration. High-level opposition manifested itself in Weygand's trip and Doyen's letter, "Lessons of ten months at Weisbaden," of 16 July, in which Doyen told Pétain that France had given too much and received nothing. Darlan had announced German concessions in two communiqués, May 6 and May 19, concessions that were not now going to be realized.[156]

In the fall of 1941, therefore, he followed an aggressive policy at home and abroad. At home, he weeded out the opposition and established a firmer control over the French government and armed forces between August and November 1941. Abroad, he labored to reopen the Protocol negotiations on a broader political basis.

---

[155] Abetz (Paris) 2274, 31 July 1941 (T-120/386/211278); OKW Abt. Ausland 106/41, 26 July 1941 (T-77/OKW-999/5,632,895); *Mémorandum d'Abetz*, 110, 116; Ribbentrop (Berlin) 830 to Abetz, 13 August 1941 (T-120/386/211336); Woermann draft, T-120/587/243648-9.

[156] In particular, announced reduction of occupation costs on May 6. *Le Temps*, 9 May 1941, 4. Months of haggling followed.

General Doyen was forced out as French delegate to the Armistice Commission at Wiesbaden in the middle of July. As for General Weygand, the suspicion that had surrounded him in German circles from the beginning was intensified by Darlan's rivalry with him and by Darlan's eagerness to obtain direct control over the armed forces. Although it was a German ultimatum that forced the retirement of Weygand in November 1941, it is clear from German sources that Darlan had encouraged it. Darlan also established his direct control over the armed services in August 1941 when he assumed Weygand's former office of minister of defense, over the opposition of other service leaders.[157]

Darlan's efforts to reopen the broad political discussions with Germany that had been interrupted in July were less successful. Having announced the "first positive results" since the armistice, Darlan had to make good. He was desperate for a major breakthrough with the Germans. There is no doubt, from the German archives, who was the suitor and who was the wooed. On August 8 Darlan saw Abetz and stated France's willingness for military collaboration with Germany. He outlined his plans for getting rid of Weygand and establishing his own control of the armed forces. On August 13, however, came new instructions from Ribbentrop: Abetz was to tell Darlan that Germany could not entertain his request for new negotiations on outstanding questions, because she was completely tied up with the Eastern front. Meanwhile, on August 12, the release of prisoners of war, announced so proudly in the French press on May 19, was halted. The "stillstand" imposed on Franco-German relations by the change of strategic interests and by Ribbentrop was complete.[158]

Marshal Pétain seconded Darlan's efforts to reopen negotiations in a way that cannot be regarded as hesitant or ventriloqual. He was as clearly excited by the anti-Bolshevik turn that the war had taken as was Darlan. If Hitler would only make a gesture of equality to France, Pétain told a Rumanian visitor on August 15,

---

[157] For army hostility to Darlan, General Emile Laure, "Des Fronts de 1939–40 à la Haute Cour de 1948 (Notes militaires et politiques)," 10 August 1941.

[158] *Le Temps,* 9 May 1941, 4; T-120/386/211317–18; T-120/1217/33009.

1941, Pétain would then receive the mandate from his people for close cooperation with Germany. On September 25 he told the same visitor that if French territory were unified under his administration (i.e., the Demarcation Line abolished and French administration fully operative in the Occupied Zone), France would work for the new Europe. Pétain now stressed Bolshevism as the common enemy of France and Germany, and their common interest in defending "a higher culture" together, as he wrote effusively to Hitler on the anniversary of Montoire, 22 October 1941. Hitler's response was an ill-tempered diatribe against the assassination of Germans on French soil.[159]

Pétain spoke even more vigorously and unmistakably when the funeral of General Huntziger on 16 November 1941 brought a number of high-ranking German officials to Vichy. (It was the second and last visit of Abetz to Vichy, and the only friendly one.) The marshal reminded Abetz and Vogl of all that France had done against England and said that he was ready to acknowledge Hitler publicly as the leader of Europe. But he could move French public opinion only after agreement on some broad plan showing how the German victors foresaw the eventual Franco-German peace terms. Abetz understood this reference to a "plan" as a reversion to the 14 July *note verbale,* and he bristled. Germany also had a plan, he said: defeat the Allies and make peace afterwards. Only after total German victory could these more distant matters be discussed.

Darlan was equally blunt on this occasion. He said he was disappointed that Germany had denied so many French requests. He told Abetz how eager he was to find a satisfactory solution to the Franco-German problem and suggested that the long-deferred offensive against British colonies in Africa, with German help, after Weygand's removal, might be the occasion. Thus the Chad operation, over which Laval is supposed to have been dismissed in December 1940, was being discussed in Pétain's presence in November 1941. Darlan amazed General Vogl

[159] T-120/386/211346, 211426; T-120/405/213935–36, 214059–61 for the Pétain-Hitler letters of October 1941. The first assassination of a German serviceman in France had occurred in Paris on 21 August 1941.

with his hatred of the British.[160] But Berlin was still afraid to let Darlan buy France off.

German conditions for reopening Franco-German negotiations in the fall of 1941 were prompt French fulfillment of at least Part II of the Protocols of Paris. Darlan was unwilling to do this without a vision of a generous peace to come. It was General Alexander's British Eighth Army and the hard-pressed Italians who finally reopened the stalled Protocol negotiations in November and December 1941. British victories in the desert made supply through Bizerte seem more essential than ever. Italy, who heretofore had always urged a harder line against France and who had to be reassured whenever Franco-German collaboration loomed as a threat to Italian aims in North Africa and Corsica, was willing in November 1941 to make some concessions in order to gain supplies through the Tunisian port. The post-Protocol negotiations finally revived on 19 December 1941, only to deadlock over Darlan's insistence on putting political concession first: larger autonomy and replacement of the armistice with normal Franco-German relations, and the promise of a lenient peace.[161]

It is in the context of the permanent French campaign for general high-level negotiations that the famous Pétain-Goering interview at Saint-Florentin on December 1 must be viewed. More immediately, the Saint-Florentin meeting was an outgrowth of the dismissal of Weygand. Pétain asked on November 3 that he be permitted to meet some high-level German figure, such as Goering, to make the German removal of Weygand seem less humiliating. This was accepted on November 18, and Pétain acknowledged the "invitation" on November 21.[162] On the French side, this was hailed as the breakthrough so long sought since the "stillstand" of July 15. Darlan and the cabinet ministers

---

[160] For various meetings with Pétain and Darlan on Nov. 16–17, T-120/405/214056–65. Both General Vogl and Welck commented on Pétain's freshness and vigor.

[161] *DFCAA*, V, 387–401, dossier of Colonel Vignol on French efforts to reopen talks, July–Dec. 1941. For German reluctance for political talks, T-120/405/214186–88.

[162] T-120/405/213982–85, 214071–72, 214082–83.

prepared an enormous dossier of economic, social, and political steps that would normalize Franco-German relations. Each minister prepared a list of concessions needed in his area of responsibility. Pétain tried to deliver this memorandum to Goering, who wanted only to discuss the ways in which France could help the beleaguered Afrika Korps if Rommel had to retreat as far west as Tunisia. The meeting was a complete fiasco, and on December 4 the French government quietly withdrew the memorandum. It continued to circulate at Berlin, where a copy was annotated by Admiral Dönitz, until Ribbentrop ordered it filed and forgotten.[163]

The use of Bizerte was urgent enough, however, for new negotiations on Part II of the protocols to be opened on 19 December. General Alphonse Juin was sent to Berlin on December 21 at the same time to work out the military implications of Rommel's retreat toward Tunisia.[164] It is apparent that Berlin was interested only in French military aid in Africa, which they could obtain under the armistice without any of the concessions that Darlan was pleading for.

In the end the Germans got much of what they wanted from the Darlan regime. Since the British advance petered out before they reached Tunisia, the question of French hospitality for Rommel was never raised. But Vichy did supply military equipment to Rommel through Tunisia. Trucks, guns, and oil were delivered to German supply officers by French officers at the Tunisian-Libyan frontier in January–February 1942. United States observers found out about them, and U.S. pressures brought them to a stop. Darlan had been forced, however, to accept the German interpretation of Part II of the protocols. On the other hand, German bases had never in fact been established

---

[163] For the French retraction, T-120/405/214111–12, 214118. Dönitz' copy is T-120/852/284443–503. Ribbentrop's order may be found at T-120/852/284537–38. So much for the somewhat exaggerated story that continues to circulate, e.g., Georges Blond, *Pétain* (Paris, 1966), of Pétain's getting the best of Goering.

[164] This is entirely misleading in Juin's memoirs, which obscure the relation of his Berlin mission to Part II of the protocols. German minutes of the visit are found at T-77/OKW-2012/5, 595, 950 ff. See also T-120/F9/264–66.

in the empire. Germans had entered the empire or used it only as part of what Darlan hoped would be an important bargain. But in the end his bargaining led nowhere because Hitler had lost interest in the Mediterranean world. Hitler thought he did not need French voluntary assistance in a maritime and colonial program of joint interest.

While the Tunisian problem was solving itself by Alexander's failure to push Rommel west onto French territory, another embarrassment for Darlan's Grand Design was opening across the Atlantic. Germany's declaration of war upon the United States immediately following the Pearl Harbor raid posed once again the question of Vichy neutrality. Must France break the Washington connection, useful materially as well as diplomatically?

Darlan was explicitly opposed to any break. French interests were certainly linked to Franco-American neutrality, for in the event of hostilities, the United States could seize much of the French Empire (especially in the Caribbean), not to mention the French gold in the United States.[165]

Hitler does not seem to have been greatly interested in promoting a French declaration of war against the Allies in December 1941. But the subject was raised by subordinates on both sides: Abetz on the German side, Benoist-Méchin on the French, for example. It is here that one finds the curious tale of a Vichy cabinet meeting on January 9, 1942, in which a majority of ministers are alleged to have decided to declare war on the Allies. The real issue, of which the Benoist-Méchin–Abetz exchange was a distorted reflection, was whether France should break relations with the United States. She did not. (A detailed discussion of this episode and the issues and personalities involved will be found in Appendix A.) In any event, Hitler and Darlan got

[165] Lucien Romier told Roland Krug von Nidda on December 19 that France, fearing the loss of her colonies, must pursue an attitude of "watchful waiting" toward war with the United States. Schleier (Paris) 4049 to Abetz (Berlin), 19 December 1941 (T-120/405/214177–78). Darlan's attitude, as explained to Schleier on 29 January 1942, was that Germany would gain nothing by a French declaration of war on the Anglo-Saxons. Schleier (Paris) 423 to Abetz (Berlin), 30 January 1942 (T-120/405/214294–95). The Germans seem to have agreed.

their way, as was to be expected. Hitler had the status quo in France, and Darlan had neutrality. But Darlan had got no concessions.

Furthermore, a belligerent United States was much harder to get along with than the neutral one had been. Washington began putting pressure at once upon French shipping and bases in the Caribbean. The Greenslade-Robert agreement that had governed Franco-American relations in the Caribbean since August 6, 1940, was now changed to reflect American belligerent status and American concern that the Germans might use French bases in the area. American daily patrols in the French Antilles were the main innovation of the new Horne-Robert agreement of December 17, 1941. In February 1942, however, a damaged German submarine landed a couple of wounded crew members at Martinique, and Washington insisted that the French bar the Axis from her Caribbean possessions. The Vichy reply, barring *all* belligerents from French Caribbean possessions in a declaration of total neutrality, was rejected by Washington. On the other hand, Germans were putting pressure on Darlan to refuse any United States demands in the Caribbean. By late March, Darlan had managed to mollify both Hull and Abetz by making conflicting promises. He assured Abetz that no planes or ships from any belligerent could use the French Antilles and that French ships would be scuttled if Americans sought to use them. At the same time, he instructed Admiral Robert to keep negotiating with the United States. On this precarious basis, he kept a fragile neutrality between the ever more exigent belligerent coalitions, but it was clear that his ground for maneuver was greatly restricted. The French Antilles were sufficiently threatened by Washington to alarm even General de Gaulle about their eventual sovereignty. It was a measure of the narrowing possibilities of success for Darlan's attempts at neutrality.[166]

---

[166] The Greenslade-Robert agreement of 6 August 1940 and the Horne-Robert agreement of 17 December 1941 may be found in *FRUS*, along with the exchanges of notes of February–March 1942. The Franco-German side to this controversy appears most fully in the Weizsäcker papers, T-120/112. Laval faced even tougher pressures in May. See below, p. 312.

By the spring of 1942, therefore, Darlan was caught in a tightening vise. One pincer was his failure to improve the conditions of French life by loosening the armistice constraints. He had failed to win any concessions from Hitler, despite the most dramatic offers of the whole Vichy period. The other pincer was the rising threat to French neutrality posed by escalating American and German pressures on the fleet and the empire. Darlan seemed likely to lose even those two bargaining cards that had so far proved inadequate but that were all France had to buy her independence.

Nor could it be said that French life was much easier in the spring of 1942 than it had been in the spring of 1941. In some senses, there was some reestablishment of normalcy. Production was rising. Unemployment had been turned into a labor shortage. But food was short, the prisoners were not home, and France remained cut in two. All the most galling aspects of the occupation remained unchanged. Darlan had failed in every positive test. His efforts to thaw German reserve had failed. Darlan's successes were negative ones: France had not returned to war and had not yet been fully occupied. These were not enough to keep him in power.

Darlan's Fall and Laval's Return: April 1942

DARLAN'S FALL GREW OUT OF A VICHY DECISION, NOT A German demand. The basic Vichy calculation from the beginning had been built on successful negotiations with Germany. Darlan had been chosen because his contacts seemed better than anyone else's in February 1941. Who else, Laval excepted, had talked to Hitler and had contacts with Abetz at that frightening time after Laval's fall? Darlan had not made good on those hopes, however, and Marshal Pétain began casting about for somebody new. Although Pétain met Laval secretly in the Randan Forest near Vichy on March 26, 1942, he wanted to replace

Darlan not with the former foreign minister but with a cabinet of traditionalist, clerical, neutralist friends.

Personal relations between Pétain and Darlan were not bad; Darlan's manners did not jar the marshal as had those of Laval. But Pétain is supposed to have been disgruntled by the admiral's penchant for high living and his cynical scorn for the National Revolution. The deeper reasons for Pétain's dissatisfaction, however, may be learned from the persons whom he wanted to include in a new government. Pétain wanted to make a new assertion of neutrality acceptable to both Hitler and Roosevelt, and he wanted to surround himself with a socially more reassuring crew than either Laval's cronies or Darlan's experts had been. These are the purposes that one can read between the lines of the ministerial list that Pétain submitted secretly to German security officials in Paris, bypassing the embassy, in March 1942.

As before, when Pétain wanted to approach high-ranking Germans unofficially, he turned to the World War I air ace, Colonel René Fonck. Fonck had already been the marshal's messenger in the fall of 1940, when Pétain was trying to meet Goering or Hitler, in the days before Montoire. Fonck was on good terms with both Goering and Air Marshal Udet. He brought Pétain's proposed cabinet list to Paris, and Achenbach checked it with Berlin and with the SD.

The leading figure of the new government, the vice-president of the Council, was to be Joseph Barthélemy, heretofore minister of justice, long-time professor of constitutional law at the University of Paris, and a laissez-faire liberal bitterly opposed to the Popular Front experiments. He had published a legal defense of the Munich agreements. His tenure as minister of justice had been an uphill effort to apply the rule of law to exceptional circumstances.

The other proposed ministers were a mixture of "experts" and old-fashioned patriots and clericals. There were five high-level civil servants who had been serving as secretaries-general of ministries: Deroy, Dayras, Charles-Roux, Terray, Arnoux. The royalist Catholic Jean Le Cour Grandmaison was proposed for a Ministry of Social Affairs, and François Charles-Roux (proposed for Foreign Affairs) had been ambassador to the Vatican as well as Secretary-General of the Foreign Ministry. The military posts were to go to Admiral Le Luc (who had signed the armistice) and General Revers (Darlan's chief of staff and still, at this stage, a loyal supporter of the regime, although he was to become a distinguished Résistant by 1944). Pétain's Senate friends Charles Reibel and Henry Lémery reappeared as prospective ministers, respectively, of the interior and of colonies.

The Paris collaborators were appalled. Fernand de Brinon described the candidates as "clerico-Gaullist" or "patriotarde-attentiste," accolades that some of these gentlemen did not really merit. Darlan, Laval, and Benoist-Méchin all saw the proposal, the Germans reported to Berlin, as "Gaullist-reactionary." [167]

The Vichy government also tried this list out on the United States. Du Moulin de Labarthète, Pétain's *chef de cabinet* and a participant in drawing up the plan, conceded to Leahy the day after the Randan meeting that there was some German pressure to restore Laval, but he said the main intention was to clean house within the ministry.[168] Du Moulin wanted Darlan removed too, because he was incompetent. Du Moulin mentioned Barthélemy to Leahy—the substitute ministry was being cleared in Washington indirectly.

Darlan's counterattack sealed his own doom. The United States note of March 27, expressing displeasure at the possibility of Laval's return, was shown to Benoist-Méchin, who told Abetz about it. Then there began a contest of wills between Abetz and Washington.[169] Thus Laval entered the picture seriously again only after the question of replacing Darlan had already arisen, and German pressure (Abetz' pressure, not Berlin's) was applied only

[167] Achenbach's report on this is found in T-120/5586/E401095–98. Du Moulin de Labarthète, *Le Temps des illusions* (Paris, 1946), 398–99, has a totally different list.

[168] U.S. Dept. of State Serial File 851.00/2727. Admiral Leahy (Vichy) 866 to Dept. of State, 24 March 1942.

[169] Dept. of State Serial File 851.00/2727. Leahy's information as of April 15 thus supports Du Moulin on this point. Aron, 478 ff., argues the more traditional view that Laval's return followed months of German pressure.

after American pressure had already manifested itself. Darlan, after all, was not thrown out. He remained a leading figure of the regime as commander in chief of the armed forces.

The Laval government was formed on 26 April 1942. Pétain had thus got half of what he wanted: a new cabinet, with German contacts. But he lost much: although he wanted to keep good American contacts, Roosevelt called Leahy home. Laval now took the office of prime minister from Pétain, leaving the marshal only as head of state. Experts still dominated the government, joined now by some of Laval's cronies. Pétain's dream of a Catholic traditionalist cabinet was farther from reality than ever.

The first two years after the armistice form a kind of unity. Like Laval before him, Darlan had tried to win an autonomous neutral place in Hitler's Europe. Both men had tried to interest Hitler in the useful role France could play if given her head: keeping the Allies out of the empire, contributing colonial and maritime weight to a new continental bloc. They were supported by the cabinet, in spite of postwar efforts by cabinet members to insist that the two late vice-premiers had worked alone. Marshal Pétain had also participated actively in the search for a settlement. Yves Châtel, governor-general of Algeria, once bragged to an American representative that Pétain was known to the Germans as "Marshal Nein," [170] perhaps in view of the Germans' exalted expectations of how defeated peoples should behave. But there is no remark of that kind in the German archives. There Pétain appears rather as "Marshal Bitte": Give us normalcy and hope for a generous peace, and we will participate in the New Europe.

It is salutary to reflect on Hitler's blind arrogance. One can only speculate on what would have happened if he had been less vengeful, less wedded to forceful solutions, quicker to sense others' needs and aspirations. If he had given France enough to eat, arms to defend her empire, and the promise of territorial integrity, France might well have become the neutral "west wall"

---

[170] *FRUS,* 1942, II, 297.

that Pétain was to talk about later in 1942. If German dominance meant abundance, Gide observed cynically on 9 July
1940, nine-tenths of Frenchmen would accept it, three-fourths of
them with a smile.[171] Hitler's arrogance of power never gave that
speculation a test.

[171] *The Journals of André Gide,* translated and edited by Justin O'Brien,
vol. IV (New York, 1957), 30. For Pétain's desire to be the continent's
neutral west wall, see chapter 4.

The total revolution of France has been prepared by twenty years of uncertainty, discontent, disgust, and latent insurrection. . . . The war has burst open the abscess. . . . This possibility of doing something new thrills men of every walk of life.

—Paul Baudouin, July 1940 [1]

We Frenchmen must try something new.

—Paul Valéry, June 1940 [2]

Reform was possible only through catastrophe.

—Frédéric Le Play [3]

II / The National Revolution

THE FRENCH QUEST FOR A SETTLEMENT WITH GERMANY was only one side of collaboration. Collaboration is not seen as a whole without its domestic dimension. Externally, the armistice position rested upon a certainty of German victory and a preference for peace and stability over a last-ditch resistance to the finish. Internally, the armistice position offered a historic opportunity for change such as France had not seen since 1870—indeed, perhaps not since 1789.

Even if few Frenchmen had wanted change before the defeat, the loss of the war would have turned jaundiced eyes upon the Third Republic. Discredit to the regime was bound to be no less than in 1870. Even more than in 1870, France had seethed already with dissatisfactions and proposals for change before the war, change which had been largely frustrated by the incoherence of oppositions and the negative balance that held the Third Re-

---

[1] Interview in *Journal de Genève,* quoted in *Le Temps,* 19 July 1940.
[2] *Cahiers,* vol. 23 (Paris, 1960), 429.
[3] Quoted by Yves Bouthillier, *Le Drame de l'armistice* (Paris, 1948), II, 282.

public in stalemate. The defeated republic, so substantial in its inertia only a few days before, evaporated like the dew. The pent-up frustrations of the 1930's burst out into the exhilaration of one of those rare moments when things are malleable. Even those dedicated to the status quo thought it could be preserved only by radical change. In their excitement, Frenchmen committed the most elementary imprudence. In their impatience to avenge old wrongs and transform the conditions that had led to defeat, they made major structural changes during an enemy occupation.

It is hard to remember today how intense and how widespread was the excitement of these projects. For some it was the exhilaration of vengeance: the hated republic, "la gueuse," was dead. But that sense of exhilaration extended far beyond the old antirepublicans. Some of it was a sense of liberation from encrusted procedures and political immobility. It had taken more than two hundred bills between 1871 and 1909 to get an income tax adopted in France on 15 July 1914.[4] Some twenty-four bills had proposed old-age pensions since 1936, the latest of which had passed The Chamber on 14 March 1939 only to fail in the Senate.[5] How much easier it was simply to issue an old-age pension law by government authority on 14 March 1941, with Marshal Pétain declaring that "we keep our promises, even those of others."

"Reform is in the air," wrote Louis Rivière of the Cour d'Appel of Rouen in 1941. "The National Revolution has done in one year what the former regime failed lamentably to do in more than a century," wrote Professor de Nesmes-Desmarets of the law faculty at Montpellier, referring to the Civil Service Statute of 1941 that had been in the political mill for a generation. "We accused the old regime, with justification, of obstructing major reforms," wrote Paris law professor Georges Ripert in the *Revue de droit commercial*. "That obstacle has disappeared."[6]

[4] J. M. Jeanneney and M. Perrot, eds., *Textes de droit économique et social français* (Paris, 1957), 306.

[5] Michel-Henri Fabre, "La retraite des vieux travailleurs," *Annales de la faculté de droit d'Aix*, Nouvelle série, no. 37 (1944), 156.

[6] *Gazette du palais*, 1941, 2e semestre, I; *Les lois nouvelles*, 1943, 51–69; *Revue de droit commercial*, 5e année, 1943, 89–108.

For still others, it was a heady "ferment of technical progress," the "insertion of the future into the present," as it was put by Jean Bichelonne, Laval's minister of industrial production and the enthusiastic partner of Albert Speer in 1943 in projects of Franco-German economic integration. Railroad engineer and Communications Minister Jean Berthelot, who had been frustrated by entrenched bureaucrats in his efforts to rationalize the Paris municipal transportation agencies in the late 1930's, recalled in 1968 how satisfying it had been to create the unified Paris municipal transit system (the R.A.T.P.) in 1942 by the unfettered application of technical good sense. Senior civil servants, such as André Bisson, a postwar president of the Cour des Comptes, rejoiced at how much easier budget-making had become without the punctilious scrutiny of the parliamentary finance committees—a sentiment that American presidents might secretly share.[7]

Conservatives had the power that universal suffrage had denied them since 1924; technicians had power that politicians had never given them. The genuine excitement aroused by those possibilities has to be reasserted now after so many postwar efforts to pretend that Vichy was merely a caretaker regime of "presence." Pétain himself could assert in his one statement at his trial in July 1945 that "France may change words and labels. She is building but she can build usefully only on the bases I have laid down."[8]

Indeed the Resistance was no less determined to sweep away what de Gaulle called "the anarchic abuses of a regime in decay." Léon Blum wrote to him on 15 March 1943 about the future France, as socialists saw it. France must be democratic. "That doesn't mean—any more for us than for you—that the Constitution and prewar institutions must be restored in their integrity, that after this long interval the old machine must simply start up again." It was a "new republic," not the old one, that

[7] Bichelonne, preface to Robert Catherine, *Economie de la répartition des produits industriels* (Paris, 1943); Jean Berthelot, *Sur les rails du pouvoir* (Paris, 1968), 219; André Bisson, *Finances publiques françaises* (Paris, 1943), 271–72.

[8] *Procès du maréchal Pétain* (Paris, 1945), 9.

glimmered in the various postwar blueprints of Resistance movements.[9]

Another measure of the intensity of those prewar frustrations and resentments that emerged in 1940 in a geyser of change can be found in a comparative look at other occupation regimes. No other defeated state set out as ambitiously during World War II on fundamental changes. To find a similar exploitation of defeat, one would have to turn to formerly stateless peoples like the Croats of Yugoslavia and the Slovaks of Czechoslovakia for whom Hitler's destruction of the eastern European status quo meant the chance for ethnic statehood. Charles Maurras' remark that the events of 1940 were a "divine surprise" is too authentic not to be quoted one more time out of context.[10]

But in what direction would these released energies flow? What forms would the new France take? Which of the multiple interests clamoring for attention would be served? Those who make a revolution are often not those who reap the benefits. We shall look first at the Vichy programs and then at the personnel who created them and who profited by them.

Competing Visions

VICHY WAS NOT A "BLOC." INFLUENTIAL WRITERS HAVE reduced it to imported nazism, to the triumph of Maurras, or even to an outgrowth of 1930's Personalism.[11] But no single-factor account of the National Revolution gets us very far. Vichy was as complex as the various groups that stepped from the

[9] Henri Michel and Boris Mirkine-Guetzevich, *Les Idées politiques et sociales de la Résistance* (Paris, 1954), 80, 82, 217. See also Henri Michel, *Les Courants de pensée de la Résistance* (Paris, 1962).

[10] Maurras was actually rejoicing in his discovery that Pétain had political sense as well as symbolic value. The phrase does not appear until 9 February 1941. See Eugen Weber, *Action Française* (Stanford, California, 1962), 447.

[11] Lawmakers of the Liberation expressed a national urge to dismiss Vichy programs as foreign doctrines "imported into the country by the tanks of the invaders." *Journal officiel, lois et décrets,* 13 October 1944, quoted in Gordon Wright, *Rural Revolution in France* (Stanford, California, 1964), 224. Robert Aron, *Histoire de Vichy* (Paris, 1954), 196 ff., at

wings onto the stage vacated by the Third Republic's "middlingness." Disparate as they were, however, the competing visions of the Good France were not altogether lacking in pattern in 1940. While any classification of human feelings does some violence to their rich variety, it helps to sort out the Vichy tendencies around several sets of alternatives: integral Catholic moral order—the pagan nationalist moral order of some prewar protofascist leagues; federal state—centralized state; communal economy—capitalist economy; persuasive means—coercive means.

An integral Catholic vision of the moral order summoned France to return to the traditional faith of her years of glory, with its acceptance of authority and social hierarchy and its solution of social conflicts by charity. At the opposite pole was a post-Christian ethic of self-realization in group action proclaimed by some younger fascist intellectuals like Robert Brasillach.

> We have thought for a long time that fascism was a kind of poetry, the poetry of the twentieth century (along with communism, no doubt). I tell myself that it cannot die. Little children who will be boys of twenty later will marvel to learn of the existence of this exaltation of millions of men, the youth camps, the glory of the past, parades, cathedrals of light, heroes struck down in combat, José Antonio, vast red fascism. . . . I shall never forget the radiance of the fascism of my youth.[12]

A Tocquevillian federal vision of the state attributed defeat to the sloth of a passive citizenry and wished to replace a numbing centralization with a revitalized local self-administration. The local *notables* would regain their old influence from both the encroaching bureaucrats and the Third Republic's Paris-oriented cliques of deputies. At the other pole, a Napoleonic vision, equally impatient with what Robert de Jouvenel called the "republic of pals," wanted to replace the ignorant amateurs of a parliamentary system with trained expert civil servants, oper-

---

least acknowledged Vichy's indigenous quality, but he treated the National Revolution very briefly as an extension of Emmanuel Mounier's Personalism.

[12] Robert Brasillach, writing in prison in 1945, quoted in René Rémond, *La Droite en France* (Paris, 1968), II, 384.

ating a state apparatus ever more centralized as required by the pace of modern life.

A communal vision of the economy dismissed laissez-faire capitalism as a harmful "foreign product, imported from abroad, which France, herself again, spontaneously rejects."[13] One form of this vision, derived from syndicalism, found a solution to the alienation of workers and the class conflicts of modern capitalism in the formation of joint worker-employer organizations to run the economy. A more traditionalist form simply "declared war on the world of money" and longed to revive a preindustrial world in which "the fields were plowed, sown, planted and harvested; and the organization of life did not separate men into categories, but they were all engaged in living on this earth as a single community."[14] Although partisans of this vision were not agreed on whether to reform or abolish the factory system, they all sought to restore some kind of personal wholeness to an atomized way of life. An opposite vision, with far less fanfare, simply adapted the business world to modern crises by allowing businessmen to organize for their own protection, under the umbrella of a benevolent state. Its partisans accepted the division of labor, the factory system, and the almost unlimited power of owners without question. They rejected only the free-swinging competition of 19th-century liberal capitalism.[15]

Finally, there were competing means of realizing these visions. On the one hand were the technicians of persuasion: organizers of mass rallies, youth and veterans' movements, stagers of ceremony, purveyors of a sentimental propaganda about the marshal greeting schoolchildren. At the other pole were the partisans of increased police power and tougher courts.

The National Revolution was not totally paralyzed by these polarities of vision. Action was possible because the visions overlapped at a number of points. They fought the same enemies,

[13] Marshal Pétain, "La Politique sociale de l'avenir," *Le Temps,* 20 September 1940. A similar text appears in *Revue des deux mondes;* both were probably drafted by Gaston Bergery.

[14] Emmanuel Mounier, "Programme pur le mouvement de jeunesse français," *Esprit,* 9e année, no. 96 (January 1941), 152–67; Jean Giono, *Ides et calendes* (Paris, 1942), 31.

[15] See the section on corporatism below.

though for different reasons: laissez-faire economy, parliamentary government, mass society. All sought a more elitist social order, though their candidates for the elite differed. None challenged the sanctity of property, and all believed that class harmony was natural when agitation was suppressed. All defended the virtues of social order, which they agreed was best maintained by authority and hierarchy at home and caution abroad. They saw more danger than hope in a liberation from the Germans by force. And so they could work together. On many points, of course, the Vichy visions clashed irreconcilably. The history of the National Revolution is, therefore, a history of the gradual gathering around one set of poles: integral Catholicism, Napoleonic centralism, more concentrated capitalism, and coercion.

One major misapprehension remains to be corrected. The National Revolution was not Hitler's project. It was not "imported on German tanks" in any direct sense.[16] After the war, Vichy participants tried to shift the blame for their domestic programs to German pressures, as it was expedient to do in 1945. Pierre Laval, for example, the star witness at Pétain's trial on 3 August 1945, agreed that the laws discriminating against Freemasons went too far but said that the Germans had insisted upon strong measures. Marcel Peyrouton traced the anti-Jewish legislation of 1940 to German pressures and said that the Germans threatened 10,000 hostages in 1942 if the French did not tighten those laws even further.[17] This alibi runs through all the postwar trials and memoirs, and it has rooted itself successfully in general opinion about Vichy. The archives of the German occupation contradict it. Neither diplomats nor soldiers at Berlin cared a fig for Vichy's internal acts as long as order was maintained and French wealth poured into the German war machine. In most of the embryonic German postwar plans, France was not "honored" with a place in the New Europe. The Germans cared little enough about France's internal composition to "dump" German Jews there in the fall of 1940. A few ideologues in the German embassy

---

[16] See footnote 11.

[17] *Procès du maréchal Pétain*, 191; Marcel Peyrouton, *Du Service public à la prison commune* (Paris, 1950), 155.

at Paris, notably Abetz himself and Dr. Friedrich Grimm, took the creation of a national socialist France seriously, but their office had barely begun to function in the summer of 1940. I have been unable to turn up any direct German order for French anti-Masonic, anti-Semitic, or other legislation during the most active period of Vichy legislation in 1940. There were strong indirect pressures upon the content of French legislation when Resistance sabotage increased sharply in August 1941 and when Vichy tried to substitute its own legislation about Jewish property for German decrees in the Occupied Zone in June 1941. Direct pressures to apply the Final Solution to Jews and to draft young Frenchmen to work in German factories began in the summer of 1942. By then the National Revolution was two years old. Even at their most brutal, German exigencies focused narrowly upon anti-Semitism, public order, and the provision of maximum resources for the German war effort. Hitler ignored or scorned the rest of the National Revolution. The National Revolution tells us about France, not Germany. It was the expression of indigenous French urges for change, reform, and revenge, nurtured in the 1930's and made urgent and possible by defeat.

Emmanuel Berl errs in the other direction. He has asserted that Vichy and the Resistance were a ritual quarrel that can be studied without reference to the course of the war.[18] The German occupation did shape the National Revolution, even if German officials did not dictate its concrete form.

First, Germany shaped the National Revolution by a mounting requisition of French goods, services, and manpower. "Kollaboration" meant booty. French wealth was harnessed to the German war effort by several reins. The tightest economic curb was occupation costs. By Article 18 of the armistice, a mirror image of Article 9 of the armistice of 1918, France bore the costs incurred by the occupying army. These were set in August 1940 at 400,000,000 francs per day (20,000,000 marks at the imposed rate of exchange), payable retroactively to 25 June 1940. In all, France paid 400,000,000 francs a day from the armistice until 10 May 1941, 300,000,000 francs a day from 11 May 1941 to 11 No-

[18] *La France irréelle* (Paris, 1957), 154–55.

vember 1942, and 500,000,000 francs a day from the full occupation of France until 3 September 1944: a grand total of 631,866,-000,000 francs, amounting to about 58 percent of the French government's income between 1940 and 1944. To this were added the costs of quarters and the burden of clearing the foreign exchange deficit with Germany, which raised the total occupation costs by another fourth.[19]

In addition, there were piecemeal agreements for the delivery of foodstuffs and strategic raw materials to Germany, and a number of French factories produced goods for Germany under contract. By the beginning of 1944, France had shipped 4,127 tons of magnesium and 518,684 tons of bauxite to Germany. Through the end of 1942, when the French colonies were cut off by Allied military action, a little over 10 percent of French colonial imports—phosphates, vegetable oils, coffee, etc.—went on to Germany. Eighty-five percent of the French automobiles produced during the occupation went to Germany. The Germans used the income from occupation costs to buy heavily in French agricultural markets, so that by 1944 the annual drain had risen from 6 to 8 million quintals of grain, from 2 to 3 million hectolitres of wine, and from 135,000 to 270,000 tons of meat. The Germans got 4,320 of some 16,000 locomotives in France. And with their surplus of francs, they purchased some 121,000,000 marks' worth of shares in French companies and overseas holdings. As Franz Richard Hemmen, chief economic delegate to the Armistice Commission at Wiesbaden, put it in January 1942, "French workers in industry, railroads, internal shipping, and most overseas shipping are working almost exclusively for Germany." "No other European country," he reported, "contributes nearly as high a balance [as France] for German armaments and even goods imports. . . . German orders in France are the dominant factor in the French economy."[20]

[19] Alfred Munz, *Die Auswirkung der deutschen Besetzung auf Währung und Finanzen Frankreichs,* Studien des Instituts für Besatzungsfragen in Tübingen zu den deutschen Besetzungen im 2. Weltkrieg, Nr. 9 (Tübingen, 1957), 25–77; Cour des comptes, *Rapport au président de la République, 1940–44* (Paris, 1947), 25.

[20] "Dritter Tätigkeitsbericht der deutschen Waffenstillstandsdelegation für Wirtschaft, 1. Juli–31. Dezember 1941" (Nuremberg document 1988–

The French economy was on short rations, and French finance had to support a massive hemorrhage of francs to Germany. Part of the National Revolution, therefore, was simply a particularly stringent war economy. Strict control and planning were unavoidable, though some public officials such as Bichelonne made that necessity into a virtue: an experience in the guided economy that would continue to practice in affluence the lessons it had learned in penury.

Growing German security needs also influenced the National Revolution directly, as we shall see in more detail, when Resistance acts began to multiply in 1941.

Ideologically, German influence upon the National Revolution was only indirect. No doubt there were temptations to share the opinion of Camille Chautemps quoted in the Prologue, that France would get more lenient peace terms if she conformed to the victor's style. Others, it can not be denied, were impressed by the successes of fascism contrasted with the lamentable performance of liberal democracy in all the tests of the 1930's: depression, diplomacy, and war. The dominant note struck in National Revolution propaganda at Vichy, however, was the return to French roots and the search for another way between fascism and communism. There were no Germans to object to, and few even to notice, such a position.

We shall examine the various programs of the National Revolution in turn, therefore, as the product of indigenous grievances and interests.

PS), 5; "Fünfter Tätigkeitsbericht der deutschen Waffenstillstandsdelegation für Wirtschaft, 1. Juli 1942–30. Juni 1943," (Nuremberg document 1990–PS), 8–9; "Sechster Tätigkeitsbericht . . . 1. July 1943–17. August 1944," (Nuremberg document 1991–PS), 63. The periodic reports of Franz Richard Hemmen are the most valuable source for Franco-German economic relations. The locomotive figures come from *Ministère public c/Berthelot,* fascicule 2, 45 n. The foodstuffs figures come from Cour des Comptes, *Rapport au président de la République, 1940–44* (Paris, 1947), 11 ff. Alan S. Milward, *The New Order and the French Economy* (New York, 1970), now provides the fullest general account of the economic side of collaboration.

An Answer to Decadence

I am a fascist because I have measured the progress of decadence in Europe. I have seen in fascism the sole means of limiting and reducing that decadence.

—*Drieu la Rochelle, February 1943* [21]

A FRENCH CITIZEN DID NOT HAVE TO SHARE DRIEU'S fascism to feel a sense of decadence, a running down of the mainsprings of civilization, in the modern world. Nowhere else in Europe, except perhaps in Vienna, had the Enlightenment faith in progress been so widely replaced by premonitions of decline by the end of the nineteenth century. The new conservative nationalism of that generation was, as Raoul Girardet observed, "a meditation upon decadence." The spread of such premonitions is not surprising in an increasingly elderly population in a nation whose real power position fell increasingly short of its sense of world mission between 1890 and 1940. The victory of 1918 had only deepened the gloom by proving too expensive ever to repeat. The decline of France made sense only as part of a cosmic decline. It was the whole modern world that was going wrong, a modern world often identified in interwar France with American mass production and Soviet statism. Between the rising empires of regimented uniformity, France seemed to count for less and less. After a war of bombed cities and poison gas, Georges Bernanos was already sure in 1931 that the next peace would belong not to Lenin but to

some little Yankee shoe-shine boy, a kid with a rat's face, half Saxon, half Jew, with a trace of Negro ancestry in his maddened marrow, the future King of Oil, Rubber, Steel, creator of the Trust of Trusts, future master of a standardized planet, this god that the universe awaits, god of a godless universe. [22]

[21] "Bilan," *Nouvelle revue française,* January–February 1943.
[22] Georges Bernanos, *La Grande peur des bien-pensants* (Paris, 1931), 454. See also Georges Duhamel, *Scènes de la vie future* (1930), translated as *America The Menace,* and Robert Aron and Armand Dandieu, *Le Cancer Américain* (1931).

The battle of France was an appropriate moment to reflect even more bitterly upon French decline in an uglier world. Paul Valéry entered a "stock market report on the values of civilization" in his notebooks during May 1940. Rising values were force, statism, the masses. Declining values were trust, leisure, perfection, comprehension, knowledge, humanity, measure, proportion, individualism, and law.[23] France and humanistic civilization were going bankrupt together.

Everything done at Vichy was in some sense a response to fears of decadence. More particularly, the defeat gave cause and opportunity for more radical measures designed to reverse that long moral decline.

The more naive the diagnosis of moral decline, the more simple-mindedly direct were the proposals for legislating a new moral climate. Like every sudden promotion to power of outsiders, the National Revolution had its share of puritanical zealots. Some at Vichy simply tried to root out modern mass culture. The veterans' movement, the Légion Française des Combattants, denounced the corruptions of "swing" and managed to prevent that prophet of hedonism, André Gide, from giving a lecture on the poet Henri Michaux at Nice in May 1941. The obligatory forest work camps for all young men of twenty, the Chantiers de Jeunesse, preached austerity to blasé city youths around a thousand campfires.[24]

Vichy waged a serious campaign against alcoholism, some of whose legislation is still in effect. The alcohol lobbies, the sugar beet growers and the home-distillers or *bouilleurs de cru,* had been untouchable under the Third Republic. The tax exemptions of the *bouilleurs de cru* were suppressed on 7 August 1940, and on 24 August 1940 apéritifs stronger than 32 proof (16°) were forbidden, and all apéritifs were forbidden to persons below twenty. Later no one below fourteen could be served in a bar at all. The law vigorously denied any prohibitionist purpose, but *Le Temps* pointed out how much healthier French-

---

[23] Paul Valéry, "Tableau de Bourse des valeurs de civilisation," *Cahiers,* vol. 23 (Paris, 1960), 306.

[24] For "swing," see *La Légion,* no. 9, February 1942.

men had been in periods when alcohol was limited (as in 1913–19) and linked defeat to the fact that France had a bar for every 80 persons, as compared to 270 in Germany, 430 in Britain, and 3,000 in Sweden.[25]

Much of Vichy's promotion of a better moral order was a whited sepulcher. Cynics had no trouble noticing its care for the outward signs over the inward substance. One thinks of Marshal Pétain, twenty-one years after his civil marriage ceremony to a divorcée, going through an annulment and a church wedding (by deputy) before the Archbishop of Paris in 1941. Far more important was Vichy's attention to two bulwarks of the social order, the church and the family, and its effort to surround young people with a different climate.

Moral Order: The Church

> If we had remained victorious, we would probably have remained the prisoners of our errors. Through being secularized, France was in danger of death.
>
> —Cardinal Gerlier, Archbishop of Lyon [26]

> Our Father,
> Who art our leader,
> Hallowed be thy name.
> Thy kingdom come.
> Thy will be done
> On earth, so we may live.
> Give us each day our daily bread.
> Give France back her life.
> Let us not fall back into vain dreams and falsehoods,
> But deliver us from all evil,
> O Marshal!
>
> —Georges Gérard [27]

[25] *Le Temps,* 9 and 25 August 1940.

[26] Quoted in Harry W. Paul, *The Second Ralliement: The Rapprochement between Church and State in France in the Twentieth Century* (Washington, 1967), 181.

[27] Le Marquis d'Argenson, *Pétain et le pétinisme* (Paris, n.d. [1953]), 170.

. . .

THE CATASTROPHE OF 1940 HAD BEGUN TO LIFT FRENCH eyes to heaven even before the Third Republic came to an end. On May 19 the next-to-last cabinet of the republic attended a special high mass at Notre Dame. Relics of the saints of France were carried in procession before these predominantly free-thinking worthies while Monseigneur Beaussart prayed, "Come, saints of France, expel the enemy attacking this nation which belongs to Christ and wishes to remain in Christ." The Marseillaise concluded this incongruous ceremony. The new regime practiced a religiosity that went far beyond foxhole prayers, however. As the old godless Third Republic lost its legitimacy, few groups found revenge sweeter than the French clergy and the faithful, nursing long grudges against the results of the French Revolution and against sixty years of official republican anticlericalism.

Although traditional Catholics and the small Catholic left had quarreled bitterly before the war, they agreed in loathing the secularism of the Third Republic and in rejoicing at the possibilities of change. Most Catholics longed for official support for religious values and for undoing old wrongs that still smarted: the "expulsion of God" from public schools in the 1880's, the quarrel over church property at the time of the separation of church and state in 1905, laws that discriminated against religious orders. The new Catholic left, while it horrified traditional Catholics by its denunciations of capitalism and the laissez-faire state, was if anything more hostile to the secular republic than the others. And so Monseigneur Delay was speaking for most Catholics when he told Pétain at the end of 1940 during one of the marshal's triumphal tours, "God is at work through you, M. le maréchal, to save France." [28]

The Pétain governments, at least the early ones, were eager to reciprocate. Maurras had accustomed conservatives to value the church as an instrument of social conservatism whether they were believers or not. Religion also seemed to promise to

[28] *La Revue des deux mondes,* 1 February 1941, 126–36.

reverse the long decadence of the secular years. Only a return
to traditional Catholic values, said one witness at Pétain's trial,
could restore a greatness that had been lost not in 1940 but long
before. Such people were "grateful because the marshal permitted the restoration of spiritual values." [29]

The result of this meeting of minds was the closest church-
state harmony since the "moral order" regime of the Duc de
Broglie and Marshal MacMahon in 1873–74, the era when the
Sacré Coeur was built on Montmartre and pilgrimages to
Lourdes became big business. Pétain would have "crushed the
church under the weight of his favor" if he had had time, said
Education Minister Jérôme Carcopino. The church's response is
usually described in friendly works as the traditional obedience
due any legitimate regime. But one has no trouble telling the
difference between the alacrity of obedience to this friendly
regime and relations with the republic.[30]

Vichy's policy toward the church was shaped by reaction to
Third Republic acts. The main battlegrounds had already been
laid out by Robespierre, Jules Ferry, and Emile Combes. Vichy
restored; it did not innovate in church policy.

Education and influence over the young had been the sorest
point since the Revolution had taken schooling from the church
and made it a state monopoly. The nineteenth century had be-
queathed two hermetically separated parallel school systems:
the "free" or parochial schools, permitted since the Falloux law
of 1850 (1,300,000 pupils in 1939), and the state schools, made
free and universal by Jules Ferry in the 1880's (5,800,000 pupils
in 1939). The state schools had been made militantly secular
by republican teachers. The two school systems had been forward

---

[29] Testimony of Donati, Inspecteur des finances and former prefect,
Procès Pétain, 292. See also André Chaumeix' diagnosis of "moral
decadence" since Emile Combes' anticlerical crusade of 1903–05, in
Revue des deux mondes, 1 October 1941, 379–84.

[30] Jérôme Carcopino, *Souvenirs de sept ans, 1937–44* (Paris, 1953),
318. The obedience theme is stressed in Monseigneur Guerry, *L'Eglise en
France sous l'Occupation* (Paris, 1947). Jacques Duquesne, *Les Catholiques
français sous l'occupation* (Paris, 1966), 55, distinguishes more subtly
between observance of the laws and active support for the regime.

posts in a long battle of values and life styles. Just as the republic had stopped short of enforcing an absolute state monopoly of education, so Vichy merely made changes in both systems.

Most striking was the end of the "godless school." On 6 December 1940, Education Minister Jacques Chevalier, philosophy professor at the University of Grenoble and Pétain's godson (Chevalier's father had been a general), restored religious instruction to the state schools. During Darlan's more technocratic regime in 1941, however, this forward position was judged to be too exposed at a time when there was so much else to affront public opinion. Darlan, anti-clerical himself, was willing to sacrifice Catholic policy to ease his regime's other efforts. Education Minister Jérôme Carcopino, the great Sorbonne classicist, merely allowed free time in the school program for voluntary religious instruction off school premises, claiming to have "won religious peace by the neutrality of public schools." [31] But the old republican schoolroom laicism had lost ground it would never regain.

Catholics had more success with state subventions to parochial schools, one of the earliest and most pressing requests of the church hierarchy. They had worked eagerly for state aid in the 1920's; immediately after June 1940 they returned to the charge. The clergy proposed a system of "bonds" granted each head of family that would permit him to send his children to the school of his choice. Marshal Pétain urged quick action on his government. The eventual law issued on 2 November 1941 by Jérôme Carcopino fell somewhat short of these hopes. State aid was granted directly to the bishops for educational purposes, and it was explicitly an emergency grant, not a recognition of the principle of permanent state aid to parochial schools.[32] But another sacred republican principle had been breached for good.

---

[31] *Ministère public c / Chevalier;* Carcopino, 300. Duquesne, 104, argues that some Catholics, including the Papal Nuncio, Mgr. Valerio Valeri, already had doubts about the wisdom of associating favors to the church with a regime that might be transitory.

[32] Duquesne, 93–100; Carcopino, 330.

Many members of Catholic orders had been prevented from teaching, and the orders themselves required to obtain governmental authorization by the legislation of Emile Combes in 1901. Minister of Justice Raphael Alibert, "a convert who burned with the ardor of a neophyte," permitted members of religious orders to teach by the law of 3 September 1940. Somewhat more cautiously, a further act on 8 April 1942 permitted religious orders to exist under the same terms as any other organization, requiring state authorization only if they wished to enjoy legal personality. Church property that had been seized at the time of separation of church and state in 1905 and that was still unappropriated thirty-six years later was restored to the dioceses on 15 February 1941. For example, the Grotto at Lourdes was returned to the direct care of the Bishop of Tarbes. Thus some of the rancorous issues that had festered since the battles of the Separation, in which the French Army had been called out to help enforce the property inventories and in which several people had been killed, were settled in a way much more favorable to the church than could have been imagined a few months previously.[33]

The most important changes were matters of tone. The regime cultivated churchmen, sought their advice, and made the church's teachings about the family, moral decadence, and spiritual values its own.

But although there was some talk of a new Concordat in the hierarchy and among some more traditionalist circles at Vichy,[34] the eventual settlement was really a favorable resolution of questions arising out of the Separation of 1905 rather than a fundamental challenge to the Separation itself. Here, as in so many other areas, Vichy programs built upon a modified nineteenth-century liberalism, distorted by defeat and fear of communism, rather than upon Restoration or *ancien régime* doctrines.

[33] Duquesne, 102, points out the disappointment of some church groups with the caution of these restitutions. Jean Le Cour Grandmaison praised these arrangements as "a breath of liberty" in *Figaro*, 26 May 1942. For the return of Lourdes, see Ministère de l'Intérieur, *Bulletin officiel*, February 1941.

[34] Duquesne, 104, says the Vatican was reluctant.

Restitution to the church remained limited, also, because the Vichy-church embrace of 1940 loosened with time. Traditionalists lost ground at Vichy after 1940. On the church's side, the universal delight of 1940 covered deep internal divisions. The Catholic left was soon disenchanted with the triumph of statist and big business influences over their communal hopes. Still wider Catholic discontent was aroused by the deportation of Jews, which became massive in the summer of 1942. This was the first issue upon which bishops (like Monseigneur Salièges of Toulouse, Monseigneur Théas of Montauban, and Cardinal Gerlier of Lyon) expressed open opposition to the regime. Henceforth, Vichy divided the church as much as it divided France itself.

Moral Order: Education and the Young

SCHOOL IS A FREQUENT SCAPEGOAT FOR NATIONAL setbacks. Sputnik produced major school reforms in the United States after 1957. The French generation of 1870 made more changes in schools than in any other civilian institution. Blame was even sharper in 1940, for it was mixed with antisocialism. André Delmas' National Teachers' Union (Syndicat National des Instituteurs) had organized teachers for socialism and for pacifism. Pétain, as we have seen, thought that France had lost the war because her reserve officers had been taught by socialist teachers.[35] Vichy wanted not to dismantle mass schooling, however, but to capture it. The centralized nature of French education made that task easier. The republic's teachers had already sought to create citizens as well as scholars. They brought a crusading fervor to the spread of a militant republican ideal: rationalist, progressive, freethinking, confident in the progress of

[35] *FRUS*, 1940, II, 384. Particular hostility was focused on Popular Front Education Minister Jean Zay, murdered in 1944 by Miliciens. Céline liked to spell 'I hate you' as 'Je vous Zay.' See *L'Ecole des cadavres* (Paris, 1938), 22.

science, patriotic.[36] Convinced that the public schools' liberating efforts were threatened by church and monarchists, republican educational leaders like Ferdinand Buisson spiced their language with the metaphors of an antichurch and an antiarmy. Teachers were the "hussars of the republic," schoolchildren were the "little missionaries" who would spread liberal republicanism back to their parents.[37]

This old but persistent quarrel was overlaid by more recent school disputes of the interwar period. These too worked themselves out in the new freedom to change after 1940.

Non-French readers must recall that the French primary and secondary education systems of the Third Republic were not sequential but parallel. Most children began in free primary school and continued there until the age of thirteen, finishing with a certificate. The most intellectually gifted among them could go on to an *école normale* to become, in turn, a teacher in the primary school system. But there was no access from the top of the primary system to the university or the liberal professions. The secondary school system led to these, and the secondary school system cost money. Parents who could pay started their children in the elementary classes of the secondary school system, which prepared them from the beginning for entry into a *lycée*. Graduated from a *lycée* at eighteen with a *baccalauréat,* they were eligible to enter a liberal profession through one of the *grandes écoles* or the university. About 2.5 percent of French schoolchildren passed through the secondary system. A handful of exceptional young scholars won transfer from the primary track into a *lycée,* and a few poor children were supported in the *lycées* by scholarships. But by and large, the secondary system, with its fee-paying boarding schools, was a preserve of the well-to-do. Teachers in the primary system ("instituteurs") were produced by that system and had little more in common with the "professeurs" of the secondary system

[36] Georges Duveau, *Les Instituteurs* (Paris, 1957), 107–67; Jacques Ozouf, *Nous, les maîtres d'école; autobiographies d'instituteurs de la 'Belle Epoque'* (Paris, 1967).

[37] Ferdinand Buisson, quoted in Antoine Prost, *L'Enseignement en France* (Paris, 1968), 397.

than had the students of these "two separate worlds." [38] The great mass of French youth passed through the primary system, taught by "instituteurs" who were themselves products of that system.

The primary school "instituteurs" had become a rather homogeneous and inward-looking body by the interwar years. They were of modest social origins and were strongly marked by the secular rationalist progressivism of their founders' generation. To their traditional anticlericalism and positivism was added a strong current of pacifism after 1914. Already bound together by shared views and by the isolation of village intellectuals elevated from a modest social background, they also became politically organized in the twentieth century. The *Cartel des gauches* government of 1924 finally recognized the teachers' long-claimed right to unionize, and the National Teachers' Union became a mainstay of the non-Communist unions, the CGT. The teachers staged a twenty-four hour strike on 12 February 1934 in reaction to the antiparliamentary demonstrations of the 6th and were prominent in the strike of 30 November 1938 against Reynaud's decree-laws. The Teachers' Union also helped found the Comité de Vigilance des Intellectuels contre le Fascisme in 1934 and was thus a grandparent of the Popular Front. After 1936, however, their intransigent pacifism made them one of the two CGT branches (along with postmen) who opposed aid to the beleaguered Spanish Republic. The Teachers' Union was a conspicuous supporter of concessions to Hitler over the Sudetenland and continued to oppose war right up to 1939. The union did not represent all primary school teachers, of course (some were Communist and were bitterly opposed by Delmas' union; a few were Catholic), but the union made a convenient target for labeling the whole teaching profession as antipatriotic and dangerously left.[39]

---

[38] See John E. Talbott, *The Politics of Educational Reform in France, 1918–40* (Princeton, N.J., 1969), 30, for the clearest description in any language.

[39] André Delmas' rather thin memoirs of the Teachers' Union, under his leadership in the 1930's, *A Gauche de la barricade* (Paris, 1950), 47–48, attributes about 90,000 teachers to his union (SNI) and about 3,000

Vichy tried to uproot the "primary school spirit," as embodied in its "dangerous and disloyal" body of teachers.[40] There is little information on the purge of teachers after 1940, partly because four of the six Vichy education ministers were acquitted after the war, and their trials do not go into such matters. The law of 17 July 1940 permitted the state to remove any civil servant without formality during the next three months, if he seemed likely to be an "element of disorder, an inveterate politician, or incapable." The law excluding Freemasons from public service seems to have removed at least 1,328 teachers, going by the names published in the *Journal officiel* in the fall of 1941. Jews were forbidden to teach on 3 October 1940. Teachers who remained had to take a loyalty oath to the regime. The purge climate among teachers is probably best recaptured in an exchange of letters between Youth Minister Jean Ybarnégaray and the prefect of the department of the Basses-Pyrénées where Ybarnégaray was a local political power. Naming two teachers who seem to have uttered threats of revolution against the Germans, Ybarnégaray ordered these two "female moujiks" fired, not merely transferred, and an immediate investigation to locate other "undesirable teachers." [41]

Politicized school teachers also had to be shut off at the source. In July 1940 Vichy's second minister of education, *Le Temps* editor Emile Mireaux, abolished the departmental Consultative Committees for primary education that had "encroached" on the educational bureaucracy with local political pressures. On 20 September 1941, in a step long predicted, the *écoles normales*—the provincial training schools for primary teachers—were abolished. The Cercle Fustel de Coulanges, a conservative pressure group on educational policy, had long proposed that primary teachers go to *lycées* and get a good classical education. This was partly another blow for quality by classicists

---

to the teachers' branch of the Communist CGTU before the reunion of 1936.

[40] The words are Pierre Pucheu's. *Ma Vie* (Paris, 1948), 281–86.

[41] Ministère de l'Intérieur, *Bulletin officiel,* (1940), 151, and Darlan circular of 6 June 1941; *Ministère public c/Ybarnégaray,* 47–58. I owe the figure on the number of teachers purged for masonry to Mrs. Mary Lynn McDougall.

against modernists. But it was undeniably mainly a blow against those "antiseminaries," those "evil seminaries of democracy" that "for sixty years had separated French children from their priests." [42]

This brings us to the elite educational system, the secondary system of *lycées:* fee-paying public boarding schools leading to the liberal professions and the university. *Lycée* professors in 1940 included some of France's most distinguished intellectuals, some (but not all) as closely identified with the Third Republic as the *instituteurs.*

Indeed, *lycéens* and graduates of the Ecole Normale Supérieure in Paris had been so prominent in Third Republic politics from Jaurès through Herriot to Blum that Albert Thibaudet christened the regime since the Dreyfus Affair as "the republic of the professors." The *lycées* too were bound to be touched by the personnel purges and loyalty oaths of the new regime. [43]

The picture is complicated, however, by the fact that the elite secondary education system had been under attack between the wars from the Left as well as from the Right. Its selectivity operated on two levels—cost and classical curriculum—to screen out all but a handful of poor children from the route that led to high professional and intellectual careers. A group of *lycée* professors who met on Pétain's staff in 1917 formed a movement to democratize French education by combining the primary and secondary systems in a single track, abolishing fees for the secondary system and basing selection to the elite *lycées* solely on intellectual merits. This program, summed up in the catch-phrase "école unique," became the mainstay of Radical and Socialist educational projects between the wars. Some of the "école unique" program was enacted into law. The secondary school system became free in the years 1930–33.

Popular Front Education Minister Jean Zay tried to carry

---

[42] Haute Cour de Justice, Arrêt de non-lieu: Mireaux; *Le Temps,* 23 September 1940, 1 January 1941; Pucheu, 299, 286; Charles Maurras, *La Seule France* (Lyons, 1941), 241.

[43] See Jean Guéhenno, *Journal des années noires* (Paris, 1947), 21 September 1943, for his demotion for political reasons; Haute Cour de Justice, Arrêt de non-lieu: Mireaux, names some university professors removed for being aboard the *Massilia.*

through the rest. He wanted to reorganize the overlapping primary and secondary systems into a single set of successive stages. This meant integrating the upper levels of the primary system into the secondary system and merging the lower levels of the secondary system into the primary. He also set up final courses for students leaving school at sixteen, which were criticized as socialist propaganda (Zay himself belonged to the Radical party). Above all, Zay wanted to leave options open to promising late starters. This meant permitting transfers between technical, modern, and classical tracks at all stages. Some of this could be enacted by decree, but Zay's legislative project, finally submitted to parliament on 5 March 1937, arrived after the Popular Front had already lost its élan.

Furthermore, it aroused a disparate cluster of hostilities typical of the Third Republic's difficulties with sweeping reform. The National Teachers' Union was opposed to the secondary system's swallowing up the upper levels of the primary system, to losing its best students even earlier, and to the concentration of the minister's attentions on the secondary system. Professors were dismayed by the flood of new students pouring into the secondary system after the abolition of fees and by the whole assault on quality that democratization seemed to threaten. Having remained stable from 1880 to 1930 while the upper reaches of the primary system absorbed the numbers, the secondary system began to grow steeply after 1930, smashing a comfortable stability and launching the "school explosion" that has not to this day been resolved by any pedagogically and politically acceptable principle of selection for higher schooling.[44]

Cutting across these professional resentments was the pedagogical quarrel of classical education against modern and tech-

[44] For all the preceding, the most interesting accounts are Antoine Prost, *L'Enseignement en France* (Paris, 1968), and John E. Talbott, *The Politics of Educational Reform in France, 1918–1940* (Princeton, N.J., 1969). See also David Watson, "The Politics of Educational Reform in France during the Third Republic, 1900–1940," *Past and Present,* no. 34 (July 1966), 81–99, who draws upon work by Christian Peyre in *Ecole et Société,* to which I have not had access, to show a rise in lower class pupils in secondary school from 3 percent to 12 percent between 1936 and 1942. The *Annuaire statistique* for 1938 shows that *lycée* enrollment jumped from 119,000 to 128,000, by almost 8 percent, in the one year 1929–30.

nical curricula. Latinity, of course, nicely reinforced the elitism of the old *lycée* system. It is no accident that its defense was associated with political conservatism. It was Léon Bérard, later one of Vichy's ambassadors to the Holy See, who, as education minister, had restored obligatory Latin in 1922, and Edouard Herriot who had gone back to the Dreyfusard program of optional Latin in 1924.[45]

These swirling currents, held at deadlock under the Third Republic, took a more positive direction after 1940. The Vichy solution was a return in the direction of both elitism and classicism in secondary education. This was what one would have expected of the Vichy ministers of education. Vichy, as usual, left things to top professionals. The politician-ministers of the Third Republic were replaced by conservative university professors: Albert Rivaud, philosophy professor at Strasbourg; Emile Mireaux, professor and codirector of *Le Temps*, Georges Ripert, dean of the Paris law faculty, Jacques Chevalier, professor of philosophy at Grenoble (all in 1940), and Jérôme Carcopino, Sorbonne classicist (February, 1941–April 1942). Only Abel Bonnard (1942–44) was not an academic but rather an essayist and writer, but he had been active in a conservative teachers' group, the Cercle Fustel de Coulanges, before the war. Teachers or officials from the primary system were of course conspicuously absent.

First, there was an attempt to arrest the alarming swarm of students into the free *lycées*. The law of 15 August 1941 reestablished fees for the higher classes of secondary education, and although Jérôme Carcopino has pointed out that some scholarships were available and that free *lycées* had favored city children, it remains clear that the main motive for return to *lycée* fees was the desire to save the idyll of the small, elite *lycée* of the halcyon days of 1880–1930.[46] Then, predictably, there was a return toward the superiority of the Latin curriculum, although a qualified one. Carcopino in 1941 gave up on the Third Re-

[45] Talbott, 78–86, 98.

[46] Carcopino, 412; Haute Cour de Justice, Arrêt de non-lieu: Jérôme Carcopino, 1. Prost, 330, is most eloquent on the stability of the *lycée* system until 1930.

public's efforts to have an equal dose of sciences in all secondary school options and set up four sections of which three required Latin and one permitted modern languages. Finally, there remained the tangled questions of the "école unique." Carcopino went back to allowing the secondary system to have its own elementary classes, a revival of part of the old twin systems. But his law of 15 August 1941 also suppressed the upper sections of the primary system and joined them with the secondary. This actually moved in the same direction as Zay's efforts and the eventual reforms of 1945, but for a different reason. The intention was to suppress yet one more vehicle of the dangerous "esprit primaire."

The main question was what was taught. The regime's efforts to end the Third Republic's militant laicism had swerved through Jacques Chevalier's restoration of religious instruction to the benevolent neutrality of Carcopino. The Third Republic's schools had sought to form citizens in its own image; Vichy schools would do no less. The school program of 15 August 1941 established different curricula for city and country, boys and girls. The Enlightenment "citizen" had given way to members of unlike communities. There must also be, as Carcopino wrote, a primacy of "national education" over "public instruction." A letter survives in which Admiral Darlan requests his education minister in October 1941 to have the school instill love of France and help block Gaullism. As late as 1943, the prefects were still instructing teachers as public servants to support the government actively.[47]

It was not enough, of course, to rely on teachers and professors, even after a purge and the requirement of an oath to Pétain. A major part of the Vichy effort to capture the young went on out of school. The young individual was supposed to be conditioned by enrollment in a healthy group experience. Youth organizations—and, indeed, the very concept of adolescence as a particular stage of life with its own properties, neither child nor adult—were spreading in the twentieth century. The scout

[47] Carcopino, 417; Guy Raïssac, *Un Combat sans merci* (Paris, 1966), 335-36; a sample prefect's letter to teachers in 1943 appears in the trial of Angéli, prefect of Lyon.

movements and the youth hostel movement (introduced into France in 1929) had already gained ground. Uniformed youth groups had become important devices between the wars for the Left and the Catholic church as well as for fascists. The Vichy regime, nervous about restless young people in 1940, adopted a technique already used by the Socialists' "Red Falcons" and the Catholic Jeunesse Ouvrière Chrétienne as well as by the Young Communists and the Hitler youth. Where Vichy innovated for France was the prodigality of its support for youth movements. The number of young people belonging to organizations more than doubled in the year after the armistice until it seemed that there were uniformed groups everywhere.[48]

At first, it was widely expected that the new France would set up a single national youth organization.[49] But Vichy achieved unity here no more successfully than in any other realm. The church worked against it, reluctant to see its own youth organizations, which had grown so prominently in the 1930's—JOC, JAC, etc.—swallowed up in some state enterprise.[50] The division into two zones did the rest, for the German authorities, fearful of the militarist and chauvinist tone of the Vichy youth organizations, forbade them in the Occupied Zone.

So there existed some fifteen or twenty "free" youth organizations—mostly church groups or scout groups—alongside the official but voluntary Compagnons de France. The Compagnons, boys of fifteen to twenty, were supposed to be the "avant-garde of the National Revolution," as Pétain told them in September 1941.[51] The Compagnons included several different kinds of "companies": rural companies sheltering the young unemployed who were put to farm work, city companies whose objective was to "unite all social classes," eight itinerant companies of

---

[48] *Le Temps*, 9 August 1941. *Espoir français*, nos. 357–58, estimated that about one French youth in seven belonged to a youth organization. For lavish government support, see Cour des Comptes, *Rapport . . . 1940–44* (Paris, 1947), 12–17.

[49] E.g., see Edouard Lavergne, "Pour une jeunesse nationale," *Revue universelle*, 18 January 1941.

[50] Paul Baudouin, *Neuf mois au gouvernement* (Paris, 1948), 396, notes the opposition of Cardinal Gerlier of Lyons to a single national youth organization.

[51] *La France militaire*, 10 September 1941.

young artisans, and an itinerant theater company. There were supposed to be 25,000 Compagnons, but German intelligence estimated their number at about 8,000 in March 1941 with only 3,350 actually in camps in June 1942.[52]

The Compagnons were intended to save young Frenchmen not only from the risks of unemployment but also from the viruses of dissidence. Some hints about its indoctrination efforts may be drawn from its leadership. Youth affairs was a cabinet post at Vichy. The first minister of youth, the family, and sports was the prominent Basque sportsman Jean Ybarnégaray. Ybarnégaray was president of the National Pelota Association, an avid shot in his native Pyrenees, and a man who took pride in his sporting exploits. Politically, he was a lifelong militant in right-wing leagues: active in the Jeunesses Patriotes of the 1920's, a leader of Colonel de la Rocque's Croix de Feu, and the most prominent deputy of La Rocque's *Parti Social Français* after 1936. He stumped France after the rightist demonstrations of 6 February 1934 calling for a French "revival in work, order, authority, and honor" and an answer to "that appeal of the race" that had been heard in Italy and Germany but not yet in France. "Is the old Gallic blood so anemic?"[53] He brought in Jean Borotra, the Basque Olympic tennis star and a fervent apostle of moral reeducation through sports.

When youth matters were placed under the Education Ministry in September 1940, Georges Lamirand became secretary-general in charge of youth affairs. Lamirand, a practicing engineer, had a career in the steel business and became the director of the great Renault works at Billancourt after the armistice of 1940. What recommended him as director of Vichy's

---

[52] General A. Niessel, "Les Compagnons de France," *Revue des deux mondes,* 15 October 1941; Wako, "Übersicht über die französischen Jugend-organisationen," 1 April 1941 (T-77/OKW-685/2,499,479 ff.); OKH Gen. St d H/Abt. Fremde Heere West (11), "Lagebericht West Nr. 701: Frankreich," 24 July 1942 (T-78/H2-184/6,428,822 ff.).
[53] Jean Ybarnégaray, "Le Grand soir des honnêtes gens: le 6 Février 1934," *Les Grandes conférences des ambassadeurs,* 23 February 1934. Information drawn also from *Ministère public c/ Jean Ybarnégaray.* It is only fair to add that Ybarnégaray was arrested by the Germans in 1943 for helping some people cross the Pyrenees to Spain and was deported to Planze (Tyrol).

youth programs, however, were his place among the fervent disciples of the late Marshal Lyautey and his active Catholicism. Lyautey's numerous disciples at Vichy (Lamirand, veterans' leader Francois Valentin, social organizer Robert Garric, Ambassador to the Vatican Vladimir d'Ormesson) were dedicated to applying the master's ideals of social paternalism to the problems of industrial society. Lamirand's 1932 book on the social role of the engineer, with a preface by Lyautey himself, consciously paralleled Lyautey's famous 1890 essay, "The Social Role of the Officer." Like Lyautey's officer with his soldiers, Lamirand's engineer was a "leader" who knew how to bring his men to a sense of participation within "the present order of things" by a mixture of warm human relations and sense of command, thereby creating a "stable social balance." [54] Lamirand believed that his style of "serve and command" was a middle way, going beyond both "liberal opportunism" and impersonal material paternalism to provide "a new order built on justice and solidarity, calmly and peaceably." In particular, he thought it would have prevented the workers' upheaval of May–June 1936. [55] Lyautey and Pétain had got along badly, but a young man who promised to win social peace through leadership was welcome at Vichy. Lamirand remained in charge of Vichy youth programs from September 1940 to February 1943, an exceptional length of service for that regime.

A young inspector of finance, Henri Dhavernas, was director of the Compagnons for a time. He was replaced in the fall of 1941 by a more positive figure, Colonel Tournemire, an officer on armistice leave. Colonel Tournemire had belonged to an officer's group working secretly after 1936 to root communism out of the army. [56]

It was the army that eventually came closest to creating a single Vichy youth movement. The Chantiers de la Jeunesse

[54] Georges Lamirand, *Le rôle social de l'ingénieur* (Paris, 1932), with subsequent editions in 1937 (after the fright of June 1936) and again in 1954; Hubert Lyautey, "Le rôle social de l'officier," *Revue des deux mondes* (1890).

[55] Ibid., 1954 edition, v, 263.

[56] Like many other conservatives, he wound up in the Resistance in 1944.

began in the summer of 1940 as an emergency measure to remove draft-age unemployed from dangerous cities and put them to work in the forests. By January 1941 it had become a form of national service. With the draft suspended, all young men were required to spend eight months of their twenty-first year in a Chantier. There they did needed forestry work, but the chief intention was moral education. Under artillery officer and former scout leader General de la Porte du Theil, the Chantiers spent part of the day at physical labor and part attending courses on the social order and on a view of French history that, German intelligence found to its unease, derived from the *Action française* nationalist historian Jacques Bainville. Eventually the whole young male population of the unoccupied zone spent some time in the Chantiers.[57]

It is doubtful that Vichy's efforts to indoctrinate French youth bore much fruit. Only the Chantiers affected large numbers, and there a good bit of time was spent producing a desperately needed substitute fuel, charcoal. Its saccharine moralism didn't appeal to all youths. More disastrously, the Chantiers were drawn up by 1943 into the maw of factory work in Germany. What must be stressed is that the Chantiers and other youth groups were not a clandestine force for a return to war with the Allies, but an instrument of indoctrination. Despite their high suspicions, the Germans could find nothing out of line at the Chantiers. General de la Porte du Theil himself was in North Africa on inspection when the Allies landed in November 1942, and he returned to Vichy to pursue what he regarded as his real work: the supervision of the young. The North African Chantiers went over in a body to the Allied side, and indeed General de la Porte du Theil was deported in December 1943, but his aim had always been social order in a neutral France.[58]

[57] Robert O. Paxton, *Parades and Politics at Vichy* (Princeton, N.J., 1966), 202–13; Jean Hervet, *Les Chantiers de Jeunesse* (Paris, 1962), highly sympathetic.

[58] German intelligence reports on the Chantiers de la Jeunesse may be found in T-77/OKW-1397, T-77/OKW-1434, T-77/OKW-1400, and T-78/H2–184. General de la Porte du Theil told the author in 1960 that the Chantiers were not a secret army.

At the most sophisticated level, Vichy also set up a half dozen *écoles de cadres,* or leadership training schools, the most celebrated of which was the school at Uriage, a chateau near Grenoble. Here, under the leadership of Major Pierre Dunoyer de Segonzac, the cream of young civil servants and intellectuals camped and studied in an exalted atmosphere strongly colored by Emmanuel Mounier's "Personalism": the effort to restore individual human worth lost in the industrial revolution. They tried to prepare leaders for the Vichy youth movements not from books but by "lived experience." The Uriage school went underground in a body when France was totally occupied in November 1942, but it had been no less committed to its version of the National Revolution.[59]

Moral Order: The Family

MARSHAL PÉTAIN, A DISCREET ROUÉ, HAD MARRIED A divorcée in 1920, at the age of 64. He was childless. His 1940 government included two upper-class illegitimate children, Paul Baudouin and General Maxime Weygand. Under this somewhat dubious patronage, the Vichy government worked to promote the solidarity and fecundity of the French family.

The declining French birthrate lay at the very core of French alarm about decadence in the early twentieth century. The concern aroused by the census results of 1891 and 1896 had already produced some action during the Third Republic. The post-World War I "horizon blue" parliament had outlawed birth

---

[59] Janine Bourdin, "Des intellectuels à la recherche d'un style de vie: L'Ecole de cadres d'Uriage," *Revue française de science politique,* December 1959; Paul Delouvrier, "Uriage," in *Gazette de l'inspection,* No. 7 (Oct. 1941), 11–15. Delouvrier was mayor of Algiers in the 1960's when General Dunoyer de Segonzac was in charge of a program to win Algerian youth to France. Other *anciens* of Uriage include Hubert Beuve-Méry, later editor of *Le Monde,* and Emmanuel Mounier's successor as editor of *Esprit,* Jean-Marie Domenach.

control in 1920. A long campaign for some more positive governmental promotion of larger families finally produced a system of incentive payments, the family allowances of the Family Code of 29 July 1939. Much of Vichy's family program simply continued this interwar campaign more vigorously along the same lines. Daladier's 1939 Family Code, for instance, had already favored resettlement of farms by providing loans to young settlers whose interest and payments decreased with each successive child; it had breached the Napoleonic concept of equal inheritance by providing that the son who stays home and works a farm inherits a greater share of it than his city brothers and sisters; it had tightened the laws against abortion and had gone back to an earlier concept of adoption in which the child was totally integrated into his new family and totally severed from his old, putting the emphasis on the solidarity of the new family rather than on the identity of the adopted child as an individual. Traditionalists at Vichy were delighted to carry these lines of policy forward.[60]

Vichy family policy rested on much franker organicist social theory, however, than Daladier's essentially pragmatic Family Code. Expanding Frédéric Le Play's nineteenth-century arguments that the Revolution of 1789 had begun the decline of the French family by equal inheritance and overemphasis upon the individual, Vichy family theorists blamed the Third Republic for an antifamily climate of high divorce, legalized prostitution, alcoholism, and rampant individual license. The remedy was a replacement of republican individualism with a reemphasis upon "real" organic social units, intermediary bodies rooted in the biological and social nature of things, such as the family. The right of families, declared Pétain, "takes precedence over the state as well as over the rights of individuals." The family is the "cell of French life." Jean Ybarnégaray promised to make the Ministry of Health and the Family a Ministry of Population, proposing a campaign against venereal disease and also threatening "sanitary and racial control" over immigration and naturalization.[61]

An obvious target was divorce. The law of 1884 permitting divorce had been untouchable under the Third Republic, and indeed even the Vichy regime could not go as far as Italy and outlaw divorce altogether. The 1884 law, however, had been the work of a Radical Republican and a Jew, Alfred Naquet (he was also a Boulangist, but that fact spoiled the argument), and so could be drastically modified. The law of 2 April 1941 forbade any divorce during the first three years of a marriage. After that, mistreatment or serious injury were possible grounds. Adultery was not an explicit ground for divorce, although Justice Minister Barthélemy instructed the courts to be more rigorous in its repression. He also instructed the courts to interpret the divorce law as strictly as possible and to apply the new law retroactively to cases already under way.[62]

The regime also favored fathers of large families and discriminated against fathers of small ones. In Vichy's concept of functional representation, the function of paternity was given high place. Alongside representatives of such other "healthy elements" as veterans, officers, and peasants, fathers of large families were given statutory seats on all sorts of committees, from the Budget Committee that replaced parliament's finance committee down to city councils.[63] Childless fathers, by contrast, got poorer jobs. In the judicial system, for example, single or childless men were not considered for better posts unless they indicated a willingness to serve wherever the government chose to assign them.[64]

Maternity was glorified at home but accorded no public role outside. There was a pragmatic reason in times of unemploy-

---

[61] *Ministère public c/ Jean Ybarnégaray*, 41. M. Ybarnégaray evidently chose fecundity over family solidarity where the two values conflicted. He had four legitimate children and recognized one illegitimate child.

[62] Circulaire of 26 May 1941, Ministère de la Justice, *Bulletin officiel*, 1941, 62–67; Circulaire of 25 April 1942, *ibid.*, 1942, 44.

[63] André Bisson, *Finances publiques françaises* (Paris, 1943), 271–72; for the *conseil municipal* of Nice, see T-586/441/023605.

[64] Circulaire of 25 March 1942, Ministère de la Justice, *Bulletin officiel*, 1942, 26–29.

ment to reduce the number of working women, as was done by a law of 11 October 1940.[65] But contemplating the different elementary education offered girls by the 15 August 1941 school program, for example,[66] one is forced to conclude that Vichy preferred women barefoot and pregnant in the kitchen. Women had not had the vote under the Third Republic, of course (they were enfranchised in 1946), though Léon Blum had appointed women to two minor cabinet posts in 1936.

The occupation was an unpropitious time to try to raise the birthrate. Two million Frenchmen were in prisoner-of-war camps, many families were divided by ·the Demarcation Line, and other interruptions of young lives such as labor service in Germany were to come. Nevertheless, signs of an increased birthrate were already apparent from the beginning of the war.[67] By the war's end, the French birthrate had reached its highest point in a century. Prosperous families as well as poor ones began having more children, so the family allocations are certainly not the only explanation. Neither is the usual birthrate rise that comes at any war's end, for it began in the darkest days. Vichy's family policy was closer to republican policy here than in most other areas, and it is likely that together they touched some national response that prepared the way for the great postwar baby boom.

France for the French [68]

DEFEAT SHARPENED A DEFENSIVE XENOPHOBIA THAT had been already growing through the 1930's. A depression di-

---

[65] Jacques Desmarest, *La Politique de la main-d'oeuvre en France* (Paris, 1946), 130–31.

[66] *Journal officiel,* 2–3 September 1941, 3694–3715.

[67] Institut national de la statistique et des études économiques, *Recensement général de la population effectué le 10 mars 1946* (Paris, 1949), viii.

[68] This phrase of Edouard Drumont, revived by Maurras and shouted in the streets in the demonstrations of 6 February 1934, reached final respectability as the title of an editorial in *Le Temps,* 25 July 1940.

minishes hospitality. Before the depression, France had relied on large numbers of foreign workmen to round out her own insufficient labor force, especially Poles in the mines of the north and Spanish and Italian agricultural labor in the south. In 1930, no less than 7 percent of the entire French population consisted of foreign workmen. That proportion was of course much higher in areas where they were concentrated, such as the Polish communities in the Nord.[69] Then unemployment turned foreign workmen into an object of hostility and retaliation. Quotas were imposed, beginning in 1932. Foreign labor became a frequent scapegoat in radical right newspapers, such as Colonel de la Rocque's *Le Flambeau.*[70]

To labor was added a flood of refugees in the late 1930's. Thousands of Spanish loyalists managed to cross the Pyrenees when the Spanish Republic ended its struggle against Franco in 1939. Jews from Germany and Austria had increased with the Nuremberg decrees of November 1938. The Polish campaign of September 1939 sent another wave to the west. Of some 300,000 Jews in France in 1939 (mostly in the Paris region), about half were foreign, and about half of those who were French citizens had one or more foreign parents. Xavier Vallat, among others, thought France was approaching "saturation." [71]

France had been the traditional refuge for exiles. The war, however, made them an embarrassment. They endangered neutral relations with Spain, for example. When Pétain was sent to be the first French ambassador to Franco in 1939, the control of Spanish republican exile movements in France was one of the major issues to be settled. The main purpose for which Daladier recognized Franco, after all, was to keep Spain neutral in case of a war between Germany and France.[72] Furthermore, the pres-

---

[69] Jacques Desmarest, *Le Politique de la main-d'oeuvre en France* (Paris, 1946), 60 ff. Desmarest is particularly well informed about Vichy labor policies, having served as *chef de cabinet* to Gaston Bruneton, commissioner for French labor working in Germany, 1942–44.

[70] Desmarest, 131. *Le Flambeau,* 27 June 1936.

[71] Joseph Billig, *Le Commissariat général aux questions juives, 1941–44* (Paris, 1955–60), I, 226; *Le Procès de Xavier Vallat présenté par ses amis* (Paris, 1948), 116.

[72] Senator Léon Bérard's negotiations for renewal of Franco-Spanish relations on February 4–6, 1939, are described in German embassy, Madrid,

ence of so many Spanish "Reds" made French conservatives nervous. They could remember that Pétain had had to shut Russian soldiers up in Courtines during the mutinies of 1917. As for the Jewish refugees, they also were politically suspect, and a source of trouble. German refugees led to Article 19, perhaps the most humiliating section of the armistice, which required France to hand over German citizens to Germany on demand, thus abridging France's right to provide political asylum.

The Third Republic had already imposed stringent security measures on foreigners before the outbreak of the war (laws of 2 and 14 May 1938). Arthur Koestler describes his four months in 1939–40 in the "Concentration Camp for Undesirable Aliens" (mostly German Jewish and Spanish refugees) at Le Vernet, in the foothills of the Pyrenees, in *Scum of the Earth*. And one will recall the internment of Ernie Levy's family in the camp at Gurs in May 1940 in André Schwarz-Bart's *Last of the Just*. The Vichy government went further. With unemployment even higher than in the depression, and fearful of the refugees' potential for disorder, the government voted itself the power to intern all foreign men between the ages of eighteen and forty-five as long as there was an excess of labor in the economy.[73] Thus Vichy had already set up its own concentration camp system.

The next step was to roll back the naturalization process by which a number of these refugees had become French citizens. A simplification of the naturalization procedure in 1927 had allowed many "to become French too easily." No doubt, some of them had not acquired perfect purity of tongue along with their naturalization papers. On 22 July 1940 Justice Minister Raphaël Alibert, an avowed monarchist whose sourness toward republicans was heightened by his successive failures in business after resigning from the Council of State in 1923, set up a Comsion for the Revision of Naturalizations to review all new grants

---

"Akten der deutschen Botschaft in Madrid betreffend Frankreich und Beziehungen zu Spanien," vol. 1 (T-120/454/223634–223674). German intelligence also kept a close watch on Spanish refugees after June 1940.

[73] Ministère de l'Intérieur, *Bulletin officiel*, 1940, no. 10 (October 1940).

of French citizenship since 10 August 1927. Of some 500,000 dossiers examined, 15,154 new Frenchmen had their citizenship revoked. Of these, 6,307 were Jews. The first step in the "purification" of the French nation had been taken.[74]

Inexorably, purification turned inward to single out what Maurras liked to call "internal foreigners," un-French Frenchmen. It was perhaps the counterpart to Fifth Column thinking on the other side. But the habit of accusing certain groups of Frenchmen of being corrupting influences in the nation had been ingrained in conservatives by forty years of Maurrassian attribution of all French decline to the *métèques*—an ugly word suggesting animal breeding that Maurras applied to the three parts of "anti-France": Protestants, Masons, and Jews. Defeat cried out for scapegoats, and scapegoats were ready to hand.

Among Maurras' *métèques,* Protestants no longer offered a target to conservatives. Indeed, the rather closed, austere Parisian world of Protestant banking and high civil servant families was well-represented among the notables who stepped forward to replace the Third Republic politicians. By 1940 the religious issue that divided Catholic and Protestant in 1900 had long since given way to an antisocialist issue that united them. One finds such Protestant notables at Vichy as Maurice Couve de Murville, the highly capable director of foreign exchange at the Finance Ministry until the spring of 1943 (and twenty-five years later, prime minister of the Fifth Republic); François Charles-Roux, secretary-general of the Foreign Office in late 1940; General Brécard, grand chancellor of the Légion d'honneur; Gaston Bruneton, commissioner for French laborers working in Germany, and so on. The leading Protestant pastor, Marc Boegner, was a member of the National Council. The only anti-Protestant remark I have found during the whole Vichy period is a suggestion to the Papal Nuncio by Yves Bouthillier that

---

[74] *Le Temps,* 25 July 1940; *Ministère public c/ Alibert; Les Procès de la collaboration* (Paris, 1948), 119. Judge André Mornet, the prosecutor of Pétain in 1945, sat on the commission. For other samples of xenophobia mixed with professional jealousy, see the complaint about the number of foreigners in the medical profession, *Revue universelle,* 10 September 1941, 344.

Charles-Roux' Protestantism made him sympathetic to England.[75]

The other *métèques* were less fortunate. The Vichy regime took seriously the conspiratorial view that Masonic Lodges, those small-town meeting places of politicians and businessmen from the Third Republic's center, were a kind of clandestine shadow government. They were reputed to intervene in personnel questions, advancing the careers of radicals and moderate socialists and retarding those of good Catholics. The virulence and ubiquity among French conservatives of a Masonic devil-theory is baffling to foreigners until one remembers that the lodges and the church had been fighting each other tooth and claw since the late eighteenth century. Unlike the Scottish-rite Masons of North America, the Grand Loge de France and the Grand-Orient de France had gone beyond anticlericalism to outright antireligion after 1877. The church, in turn, forbade any good Catholic to belong. By the late nineteenth century, the lodges were indeed more than just social clubs. They were part of the web of friendship, shared views, and organization that bound together the partisans of the militant lay Republic—village teachers, shopkeepers, and doctors—against the village curé, nobleman, and monarchist notables. Indeed it is established that the lodges did operate an unofficial intelligence system for the pro-Dreyfus majority after 1899, collecting information about which army officers in the provinces were republican and which went to mass. The revelation of these secret card files in 1905 (the "affaire des fiches") allowed frightened conservatives to imagine what other horrors went on behind the lodges' sealed doors. More than just an old enemy, the lodges were a surrogate of the militant anticlerical petit-bourgeois republic, a voodoo doll into which one stuck pins in order to get at the real body.

Justice Minister Raphaël Alibert attacked the lodges at once. There is no evidence of the German pressures on which Laval later blamed the whole business.[76] On 13 August 1940 all

---

[75] *Actes du Saint-Siège relatifs à la seconde guerre mondiale* (Vatican City, 1967), IV, 175.

[76] *Le Procès du maréchal Pétain* (*Journal officiel*, 1945), 191. Abetz thought the Vichy anti-Masonic organizations around Bernard Faÿ and

secret societies were abolished. Public officials and civil servants were required to swear that they were not (or were no longer) members. Further acts were taken against Masons in the general tightening up of August 1941. The names of some 14,600 office-holders in the lodges were published, presumably to reveal those who brazenly and illegally continued to hold official functions and also to expose them to public obloquy. Bernard Faÿ, director of the Bibliothèque nationale and scholar of the eighteenth-century Masonic precursors of the French Revolution, began going through seized documents to unearth the secrets of Masonry under the Third Republic. These were to be published in *Les Documents Maçonniques,* which appeared for about a year after October 1941 under the editorship of Robert Vallery-Radot. There were a few surprises: Marcel Peyrouton, Vichy interior minister in the fall of 1940 and then ambassador to Argentina, had to be given special exemption from the law of 13 August 1940.[77] But by and large, the results were as disappointing as were the contents of the Yalta documents in 1955 to Senators Joseph R. McCarthy and Styles Bridges, who had forced the State Department to publish them early out of series. The main effect was to discredit a legend, to antagonize thousands more middling Frenchmen who would probably otherwise have supported the regime, and to reward a few more conservatives with vacant places.

This brings us to the blackest mark on the whole Vichy experience: anti-Semitism. It is vital to expose the French roots of early Vichy anti-Jewish measures, for nowhere else has the claim of German pressure and French passivity been more insistent. It is true that, from 1942 on, the German project of deportation was imposed upon France by fiat and despite a certain amount of Vichy foot-dragging. At the beginning, how-

Robert Vallery-Radot were too clerical and hostile to German influence, but he subsidized the periodicals and exhibitions of Henri Coston's Centre d'Action et de Documentation anti-Maçonnique in Paris. See Paris telegram 3218 of 27 July 1942 (T-120/434/220208–11).

[77] *Le Figaro,* 6 February 1942. See Bernard Faÿ's lecture on his discoveries in the "120 tons of documents," *Le Temps,* 2 December 1941. Lists of Masonic dignitaries appear in the *Journal officiel,* 14 August–22 October 1941.

ever, the Germans cared so little for French internal matters that France was used as a dumping area for German Jews. On 23–24 October 1940, over intense French government objections, six thousand German Jews were sent into France from Western Germany.[78] Just as France was not included in the "Middle European Great Economic Region" of German peace plans, so it was not considered part of the area to be "purified" of Jews.[79] In 1940, therefore, an indigenous French anti-Semitism was free to express its own venom.

Long before the Germans began to apply any pressure, the Vichy government began setting up a purge and quota system. A law of 3 October 1940 excluded Jews from elected bodies, from positions of responsibility in the civil service, judiciary, and military services, and from positions influencing cultural life (teaching in public schools, newspaper reporting or editing, direction of films or radio programs). A law of 4 October authorized the prefects to intern foreign Jews in special camps or assign them to forced residence. A law of 7 October repealed the Crémieux law of 1871, which had extended French citizenship to the indigenous Jews of Algeria. A law of 27 August 1940 had already repealed a law of 21 April 1939 that penalized anti-Semitic excesses in the press. From the beginning, the government singled Jews out for special penalties and sanctioned hostile attitudes toward them. Jews were excluded altogether from the department of the Allier, where Vichy was located.[80]

In view of what was to come, it may seem casuistical to observe that Vichy anti-Semitism rested upon different bases from Nazi anti-Semitism. Left to itself, Vichy would probably have stopped short at job discrimination and measures calculated to hasten the further emigration of foreign Jews. Vichy xenophobia

[78] T-120/368/207282–85; *DFCAA*, II, 244.
[79] Eichmann thought he could threaten France with being omitted from the "area of evacuation" if the French did not cooperate more fully in July 1942. See report of Röthke telephone conversation, *CDJC*, document no. XXVI-45 (also Nuremberg document RF-1226). See peace plans referring to the Mitteleuropäischen Grosswirtschaftsraum in T-120/363/206135–53.
[80] Most works, including Gerald Reitlinger, *The Final Solution*, 2d ed. (London, 1968), 73, assume erroneously that these laws were exacted by the Germans.

was more cultural and national than racial, in a French assimilationist tradition. Vichy displayed no more intolerance toward blacks, for example, than had the Third Republic. Henry Lémery, the Martinique lawyer who was among Pétain's closest cronies in the Senate, was minister of colonies in June–July 1940 and a confidant thereafter. Senegalese units were excluded from the Armistice Army only upon German order, in memory of their presence in the Rhineland in the 1920's.[81] What most Frenchmen required of outsiders was assimilation, the unreserved adoption of French culture. A black man like Lémery was altogether French, but even the republic had had running battles with gypsies, whose mobility confounded the *état civil,* and with Breton mothers who insisted upon giving their children names unpronounceable in Paris. Traditional conservative French xenophobia demanded cultural conformity (which any individual may acquire) more insistently than physical resemblence.

Vichy's anti-Semitic legislation, therefore, always exempted Jewish war veterans and long-established families from some of the rigors of the law. As Darlan explained to a scornful Abetz on 5 March 1941, Marshal Pétain insisted upon treating those who had served in the French Army differently from foreign Jews. The French are not a race, argued Thierry-Maulnier in the *Revue universelle,* but a melting pot of diverse peoples welded into a nation. Pétain seems to have consulted the Vatican on the permissible limits of anti-Semitism. Ambassador Léon Bérard wrote him a long personal letter on 2 September 1941 assuring him that an "authorized person at the Vatican" had said that the church would not start any quarrel over restricting certain citizens' access to jobs or over limiting Jews' actions in society. The church's quarrel with fascist and Nazi "racism" rested on their refusal to agree that a Jew ceased to be a Jew upon conversion to Catholicism and on their refusal of intermarriage even after conversion. The Vatican spokesman took issue only with the first article of the law of 3 October 1940 (which clashes in spirit with the exemptions elsewhere in the text) defining Jews racially

---

[81] Robert O. Paxton, *Parades and Politics at Vichy* (Princeton, 1966), 45.

as anyone with three Jewish grandparents, whatever the religion of the present generation. There were racist anti-Semites in France, and with Darquier de Pellepoix in 1942 they even entered the government. But, as long as Vichy had a free hand in Jewish matters, a Catholic and national anti-Semitism rather than a racial anti-Semitism lay at the base of French policy.[82]

Meanwhile, the German authorities were going their own way in the Occupied Zone. From 20 May 1940 on, they assigned provisional administrators to enterprises whose owners had fled and forbade Jews who had fled to return. A census ordered on 18 September 1940 was the first German ordinance to single out Jews. Then, on 18 October 1940, provisional administrators were assigned to all Jewish property. The third ordinance of 26 April 1941 gave the provisional administrators the power to sell Jewish properties to Aryans or to liquidate them, with proceeds going to the state. Thus a number of Frenchmen in the Occupied Zone became beneficiaries of an act of spoliation no less direct than the Rosenberg office's seizure of Jewish art treasures in Paris at the same time. By July 1943 provisional administrators were running 39,000 Jewish enterprises in the Occupied Zone (28,000 businesses and 11,000 buildings), of which 12,700 (12,000 businesses and 700 buildings) had already been "Aryanized" or liquidated, often at a fraction of their prewar worth. As in the French Revolution, a new class of purchasers of *biens nationaux* was being created, and, as was done in 1815, the Germans expected to write the legitimacy of these new property titles into the peace treaty.[83]

Efforts to block these German practices in the fall of 1940 having failed, the Vichy government in 1941 succumbed to the

[82] Abetz telegram 763 to Ribbentrop, 6 March 1941 (T-120/221/149146); Thierry Maulnier, "L'Avenir de la France," *Revue universelle*, 10 May 1941, 570 ff.; Léon Berard letter to Marshal Pétain, 2 September 1941 (*CDJC*, document no. XLII-10).

[83] Figures are from Militärbefehlshaber in Frankreich, "Lagebericht über Verwaltung und Wirtschaft, April–June 1943," Nr. 462/43g, Paris, 21 July 1943 (*CDJC*, document no. LXXV-219). Also see similar figures in Joseph Billig, *Le Commissariat Général aux questions juives* (Paris, 1955), III, 325. The commander of *Verwaltungsgruppe 531* assured the Chamber of Commerce of Troyes of the second point in a letter of 26 February 1941 (*CDJC*, document no. CCXLVI-15).

temptation to try to restore French sovereignty over Jewish affairs in the Occupied Zone. Not that Vichy regretted German efforts to reduce Jewish influence in the economy. But "Aryanization" all too often meant Germanization. Already, in the fall of 1940, General de la Laurencie, the French government's representative in Paris, concentrated his efforts upon obtaining assurances that almost all the provisional administrators would be French. In early December a Service du Contrôle des Administrateurs Provisoires within the Ministry of Industrial Production, under Pierre-Eugène Fourrier, former governor of the Bank of France, attempted to "oversee in the name of the French government the organization of Jewish enterprises demanded by the German authorities." [84]

As soon as his position was assured after the crisis over Laval, Darlan took further steps to recapture French initiative over policy toward Jews. In his first serious talk with Abetz on March 5, 1941, Darlan discussed the creation of a central office for Jewish affairs within the French government. The project was all the more acceptable to Abetz since German security and police officials at Paris had been urging the same thing.[85] On 23 March he named Xavier Vallat commissioner-general for Jewish affairs, with rank of under-secretary in the French cabinet. Vallat, a nationalist deputy frightfully mutilated in World War I, who played a flamboyant role in right-wing veterans' organizations and in General Curières de Castelnau's *Fédération Nationale Catholique* between the wars, had never hidden his anti-Semitism. In June 1936, as Léon Blum assumed the office of premier in the Popular Front, Vallat had risen to note this

[84] Letters of General de la Laurencie, 16 October 1940, 19 October 1940 (*CDJC,* document no. CCLXVI-19); first circular of S.C.A.P. to provisional administrators, 22 December 1940 (*CDJC,* document no. CCXVI-14). Fournier suggested that provisional administrators form a corporation and keep the original owner as a technical advisor.

[85] Abetz (Paris) no 763 to Ribbentrop, 6 March 1941 (T-120/221/149146–47); Billig, I, 51 ff. This was the same meeting at which Darlan stressed Pétain's insistence upon different treatment for French Jews, especially war veterans, and foreign Jews. In a long report on Jewish policy on 22 February 1942, Theodor Dannecker, the SS officer responsible for Jewish affairs in France, took credit for this step and stressed the value to Germany of having France take the initiative. *CDJC,* document no. XXIV-13.

"historic moment" on which, for the first time, this "ancient Gallo-Roman country" was to be governed by "a subtle Talmudist." As Pétain's first minister for veterans' affairs, he had realized the interwar activists' dream of a single veterans' organization, the Légion Nationale des Combattants, assigned a leading role in public affairs. His chauvinism in this office had made the German authorities in Paris nervous. He was no less blunt as commissioner-general for Jewish affairs. He once lectured the SS officer Theodor Dannecker with the assertion that "I am an older anti-Semite than you. I could be your father in these matters." [86]

Vallat's assignment was to restore French law and administration over Jewish matters in the Occupied Zone, or as he put it to Dr. Werner Best of the German military administration, to "harmonize the two zones." This seemed the best way to stop the German infiltration of the French economy through "Aryanization" and to forestall possible further future dumping of foreign Jews in the unoccupied zone. Vallat asked Dr. Best on 23 June 1941 to "withdraw" the German ordinances when proposed new French laws went into effect.[87] The law of 2 June 1941 tightened up the Vichy quota system already set up by the law of 3 October 1940. The list of jobs entirely forbidden to Jews was expanded beyond senior public service, education, and cultural affairs to include advertising, banking and financial matters, and real estate agencies. Quotas were imposed on Jews in a nearly total range of jobs—"liberal, commercial, industrial, or artisanal professions" and lower public posts and functions in the legal-judicial system. Limits of 2 percent were set for various professions in a series of decrees over the following months: lawyers (16 July 1941), doctors, pharmacists, and midwives (11 August 1941), architects (24 September 1941), and dentists (5 June 1942). The stage, film, and concert worlds were sup-

[86] *CDJC*, document no. LXXV-147. Vallat also referred to the German "invasion" and warned that he could not forget being treated as a subordinate. Dannecker called it an "unheard-of effrontery." Vallat was removed from office soon after, in March 1942. For Vallat's career, see *Le Procès Vallat présenté par ses amis* (Paris, 1948), and Xavier Vallat, *Le Nez de Cléopâtre* (Paris, 1957).

[87] Xavier Vallat letter to Dr. Werner Best, 23 June 1941 (*CDJC*, document no. CX-65); Report of the Institut des Questions Juives, 8 August 1941 (*CDJC*, document no. XIb-172). See also Billig, I, 108, 177.

posed to be closed altogether to Jewish performers (except by special permission) by a decree of 6 June 1942. Jewish students were limited to 3 percent in secondary school and universities on 21 June 1941. This meant, to take one example, that alongside 5,410 non-Jewish doctors in Paris, 108 Jewish doctors (2 percent) could be licensed to practice. The German authorities were complaining in March 1943 that there were in fact 203 Jewish doctors still in Paris. The Vichy government did, however, take the Jewish purge seriously. After his first six months, Vallat could boast that 3,000 civil servants had been dismissed, with similar proportions dismissed from positions in the press, radio, movies, and "in all the areas where their functions gave them power . . . over minds." [88]

Jewish power in the economy was an even more sensitive area. Determined to wrest "Aryanization" from German hands, Vallat forced through the law of 22 July 1941 on the basis of a German promise to cancel their own ordinances in the Occupied Zone.[89] The law's stated purpose was to "eliminate all Jewish influence in the national economy." It empowered the commissioner-general to name a provisional administrator to any Jewish business or real estate. The provisional administrator took the owner's place in every respect. He could sell the property to a non-Jew, depositing the purchase price in a blocked government account, or if he could find no seller and the enterprise was not of value to the national economy, he could liquidate it. Some of the proceeds were to go to the support of "indigent Jews." Thus the sordid business of forced sale of Jewish property, and the development of a Vichy clientele of jackal-like profiteers, was extended to the unoccupied zone. Statistics of the total spoliation of Jewish properties in the unoccupied zone are not so complete as those for the Occupied Zone, but figures of 231

[88] Billig, I, 157–66, 327–30; III, 12–60.

[89] See Vallat letter to General von Stülpnagel, 9 October 1941, accusing the Germans of reneging on that promise which had "helped me obtain the agreement of my government to the changes you wanted in the text of 22 July." (*CDJC,* document no. LXXV-62). See also Vallat's letter to Darlan, 7 July 1941, denying that the text proposed a "general spoliation of the Jews, as some fear." The letter seems to have been used to sway the cabinet to accept the law. Billig, I, 171 ff.

businesses placed under provisional administrators at Toulouse, of which 117 were actually "Aryanized," may give some idea of its extent.[90]

The Darlan government returned from this particular ride on the inside of the tiger. Far from reasserting French sovereignty over the Occupied Zone, anti-Semitism became a major avenue for German influence over Vichy. From their early stance of lofty indifference to France's share in the "purification" of Europe, the German authorities turned, with the new policy and with Abetz' genuine interest in collaboration, to trying to bring France into the pale of the New Europe. The veiled German promptings of early 1941 become a direct German share in preparing the new legislation of mid-1941, through French hopes that it would be applied to the Occupied Zone. It never was. Then the Germans used the new French machinery to impose their own more drastic "final solution" on the unoccupied zone.

The over-chauvinistic Vallat having been boycotted by the Germans in March 1942, he was replaced in April by Louis Darquier de Pellepoix (the noble patronymic was phony), a genuine genetic racist and street brawler, president of the Association of the Wounded of 6 February 1934, and a member of the Paris City Council. Darquier had quit the Croix de Feu in December 1935, accusing Colonel de La Rocque of being a "rosewater dictator." He had served three months in prison in 1939 for "excitation to racial hatred" in his newspaper, *La France Enchaînée*. In the fall of 1940, he founded a French Union for the Defense of the Race, to replace his prewar Rassemblement Anti-Juif. Darquier's regime was scandalous financially as well as ideologically, according to surviving papers in the Centre de Documentation Juive Contemporaine in Paris, but he could be removed only if he were replaced by someone equally fanatical. Laval seemed to have found the man in February 1944 with Charles Mercier du Paty de Clam, a lawyer and former French official in Syria, son of the notorious anti-Dreyfusard officer. Du Paty won acquittal after the war by proving that the administrative disorder of the Commissariat for Jewish Questions

[90] Billig, III, 301.

Marshal Pétain and his cabinet, July 1940. LEFT TO RIGHT: *Pierre Caziot,
agriculture; Admiral François Darlan, navy; Paul Baudouin, foreign affairs;
Raphaël Alibert, justice; Pierre Laval, vice-premier; Adrien Marquet,
interior; Yves Bouthillier, finance; Marshal Philippe Pétain, premier and
head of state; Emile Mireaux, education; General Maxime Weygand,
national defense; Jean Ybarnégaray, youth and the family; Henri Lémery,
colonies; General Bertrand Pujo, aviation; and General Louis Colson, war.*

The French cruiser Mogador *burns after the British naval attack upon the French Mediterranean fleet at Mers-el-Kebir, Algeria, on 4 July 1940.*

*The Demarcation Line. A
German officer checks papers at
the crossing into the occupied
zone at Moulins, near Vichy.
The automobile has been
adapted for substitute fuel.*

*Admiral William D. Leahy,
United States Ambassador to
Vichy France, received by
Marshal Pétain on his arrival in
January 1941.*

*Church and State at Vichy. Emanuel Célestin Cardinal Suhard, Archbishop
of Paris, and Pierre-Marie Cardinal Gerlier, Archbishop of Lyon, with
Pétain and Laval at the entrance to the makeshift executive offices in Vichy's
Hôtel du Parc.*

After a cabinet meeting at Vichy in May 1941, during the discussion of the Protocols of Paris, Admiral Darlan (left) talks with Finance Minister Yves Bouthillier (center) and War Minister General Charles-Léon Huntziger.

OPPOSITE TOP: *Admiral Darlan makes a point to Hitler at Berchtesgaden, 12 May 1941. Between them is Ambassador Otto Abetz and behind Darlan is his foreign affairs liaison officer in Paris, Jacques Benoist-Méchin.*

OPPOSITE BOTTOM: *German Ambassador Otto Abetz (center) at Vichy, with Pétain and Darlan, on the occasion of General Huntziger's funeral, November 1941.*

An inconclusive summit meeting. Marshal Pétain meets Marshal Hermann Goering at Saint-Florentin (Yonne), 1 December 1941. Admiral Darlan walks behind Pétain, and the German interpreter Dr. Paul Schmidt is at the left.

Pierre Pucheu, France's Minister of the Interior, with over one hundred prefects at Vichy, as the gathering pledged their loyalty to Marshal Pétain (center). Admiral Darlan is seated next to Pétain.

The struggle against the Resistance. Laval (right) and Joseph Darnand, Secretary of State for the Maintenance of Order, review a special unit of the Milice, spring 1944.

Retribution. A suspected collaborator, beaten by the crowd, is taken into custody by police and soldiers during the liberation of Paris, August 1944.

Laval (standing) testifies at the trial of Marshal Pétain in Paris, August 1945, as the marshal (seated at right, hand to face) listens.

under his guidance was intentional. But long before then, all real initiative had passed to German hands.[91]

Through Darlan's regime, it seems arguable that the Vichy government wanted only to hasten the reemigration of foreign Jews and the assimilation of long-established French Jewish families. Even Hitler had exempted the Nobel Laureate biochemist Dr. Otto Warburg because he was afraid of cancer. In Vichy France, exemptions were legion: Professors Louis Halphen and Marc Bloch; General Darius-Paul Bloch; the deputy Achille-Fould, descendant of Napoleon III's financier, who had voted "yes" in July 1940, for example.

Meanwhile, in Berlin something far more ruthless was taking shape. There were forewarnings even in 1941, when the French police agreed to cooperate in the first mass internments in the Occupied Zone: 3,600 Polish Jews around Paris in May 1941, another group of foreign Jews in August 1941. Then, during the wave of assassinations in late 1941, came the arrest on 14 December of a thousand Jewish notables and the imposition of a fine of a billion francs on the Jewish population of the Occupied Zone. Hitler gave up his Madagascar resettlement scheme and laid plans for extermination at the Wannsee Conference at the turning of 1941–42. The first systematic deportations of stateless Jews from camps in the Occupied Zone began in May and June 1942. Jews in the Occupied Zone were required to wear a yellow star after May 28, 1942, as in the rest of Hitler's Europe. Finally, on June 11, 1942, Himmler set massive quotas for deportations from the west to the extermination camps at Auschwitz: 15,000 from Holland, 10,000 from Belgium and Northern France, and 100,000 from France, "including the Unoccupied Zone."[92] The Final Solution had begun, and the Vichy zone was about to be drawn into it.

The first mass deportations began with the notorious roundup of some 13,000 Jews in the Vélodrome d'Hiver in Paris on July 16, 1942, before being shipped to a camp at Drancy and then on to

[91] Darquier seems to have escaped to Spain during the Liberation; I have found no trial record. The best source for his work is the archives of the *CDJC*. For du Paty, Haute Cour de Justice, "Arrêt de non-lieu: Mercier du Paty de Clam."

[92] Billig, I, 239–40, 364–65; Reitlinger, 327–51.

the east. That spectacle of human misery, which prompted formal opposition from the Catholic hierarchy, was only the beginning. Laval was caught in the trap of trying to maintain some French participation. He agreed in July to deliver 10,000 foreign Jews in the unoccupied zone to the German authorities on the understanding that French Jews would be deported from the Occupied Zone only if foreign Jews fell short of Himmler's quota. On 2 September 1942 General Oberg assured him that there would be "no further demands in this area" after France had handed over all German, Austrian, Czech, Polish, and Hungarian Jews. In February 1943 Laval was still trying to hold the line at foreign Jews but was offering to go further if France could get "some kind of political security" (Zusicherung) about French territory as advantageous as that which an American victory would offer.[93]

Pawns in these fruitless bargains, Jewish refugees in the Vichy zone were divided rather between rich and poor than between French and foreign. Those with money and connections still managed to hang on in southern cities, trying desperately to get visas and boat passage to a new world that was doing little to help them. The poor were already in work camps, helpless. The German occupation of the rest of France exposed them to direct Nazi presence after November 1942.

There remained one unexpected asylum. Mussolini's Italy, never more than lackadaisically imitating the 1938 Nuremberg decrees, took up active defense of Jewish refugees in the Italian occupation zone east of the Rhône in 1943, partly because of the important Jewish contribution to the Italian imperial presence in Tunisia. The Italian government had objected strenuously to French anti-Semitic measures in Tunisia, seeing them as another aspect of French anti-Italian actions there.[94] When deportations from the coastal zone increased in early 1943, the Italian occupation authorities obstructed them east of the Rhône, warning

---

[93] Abetz (Paris) telegram 2784, 2 July 1942 (T-120/434/220086); Nuremberg document RF-1226 also refers to this agreement; Laval-Oberg conversation, 2 September 1942 (*CDJC,* document no. XLIX-42); Knochen report, 12 February 1943 (*CDJC,* document no. I-38).

[94] Weizsäcker memorandum St. S. 507, Berlin, 2 September 1942 and enclosed note from Italian Ambassador Alfieri (T-120/434/220334).

the French government that while it could do what it wanted with French Jews, foreign Jews in the Italian-occupied zone were exclusively a matter for the Italian authorities. In March the Italian authorities stepped in to prevent the French prefects of Valence, Chambéry, and Annecy from arresting foreign Jews there. In June 1943 Italian police prefect Lospinosa blocked the French arrest of 7,000 foreign Jews at Mégève. That a fascist Italian police prefect should have to point out to Antignac, Darquier de Pellepoix's hatchet man in the Commissariat-General of Jewish Affairs, that Italy "respected the elementary principles of humanity" is some measure of judgment upon Vichy anti-Semitism.[95]

With Italy out of the war in July 1943, the last barrier to mass deportations was down.

> I saw a train pass. In front, a car containing French police and German soldiers. Then came cattle cars, sealed. The thin arms of children clasped the grating. A hand waved outside like a leaf in a storm. When the train slowed down, voices cried "Mama!" And nothing answered except the squeaking of the springs. . . . The truth: stars worn on breasts, children torn from their mothers, men shot every day, the methodical degradation of an entire people. The truth is censored. We must cry it from the rooftops.[96]

In the end, some 60,000–65,000 Jews were deported from France, mostly foreigners who had relied upon traditional French hospitality. Perhaps 6,000 French citizens also took that gruesome journey. Some 2,800 of the deportees got back.[97]

Vichy's share of responsibility for the bestial deportations of 1942–44 was probably greater than the German documents themselves would suggest. Because French cultural anti-Semitism, with its acceptance of assimilated Jews, was built upon bases entirely foreign to Nazi racial anti-Semitism, it seemed to Abetz—and indeed to French racial anti-Semites like Darquier and Antignac —that the Vichy people were lukewarm, obstructionist, or even

---

[95] Antignac report, *CDJC,* document no. I-53. The whole CDJC dossier I is the source for this paragraph.

[96] Edith Thomas in *Lettres françaises,* no. 2, quoted in Claude Lévy and Paul Tillard, *La Grande rafle du Vel d'Hiv* (Paris, 1967), 176.

[97] Reitlinger, 327, 538, probably has the last word on the shaky German statistics.

"philo-semitic." German authorities were angry because Vallat had indeed tried to block the German use of "Aryanization" as an undercover device to gain control of important parts of the French economy, or because they suspected that "Vichy Jewish legislation parallels ours only in order to soften the German decrees." [98] But Vichy's cultural and economic anti-Semitism was no less real for being scorned by Nazis. Such a regime, even if the German troops had soon withdrawn, would have made life difficult for Jews in France. Darlan and Vallat had tried to regain the initiative not out of concern for Jews but out of fear that the Germans would dump more foreign Jews into unoccupied France or would take over Jewish property in the Occupied Zone.

Furthermore, the French laws of 1940 and 1941 made the Final Solution much easier. By the summer of 1942, some 20,000 Jews had already been interned in French concentration camps in the unoccupied zone under the law of 4 October 1940. [99] The census of all Jewish persons and property ordered under the law of 2 June 1941 made escape harder. The creation of the Union Générale des Israélites Français on 29 November 1941, the obligatory welfare and representation organization of all French Jews, helped set them apart even more clearly. Expulsion from jobs and "Aryanization" of businesses reduced more to destitution. Finally, the official government attitude and the gutter press lent an air of respectability to Vichy anti-Semitism from which Nazi anti-Semitism profited.

It is true that the Vichy government had not planned to turn discrimination into genocide. Vichy clearly blocked some German measures. Pétain forbade the extension to the unoccupied zone of the yellow star worn by all Jews in the Occupied Zone after 28 May 1942; it was not applied there even after the total occupation of November 1942. At lunch with SS Colonel Oberg on 2 September 1942, Laval warned that Jews couldn't be handed over "as in a supermarket, as many as you want for the

---

[98] Unsigned memorandum, 23 January 1942 (*CDJC*, document no. LXXV-38). Knochen's report of 12 February 1943 (*CDJC*, document no. I-38) accused Pétain, the French clergy, and Police Commissioner René Bousquet of "doing everything to hinder the deportation of French Jews."

[99] T-120/405/213960–63.

same price." That day, as always, he tried to get Oberg to limit further deportations to Jewish refugees from countries now controlled by the Nazis: Germany, Austria, Poland, Hungary, and Czechoslovakia.[100] In July–August 1943 Laval stubbornly refused to issue a proposed law depriving all French Jews who had become citizens since 1933 of their citizenship so that they could be deported, in spite of German efforts to "force" its promulgation. Laval's tortuous explanations and postponements are annotated by German officials with remarks such as "the fox" and "where insolence becomes a method."[101] Outside the immediate Vichy circle, the French Catholic hierarchy made public its opposition to the deportations in the summer of 1942. And shelter and help to Jews by thousands of French citizens are among the most honorable acts of the Resistance.

The fact remains that the Vichy government had tried to single out a group for special contempt and for measures of discrimination. Those measures were a great help to the Germans when the more bestial program of the Final Solution began.

The State: Liberty and Authority

> In a world growing harder, the democracies . . . must tighten their spring.
>
> —*Paul Baudouin, 1938* [102]

> I won't hesitate to agree that the French governmental system suffered excessively from internal ills, that it bore within itself inherent elements of instability, discontinuity, inefficiency.
>
> —*Léon Blum, 1941* [103]

MARSHAL PÉTAIN DID NOT SEIZE AUTHORITY IN THE summer of 1940. It descended upon him like a mantle. Within

---

[100] Notes of Laval-Oberg conversation 2 September 1942 (*CDJC,* document no. XLIX-42).

[101] *CDJC,* dossier no. XXVII.

[102] "Les données du problème français," *Revue de Paris,* 1 February 1938.

[103] Léon Blum, *A L'Echelle humaine* (Paris, 1945), 57.

the Third Republic itself a movement for a stronger executive had been frustrated but not diminished between the wars. Then the war governments of 1939–40 set up authoritarian machinery within the republic that an occupation regime could not dispense with. Finally, Pétain's symbolic meaning for Frenchmen—a paternal substitute for politics—simply left no room for a legitimate opposition.

The Constitution of 1875 had proven remarkably resistant to amendment after the primacy of parliament over president had been established with the crisis of 16 May 1877. Neither of the partisans of further revision—monarchists on the one hand, intransigent radicals unreconciled to the existence of a Senate on the other—still had significant parliamentary support by the turn of the century. Then a new revisionism appeared, dedicated to strengthening the executive. It fed upon the experience of World War I and upon the crises of the interwar years. No one could argue that French parliamentarism had responded well to the major problems of the interwar period—military, diplomatic, or economic. Shorter-lived ministries and longer tractations around the formation of new ones were the clearest external signs of powerlessness at the top at just the moment when decisive action was needed. While the average length of Third Republic ministries was about a year, it fell during periods of economic crisis (1925–26, 1931–36) to six months. There was a caretaker ministry or no ministry at all at such moments as the German remilitarization of the Rhineland in March 1936 and the Anschluss in 1938. Twice in the 1920's and nine times in the 1930's parliament voted "pleins pouvoirs" to permit ministers to dictate unpleasant actions on which the deputies would prefer not to vote, but these exceptional measures usually followed prolonged periods of emergency and were themselves recognition that the system wasn't working. The "system" had let France slip from the heights of 1918 to the depths of 1939.[104]

Proponents of a stronger executive came from all quarters of

[104] Poincaré was the first to enjoy this extraconstitutional device, on 22 March 1924; *pleins pouvoirs* had been denied Briand during World War I, on 30 December 1916. Jacques Soubeyrol, *Les Décrets-lois sous la Quatrième République* (Bordeaux, 1955).

the political spectrum. Léon Blum, as a young councilor of state fresh from a sobering experience as *chef de cabinet* to the Socialist Minister of Public Works Marcel Sembat, wrote an elaborate plan for providing the French premier with more staff and an office of his own, like a British prime minister. On the other side of the chamber, André Tardieu, who had tried and failed to form a strong ministry in 1931, wrote of the "captive sovereign" and of the "revolution to do over again." [105] Technicians and senior civil servants found their lives complicated by frequent changes of direction and the necessity for political maneuvering instead of arguing for programs on their technical merits. The technical efficiency argument could be heard from a *président de section* at the Council of State, Henri Chardon (France has been "out of balance for fifty years. She has given an excessive preponderance to political powers"); from a *conseiller-maître* at the Cour des Comptes ("Whereas politics dominated the deliberations of [the Finance Committees of the Chamber and Senate], only technical considerations and conclusions drawn from the examination of precise facts inspire the judgments of the Budget Committee [set up on 16 November 1940]"); and even from a republican *lycée* professor, Jean Guéhenno ("electoral politics continued to forbid great projects and long-term designs").[106]

For most proponents of a stronger executive, however, authority was an answer to social fears. A regime that permitted the strike wave of May–June 1936 and the Popular Front government was, as the *Action française* had been telling its readers for years, "established disorder." Constitutional reform was, for some, an escape from an electorate turned dangerous. The electorate had made the Socialist party the largest in France by 1936, and the Communists had grown from nothing to one voter out of five. Even the Radicals, who had come close before

---

[105] Léon Blum, *La Réforme gouvernementale* (Paris, 1918, reissued 1936); André Tardieu, *La Révolution à refaire,* I. *Le souverain captif* (Paris, 1936).

[106] *Le Réforme de l'état,* Conférences organisées par la société des anciens élèves et élèves de l'Ecole libre des Sciences Politiques, (1936); André Bisson, *Finances publiques françaises* (Paris, 1943), 271–72; Jean Guéhenno, *Journal des années noires* (Paris, 1947), 25 October 1942.

World War I to winning the absolute majority that only the Gaullist party has actually managed to attain in French history, watched nervously as the SFIO passed them in 1936 and the number of Radical seats declined. For some of the most traditionally solid republicans, the bloom was off the rose of election. A stronger executive would no doubt be in more reassuring hands than a parliament.

The movement for strengthening the executive produced a massive literature between the wars. But its authors worked mostly outside the world of established political parties: in veterans' movements, labor unions, or intellectual study groups like the "X-Crise" of Ecole Polytechnique alumni. The Chamber, comfortable in its old ways, gave serious attention to constitutional reform only during the emergency government which followed the right-wing demonstrations of 6 February 1934. The constitutional reform plan of 1934, however, like the others, fell into oblivion with the Doumergue government at the end of that year. Thus France went to war under a constitution that was already strenuously criticized and that seemed unreformable from within. Defeat raised those voices to a roar: down with "la démocrassouille." [107]

Beyond the mere "pleins pouvoirs" of his predecessors, therefore, Marshal Pétain received the charge from the National Assembly on 10 July 1940 in the Casino at Vichy to draft a new constitution. There can be no doubt that legally and actually Pétain had a very broad mandate to draft a new constitution for France.

It was clear from the first that parliament would play an effaced role. Unlike World War I, when the committees of the chambers reasserted their authority over the nearly absolute war government of the first months, the war government set up by Daladier and Reynaud in 1939–40 continued under Vichy without any parliamentary share at all. Parliament was not abolished; the deputies and senators continued to draw their salaries (until August 1941, at any rate), and the permanent bureaux of the two chambers remained in operation (until September 1942). A few

[107] The word is Pierre Pucheu's. See General Schmitt, *Toute la vérité sur le procès Pucheu* (Paris, 1963), 166.

favored deputies even entered the new regime. Some were named *chargé de mission* to report on the state of the provinces.[108] Others (Parmentier, Potut) followed the prevailing wind from legislation to administration and became prefects. Some deputies were even still ministers. The general antiparliamentary drift was clear, however. Deputies most closely connected to the Popular Front (Blum, Zay), the defeat (Daladier, Reynaud), or the proposed move to North Africa (Mandel) were imprisoned. Most strikingly of all, in a return to Bonapartist practice, a constitution was about to be drafted by commissions of experts instead of by a national assembly.[109]

That the new constitution would restore "authority and hierarchy," a "sense of the state," became a cliché. The new regime's style, under the guidance of neomonarchist Justice Minister Raphaël Alibert, set out to prove it at once. The government legislated by fiat, beginning each new law with the quasi-royal "We, Philippe Pétain, Marshal of France, Head of the French State, decree . . ."[110] The creation of specific new governmental institutions, however, was bound to open up the latent conflicts within the appeal for authority.

A major problem was how to balance that authority with some kind of link to the public. The single party idea, that stock-in-trade of authoritarian regimes of the 1930's, was frequently mentioned in the summer of 1940, both by Laval and by people closer to Pétain, like Ambassador to the United States Gaston Henri-Haye. But it was soon quietly abandoned. The very word *party* sounded more factious than national to everyone except those likely to control such a party, and, in practice,

[108] For example, the PSF deputy from St.-Etienne, Creyssel. *Ministère public c/Creyssel,* 18.

[109] It was the method also used by General de Gaulle in 1958.

[110] The pretender, Henri Comte de Paris, told the U.S. consul at Tangier that he believed there was a chance of a monarchical restoration upon Pétain's death. J. Rives Childs (Tangier) to Department of State, 11 July 1941 (U.S. Dept. of State Serial File 851.00/2311). But when he got German permission to visit Pétain at Vichy in the summer of 1942, Pétain seems to have angrily rejected any talk of restoration. (T-120/112/116360–62, 116385; T-120/434/220261–62). By November 1942 the Comte de Paris was on hand again in North Africa awaiting another change of regime.

all the contending groups at Vichy feared that a single party would be controlled by someone else.[111]

Veterans' organizations as a more broadly based "transmission belt" between regime and population seemed an even better idea than a single party to Pétain himself and to some of his more traditionalist advisers. The interwar veterans' organizations, fragmented and ineffectual, had persuaded themselves that the "generation of the trenches" had been done out of their victory after 1918 by the old political crowd. Under Xavier Vallat as first minister of veterans' affairs, the rival interwar veterans' organizations were forcibly united into a single Veterans' Legion (Légion Française des Combattants) intended to play the civic role that had eluded them before 1939. Veterans "must form groups down to the uttermost village in order to have the wise counsels of their leader of Verdun heeded and carried out." [112] This appeal to vigilantism did in fact produce local incidents in which legionnaires took it upon themselves to denounce prewar leaders to the authorities, to forbid public appearances that displeased them, and in general to act like a pseudogovernment. It was the local Legion that prevented André Gide from giving a lecture at Nice in May 1941. The Legion claimed to be agents of patriotism and loyalty to the new regime in the provinces. Jean Guéhenno gave a sourer description of one Legion chief, "the local pharmacist getting his revenge for having exerted no influence for the rest of his life," joined in a patriotic ceremony by the ex-radical mayor, "who doesn't want to miss his legion of honor award," and the schoolteacher, "fearful of losing his

---

[111] Laval, who was rumored in July 1940 to be planning to form a single party with Marquet, Déat, and Weygand, opposed the idea afterwards for fear that Doriot would control it. (T-120/121/119723; U.S. Dept. of State Serial File 851.00/2918). Henri-Haye expected on 31 July 1940 that a single party including Déat and Bergery would shortly be formed (U.S. Dept. of State Serial File 851.00/2046). Abetz, on the other hand, worked in the Occupied Zone, according to instructions, "against a unified political will in France" [Abetz (Paris) telegram 5295 to Ribbentrop, 19 November 1942, T-120/928/297509–11].

[112] Xavier Vallat, quoted in *D'Ordre du maréchal Pétain. Documents officiels réunis et commentés par Jean Thouvenin* (Paris, n.d. [1940]). The veterans' Légion Française des Combattants must not be confused with the Légion des Volontaires contre le Bolshevisme, which sent French volunteers to fight Russia.

job." [113] Guéhenno's version probably comes closer to the web of local pressures and interests that lent force to the Legion in many localities than does the Legion's own overblown propaganda.

These officious and impetuous local initiatives soon antagonized the prefects, however. A subterranean tug-of-war between the Legion's spontaneity and the prefectoral corps' system surfaced in early 1941 in sterner and sterner orders to the legionnaires to keep out of the official administration's hair. Instruction No. 1 of 26 February 1941 reminded the legionnaires that the "representatives of the central power are the only responsible repositories of the central power's constitutional authority" and that the Legion must perform its vital role in close cooperation with the official administration and "at its request." Instruction No. 2 of 30 April 1941, designed to "appease" legionnaires who had apparently complained of a diminution of their role, nevertheless reminded them that their role was "moral and social" and warned them against an "exaggerated" use of that role in "direct civic police actions" in their localities. [114] The prefects had clearly won game and set—a forecast of the professional administrators' eventual victory over all of Vichy's various experiments with functional representation.

At stake was a dim groping toward another conception of representation to replace the Third Republic's equal and atomized voters. According to the traditionalists' theory there was a fatal conflict in parliamentarism between getting elected and serving the country. [115] Some kind of advisory or consultative body was essential, however, and the traditionalists wanted to people it with another kind of representative, those who excelled in certain functions prized by the regime: veterans, those "aristocrats of courage"; fathers of large families; spokesmen for patriotic and religious values; prominent members of "real" social groups (artisans, peasants, professions). Elites were the only real representatives, according to René Gillouin. As Pétain himself

[113] Jean Guéhenno, *Journal des années noires* (Paris, 1947), 23 August 1942.

[114] *Almanach de la Légion française des combattants, 2e année* (1942), 111–12. "Published with the express approval of Marshal Pétain."

[115] Jean Le Cour Grandmaison, "Le Parlementarisme et la révolution nationale," *La Légion, revue mensuelle illustrée*, no. 1 (June 1941).

explained on October 18, 1941, he needed "continuous circuits between the authority of the state and the confidence of the people, . . . intermediaries who will discover the express wishes of their constituents, make known their needs, and will answer to the leaders' need to be informed." He wanted to "bring forward competences and to replace the power of mere number by the notion of value." War veterans were not enough. The regime was still groping for some other alternative to elections as a way to enlist the loyalties of local notables and to manufacture public support for the regime.[116]

The final attempt to create some new form of representative body was the National Council. The creation of a "consultative assembly" was announced on 24 January 1941 during the Flandin interregnum.[117] The government chose its members, whose roster reads like an honors list of "la vieille France." There were Alfred Cortot, the pianist, the physicist Prince Louis de Broglie, three Third Republic ministers (Georges Bonnet, Germain-Martin, Lucien Lamoureux), two members of the French Academy (Joseph de Pesquidoux, Abel Bonnard), Monseigneur Beaussart, coadjutor of the Archdiocese of Paris, and Pastor Marc Boegner, president of the French Protestant Federation, along with some presidents of local chambers of commerce, some Third Republic deputies and senators, heads of agricultural societies, and cooperative union officials.[118]

Through 1941, committees of the National Council set to work drafting major pieces of the new constitution. As Justice Minister Barthélemy reminded Frenchmen, even though the new constitution could not be ratified until the peace, the revival of French authority could not wait. The first committee met from 6 May to 10 June 1941 to draft a plan for reviving the

[116] René Gillouin, "Souveraineté et représentation," *Revue universelle,* 25 November 1941, 617; *Le Figaro,* 18 October 1941. It was Xavier Vallat who called war veterans the "aristocrats of courage."

[117] *Le Procès Flandin devant la Haute Cour de Justice* (Paris, n.d.), 203 ff. The Senate and Chamber of Deputies were not to be dissolved, however.

[118] The members of the National Council (*Conseil national*) are listed in Henri Coston, *Partis, journaux, et hommes politiques* (Paris, 1960), 166 ff. See also *Le Temps,* 27 April, 22 May, 15–19 September, 15 October 1941.

French provinces; the second committee discussed municipal government after 10 June 1941. The third committee discussed the political structures of the new constitution in July, and from September 16 to 18 a committee on "general information" sought ways of improving mutual understanding between country and government. Plans were laid for a Chamber of 200, entirely named by the head of state, and a Chamber of 300, half named by the head of state and half elected by the provincial assemblies from among war veterans, professional groups, fathers of large families, and other "real" organized social units. It is this last feature of functional representation that places Vichy's traditionalist constitution-making closer to Tocquevillian "intermediary bodies," Orleanist "best people," or the Duc de Broglie's scheme for an elite council in 1874–75 than to the complicated set of parliamentary bodies the Abbé Siéyès set up for Napoleon. Peace never came however, and these constitutional plans stand as a kind of monument to Vichy's efforts to base its authority on elite councils of local notables.[119]

In the meantime, into the constitutional vacuum stepped provisional measures of wartime bureaucracy that became the real face of Vichy authority. Vichy, as Yves Bouthillier proudly said, was the primacy of public administration over politics. In the most elementary sense, there was the sheer numerical growth of bureaucrats. After remaining stable in the years of deflation, the total number of people in French public services grew by nearly 50 percent, from about 600,000 to about 990,000 between 1936 and 1947. There was also an expansion of function. The Third Republic's war government of September 1939 had created a Ministry of Propaganda; Vichy created a Ministry of Industrial Production to assume new economic functions, as the Popular Front's Ministry of National Economy had done in 1936. The

---

[119] Abetz (Paris) telegram 3022 to Berlin of 6 October 1941 criticizes these plans as too clerico-bourgeois-reactionary to fit his ideal of a "socialist Europe" (T-120/405/213889–90). Xavier Vallat, "La Constitution voulue par le maréchal," *Revue de Paris,* refers only to efforts to assure continuity in 1944. Peyrouton's claim in *Du service publique à la prison commune,* 161, that the *National Council* was appointed only because the occupation prevented elections ignores the distrust of elections shown in all Vichy constitutional arrangements.

need to block prices, to ration and allocate scarce resources, to control production and the market through 321 Organization Committees (*comités d'organisation*), all increased the number of things civil servants were called upon to do. At the top, high civil servants stepped directly into positions of command, replacing the politicians whom they had once merely advised from behind the scenes.[120]

Civil servants were as ready as any interest group to exploit the new climate for change. They carried out long-discussed and long-deferred reforms in the structure of public administration. Steps were taken toward replacing the various examinations for entry into the various *grands corps* of the upper bureaucracy with a single examination. The knotty business of budget-drafting was taken from the powerful budget committees of Chamber and Senate and entrusted to a purely technical body on 18 November 1940, and men like Conseiller-maître André Bisson of the Cour des Comptes were delighted to see "the examination of precise facts" replace "politics" in these deliberations.[121] A permanent secretary-general, formerly a normal feature only of the Foreign Ministry, was assigned to every ministry to provide bureaucratic continuity by a law of 15 July 1940. The Cour des Comptes, which audits public accounts, had its work rationalized by a law of 16 May 1941, under which the accounts of all public funds, including organizations subsidized by the state, were submitted to its scrutiny automatically, and not—as under the Third Republic—case by case. The Council of State, the highest administrative court in France, had resumed the legislative function it had enjoyed under Napoleonic regimes (and was to enjoy again under the Fifth Republic). The law of 18 December 1940 added a fifth section to the Council of State responsible for drafting legislative projects. The council had to be consulted on all new legislation, and it could initiate legislation by calling

[120] Yves Bouthillier, *Le Drame de l'armistice,* 1. *Face à l'ennemi, face à l'allié* (Paris, 1950), 13; Lucien Mehl, "Die Zunahme des Personalbestandes im öffentlichen Dienst Frankreichs," in Carl Hermann Ule (ed.), *Die Entwicklung des öffentlichen Dienstes* (Berlin, München, Bonn, 1961).

[121] Maurice Duverger, *La Situation des fonctionnaires depuis la révolution de 1940* (Paris, 1941), 70 ff.; Andre Bisson, *Finances publiques françaises* (Paris, 1943), 271-72.

attention to matters that needed settlement in law. The prefectoral corps, whose group spirit was enlarged by the exceptional independence it enjoyed during the moment of the defeat, was given wider responsibility. Under the Third Republic, local branches of specialized agencies had increasingly dealt directly with Paris, bypassing the prefects. Now the law of 23 December 1940 restored to prefects the role of "sole representative of the state" in the departments, with every public servant except judges under their express control. As Interior Minister Pucheu told them in February 1942:

> They [the prefects] know that in the past the decay of our political institutions had bit by bit eroded the high character of their functions. Their role had been too degraded by temporary tasks of electioneering, without continuity, without grandeur. They know, too, how much you [Marshal Pétain] have insisted that their mission be restored in all its grandeur. And they have renounced with relief the game of short-run favors in order to consecrate all their force to the exercise of a supreme command.[122]

The regime also strengthened the authority of senior civil servants over the mass of lower civil servants. Public employees had been campaigning since before World War I for a "statute" regulating the conditions of their employment and recognizing the right to organize and strike. They got their Civil Service Statute on 15 October 1940, but action on this log-jammed issue had become possible only after the political climate had changed the meaning of such a step. Although civil service associations were recognized as legitimate, they were forbidden to strike or "demonstrate." Civil servants were required to show active support for the regime and were subordinated to more direct control by their superiors. Promotion by merit gained ground on promotion by seniority.[123] In general, Vichy freed the high civil

---

[122] Pierre Doueil, *L'Administration locale à l'épreuve de la guerre, 1939–49* (Paris, 1950), 283–85. Gaullist law professor René Cassin is mistaken in asserting that the Conseil d'Etat's role in preparing legislation was "a striking innovation" of the Fourth Republic. See his "Recent Reforms in the Government and Administration of France," *Public Administration* XXVIII:3 (Autumn 1950), 179–87.

[123] See the approving account of this legislation in Maurice Duverger, *La Situation des fonctionnaires depuis la révolution de 1940* (Paris, 1941).

servants from the threat of mass action by their subordinates and enhanced their personal authority. As a final sweetener, the high civil servants, whose pay had been increasing less rapidly than that of lower civil servants since World War I as salary pyramids generally grew more truncated, had hopes of reversing that trend.[124]

Public officials encroached upon new functions all the way down to the lowest level of local government, the 90 departments and the 36,000 communes of France. On 12 October 1940 elected departmental councils were replaced by appointed administrative councils. As for the communes, "amateur mayors" presiding in their spare time, wrote Francis Ripert of the law faculty at Aix in 1942, were no longer adequate to the demands of public affairs.[125] The greater a commune's degree of urbanization, the greater the need for expertise and the greater the risk of civil disturbance. The regime was also interested in dispersing that fortress of Third Republic radicalism, the mayors of southern towns. Paris and the other great cities had never enjoyed the 1884 democratization that made mayors elected instead of appointed officials. The law of 16 November 1940 returned to appointed mayors for all towns with a population over 2,000. Municipal councils in such communes were named from a list supplied by the new mayor, and, furthermore, elected municipal councils in smaller towns could be dissolved at the discretion of the prefect.

We need more local studies to discover just which municipal councils survived and which were dissolved, and which prewar mayors survived. But it seems a safe bet that Interior Minister Marcel Peyrouton's postwar explanations were special pleading. This was no Tocquevillian return to local-notable rule, "en père de famille," as he claimed, nor a move dictated entirely by the need of larger cities for technical administration "independent

---

[124] At the end of the nineteenth century, a Conseiller d'état received eight times as much as an auditeur de 2e classe just beginning his career in the Conseil d'Etat; in 1939 he received four times as much; in 1954 he received twice as much. On the "closing of the fan" of salaries, see Christian Chavanon, "Les Hauts Fonctionnaires," in *Aspects de la société française* (Paris, 1954), 165.

[125] Francis Ripert, "Le Régime administratif de la ville de Marseille," *Annales de la faculté de droit d'Aix,* Nouvelle Série No. 25 (1942).

from private interests." It was a purge of the Third Republic's local cadres. Later, after 7 August 1942 when Laval tried to have more former elected departmental councillors named to the appointed departmental council, some Third Republic departmental councillors reappeared in departments with formerly conservative majorities (in Brittany or the east) or where there was strong personal influence of a Vichy leader (as in Adrien Marquet's Gironde). By and large, however, the elected local officials of the classic Third Republic small-town Left—the radical and moderately socialist local schoolteachers, lawyers, and merchants who formed the "republic of pals" at the local level between the wars—either conformed or lost office.[126]

The march of "statism" was profoundly disturbing to the traditionalists at Vichy. The traditionalists had called for a restoration of the state's authority but not for an increase in its attributes. They wanted a stronger night-watchman state, not a leviathan; they wanted protection, not *dirigisme*.

Traditionalists as irreconcilable as Charles Maurras and Emmanuel Mounier thought that the National Revolution would reduce the number of state officials. The state shouldn't meddle in everything; it should be absolute within its narrow domain, but that domain should contract. A "deflation of the state" should accompany a "restoration of the sense of the state."[127] Equally disappointed were the businessmen who wanted corporatism to be a form of businessmen's self-regulation, and they complained bitterly at the economic constraints that tightened with every month. Anatole de Monzie saw the whole development as an inverted Jacobinism in which Vichy had simply replaced one set of masters by another. More naive and conspiratorially minded

[126] Pierre Doueil, *L'Administration locale à l'épreuve de la guerre, 1939–49* (Paris, 1950), 153 ff., has the most information. Some studies of local government were made for the conference on Vichy at the Institut des Sciences Politiques at Paris, March 1970, but have not yet been published.

[127] Charles Maurras, *La Seule France* (Paris, 1941), 167; René Gillouin, "Doctrine de l'état français," *Revue universelle*, 25 July 1941, 77–78; Emmanuel Mounier, "D'Une France à l'autre," *Esprit*, 8e année, no. 94 (Nov. 1940). The PSF leader Ybarnégaray expected a major purge of administrators, *Ministère public c/Ybarnégaray*, 31. See also Maurras' denunciation of a "biscornu et minutieux" statism in *Action française*, 27 August 1942.

men like Déat thought there had been a silent *coup d'état* by a secret society of "technocrats," which he linked to a Masonic sect called Synarchie.[128] There was no synarchic plot, but simply a clearer understanding by technical experts like Minister of Industrial Production Jean Denis Bichelonne that France's wartime economic management in a period of penury was going to lead to a postwar managed economy of plenty.[129]

The traditionalists were equally disappointed by the outcome of regionalism at Vichy. Most of the propaganda about regionalism came from the traditionalists. There was talk in 1940 and 1941 of restoring the ancient provinces destroyed in 1789 and of appointing a governor to each, thus restoring links to the organic past. Behind the rhetoric lay a design to displace both the Third Republic "pals" and the encroaching Paris bureaucrats by revived local notables.[130] Their efforts produced the nearest thing to a replacement of the department structure between the revolution and the Fifth Republic. The first committee of Pétain's National Council convened on 6 May 1941 to draft the new regional constitution. Lucien Romier, the historian, economic journalist, and close advisor to Pétain, was chairman. Although the committee was supposed to be "functionally representative," it was no cross section. No technical experts took part. One of the "farmers" was better known as Joseph de Pesquidoux of the Académie Française, the folklorist. There were also four conservative parliamentarians, a scattering of local government officials, two professors, and Charles Brun, "father of French regionalism," who had been propagandizing for regional reform since 1901. Emulating Napoleon in the Council of State, Marshal Pétain himself visited its sessions on 16 May. A plan appeared on 18 August 1941 to set up twenty provinces based on economic

[128] Anatole de Monzie, *La Saison des juges* (Paris, 1943). The best account of the origins and vagaries of the legend of Synarchie is Richard F. Kuisel, "The Legend of the Vichy Synarchy," *French Historical Studies* VI: 3 (Spring 1970), 365 ff.

[129] See *Conférence de M. Bichelonne, Ministre-Secrétaire d'état à la production industrielle et aux communications* (Paris, 1943) [BN 8⁰ L¹⁸ k.4003(4)].

[130] Félix Ponteil, *Les Classes bourgeoises et l'avènement de la démocratie* (Paris, 1966), 449, observes that regionalism had been a club to batter the "république des camarades" since the nineteenth century.

as well as historical considerations. Each province was to be run by a governor, assisted by an appointed "conseil des notables." Shades of the Duc de Broglie's "grand conseil" plan of 1874! Here we approach a genuine displacement of power from Paris-based administration to local notables.[131]

Words came from the National Council. Deeds, however, had already come from Admiral Darlan's government. Official regionalism was based firmly on technical considerations. Darlan created the new office of regional prefect on 19 April 1941 to cope with two pressing practical problems: order and the food supply. Order, already causing concern in the spring of 1941, seemed to require the exchange of information and the movement of motorized gendarmerie over a larger area than the 1791 department. Smoothly functioning food supply required some means of overcoming departmental chauvinism and hoarding and of planning food distribution on a broader regional scale. Each regional prefect, therefore, was flanked by two assistants, one for police and one for food supply. This change moved no functions from the center outwards. It simply added a new bureaucratic level more convenient for an age of faster travel and communication than had been available in 1791. As we shall see, the regional prefect arrangement was continued after the Liberation.[132]

The final bitter disappointment was Vichy's failure to realize its promise of stability and permanence. Failing to find any stable basis other than Pétain's symbolism, suffering increasingly from the blame the regime assumed for mounting hardships, ministries came and went at speeds even more dizzying than at the worst moments of the Third Republic. German orders accounted for far less of the turnover than was claimed after the war, when every Vichy participant's liberty or life depended upon proving that the Germans had thrown him out. Before the period of direct control in 1944, the Germans really removed

[131] *Le Temps,* 5 May 1941, contains a list of members and an outline of the committee's methods of operation. The committee's minutes have been used by Pierre Bancal, *Les Circonscriptions administratives de la France: leurs origines et leur avenir* (Paris, 1945), 258 ff.

[132] Pierre Doueil, *L'Administration locale à l'épreuve de la guerre, 1939–49* (Paris, 1950), 22–72, has the clearest sympathetic account. See also Brian Chapman, "A Development in French Regional Administration," *Public Administration* XXVIII:4 (Winter, 1950).

only Ambassador Léon Noel, General Weygand, possibly Xavier Vallat, and some of those most closely involved in Laval's fall on 13 December 1940: General de la Laurencie, Alibert, Peyrouton. The quarrels of factions, sometimes playing upon German aid, accounted for most of Vichy's transience. There were three major governmental shifts in the last half of 1940 (July 16, September 6, and December 13), two in 1941 (February and August), two in 1942 (April 18 and November), and two crises in 1943 (April and November). In the first year of Pétain's regime, there were four ministers of foreign Affairs, five ministers of the interior, five ministers of education, and six ministers of industrial production. Propaganda functions wore out particularly rapidly; there were fifteen ministers-secretaries of state for radio and eight for information between 1940 and 1944. One would have to turn to the most hectic years of the Third Republic for a comparable display of instability (1925–26, for example, or the early 1930's).

Authority there was, in the form of powerful police, inhibited public expression, and special courts. But in the sense of stable political structures, Vichy was worse than the "old regime." Awaiting the peace, forced to improvise, based on a fatal geopolitical miscalculation, Vichy became, in that vivid French expression, a basket of crabs.

Return to the Soil

The idiocy of rural life . . .

—*Karl Marx*

He takes a handful of that rich soil, full of air, which bears grain. It is good soil. He feels the goodness between his fingers.

—*Jean Giono* [133]

IT WAS AN ARTICLE OF FAITH AMONG FRENCH SOCIAL conservatives that self-supporting peasants made countries strong

[133] The Communist Manifesto, 1848; Jean Giono, *Regain* (Paris, 1930).

while city populations made them insecure. Fecund, practical, rooted in a traditional social hierarchy, the peasant family was the antidote to the decadent, abstract, rootless culture of city masses. Peasant battalions had snuffed out every revolution since June 1848. Peasant tenacity had, it was argued, won at Verdun. In the early 1930's when France seemed less subject to depression than Germany, Britain, and the United States, social conservatives like Lucien Romier gloried in the agrarian self-sufficiency that spared France the frantic swings of credit-based consumer economies.[134] Family agriculture, wrote Romier at about the same time, "assures better than anything else the duration of nations and societies." [135]

The vanishing peasant had been a subject for concern since the French census of 1891 revealed the steady decline of the rural population. Concern turned to alarm as Franco-German tensions called attention to the relative decline of Frenchmen as compared to Germans, and when the First World War scythed out the best of a whole generation. In the 1890's Maurice Barrès had already discovered that cities uproot young people while attachment to "la terre et les morts" solidified their character. After World War I, the novels and plays of Jean Giono praised primitive rural life as ennobling rather than stultifying. What Karl Marx, Honoré de Balzac, and Emile Zola had agreed was the "idiocy of rural life" now came to seem the fragile and precious fountainhead of a dwindling national vigor.[136]

Some of this sentimental rural nostalgia spent itself between the wars in a folkloric revival. Folklorists such as Joseph de Pesquidoux set out to revive local songs and dances, as Cecil Sharp had recently done in England. The youth hostel movement spread to France in 1929, at about the same time as several variants of the boy scout movement. Emotionally and symbolically, some of this rural nostalgia set itself against the Third Republic's urban style. "With him [Doriot]," wrote Pierre Drieu

[134] Lucien Romier, *Problèmes économiques de l'heure présente* (Montréal, 1933), 135, 170.

[135] Lucien Romier, *Plaisir de France* (Paris, 1932), 84, quoted in Pierre Barral, *Les Agrariens français de Méline à Pisani* (Paris, 1968), 201.

[136] Pierre Barral, 201-2, 260-63 has a good bibliography of literature praising rural life.

La Rochelle, "the France of camping-out will vanquish the France of the apéritif and party congresses."[137]

Some of this energy went beyond the folkloric to form a political force—peasantism. Insofar as agricultural interests had been organized before the First World War, it was a "syndicalisme des ducs,"[138] associations of large landowners, such as the aristocratic Société des Agriculteurs de France, headed by two generations of Marquis de Voguë, and the Union Centrale des Syndicats des Agriculteurs de France, closer to the republican Ministry of Agriculture. Between the wars, those who cultivated their lands themselves began to assume organized political weight for the first time. In particular, in 1934 the Union Nationale des Syndicats Agricoles (UNSA) came under the energetic leadership of Jacques Le Roy-Ladurie, son of a cavalry officer who had resigned at the time of the use of the French Army to carry out the separation of church and state in 1905 and who had turned to direct exploitation of a family property in Normandy. The UNSA became the major agricultural pressure group of the 1930's. No less large proprietors than their predecessors of the SAF, this new generation had a different tone. Often expertly trained in agronomy, they cultivated their own properties and took pride in the term *peasant,* solid landowners though they were.[139]

Peasantism also moved in the 1930's from traditional pressure-group activities to direct political action. The Parti Agraire et Paysan Français, founded in 1928, staged some major demonstrations in the early 1930's and managed to elect one deputy from the Vosges in 1932 and eight in 1936, mostly from the Massif Central. Henri Dorgères' Défense Paysanne mobilized widespread rural resentments in a form of direct political action

[137] Drieu la Rochelle in *L'Emancipation nationale,* 20 August 1937, quoted in Raoul Girardet, "Notes sur l'Esprit d'un fascisme français, 1934-39," *Revue française de science politique* V (1955), 533. Girardet gives many other examples of rural nostalgia. See also Robert Soucy, "The Nature of Fascism in France," *Journal of Contemporary History* (1966).

[138] The phrase is Pierre Barral's.

[139] Barral, 232, 241, describes the evolution by which the term *peasant* evolved from epithet in the nineteenth century to acceptance and even pride in the twentieth. Vichy propagandists liked to praise the great peasants of France from Jeanne d'Arc to Marshal Pétain.

much more clearly derived from fascist models: a private militia clad in green shirts, mottos such as "believe, obey, serve," and demonstrations promising to clean out the Parisian nest of bureaucrats. Dorgères claimed 400,000 members in 1939.[140]

The fundamental stimulus for the new peasant activism of the 1930's was, of course, the depression. French farmers were no more immune than any other farmers to the world decline in agricultural prices of the 1920's, the first warning signal for the downtown to follow. But having prospered and paid off mortgages during and after World War I, their resentment had the sharper edge of those who had known better times. Their activism in the 1930's, and much of its political language (such as the repeated demand that real cultivators replace Third Republic politicos at the Ministry of Agriculture) simply expressed agricultural depression in political terms, with a strong flavoring of typical 1930's antiparliamentarism.

The precise remedies proposed by agricultural spokesmen in the 1930's link them to a protectionist and cartelizing tradition with roots in the first great modern agricultural crisis of the 1870's–1890's. Like industrialists, French producers in the most heavily capitalized, market-oriented sectors of agriculture found ways to organize their markets against competition. Most striking was the case of the growers of sugar beets. The child of wartime application of chemistry to the search for a substitute for cane sugar during the Napoleonic Wars, sugar beet cultivation struggled after 1815, when trade with the cane-sugar producing Caribbean colonies was restored. During the depression, sugar beets won a government subsidy in 1884, however, and as production multiplied twentyfold between the 1840's and 1900, a scheme was worked out whereby the French government bought excess beet sugar for distillation into alcohol. This card-house of artificial prosperity was watched over by a special lobby founded just after World War I, the Confédération Générale des Planteurs de Betterave, headed vigorously by a professional lobbyist, Jean

---

[140] The two indispensable works on French agricultural politics in the 1930's are Pierre Barral, *Les Agrariens français de Méline à Pisani* (Paris, 1968), and Gordon Wright, *Rural Revolution in France* (Stanford, 1964).

Achard.[141] Anyone who has driven through the mournful plains of northern France can see the monuments to his success stretching as far as the eye can reach. But sugar beets are only one spectacular case. The winegrowers, having learned to organize to combat the American parasite *phylloxera* in the 1880's organized to control the market when cheap Algerian wines began to force prices down after 1906.[142]

Some types of agriculture lent themselves much more effectively to market organization than others. They also suffered more from price fluctuation. One thinks of heavily capitalized monoculture, cash crops such as wine and sugar beets. Others, like milk, meat, and wheat, could be organized only by bringing very large numbers of varied units into a control system. At the other extreme, family farms and such products as fruits and vegetables could hardly adapt to cartels and self-regulated markets at all.

One finds differing emphasis in the peasantist movements between the wars, therefore. An older generation tried to shore up the declining family farm, with the enthusiastic support of social traditionalists. Pierre Caziot, for example, an agricultural economist with a long career in the land bank (Crédit Foncier) and the Agriculture Ministry who claimed that his 30-hectare family farm in the Berri went back five or six centuries, began in 1920 to promote a government program for the "internal colonization" of rural France, to stem the peasant exodus by promoting new family farms. His book, *Solution du problème agraire: la terre à la famille paysanne* (1919), sought to "reconstitute the French agricultural population." In other words, his main aim was neither higher productivity nor organization of the market against overproductivity, but restoring a labor-intensive polyculture for reasons of social stability, at whatever cost

[141] John H. Clapham, *The Economic Development of France and Germany,* 4th ed. (Cambridge, 1951), 25–26, 69–70, 181, 194; Barral, 222, 230–31. Achard served Vichy as secretary of state for food supply, 1940–41.
[142] Charles K. Warner, *The Winegrowers of France and the Government since 1875* (New York, 1960). See an excellent brief account in Emmanuel Le Roy-Ladurie, *Histoire du Languedoc* (Paris, 1962).

to efficiency. His 1920 bill died in parliament more through inertia than opposition, but the idea persisted in interwar peasantism.[143]

On the other hand, the more highly capitalized, market-oriented proprietors turned to corporatism. The piecemeal cartels set up by winegrowers, sugar-beet growers, and wheat growers in the early twentieth century became models for a whole system of public organization, in which the growers themselves would control production and halt the ravages of free competition in a glutted world market. This was the approach of Jacques Le Roy-Ladurie's UNSA. In part, they demanded the protection of French agriculture from foreigners within and without, as Le Roy-Ladurie asked in Colonel de la Rocque's newspaper *Le Flambeau* as early as 1933.[144]

By the later 1930's, however, simple protectionism, by tariffs or quotas upon immigration or imports, no longer filled the bill. At the Congrès Syndical Paysan of 1937, Jacques Le Roy-Ladurie proposed a fully corporatist system in which the existing agricultural organizations (such as his own UNSA) would autonomously run French agriculture themselves "with the arbitration of the State" and with direct representation in a corporatist legislature, or "council of corporations." The peasantry, in such a corporatist state, would be the "first order in the nation." The theoretician of agrarian corporatism Louis Salleron pointed up the political implications of this program: agricultural organizations could remain as they were in the new scheme; it was the state that would have to change.[145]

This scheme promised two great advantages. The self-administered agricultural corporations, run by leading farmers themselves, could control the market, limit production, and avoid another world price collapse. They could also help keep social order. The language of "peasant unity," like the industrial corporatists' assertion that workers and managers in a single in-

---

[143] *Ministère public c/Caziot;* Barral, 199.
[144] Jacques Le Roy-Ladurie, "La Terre et ses défenseurs," *Le Flambeau,* 1 September 1933. I owe this reference to Mrs. Judith Wishnia.
[145] Barral, 235–36.

dustry had more in common than in conflict, was a device to help control rural conflicts between landowners and laborers by denying the existence of class.[146]

The Popular Front of 1936 had attempted to organize the grain market with the Office national du blé. The ONB attempted to reach a negotiated price for wheat through a system of councils and then applied that price in a regulated national grain market. But the program was too consumer-oriented and too statist for the proprietors and their professional organizations, and agricultural lobbyists such as Pierre Hallé for the Association des producteurs de blé and Jean Achard of the sugarbeet growers' syndicate remained closer to Jacques Le Roy-Ladurie's corporatist UNSA than ever. Defeat and occupation turned the French agricultural problem upside down: from overproduction to dearth.[147] At the same time, the Third Republic's discredit opened the way for the interwar peasantists to assume power. Third Republic political ministers of agriculture, like the perpetual Henri Queuille of the Radical party, were replaced by "experts"—men with a little horse manure on their boots and corporatist doctrines in their heads. It is typical of Vichy that the flamboyant, green-shirted Henri Dorgères, the most "fascist" in style of the interwar agrarians, was shunted into a relatively minor role in the Peasant Corporation while the interwar leaders of proprietors' groups and agricultural cartels took the major jobs.

In agriculture as in other social realms, the social traditionalists dominated the early days at Vichy. Pétain's 12 October 1940 speech on social policy described "family agriculture" as "the principal economic and social base of France." Pierre Caziot, who had failed twenty years earlier to persuade parliament to revive the family farm and who held parliamentary anarchy and the "automatic antipeasant reflex" of the "citadins" responsible for the long decline of peasant populations, was minister of agriculture until April 1942. With his Vercingetorix moustaches and

---

[146] Barral, 141, for example.
[147] Michel Cépède, *Agriculture et alimentation en France pendant la deuxième guerre mondiale* (Paris, 1961), is the basic work.

rural homilies, he seemed to personify the victory of peasant proprietors over bureaucrats (though he had been a civil servant as well as a farmer all his life). He welcomed the chance to govern without parliament. "Return to the soil" was officially promoted by granting subsidies to families who would restore abandoned farms. Other programs took up the cry, such as the Chantiers de la Jeunesse, which put every French young man in a rural work camp outside the noxious influence of cities for eight months of his twenty-first year.[148]

There were, of course, good practical reasons as well as reasons of social stability for promoting a large rural labor force at a time of scarcity, when millions of peasants were still held in German prisoner-of-war camps and when there was no fuel for the occasional French farm machine. Caziot could not reject the goal of efficient production altogether. The family farm was safe, but it could also improve its yield. Most important was the law of 9 March 1941 that made it easier to regroup scattered parcels of land into unified farms (*remembrement*). World War I had heightened interest in consolidation of scattered farm plots, but the law of 27 November 1918 required the association of at least two-thirds of the villagers concerned before lands could be transferred.[149] Caziot's law permitted consolidation by majority vote and gave the state a proposing role as well. This law was retained after the war with slight modifications, and the Commissariat du Plan used it to promote a major program to regroup 500,000 hectares in 1947 alone.[150]

In addition, Caziot's legislation eased credit for rebuilding farmhouses, modified inheritance laws to make it easier to pass a farm on intact to one son who wanted to farm it (antirepublicans had long accused the Napoleonic Code of hastening the breakup of family farms by requiring equal inheritance among sons), encouraged better education in agronomy, and encouraged tenants to make improvements by obliging the owner to

---

[148] See Barral, 258, and Caziot's own *Au service da la paysannerie* (Clermont-Ferrand, 1941).

[149] J. M. Jeanneney and M. Perrot, *Textes de droit économique et social français, 1789–1957* (Paris, 1957), 219–21, 233–34.

[150] Commissariat du Plan, *Rapport*, 1946, 121, 144.

reimburse the tenant for value added if the lease were ended (ending sixty years of agitation for this provision).[151]

In the end, whatever its contribution to consolidation of plots, rural education, and to home improvement, the Caziot regime failed in its essential purpose, which was to keep Frenchmen down on the farm. Only 1,561 families actually drew "return to the soil" subsidies, of whom 409 failed to make a go of it. A look at the agricultural statistics shows that the long secular population trend away from the countryside continued more rapidly than ever after the war, after the brief pause of the war years. The perfervid propaganda for the countryside aroused, as Gordon Wright observes, "more raillery than results." [152]

In agriculture, as in industry, the evolution at Vichy was away from nostalgia toward modernization and toward power for the well-organized and efficient. It should not be surprising that the directors of prewar agricultural cartels, in the most capitalized and easily organized sectors of French agriculture, such as Achard and Hallé, found important places at Vichy. Self-regulation by the major producers was the point of corporatism, in agriculture as in industry.

Although Pierre Caziot was on rather poor terms with leading corporatists such as Jacques Le Roy-Ladurie and Louis Salleron, he acquiesced when the interwar peasantist organizations rushed forward with a Peasant Charter that the government adopted and made law on 2 December 1940. The *charte paysanne* provided essentially what the more concentrated sectors of French agriculture had been working for since the 1870's, official public machinery embodying producers' self-regulation in an organized market. But the Peasant Corporation machinery was only gradually set up. Caziot quarreled with Louis Salleron, who was removed from office as one of the general delegates of the Peasant Corporation in September 1941, over the issue of bureaucratic control vs. corporatist self-regulation. Meanwhile, Caziot was losing the support of the German occupation authorities, who found him "old-fashioned," "reactionary" and "attentiste" (they thought he was close to Weygand, who was forced

[151] Barral, 258; Wright, 90–92.
[152] Barral, 258. For agricultural statistics, see chap. 5. Wright, 227.

out in November 1941).[153] When Laval set up his second government in April 1942, therefore, Jacques Le Roy-Ladurie became minister of both agriculture and food supply, an appointment praised by the German authorities.[154]

Although Le Roy-Ladurie had been an active corporatist before the war, food shortages and the rationing system required direct state intervention. The corporations became, in effect, machinery for state administration of the market. Thus what had begun as "peasantism" progressed through corporatism to state management of agriculture, with emphasis placed upon efficiency of production rather than upon encouragement of the family farm. If Caziot represents early Vichy traditionalism, the sugar-beet cartel lobbyist Achard represents the direction of future development. Vichy's evolution moved French agriculture toward its postwar pattern.

French farmers faced great difficulties during the occupation: 36 percent of the prisoners of war were farmers; the price of fertilizer went up; the few machines lacked fuel.[155] On the other hand, farmers had at hand the most precious commodity: food. They undoubtedly got more ready cash during the war than ever before, but there was nothing to spend it on. It was sufficient advantage to anger townspeople without permanently improving the farmer's position. The wave of the future was clearly with the big modern farm rather than old-fashioned polyculture, and that movement was foreshadowed in the evolution of political power at Vichy. The little farmer was destined to decline with the traditionalists who favored him. After the war, those who were willing to sacrifice productivity to social order had been reduced to a minority.[156]

[153] T-120/405/213883-85, 214039; T-120/5586H/E401104-8; Militär-befehlshaber in Frankreich, "Politische Lage in Frankreich," 4700/41g, 25 September 1941 (CDJC LXXV-98 ff.).

[154] It should be observed that Le Roy-Ladurie resigned in September 1942 after opposing Laval's labor draft and later fought in the *maquis*. He was acquitted by the Haute Cour in 1945.

[155] *Institut National de la Statistique et des Études Économiques, Le Mouvement économique de la France de 1938 à 1948* (Paris, 1950), 65, 67.

[156] See, e.g., Roland Maspiétol, *L'Ordre éternel des champs* (Paris, 1946). Wright, 89–90, notes the evolution of the corporatists away from protection toward productivity by the end of the war.

Escape from Class and Competition: Corporatism in Power

FRENCH BUSINESSMEN FELT BESIEGED ON TWO FRONTS between the wars: labor and competition. French labor made up in class spirit what it lacked in size and organization, and businessmen, always ready to fear the worst, mistook the giant, spontaneous, and good-humored sit-down strikes of May–June 1936 for the revolution of their nightmares. Simultaneously, slumped in the trough of the Great Depression, businessmen and political economists became convinced beyond question of "the fact of overproduction": modern industry had outrun the world's capacity to purchase.[157] The enormous vogue of corporatism among businessmen and political economists in the 1930's stemmed from that doctrine's promise to solve both problems at once. Behind corporatism's defensive earthworks, French business could escape from both the class struggle and merciless competition.[158]

Corporatism proposed that all levels of the economically active population—employers, managers, workmen—be organized into natural economic groupings (by branch of industry or profession) and that these natural "corporations" govern themselves and society. Thus the artificial authoritarian state and the chaotic liberal market would be replaced by self-regulating

---

[157] See Gaëtan Pirou, *Néo-libéralisme, néo-corporatisme, néo-socialisme* (Paris, 1939), 23, and Lucien Romier works in footnotes 136–37.

[158] The 1930's French literature of corporatism is immense. The most articulate statements come from professors of law, especially at Paris. See Francois Perroux, *Capitalisme et communauté de travail* (Paris, 1938); Gaëtan Pirou, *Essais sur le corporatisme* (Paris, 1938). Among businessmen, see Auguste Detoeuf, *Passé, présent, et avenir de l'organisation professionnelle en France* (Paris, 1946). Most writers on corporatism were professors of economics in law faculties: François Perroux, Gaëtan Pirou, Louis Baudin, Maurice Bouvier-Ajam, François Olivier-Martin. See also Matthew H. Elbow, *French Corporatist Theory, 1789–1948* (New York, 1953).

"natural" groups. Artificial class groupings that emphasized conflicting interests, such as labor unions and employers' associations, would be replaced by "natural" economic units whose members all shared a common interest in the success of their product. Each economic unit would harmonize its own productive capacity with the needs of the market, and the chaos of the liberal market place would give way to the organized exchange of goods. Liberalism was dead, but a "third way" was available between the two competing statisms: fascism and socialism.

One root of corporatism was the desire to get rid of the class struggle. Denying that class conflict reflected an intrinsic inescapable clash of interests between those who own machines and tools and those who have only their muscles, the corporatists insisted on the community of economic interests within each profession, industry, or trade. Class struggle, corporatists believed, was an artificially aroused conflict. If workers and employers were organized along lines that emphasized their common interests and prevented agitators from organizing them along class lines, the class struggle would vanish. Faith in the natural harmony of interests, it should be noted, derived not from conservative doctrines of social inequality and hierarchy as in de Maistre and Bonald, but from the Enlightenment doctrines of Adam Smith and such nineteenth-century successors as J. B. Say, and the Radical Léon Bourgeois' "Solidarism." Thus they could clothe regressive legislation, such as the abolition of trade unions, in the language of nineteenth-century liberals.

The other root of corporatism was the flight from competition. In a sense, the French economy had never functioned along classical liberal lines. Indeed, had any? Mercantilist state enterprises (glass, Gobelins tapestries, armaments) survived into the nineteenth century, when they were joined by government-supported industry in the industrial revolution (railroads, beet sugar) to form a substantial bloc of subventioned enterprises. In addition, tariff protection was the rule rather than the exception in the nineteenth century (free trade lasted less than twenty years after Napoleon III's trade treaties of 1860). In France laissez-faire had historically applied mostly to employer-worker relationships.

But subventions and protection were not enough to muffle the blows of competition upon industrialists and major agricultural producers, especially after the free trade agreements of 1860 and the depression of the 1870's. Those industries sufficiently concentrated (usually the most modern, capital-intensive sectors) to permit organization began in the 1870's to restrict competition by ententes and cartels. Everyone would have preferred to escape competition; highly concentrated producers were actually in a position to do so. The Comité des forges (1864) was a precursor to what became the normal escape mechanism for European businessmen.[159]

The financial and economic disorders of the post-World War I Europe produced a steep increase in industrial ententes, which then became nearly universal in the 1930's. In practice, French governments left the initiative for producers' associations in private hands, and by tacit consent, those industries that could organize themselves effectively did so. There were probably over 2,000 ententes or agreements among producers setting prices or conditions of sale for their products by 1939, and some 60 international cartels to which French industry belonged. By 1939 the French economy was still "liberal"—i.e., with market forces beyond the control of individual firms or groups of firms—only in those fragmented or primitive sectors where there were unmanageable masses of producers or distributors.[160]

Corporatism simply suggested that these cartels, organizations, and ententes be made universal and official. Indeed, in the reigning climate of skepticism about the usefulness of parliament in economic matters, corporatists believed that such "natural" economic groups should themselves compose a legislature, or council of corporations. Even during the Third Republic, for example, the Marchandeau bill of 1935 had proposed that all sectors of industry and business organize to prevent overproduction and further price decline.

[159] See Roger Priouret, *Origines du patronat français* (Paris, 1963), and André François-Poncet, *La Vie et l'oeuvre de Robert Pinot* (Paris, 1927), for lack of something better on the Comité des Forges.
[160] For French participation in cartels, see Frank A. Haight, *A History of French Commercial Policies* (New York, 1941), 198–203; Ervin Hexner, *International Cartels* (Chapel Hill, N.C., 1945), 136, 138.

After the defeat, corporatists had a free hand. But there were three possible directions in which industrial organization could move. There might be mixed councils of working men and managers at every level of each corporation, a genuine worker participation in the administration of his branch of industry. Or corporatism could merely provide a camouflage for what was really self-regulation by the most powerful industrial owners in their own sole interest. Finally, corporatism might become subordinated to a planned statism in which bureaucrats set industrial production goals, allocated resources, and placated competing interests.

At the beginning there seemed to be a genuine possibility of bending corporatism to the first pattern. The first minister of industrial production was René Belin, a telephone workers' union official who had worked his way up to become deputy secretary-general of the Confédération génerale du travail by 1933, second only to Léon Jouhaux. He was simultaneously minister of labor. Belin's abhorrence of war reconciled him to the armistice position, and as an old syndicalist distrustful of parliamentary parties and more interested in creating a new society upon building blocks of local labor associations than in electoral politics, he saw opportunities for syndicalist progress within corporatism. Although most of the CGT subsequently became a backbone of the Resistance, much of organized labor seems to have been ready for a while to continue its wartime self-restraint and work for a syndicalist program of "free unions in organized professions" within the new regime.[161]

This was the period, it should be noted, in which the Vichy regime sounded most hostile to unregulated liberal capitalism. Marshal Pétain's major address on social policy of 12 October 1940, denouncing liberal capitalism as a foreign import that had

---

[161] The CGT leaders' offers of cooperation in the summer and fall of 1940 are stressed by Georges Lefranc, *Les Expériences syndicales en France de 1939 à 1950* (Paris, 1950), 37–40. Lefranc, who was Belin's *chef de cabinet,* claims that the Jouhaux group of the CGT, in a meeting at Toulouse on 20 July 1940, proposed a "French Community of Labor" and joint worker-management councils and that they offered to replace strikes with arbitration and to suppress the mention of class struggle in the CGT statutes.

been "degraded" by 1939 into "enslavement to the powers of money," promised a "hierarchial and social regime" that would "guarantee the dignity of the worker's person by ameliorating his conditions of life all the way to old age." It was drafted by Gaston Bergery, whose "frontist" movement in the late 1930's was a curious antiparliamentary, anticapitalist appeal for national unity against communism and against "the trusts." [162] Bergery as well as Catholic traditionalists had long proposed a revision of the 1867 law creating the limited liability corporation, or *société anonyme*. Jean Le Cour Grandmaison, Xavier Vallat, and other leaders of the Fédération Nationale Catholique had actually proposed to abolish limited liability in a March 1938 bill, while Bergery preferred to make the president of each company fully responsible for all he possessed in case of bankruptcy. Georges Bonnet proposed to limit the number of corporate directorships an individual could hold. These prewar currents triumphed in a law of 13 September 1940 increasing the personal responsibility of the president of a corporation in case of bankruptcy and limiting to two the number of companies of which one person could be a director. Although Yves Bouthillier claimed after the war that this was an alternative to nationalization (which was never dreamt of at Vichy), it was actually a moralistic attack on traditional grounds against alleged irresponsibility and corruption behind the screen of corporate limited liability.[163]

Other traditionalists hoped to go even further in dismantling

---

[162] Bergery's newspaper *La Flèche* carried a masthead appeal "for the gathering of all who want to liberate France from the tyranny of money and the interference of foreign governments." I have not been able to consult the thesis on Bergery by Michèle Cotta at the Institut des Sciences Politiques in Paris. Bergery sounds objectively fascist, but he denounced fascism for seeking "scapegoats in war-mongering and racism." *La Flèche*, no. 133, 26 August 1938. Bergery wound up as Vichy ambassador to the Soviet Union.

[163] For background, see Gaston Bergery, "Vers une réforme des sociétés," *La Flèche*, no. 112, 1 April 1938, 5; Yves Bouthillier's *exposé de motifs* for the law, in *France Nouvelle: Actes et paroles du maréchal Pétain*, 90–91, may be compared with his explanations in *Le Drame de l'armistice* (Paris, 1950), 11, 299–301. See also Georges Ripert, "Une nouvelle réforme des sociétés par actions," *Revue générale du droit commercial*, 5e année (1943), 89–108. The law was considerably softened on 16 November 1940.

the modern urban and industrial world. Pétain had not been afraid to say on 12 October 1940 that the family farm was the "principal economic and social base of France." Traditionalist social philosophers close to Pétain like Gustave Thibon and René Gillouin, at whom we shall look more closely in chapter 3, argued that France was being punished in 1940 for having departed from the balanced, individualist craft and peasant world that had made her both happy and great. On the inspiration of such ideas, Vichy took steps to revive artisan skills. Unemployment provided a practical justification, but the social dream of the traditionalists was also at work. René Gillouin, who believed that a strong *artisanat* gave a nation balance and social order, seems to have forgotten that proud artisans struggling against mechanical competition were the shock troops of nineteenth-century revolution. The regime preferred to think that "artisans represent old France, the France which had a taste for work, the sense of saving, and the sentiment of the family." By the end of 1942, therefore, the government had resettled about two hundred artisans in the French provinces. Education programs emphasized the value of handwork anew. Finally, a host of individual initiatives flourished in this climate. The Jewish essayist Daniel Halévy assisted in the reestablishment of the old artisan brotherhood, the Compagnonnages de France, whose revived headquarters one may still visit in the narrow streets just behind the Hôtel de Ville. General Jean de Lattre de Tassigny used his troops and some students from the University of Strasbourg to rebuild a deserted village, "Opme," near Clermont-Ferrand.[164]

In the atmosphere of verbal hostility to big business, it was possible to think that labor would win a participating role in the new coordinated economy. In fact, every important decision about establishing corporatism turned in favor of business. Pétain had promised to outlaw strikes and lockouts in his 12 October speech. On 9 November 1940, all economic interest

---

[164] René Gillouin, *J'Etais l'ami du maréchal Pétain* (Paris, 1968), 220–22; Marius Coulon, *L'Artisan devant l'impôt* (Lille, 1943), 105; Jacques Desmarest, *La Politique de la main-d'oeuvre en France* (Paris, 1946), 142; Alain Silvera, *Daniel Halévy* (Ithaca, N.Y., 1966), 201; Robert O. Paxton, *Parades and Politics at Vichy* (Princeton, N.J., 1966), 194.

groups, whether of workers or employers, were dissolved. Local unions continued to survive (except civil servants' unions), but the national structures of the CGT and the Christian unions (CFTC) were abolished. The workers' right to organize had been set back to before the 1884 law permitting labor unions.

The employers' association, the Confédération Générale du Patronat Français, was of course also dissolved in this seemingly evenhanded measure. The previous August 16, however, each branch of industry and trade had been authorized to set up an Organization Committee (Comité d'Organisation), a planning group designed to be the building block of the corporatist "coordinated" economy. Each Organization Committee was empowered to make a census of the capacity of all enterprises in that sector of the economy, assess stocks, close down some enterprises, allocate scarce resources, fix conditions of operation and quality of products, and propose price schedules to the government. Its operations were financed by a levy on participating companies. The members were appointed by the minister of industrial production. While the old syndicalist René Belin was minister, one might have expected some care in appointments. After February 1941, however, representatives of heavy industry (Pucheu, Lehideux) held the ministry of industrial production. The personnel of prewar trade and industrial associations reappeared in the Organization Committees. The goverment had a major influence in the presence of a government delegate and in the fact that the last word in allocation of raw materials remained with government Allocation Committees (*comités de répartition*). Insofar as Organization Committees eventually applied the war economy to some 321 branches of French business, however, corporatism meant self-regulation by businessmen themselves.[165]

---

[165] H. W. Ehrmann, *Organized Business in France* (Princeton, N.J., 1957), has worked out the continuity of personnel between prewar trade and industry associations and the Organization Committees. The basic work from a more legal point of view is J. G. Mérigot, *Essai sur les comités d'organisation* (Paris, 1943). See also Robert Catherine, *L'Economie de répartition* (Paris, 1943). A similar conclusion is drawn by Léon Liebmann, "Entre le mythe et la légende: 'L'anti-capitalisme' de Vichy," *Revue de l'Institut de Sociologie* (Institut Solvay), 1964, 110–48. While the Germans did block the creation of an organization committee in the aircraft indus-

The Organization Committees had no trade union counterpart. Although there were supposed to be labor organizations within corporatism, and labor participation on various committees, these lacked the main guarantee of independence: the right to strike. Moreover, they were much slower to be formed. The Charter of Labor, promised by Pétain in his one speech to factory workers, at Saint-Etienne on 1 March 1941, finally saw the light only on 4 October 1941, fourteen months after the Organization Committees had been set up. It followed nearly a year of secret tugging and hauling at Vichy, between the Vichy syndicalists like Belin on the one hand, and cabinet members determined to root out unionism on the other. We have only the word of Georges Lefranc and Belin about the parallel worker organizations, the single but voluntary official labor union, and the workers' participation at the unit of production which they envisaged. The final document, which Belin did not in fact sign (he had been only minister of labor since February 1941), forbade strikes and unions above the regional level and provided for worker participation only in some vague "social committees" (*comités sociaux*) at the local level. Their function was to "discipline" their members and to represent them in such matters as recreation and pension funds. No "political" function (dirty word to corporatists) was permitted.[166] Despite its stated concern for labor welfare and its injunctions of charity upon entrepreneurs, the Charter of Labor was clearly designed to break the back of trade unions in France.

Insofar as some local mixed committees were in fact set up, Vichy carefully divided them three ways instead of two so that workers were in a permanent minority. Seizing upon the unions of "cadres" (engineers, middle management) that had sprung up during the depression, corporatists included them as a separate third category in mixed committees. However bitterly the unionized managers and technicians had quarreled with em-

---

try, preferring to deal more freely with individual companies (see *DFCAA,* IV, 68–72), the main motive in creating the Committees was corporatism and not anti-German obstructionism.

[166] Georges Lefranc, *Les Expériences syndicales,* chap. 4. *Ministère public c/Belin.* The author was also able to hear M. Belin discuss these matters in March 1970.

ployers n the late 1930's, they had even less in common with labor.[167]

It is not surprising, therefore, that most workmen and especially union personnel were quick to go into opposition. Christian Pineau of the CFTC was distributing a mimeographed underground leaflet in the north by November 1940. The Jouhaux group in the CGT was clearly in opposition by early 1941. Even initially friendly observers like the former deputy of the Lot, Anatole de Monzie, complained about "this mercantile feudalism," and Marshal Pétain had to promise in his 12 August 1941 speech to check abuses within the Organization Committees.[168]

Corporatism did not, however, mean that businessmen's chosen representatives managed the economy as they wished. There were conflicting interests within corporatism. On one level, the interests of large and small businesses were not always identical, especially in a war economy. Traditionally the two had agreed to shelter from competition: big industry was happy to conform to the conditions of less efficient colleagues, in the famous "Malthusianism" denounced by critics of interwar French productivity. Under conditions of penury, however, differences arose. Who would get raw materials, labor, contracts with Germany, electricity? Which plants would be shut down in the interests of efficiency?

On another level, there was a conflict of power between businessmen and bureaucrats. Conservatives had wanted a regime that was "authoritarian but not statist"[169] or, in other words, an economy run by businessmen. Upper civil servants preferred the impartial and expert control of highly trained bureaucrats like themselves.

---

[167] On manager-technicians' unionism in the 1930's and under corporatism, see Pierre Almigeon, *Les Cadres de l'industrie et notamment dans la métallurgie* (Paris, 1943), 140 ff. This doctoral thesis, directed by Edouard Dolléans, stresses the bitterness of managers and technicians in the face of "leveling" salaries and "déclassement" in the late 1930's.

[168] *La Saison des juges,* 108. Minister of Industrial Production Lehideux announced plans in September 1941 to prosecute officials of *Organization Committees* who acted in the interests of trusts. Ministère de l'Intérieur, *Informations générales,* no. 53 (2 September 1941), 625. I owe this reference to Professor Richard F. Kuisel.

[169] *Le Flambeau,* 18 July 1936.

These interlocking disputes were both settled in favor of bigness and state power. Successive ministers of industrial production were increasingly interested in efficiency and productivity. René Belin (June 1940–February 1941), who was interested in restoring full employment, gave way to Pierre Pucheu, former official of the steel cartel (February–June 1941), who was replaced in turn by François Lehideux, Louis Renault's nephew. This was a movement toward those sympathetic to rationalization, concentration, and modernization. Three automobile firms produced almost all the French cars; textiles and shoes, by contrast, were produced by thousands of firms of varying efficiency. Policy plus wartime exigencies helped carry things in the direction of the automobile pattern and away from the textile pattern.

François Lehideux was genuinely interested in rationalizing an outmoded French industrial system and organizing European business specifically against what Jean Jacques Servan-Schreiber twenty-eight years later called "le défi américain." With Colonel Thönissen of the German automobile industry, when he was still head of the Organization Committee for the automobile industry, Lehideux discussed plans for combining French-German-Italian automobile production to reach "world supremacy." As delegate for national equipment, he produced a Ten-Year Plan for National Equipment, forerunner at least in spirit of the Monnet Plan for ordered national investment in basic productive plant. Finally, as minister of industrial production, he passed, on 17 December 1941, a law permitting inefficient firms to be closed.[170]

The statists and rationalizers certainly held all the cards. German policy in the Occupied Zone was ever more ruthless in

[170] For an expression of Lehideux' desire to organize Europe "en face du bloc américain," see François Lehideux, "La Lutte contre le chômage," Ecole Libre des Sciences Politiques, *Conférences d'information*, no. 1, 7 February 1941. The plans with Colonel Thönissen are found in *Ministère public c/Lehideux*, 16, 31, and are referred to in Auswärtiges Amt, Richtlinien Pol. II, Bundle 5/1: "Kartel Frankreich, M-Z" (T-120/5584H/E401074 ff.). For the Ten-year plan and 17 December 1941 law, in addition to the trial, see *Le Temps*, 5 and 15 May 1941, and Lehideux' own statement in Hoover Institution, *France during the German Occupation, 1940–44* (Stanford, Calif., 1959), I, 36–38.

diverting raw materials and electricity away from inefficient firms or firms not producing vital materials for them. Furthermore, they closed plants in France in order to free labor to work in Germany, at least until Albert Speer reversed German policy in 1943 and tried to raise French productivity at home. In the unoccupied zone, tight state control over the Allocation Committees and the law of 17 December 1941 both worked in the same direction. One can read the growing despair of small businessmen in the diary of their lobbyist at Vichy, Pierre Nicolle. He saw, rather simplistically, the triumph of "anonymous bureaucracy" and "international Synarchy."[171] France was being dragged through the occupation in the direction of concentrated industry and rationalization. The 1930's emphasis upon preventing overproduction was already giving way to the postwar emphasis upon seeking higher productivity. Corporatism had become central planning and *dirigisme*.

These developments reached their height during 1943, when Laval's minister of industrial production, Bichelonne, struck a happy partnership with Hitler's new economic tsar, Albert Speer. Bichelonne was one of the few people at Vichy to perceive clearly that wartime planning was more than a temporary necessity. He looked forward, as an engineer and a bureaucrat, to the application of planned state direction to the postwar economy. Speer, his equal in youth, bookish brilliance, and political naïveté, reversed the policies of Goering and Sauckel in 1943 in order to increase French production at home, away from Allied bombing, instead of bringing French workers to Germany. One more tool for combing out the inefficient was created. Major industries producing for Germany were designated *S-Betriebe* (Speer factories), and their workers were exempted from the German labor draft. Laval found this as politically useful as Bichelonne found it economically satisfying. The future was with bigness and the state.[172]

[171] Pierre Nicolle, *Cinquante mois d'armistice. Vichy, 2 Juillet 1940–26 août 1944. Journal d'un témoin* (Paris, 1947), I, 305, 372, 374. Nicolle worked for the organized "Petites et Moyennes Entreprises."

[172] Bichelonne's views of the postwar economy are most clearly expressed in his preface to Robert Catherine, *L'Economie de répartition* (Paris, 1943). The Germans were convinced of his will to Franco-German

From Persuasion to Constraint: The Emerging Police State

The National Revolution has boiled down to the social advancement of the gendarmerie.

—Anatole de Monzie [173]

NO ONE EXPECTED THE ARMISTICE REGIME TO BE SOFT. The republic had already suspended a number of civil liberties at the start of the war in 1939. Under the provisions of a "state of siege," the army assumed the supervision of order in the departments and the judicial system was modified. The Communist party, technically Hitler's ally since the Nazi-Soviet Pact of August 21, was dissolved on September 26, its newspapers shut down and its political leaders expelled from parliament the following January. [174] The post of minister of propaganda was created, and the republic entrusted the business of wartime control of opinion first to playwright Jean Giraudoux and then to Jean Prouvost, textile magnate and newspaper owner. Vichy carried all of these republican emergency devices further and accepted their authoritarian implications more frankly. [175]

The new regime wanted to be loved as well as feared, however. An immense amount of Vichy effort went into group ac-

---

economic integration (see T-120/5584H/E401074). For the Speer-Bichelonne agreements of December 1943, see *Ministère public c/Chasseigne,* 114; Alan S. Milward, "German Economic Policy Towards France, 1942–44," in D. C. Watt, *Studies in International History* (London, 1967), who finds Bichelonne and Speer "kindred spirits"; and Speer's own memoirs. Bichelonne left neither trial records nor memoirs. The only technocratic minister to hang on even after Pétain's move to Germany in August 1944, he died in Germany in December 1944.

[173] *La Saison des juges* (Paris, 1943).

[174] *J.O., Lois,* 27 September 1939, 11,770. Moscow and Vichy revived diplomatic relations after the armistice and continued them until the German attack on the Soviet Union in June 1941.

[175] On propaganda at Vichy, see Philippe Amaury, *Les deux premières expériences d'un Ministère d'Information en France (1939–49)* (Paris, 1969), and the forthcoming work on Marcel Marion by Graham Thomas.

tivities and ceremonial designed to generate public fervor. Its style was the very antithesis of that prickly refractoriness to group discipline personified in Third Republic folk heroes like Marcel Pagnol's Marseilles cafetier César or the Chaplin of *Modern Times*. Frenchmen had not designed public ceremonies with such didactic zeal since David worked for the Committee of Public Safety, nor marched in such a profusion of uniforms since the Second Empire of Napoleon III. Jean Guéhenno, coming down from occupied Paris into the Vichy zone for the first time in 1942, found it

> a strange land, a sort of principality where everyone from children of six on up, regimented into groups from "Youth" to "Veterans," wearing Francisques or symbols of the Legion, seemed to be in uniform. Where is France? [176]

Vichy ceremonial and group spirit were firmly in the hands of traditionalists. Their symbols were clerical, rural or artisan, and patriotic. Masses in the Church of St. Philippe at Vichy, parades of the tatterdemalion Armistice Army, schoolgirls lisping "Maréchal, nous voilà," young artisans with an elaborate wooden scale model of Chartres Cathedral, athletic contests among youth groups—all had some vision of *la Vieille France* behind them. Vichy's techniques of mass enlistment owed something to a Jacobin-Napoleonic tradition and something to contemporary totalitarian practice, but in detail there was an air of the old-fashioned village fête that no one could mistake for a Nazi party rally.

Persuasion might well have kept the regime above water if its major assumption, an early peace, had been proven right. At the very beginning, acquiescence was normal. A handful of prominent Gaullists were tried in absentia by court-martial without incident. Everyone commented on how well the German troops behaved (they were shot by German courts-martial if they didn't). What a relief that was, especially given the fear of disorder in the nearly abandoned cities of the north and east. Among Frenchmen, while the number of

[176] Jean Guéhenno, *Journal des années noires* (Paris, 1947), 17 July 1942.

criminal cases increased between 1940 and 1944, suicides declined strikingly, as they usually do in times of national emergency.[177]

But there was no peace. Instead, the makers of the National Revolution plunged unexpectedly down a darkening tunnel of extending war, tightening occupation, rising resistance, and finally, renewed combat on French soil. These somber developments exposed Vichy's initial miscalculations and deepened material want. As popular support and acquiescence fell away, constraint replaced persuasion.

In any chronological account of Vichy, June–August 1941 should rank as a major turning point, perhaps more significant than the more standard 13 December 1940. The Communist party's shift from "neither Pétain nor de Gaulle" to active resistance after Hitler's attack on June 22, 1941, committed the party's underground capacities to the Allied side. The party's pent-up militancy burst forth in a series of assassinations that brought the law-and-order question to a head in the last half of 1941. Eventually, the Communists worked more closely with the Gaullists, but in the first anguished months of the German blitzkrieg in the east, terror was the order of the day. It called forth a German counterterror, with Vichy rushing to keep up.

Terrorist acts against the occupation authorities climbed steeply after June 1941. Colonel Hans Speidel, chief of staff of the German military command in Paris (and later West German NATO commander), reported 54 acts of sabotage in July 1941, 73 in August, 134 in September, and 162 in October, a figure not to be reached again until May 1942.[178] Among them were a number of spectacular assassinations. The first German soldier killed in France after the armistice was the naval cadet Moser, shot in the subway station of Barbès-Rochechouart in Paris on 21 August 1941. He was followed by the NCO Hoffman, shot in the Gare de l'Est on 3 September, an army major and a

[177] Ministère de la justice, *Compte général de l'administration de la justice civile et commerciale et de la justice criminelle*, Années 1944–47 (Melun, n.d.), xvii–xxii, xxiv.
[178] Lageberichte des Verwaltungsstabs (Centre de documentation juive contemporaine, Paris, dossier LXXV).

civilian official shot in Bordeaux on October 22, and—highest-ranking of all—the Feldkommandant of Nantes on October 20. The Germans reacted with exemplary ferocity. Taking common-law prisoners and Communists already in jail as hostages, they shot them in large batches as various deadlines passed without the capture of the assassins. By October 25, six hundred French hostages were threatened, and over a hundred had been shot, 50 at Bordeaux, 48 in one group at Nantes: the most massive execution there since the Representative-on-Mission Carrier's mass drownings in 1793. "The students of my school are devastated," wrote Jean Guéhenno. "The horror overwhelms us."[179]

In the face of this horror, Marshal Pétain proposed to present himself at the Demarcation Line at Moulins at 2 P.M. on October 25 as a hostage, considering himself a prisoner until the Germans responded to his protest. Interior Minister Pucheu showed Pétain's draft speech to Abetz the night of the 24th, and although Ribbentrop dismissed the whole scheme as a bluff, Abetz urged the suspension of further executions. Pétain's bluff was not called, but Vichy was under intense pressure to stop French terrorism itself.[180]

The Darlan government had already begun to react in August to the rise in Resistance terrorism with the busiest burst of legislation since the first days. This time, however, the theme was order and not the National Revolution: a sign of evolving priorities. "Special Sections" of the departmental courts-martial were set up under a new law empowering the government to act with exceptional rigor against "Communists and anarchists." Justice Minister Barthélemy asked the Cours d'Appel to choose

---

[179] Abetz gives the figure of 600 in his telegram No. 3325 from Paris, 25 October 1941 (T-120.405/213950 ff); Jean Guéhenno, *Journal des années noires* (Paris, 1947), 24 October 1941, 25 October 1941.

[180] Although this bizarre gesture was first revealed in Du Moulin de Labarthète's *Le Temps des illusions* (Geneva, 1946), a book as tendentious as it is delightful, it is verified in German telegrams. See especially Abetz (Paris) 3325 of 25 October 1941 (T-120/405/213950–52) and a report by Walter Schellenberg on 10 November 1941 (T-120/685/259187–88). Schellenberg says Pucheu ridiculed the plan of General Laure and Du Moulin, but he thought the Germans should be informed so that they would grasp the intensity of the French reaction.

judges "known for the firmness of their character and for their total devotion to the state" for the civilian component of these courts, applied the new procedures retroactively to current cases, and singled out the "Third International" as the "first-ranking target." [181]

Laws regulating political meetings were extended to cover private meetings as well as public ones. The decision was taken to start publishing the names of prominent Freemasons in the *Journal officiel*. The pay of deputies and senators was stopped and the two chambers' permanent bureaux dissolved. The oath to Marshal Pétain was now required of military officers, judges, high civil-service officials. Darlan solidified his control of the military by reestablishing the Ministry of National Defense. A few sops were thrown to public opinion. "Commissaires du pouvoir," roving ombudsmen, were created to check up on bureaucratic abuses. The government promised to change the Organization Committees to blunt charges that businessmen were profiting from the guided economy. Food Supply Minister Achard was replaced by Paul Charbin, a Lyons silk manufacturer. Pétain created the Francisque, an emblem combining a Gallic axe and a marshal's baton, to reward loyal service. Finally, on September 10, another special court—the Tribunal d'Etat—was created to "permit the state to strike wherever acts occur which endanger its unity and security." It was designed to "escape" the limitations of the penal laws by giving the state a weapon against the planners and helpers of terrorism as well as against the actual perpetrators, and it had the power to execute an immediate death sentence without any recourse to the appeals court.[182]

Marshal Pétain set the tone of the new program by a radio address on August 12, the day the new legislation appeared in the *Journal officiel*.

---

[181] Ministère de la Justice, *Bulletin officiel,* 1941, 99–102. In the Occupied Zone, where there were no courts-martial, a "Section Spéciale" was attached to the Paris Cour d'Appel. *Ministère public c/Dayras*. See also Guy Raïssac, *Combat sans merci* (Paris, 1966), 327 *n*.

[182] Most of this legislation is found in *Journal officiel*, 12 August 1941, 3364–67, and 16 August 1941, 3438, 3450. See also *Le Temps*, 11 September 1941.

I have grave things to tell you. From several regions of France, I have felt an ill wind rising for some time. . . . The authority of my government is contested; its orders are poorly executed. . . . A genuine malaise is gripping the French people.

Pétain's speech, the press, Justice Minister Barthélemy's orders to the courts, all firmly identified opposition to regime in August 1941 with communism.

The crisis of August 1941 also shows how the armistice entrapped the Vichy regime into ever closer complicity with German repression. Germans were not the only victims. Former Vice-Premier Laval and Marcel Déat were injured by a would-be assassin at Versailles on August 29, and Marcel Gitton, former secretary-general of the Communist party who had followed Doriot into fascism, was shot on September 5. Furthermore, all the assassinations took place in the Occupied Zone. The issue of French sovereignty there, promised in Article 3 of the armistice but never effectively exercised by Vichy, came to a head also. Pétain had promised in his 25 June 1940 speech that "France will be administered only by Frenchmen." Now, over a year later, with the government still holed up in a southern mountain spa, it was more urgent than ever to seize every opportunity to re-establish French administrative sovereignty in the Occupied Zone. The Germans were demanding that the French find the assassins of its soldiers—a tempting chance to increase French police authority in the Occupied Zone. But they were also executing innocent men as hostages. Should Vichy get involved?

Justice Minister Barthélemy, professor of law dating back to precorporatist laissez-faire days, wanted Germany to choose and sentence hostages if anyone did, not French courts. Interior Minister Pierre Pucheu—steel executive and former militant in La Rocque's Croix de Feu and then Doriot's PPF—whose anti-communism was as single-minded as his care for legal niceties was slight, saw a chance to "take the police [of the Occupied Zone] back into our own hands." Pucheu was also concerned about the random nature of the German hostages. In French hands, only Communists would be killed; the Germans were using anyone as hostages, including youths caught sneaking across the Demarcation Line and even, at Nantes, three members of the Legion, as he complained to Abetz on November 6.[183]

Pucheu's view carried more weight, and the French government tried to execute enough people itself to get the Germans to stop. The Paris "Special Section" was hurried into existence on August 23 in time to sentence three Communists to death for infraction of the decree of 26 September 1939 dissolving the party (Bréchet, Tzebrucki, and René Bastard). But the German taste for vengeance was not slacked by such paltry numbers. In November Pucheu also produced a Communist terror group headed by an Alsatian Jew who he said had carried out the Nantes assassination, but one never knows how accurate the police are when they need an accused so badly. In the end, the Germans went on choosing their hostages, to Pucheu's great regret. It is ironic that Pucheu was shot in 1944 largely for something he tried to do but failed.[184]

The logic of the armistice position thus drew Vichy into trying to do the Germans' dirty work for them. Better execute the innocent yourself than let the Germans usurp the law-and-order function completely in the Occupied Zone. That logic was to lead one step further in the summer of 1942, when the SS took over German police functions in France from the Army. At that time, Laval negotiated a still larger role for the French police in the Occupied Zone.[185] With the growth of the Resistance, Vichy was locked into an ascending spiral of repression on behalf of Germany.

After August 1941 it simply took more police to keep the

---

[183] This is one of the few internal Vichy disputes for which there is good contemporary evidence. Barthélemy's views were learned in a German telephone tap. See a briefing by Colonel Hans Speidel, No. 2495/41, of 9 September 1941 (*CDJC,* document no. CCXXVII-50). Pucheu's intentions were stressed by the defense at his trial, in Butin, *Le Procès Pucheu* (Paris, n.d. [1948]), 304–5. His complaints to Abetz are contained in Paris telegram No. 3486 of 6 November 1941 (T-120/405/214002–3). This is analogous to Vallat's June 1941 efforts to assert Vichy sovereignty over Jewish matters in the Occupied Zone. See above, pp. 177 ff.

[184] *Ministère public c/Dayras* has the most information on the Paris Special Section. See also Paris telegram 3486, 6 November 1941 (T-120/405/214002–3).

[185] See chap. 4.

Pétain regime in place. Having shed blood, the regime now had to shed more and more of it to keep alive. "Travail, Famille, Patrie," said Léon-Paul Fargue, had given way to "Tracas, Famine, Patrouilles." [186]

The only common denominator was order.

The National Revolution and Fascism

WELL PAST THE HALFWAY POINT OF THIS BOOK, THE term *fascism* has hardly appeared. That omission is not meant to deny any kinship between Vichy France and other radical right regimes of the twentieth century. The trouble is that the word *fascism* has been debased into epithet, making it a less and less useful tool for analyzing political movements of our time. For the French case in particular, lumping Vichy casually with fascist regimes in Germany and Italy[187] dismisses the whole occupation experience as something alien to French life, an aberration unthinkable without foreign troops imposing their will. This mental shortcut obscures the rich variety of groups competing for influence at Vichy, conceals the deep taproots linking Vichy policies to the major conflicts of the Third Republic, and facilely passes the whole thing off as a mere foreign import.

Fascism does mean something quite specific, however. The word is not a mere bludgeon with which to belabor conservatives. Strictly speaking, as an ideal type, fascism is a mass antiliberal, anticommunist movement, radical in its willingness to employ force and in its contempt for the upper-class values of

[186] Bourget, *Un Certain Philippe Pétain* (Paris, 1966), 235. The pun loses in translation: "Work, Family, Nation" had given way to "Bother, Hunger, Surveillance."

[187] The latest influential example is William L. Shirer, *The Collapse of the Third Republic* (New York, 1969), 21, 557, 900, where the ideas of men like Baudouin and Weygand "derived mainly from Rome and Berlin" and from "reading *Mein Kampf*" and where the new regime "attempted to ape" the conqueror's doctrine.

the time, sharply distinct not only from its enemies on the left but also from its rivals on the right, traditional conservatives. Where conservatives want social structure to be hierarchical, fascist mass rallies in uniform colored shirts display a leveling egalitarianism before the leader. Economically, fascists make their appeal to the solitary "common man" against the organized "interests" of society, from bankers and landlords to trade unions. Where conservatives show distaste for mass participation and prefer government by a few established families, fascists—children of the era of mass politics instead of survivors of elitist nineteenth-century Europe—attempt to marshal mass affirmations. Fascists often prefer a Dionysiac pagan vigor to the social bulwark of established churches. They mock the softness, the conformity, the empty manners of conservatives. Totally devoid of any sentimental conservative attachment to the vanishing Europe of grandpapa, fascists revel in dynamism, change, and a "new order." There are common points, of course: authoritarianism, hatred of liberals as weak-kneed harbingers of leftist social revolution, defense of property. But that common ground tends to be drowned out by discordant clashes of tone and value, especially among fascists enjoying the freedom of those out of power.

The study of fascism is complicated by the fact that no fascist movement has ever reached power on its own terms. None has come to power without being assisted by conservatives, under conditions in which fascists and conservatives mute their differences and undergo a certain amalgamation in the face of higher interests: achieving office and staving off a communist threat. Conservatives have frequently found the organized mass support and private armies of fascism a welcome ally against the Left; fascists have frequently found conservatives holding the keys to power. Mussolini was financed by industrialists and landowners when his nationalist-syndicalist *squadristi* turned their attention to beating up reformist socialists. It was King Victor Emanuel III, with the advice of parliamentary leaders, who summoned him to form a government in 1922. Mussolini threatened to march on Rome, but he arrived in fact by Pullman car. Hitler received conservative money and support and was called to power by President von Hindenburg, on the advice of conservatives like Franz von Papen and General von Schleicher. Jose Antonio Primo de Rivera's Falange had only a minor and diminishing role in Franco's military-clerical group that destroyed the Spanish Republic. All these leaders, upon taking power, headed coalitions of fascist and conservative elements joined together in the common endeavor of obtaining office and preventing communist revolution. All of them, moreover, had to put down opposition from purer-minded fascist ideologues whose radical frenzy had helped them acquire a mass following in the first place. Mussolini had to get rid of his early syndicalist followers like Massimo Rocca. Hitler cynically liquidated Ernst Röhm and Gregor Strasser along with other inconvenient past allies and accomplices in the Night of the Long Knives, 30 June 1934. Franco gradually muted the Falange. No undiluted fascist regime has wielded power.

It helps to set up a spectrum of radical right regimes, ranging from those in which fascists dominated the partnership to those in which conservatives dominated the partnership. Hitler's Germany clearly occupies one end of the spectrum. The Nazi party and the paramilitary organizations eventually broke the power of even such conservative elite groups as the diplomatic corps and the army. In Italy, by contrast, king, church, and army retained sufficient autonomy to regain their independence and overthrow Mussolini and the party in order to make a deal with the advancing Allies in July 1943. Dr. Salazar's Portugal perhaps occupied the other end of the spectrum, in which conservative, Catholic authoritarianism was almost untinctured by mass antitraditional authoritarianism.

The Vichy National Revolution clearly occupied a place on such a spectrum nearer the conservative than the fascist end. Pétain felt himself closer to Franco and Salazar than to Hitler. Before the war, conservatives were groping for a "third way" between communism and fascism as a substitute for the parliamentarism and market economy that they judged dead; even fascist ideologues like Robert Brasillach found Nazi party rallies foreign and slightly ludicrous. After 1940, Vichy theorists like Thierry-Maulnier continued to insist upon indigenous solutions rather than "pure and simple imitation of the victors." [188] In personnel, as we shall see in the next chapter, Vichy began in the hands of French traditionalists. Even as they lost ground over time, however, traditionalists gave way not to fascist ideologues but to technicians, professional administrators, and businessmen already prominent during the Third Republic. Although fascist figures gained some ground in propaganda functions, in official anti-Semitism, and, eventually in 1944, in the Vichy paramilitary counteroffensive against the Resistance, whole vital areas of the National Revolution—finance, foreign relations, the armed services—were never in their hands.

There are several reasons for the relatively restricted role of fascists, in any strict sense, at Vichy. One is the splintered and ineffectual role of those movements before the war. The largest movement was Colonel de la Rocque's Croix de Feu, which more vigorous fascists contemptuously spoonerized as "Froides Queues." The ablest leader was Jacques Doriot, whom the others effectively blocked from predominant influence after 1940. Then the separation of occupied Paris from autonomous Vichy siphoned off most of the interwar fascist leaders to comfortable but ineffectual positions in the German-subsidized newspapers and parties and high life of the capital. With two stages to play upon, the fascists got the gaudier but less independent one.

Digging deeper, one finds more profound reasons for the peripheral position of fascists at Vichy. That old hesitancy that French authoritarian nationalists felt for drawing upon German models was not lessened by the defeat of 1940. Furthermore, France had a long tradition of unity and liberty combined, and there was less incompatibility in French history between democracy and grandeur. France had been less socially disjointed by the depression than had other, more advanced industrial countries. Her small farms and shops suffered but survived, a social cushion upon which the French middle class rode out the storm,

---

[188] For "middle way" conservatives of the late 1930's, see Jacques Bardoux, *Ni Communiste, ni hitlérien: La France de demain* (Paris, 1937). Robert Brasillach described his reaction to Nazi ritual in "Cent heures chez Hitler," *La Revue universelle* (1 October 1937). Thierry-Maulnier, "L'Avenir de la France," *La Revue universelle* (1 February–10 May 1941).

underemployed but intact. The fear of revolution had lost some of its internal immediacy as the vast sit-down strikes of May–June 1936 were succeeded by the more typically ineffectual strike of November 1938. At bottom, France's breakdown in 1940 was national more than social, unlike Germany's breakdown in 1928–33 and Italy's breakdown in 1919–22. France was shattered enough in 1940 to reject the republic, but not enough to seek its substitute outside French tradition.

While Vichy was more traditional than fascist, it was not a return to the *ancien régime*. The National Revolution drew more from Enlightenment and nineteenth-century liberal values than from nineteenth-century Restoration values. From the Restoration and romanticist imaginings about the *ancien régime* came integral Catholicism, the subordination of the individual to "natural" groupings from province to family, and an organic conception of law that could lead Marshal Pétain to pretend that the National Revolution could not be legislated from above. "The law cannot create a social order; it can only give it institutional sanction, after the solid citizens (*honnêtes gens*) have already created it. The role of the state should be limited here to give an impulse, to indicating principles and main lines of direction, to stimulating and orienting initiatives." [189]

From the Enlightenment and nineteenth-century middle-class values came the heart of the National Revolution. There was a strong dose of the Enlightenment view of natural social harmony, which the Radical party of 1901 had elevated into doctrine. A faith that good government and education would eradicate the class struggle was common to both the Radical party programs of the early 1900's and to corporatism. Léon Bourgeois' *Solidarité* (1896) is closer to the National Revolution's social and economic program than, say, to the pessimistic view of human nature of a de Maistre. Another middle-class value of the nineteenth-century, positivism, lay behind the progressive technocratic vision at Vichy of a better planned and managed industrial France. None of these people thought of changing the basic

[189] Pétain's Saint-Etienne speech on labor, 1 March 1941. He was also, of course, reassuring businessmen that the anticapitalist rhetoric of the regime was not dangerous.

presuppositions of the Third Republic's educational system, or even some of its Popular Front improvements such as the school-leaving age of sixteen. Nor was serious thought given to reestablishing the Catholic church. In these matters, Vichy was postindustrial and postliberal in a way closer to Germany and Italy than to Franco and Salazar.

The National Revolution was a heresy of Third Republic liberal and progressive doctrines. French leaders had kept their faith in such post-1789 values as the nation, science, an educated society, and general prosperity. They had lost their fathers' faith in parliamentarism and laissez-faire economics as the way to achieve them, less because of a half century of Maurras' *fascisant* propaganda (though that helped) than because those means no longer seemed capable of dealing with the twin crises of decadence and disorder from the 1930's. Hard measures by a frightened middle class—that, indeed, is one good general definition of fascism. In that broader sense, Vichy was fascist. And in that sense, fascism has not yet run its course.

III / The Collaborators

IT IS HARD TO MEASURE SUPPORT FOR AN AUTHORIT-
arian regime. Not only are the usual reflections of public opinion
missing: a relatively unfettered press, elections, parliamentary
debate, some degree of tolerance for expressions of dissenting opinion. The regime also distorts those measures of opinion one has.
Rulers equate silence with support, acquiescence with enthusiasm, and participation with loyalty. Any assessment of support
for the Vichy regime is further complicated by the almost universal joy of liberation in 1944 and by Frenchmen's failure to remember—for conscious or unconscious reasons—quite different earlier
moods more in keeping with the apparently hopeless days of 1941
or 1942.

A crude graph of French public opinion from 1940 to 1944
would show nearly universal acceptance of Marshal Pétain in
June 1940 and nearly universal acceptance of General de Gaulle
in August 1944, with the two lines, one declining and the other
rising, intersecting some time after the total occupation of the
hitherto "free zone" of Vichy in November 1942.

But the two lines would not be straight lines, and a number

of refinements are both possible and necessary. First, one must distinguish between active participation in the regime and mere favorable opinion. Within favorable public opinion, one can further distinguish among varying degrees of warmth and among varying grounds for support: personal faith in Marshal Pétain, fear of war and revolution, enthusiasm for the National Revolution. Even those who grumbled at the regime without doubting its basic legality or doing anything positive against it helped swell the tide of acquiescence. All these groups, from lukewarm to fervent, were "collaborators" in a functional sense, for they provided the broad public climate of acceptance that lent legitimacy to a more active participation.

There remain two important contemporary sources for public opinion in the two zones of France, occupied and unoccupied. Although French prefects' reports for this period are still closed to scholars, fragments of them can be found here and there.[1] The other main contemporary source is German intelligence reports, based upon intercepted mail, the statements of informers, and overheard conversations.[2] Both sources are subject to caution: official samplers of opinion often hear what they want to hear and tell their superiors what they think those superiors want to know. These sources are much more revealing than the press, however, and they have the great advantage over diaries and memoirs of not having been retouched after the war. They must suffice for drawing in some of the corrections on this crude graph of public opinion.

The most striking feature of public opinion about Vichy was the clear distinction most people drew between Pétain and his ministers. Both chief Vichy ministers were targets of assassins. Laval was wounded by a would-be assassin at Versailles on 27

---

[1] Monthly digests of prefects' reports for the Occupied Zone for March–May 1941 are published in *DFCAA*, IV, 385–96, 491–503. Monthly digests of prefects' reports for the Vichy zone for January–April 1943 may be consulted at the Centre de Documentation Juive Contemporaine in Paris, dossier CCCLXXXIII, items 2–9. Jacques Baudot, *L'Opinion publique sous l'occupation* (Paris, 1960), makes use of official material for one department, the Eure.

[2] Military inspection teams of the Armistice Commission submitted regular public opinion reports to Wiesbaden. See T-77/OKW-1432, OKW-1434, OKW-1436–39, and OKW-1605.

August 1941, while out of office. Darlan was shot to death in Algiers on Christmas Eve, 1942. Pétain, by contrast, could still draw sympathetic crowds long after the total occupation of France in November 1942, not only in traditionally nationalist towns like Nancy (26–27 May 1944), but even in *frondeur* Paris just four months before the Liberation, on 26 April 1944.[3] The presence of Pétain, the World War I victor, the cautious hoarder of French blood, the bulwark against revolution, the wise father, provided a moral cover for the regime long after all its other members had been widely discredited.

Beyond faith in the person of Marshal Pétain, there were other positive grounds for mass approval of the new regime. After all, nearly half the voters had voted against the Popular Front in May 1936 although the play of electoral coalitions in multicandidate races had given the Popular Front a large majority in the Chamber. The number of Catholic families who had felt strongly enough about the Third Republic's school to pay tuition in parochial schools (about one French secondary school pupil out of five attended a parochial school) is another measure of potential mass support for this ostentatiously Catholic regime. And no one can read much of the serious journalism of the 1930's without sensing the massive contempt for the faltering Third Republic even before the defeat.

The main ingredients for mass approval of Pétain's regime were negative ones, however: elements that simply removed any real alternative from public attention and left Vichy as the only apparently lawful French government. The circumstances of the regime's creation in June and July 1940 allowed little doubt of its constitutionality. Even General de Gaulle rejected Vichy's legitimacy on philosophical rather than legal grounds: that "France is not France without grandeur."[4] The administrative

---

[3] One can moderate the romanticized account of the Paris visit in works like Jean Tracou, *Le Maréchal aux liens* (Paris, 1948), 217 ff., without denying the extraordinary range and longevity of faith in Pétain himself.

[4] Charles de Gaulle, *Mémoires de guerre*, vol. 1, *L'Appel* (Paris, 1954). The Brazzaville manifesto of 27 October 1940 declared the Vichy regime "unconstitutional and subject to the invader" and announced that in the absence of a "government properly French," a "new power" must assume the French war effort.

apparatus of the state went on about its work, with an even higher commitment than before to doing its job. Vichy was accepted simply because it was all there was, or all there seemed to be for some time after 1940.

Vichy was assisted too, in a negative way, by the widespread apathy of public opinion after the shock of 1940. Never, wrote A'natole de Monzie in 1943, had the French public experienced so long a period of anesthesia. Léon Blum likened it to the shock of an accident victim. Political apathy born of gloom and disgust left the way clear for a controlled press and radio to manufacture public support out of what was much more often simply public lethargy. In a curious counterpoint to the official displays of ardent support—the triumphal tours of Marshal Pétain, the delegations of scouts, war veterans, and youth groups—both prefects and German intelligence agents agreed upon "the dominant political lethargy." In 1941 and 1942 the refrain of both kinds of report is "the general sentiment of lassitude and fatigue," the "great discouragement and infinite lassitude" of the population.[5]

Apathy was deepened by a growing focus of attention upon physical needs. The conditions of life in both zones of France declined from austerity in 1940 to severe want in 1944. Even the moral discomforts of a humiliated country, divided families, restrictions upon movement and information, and the presence of an occupying army eventually yielded place to physical concerns. The French had only about 35 percent of the coal of prewar years for their own use, since imports were impossible and the richest fields of the Nord and Pas-de-Calais were administered by the German army command in Brussels rather than from Paris. Oil supplies were at one-tenth their prewar level. Electric power fell unusually short because of a dry year in 1941. Shoes were soled in wood. "You get so cold you can't think of anything else," wrote Jean Guéhenno in his diary on 21 January 1942.[6]

---

[5] For example, Kriegstagebuch der D.A.S., Port Vendres, "Stimmungsbericht für die Zeit 22.8–21.9.42" (T-77/OKW-1437/5, 593, 685 ff.); *DFCAA,* IV, 394, 500.

[6] Jean Guéhenno, *Journal des années noires* (Paris, 1947), 21 January 1942. For electricity shortages in the winter of 1941–42, see *Revue des*

The main concern was food. France was eventually the worst nourished of the western occupied nations. While rural populations were at least close to the source of supply, the urban poor suffered genuine malnutrition. Roger Martin du Gard wrote Gide that he had lost 19 kilograms (over 40 pounds) by May 1942. By September, he wrote that there was literally nothing in the markets.

> There are whole families who have nothing but their daily bread ration each day. There is great unrest. You can see mothers of families weeping in the street.[7]

Even the ration allotments were hard to obtain in cities because of diminished production and transport, peasant hoarding, and German requisitions. Alfred Fabre-Luce decided that the real voice of France by 1942 had become the growling stomach.[8]

Under such conditions no one could expect very warm feelings toward Germany. Both German and French observers of French public opinion agreed that anti-German feelings were very widespread and growing. French prefects' reports warned in 1941 that German requisitions and police actions were blocking the path to collaboration and inviting the spread of communism. The German inspection teams' opinion reports were full of information about hostility to Germany, as they reported the first gestures in the spring of 1941 of public hostility: the "V" signs painted on walls and the ostentatious carrying of two bamboo fishing poles, "deux gaules." The surprising thing is how much less virulent those anti-German feelings were than they might have been. During the early days, the German occupation forces' behavior was unusually good for an occupying army. Savage reprisals against the Resistance were still far in the future. Furthermore, hopes for an early peace and the apathy of defeat helped limit anti-Germanism to grumbling. The German

---

deux mondes, 15 January 1942, and Le Figaro, 17 January 1942. Coal and oil figures are found in "Mitteilungen über die Arbeiten der WaKo," no. 68 of 13 September 1940 and, no. 94 of 15 October 1940 (T-120/368/206980, 207141).

[7] André Gide–Roger Martin du Gard, Correspondance (Paris, 1968), II, 250, 272.

[8] Alfred Fabre-Luce, "L'Oreille au ventre," in Journal de France, 1939–44 (Paris, 1946).

inspection teams consistently overestimated the extent to which the armistice was violated.[9]

Growing animosity toward the Allies also smoothed the way for collaboration in French public opinion. French sympathy for the Allies was traditional, but even for those who could forgive Mers-el-Kebir, that sympathy after 1940 was closely geared to two variables. Allied war successes in distant theaters raised French hopes; Allied war measures in the Western European theater (and especially the bombing of targets in France) raised French apprehensions. German observers reported two flurries of French enthusiasm for the Allies during 1941: in April 1941, when the Yugoslavs and Greeks gave promise of soaking up German might in the Balkans, and shortly after the German invasion of Russia in June 1941. The Balkan resistances were quickly crushed in another dazzling display of German prowess in May 1941, however, and the Russian campaign also soon looked as if Hitler were stronger than Napoleon.[10]

After the midsummer of 1941, most Allied successes seemed in France to involve French losses. First, there was the British invasion of Syria in June 1941 and the loss of that area of ancient French influence to the ancient colonial rival. Franco-British conflicts at sea over the blockade reached their peak in the spring and summer of 1941. The Allies could be blamed for food and fuel shortages. On 3 March 1942 the bombing began, with a raid on the Renault works in the Paris suburb of Boulogne-Billancourt that caused a large number of civilian casualties. Between the blockade and the bombing, it was clear that hostility to Britain was increasing no less than hostility to Germany in 1942. It was

---

[9] The French prefects' reports published in *DFCAA*, IV, 396, 500, were of course expected to be seen by German eyes. The Armistice Commission inspection teams' "Stimmungsberichte" or opinion reports for 1941–42 may be consulted in T-77/OKW-1432, OKW-1434–37.

[10] For prefects' reports on the quick excitement and disappointment of April–May 1941, see *DFCAA*, IV, 500. T-120/221/149183–86 reports a pro-Yugoslav demonstration in Marseilles in April 1941. After Yugoslavia had been crushed, Jean Guéhenno thought "for the first time" that French defeat was "definitive." *Journal des années noires* (Paris, 1947), 11 April 1941. T-120/211328–30 reports opinion in Toulouse in August 1941 about the Russian campaign. For officers' views on the Russian campaign, see Paxton, *Parades and Politics at Vichy* (Princeton, N.J., 1966), 243–44.

possible for two thousand people to demonstrate in Toulouse on 16 June 1942 against British bombing and "Communist terrorism," where a year earlier hopes of German defeat had been aroused by the new German-Russian war.[11]

Under these conditions, response to Gaullism was even less enthusiastic in 1941 and 1942 than it had been in 1940. Until General Koenig's troops held off a German attack at Bir-Hacheim, in the Libyan desert, in June 1942, no Gaullist ground troops had been directly engaged against the Axis. Free French efforts to force parts of the empire back into the war lent color to charges that de Gaulle was simply giving the French Empire to the British. At the very time that the French internal Resistance was entering a more active stage in the summer of 1941, Gaullism was approaching its low point in French public opinion. The union of Gaullism and the Resistance and genuine hopes of liberation at their hands were still in the future.[12]

The United States, too, supplier of food and possible arbiter to end the war, lost some of its appeal to neutralist French opinion after it also became a belligerent in December 1941.

Public opinion, then, offered a broad basis of acquiescence within which active participation in the Vichy regime was made legitimate. Only in the spring of 1943, after the whole of France had been occupied and after young men began to be drafted to work in German factories, do the intelligence reports consider

[11] Kriegstagebuch der D.A.S., Port Vendres, "Stimmungsbericht für die Zeit 6.6–24.6.42" (T-77/OKW-1437/5,593,696 ff.).

[12] Although German intelligence reports are confused by a tendency to equate Gaullism and communism, the Germans were clearly less nervous about the Free French in 1941 than they had been in 1940. See, for example, a report in May 1941 that Gaullism was "not noteworthy" in Oran (T-77/OKW-685/2,499,320) and also a U.S. diplomat's report that there was little Gaullism in French North Africa, FRUS, 1941, II, 420. Most of the French Forces in Syria chose to be repatriated rather than join de Gaulle after the fratricidal Levant war of June–July 1941. Between the Gaullist success in French Equatorial Africa in the fall of 1940 and the return of French Africa to the war with the American landing in November 1942, there were no mass defections from Vichy to the Free France. And even then, only 100 out of 2,000 French sailors in the French squadron interned at Alexandria eventually joined the Free French (U.S. Dept. of State Serial File 851.01/176). The one senior French officer to defect in 1942, Air Force General Odic, went to Washington rather than London.

opinion to have turned decisively against the regime. The monthly digest of prefects' reports for the formerly unoccupied zone for February 1943 stressed the "contrast to previous months." It went on to describe the "universal agitation" against forced labor and shortages, including "even merchants and businessmen to whom fraud had permitted a standard of living rare in our time. . . . In a word, never has the public been so agitated (*frémissante*)." There was, the prefects reported, still no "organized opposition." Public opinion had definitely turned the corner, however, nearly three years after armistice and a little over a year before D-Day.[13]

Ins, Outs, and Notables

Public opinion during the Vichy years can be estimated only in impressionistic terms. It is rather to the active participants in the regime that one turns to test the regime's style, temper, and character. It is tempting to assume that there was a mass replacement of "ins" by "outs" in the summer of 1940 and that the radical right that had demonstrated and paraded so noisily in the 1930's now came to power. At first glance, Vichy looks like the triumph of 6 February 1934 demonstrators, veterans' leaders, Maurrassiens and followers of Colonel de la Rocque, and a whole 1930's underworld of anti-Semitic, antiparliamentary agitators. Simultaneously, important parts of the Third Republic leadership—leaders of the Popular Front, all but a handful of deputies, a large proportion of the republican mayors and town councils—passed into obscurity. A few even went into exile or prison.

Purges of personnel at changes of regime are never as sweep-

[13] Ministère de l'Intérieur, cabinet du secrétaire-général pour l'administration, "Synthèse des rapports des préfets de la Zone Libre pour le mois de février 1943," 18 March 1943 (Centre de Documentation Juive Contemporaine, document no. CCCLXXXIII-3).

ing as they seem, however, and the Vichy regime made no exception. There were in fact few genuinely "new men" in office at Vichy, men who had held no major responsibilities already under the Third Republic. Joseph Darnand, the Nice garage owner and hero of World War I guerrilla patrols who rose from veterans' militant to the cabinet post of secretary-general for the maintenance of order in December 1943, was certainly a new man. One might also add Paul Marion, ex-Communist, ex-Doriotist, and radical right journalist who became minister of information in February 1941. Outsiders found places in the realms of order and propaganda, especially later in the regime. On the other hand, they never gained influence in the vital fields of finance, defense, or diplomacy. On the contrary, some elements of Third Republic leadership passed directly into the Vichy regime almost without change of personnel. Senior civil servants and the mass of public officials went on with their jobs, with the exception of Jews, officials of Masonic orders, some prefects too closely tied to the Popular Front, and a handful of top officials personally linked to Paul Reynaud, such as the Inspectors of Finance Leca and Devaux who had been caught on their way to Spain with the secret funds of the Reynaud ministry. The Third Republic's business elite went on virtually unchanged. Jewish businessmen, of course, were penalized, along with those who joined de Gaulle, but no leading businessman comes to mind in that category.

Vichy was run to a large degree by a selection of what French political sociologists usefully call "notables": people of already high attainment in the worlds of public administration, business, the professions, and local affairs. With deputies, senators, and local republican mayors and councils removed from center stage, the real power of the unelected French elite was made manifest. Daniel Halévy had written in 1937 with some regret of the "end of the notables" in the 1870's, that replacement of Orleanist gentlemen by village teachers, doctors, and shopkeepers with which the Third Republic began. One can speak of 1940 as a return of the notables, or perhaps more accurately as a persistence of the notables: those men of experience and training who stepped into the foreground with the disappearance of a parliamentary façade in 1940. It is not accidental that Daniel Halévy, though a Jewish intellectual, saw some good in it.[14]

The Third Republic notables did not, however, step into office at Vichy completely unchanged. Prefects, for example, were much more extensively purged than other civil servants. An important segment, but only a segment, of the prewar socialist and trade union leadership participated in Vichy. We must look back into the Third Republic to see what lines were already being drawn, what selection was beginning to operate, which would choose that portion of the Third Republic notables who remained on top after the cataclysm of 1940.

The French Civil War: 1934–37

"IT IS THE REVENGE OF DREYFUS!" CHARLES MAURRAS exclaimed when he heard his sentence to life imprisonment in the Court of Justice at Lyons on 27 January 1945.[15] The defeat in 1940 sent shock waves through all of French society, reopening old fissures that went back at least to 1789: hierarchy vs. equality, secularism vs. religion, expertise vs. election, capital vs. labor. The most important of these reopened fissures in 1940 was the rift between "order" and "revolution," still gaping from the virtual French civil war of the mid-1930's. The antirevolution, anticommunist line was firmly drawn then, and most of those who were to become Vichy notables had already taken their position at that time.

A double change came over French conservatism between 1934 and 1936. Their main enemy was switched from Germany to Russia abroad, and from pacifists to the rearming Popular Front at home. Secondly, their militancy was vastly intensified. Losing faith in the machinery of the Third Republic to defend their interests, they turned to vigilantism.

[14] Daniel Halévy, *La Fin des notables* (Paris, 1937). For Halévy and Vichy, see Alain Silvera, *Daniel Halévy and His Times* (Ithaca, New York, 1966), and the Stephen Wilson article cited in footnote 17.

[15] *Le Procès de Charles Maurras* (Paris, 1946), 371.

As late as the great demonstrations of 6 February 1934, conservative criticism of the Third Republic centered on the German menace. France had won the war and lost the peace, according to nationalist and veterans' groups. In their diagnosis, parliamentary government lacked the authority, and the Radical and Socialist parties (which had won electoral majorities in 1924 and 1932) lacked the will to maintain the dominance France had won in 1918. In 1918 French armies occupied parts of the Rhineland, the Balkans, and Russia. By 1934, the army had been reduced to training cadres and military service had been reduced to one year (law of 1928), Allied troops had been withdrawn early from the Rhineland (1930 instead of 1935), reparations had been abandoned (1932), reports of German clandestine rearmament had been suppressed and ignored by the Allied control commissions (1928), and the principle of arms parity for Germany had been recognized (1932).

The scorn of nationalist and veteran groups for the republic was sharpened to paroxysm by two other developments of the early 1930's: the beginnings of the Great Depression in France, met by deflationary measures (veterans' pensions were cut in 1934 and 1935), and a wave of scandals implicating members of parliament in financial deals and payoffs, most notoriously the widespread suspicion that political leaders had shielded the fraudulent financial promoter Stavisky from prosecution.

Nationalist and veterans groups took matters into their own hands with the street demonstrations of 6 February 1934, the wildest night Paris had seen since 1871. It no longer seems as certain as it did at the time that the organizers of this mass demonstration sought to overthrow the republic. But they coordinated their plans for a mass move on "la maison sans fenêtres," the Chamber of Deputies, with slogans like "throw the deputies in the Seine." Action Française, the largest veterans' organization, the Union Nationale des Combattants, the Croix de Feu, and other middle-class nationalist direct-action groups massed some 40,000 demonstrators in a march on the Chamber. Although the Croix de Feu on the Left Bank didn't try very hard, the Action Française and UNC groups crossing the bridge from the Place de la Concorde pressed for hours against police barricades until finally the police fired into the crowd (it is still not clear what orders had been given by Eugène Frot, the minister of the interior), killing 16 and wounding 655. The Chamber was kept inviolate, but Edouard Daladier's government resigned the next day without being voted into a minority. That act recognized that the street had at least a veto power on the composition of the government of France.

The demonstration of 6 February 1934 and its repression began the virtual French civil war of the mid-1930's. It was the Right's Dreyfus Affair. A whole generation of conservatives who had scorned political participation now became politically active. Pierre Pucheu, bright young director of the Comité des Forges' international steel sales organization and twice Vichy minister, dated his entry into politics to February 1934. It was time, he said, to "shake off our apathy at all costs." A number of young intellectuals made 6 February the base of an action cult on behalf of race, blood, nation. For Drieu la Rochelle the street-fighting was proof "that this people is not dead . . . has not entirely lost pride in its own blood." Lucien Rebatet found in the fighting "an undreamed-of opportunity for our country to recover its health, and its fortune within, its independence abroad." Robert Brasillach looked back on this "exalting night" when there were "no more opinions," only feelings; workers and bourgeois talked to each other as equals, and revolution was again possible. "That divine couple, Courage and Fear, had joined again and stalked the streets." [16]

It was not only men of the Right who were aroused against the decadent "république des petits" by the killings of 6 February 1934. Daniel Halévy, who had been one of the first Dreyfusards and a founder of *L'Humanité* before World War I, but more recently disillusioned by the uprooting of old values and by the petty futility he found in republican quarrels, was described by his nephew early the next morning

striding the streets alone . . . gesticulating as if crying vengeance: my uncle Daniel Halévy who, beside himself, losing all restraint,

[16] Pierre Pucheu, *Ma Vie* (Paris, 1948), 109, 138; Drieu La Rochelle, *Gilles* (Paris, 1939), 434; Lucien Rebatet, *Les Décombres* (Paris, 1942), 29–33; Robert Brasillach, *Notre Avant-guerre* (Paris, 2nd ed., 1955), 151–55.

throwing down the mask, publicly proclaimed himself a man of the extreme right.[17]

This aroused militancy began to be redirected against a different target after February 1934. The accusation of weakness remained, but the source of the threat was transferred from the *boches* to the Bolsheviks. Fear of revolution was, of course, a constant of French conservative politics. In the 1930's, however, men of impeccably republican background joined the conservative crusade against the Left, as their fathers and grandfathers had in 1917, 1871, and 1848. They were frightened this time by the depression, by the possibility of another war with its attendant revolution, and by the Communist party's efforts to emerge from its isolation. Their frantic antibolshevism began to prepare the alignment of 1940.

The French Left had indeed reacted to the nationalist demonstrations of February 1934 by an "opening to the left," in the form of a socialist and radical rapprochement with the previously isolated Communist party. Some Communist militants had marched against the republic with the nationalists on February 6. Over the succeeding months, however, an antifascist front united them with the democratic Left. The formation of the Popular Front coalition in time to win the elections of May–June 1936 is too familiar a part of the history of the Third Republic to need retelling here. The point is that in a popular vote divided nearly fifty-fifty, the left parties profited by their union to win a majority of seats in the Chamber and Senate. The Communist delegation, in particular, grew from ten to seventy-two seats. Conservatives felt unrepresented and turned more willingly to direct action. Furthermore, the wave of sit-down strikes that began in the aircraft factories of Paris on 26 May 1936 and that surged in a wave of postelectoral jubilation across the country until more than a million men were on strike, heightened a climate of civil war. French conservatives believe to this day that a Bolshevik takeover had begun, although it is quite clear that the leaders of both the Communist party and the CGT were

[17] Daniel Guérin, *Front populaire, révolution manquée,* quoted in Stephen Wilson, "The Action Française in French Intellectual Life," *Historical Journal* XII:2 (June 1969), 348.

taken by surprise by that spontaneous wave of jubilation and by the occupation of factories. Indeed, the workers were good-humored, damaged nothing in the occupied factories, and hadn't the remotest idea what to do next. But their demonstration of the fragility of owners' control threw owners into panic.

Left successes had already sent the Right into the streets before 1936. The victory of the "Cartel des Gauches" in 1924, combined with France's humiliating failure to gain anything by the military occupation of the Rhineland in 1923, produced a rash of direct-action nationalist groups, of which Les Jeunesses Patriotes of the champagne magnate Pierre Taittinger and the Fédération Nationale Catholique of General Curières de Castelnau, Xavier Vallat, and Jean Le Cour Grandmaison were the most conspicuous. But between 1934 and 1936, antirevolution definitively took precedence over foreign grandeur and traditional anti-Germanism as the fuel of right-wing activism.

The heightening shrillness of the conservative press between 1934 and 1936 is very revealing. Colonel de la Rocque's *Flambeau,* for example, the newspaper of the Croix de Feu, acquired larger and larger headlines and repeatedly pronounced the revolution at hand in the spring of 1936. The normally understated *Temps* habitually called the moderately reformist Popular Front program "revolutionary" during the winter of 1935–36. Daniel Halévy was still writing in 1937 that the Chamber elected in 1936 was "revolutionary." That kind of hyperbole led straight to the later assertion of Vichy propagandists that "Moscow ran France for years." [18] In effect, the National Front, the Popular Front's electoral opponent in the elections of April–May 1936, had already drawn up the alignment of those conservatives and fearful liberals whose expectation of imminent revolution subordinated everything else to antibolshevism. In their eyes, the Third Republic had lost its legitimacy by failing to protect them from Stalin in 1936 long before it failed to protect them from Hitler in 1940.

[18] Daniel Halévy, *La République des ducs* (Paris, 1937), 108; *La Légion,* no. 15, August 1942. Charles Micaud, *The French Right and Nazi Germany* (Durham, N.C., 1943), is still the best summary of this evolution in the middle-class press.

That alignment helped prevent Frenchmen from forming another 1914 "union sacrée" as war with Hitler loomed in the late 1930's. Internally, the traditional partisans of national defense feared war more than they feared Hitler while the most vigorous anti-Hitlerians stood on the traditionally pacifist Left. There was simply no political basis for a national defense coalition, even when the political temperature moderated somewhat after the end of the first Blum government in June 1937 and the vigilantism of 1934–37 abated. Externally, the most militarily obvious alliance, the Franco-Russian combination, was excluded, because, as the opponents of the Franco-Soviet Pact said in the Chamber in February 1936, official cooperation with the Soviet Army would encourage and legitimize the French Communist party at home. Behind that was the less openly stated support for Hitler as the best barrier to Stalin and the fear since 1917 that any war meant revolution. The other possible alliance, with Italy, was more welcome to French officers. In this case, it was Mussolini rather than the French who put ideological hostility above common geopolitical interests. War against Hitler, under these conditions, became "Moscow's War" to conservatives because it could hardly be waged without Russian aid.

When war actually broke out, conservatives' fears of the Left were the reverse of those of 1914. The planned arrests of pacifists (including Pierre Laval) did not have to take place in 1914, for the Left by and large rallied to the national war effort. By contrast, conservatives feared the Left in 1939 for its bellicosity. The Nazi-Soviet Pact of 25 August 1939 provided an unexpected pretext for police action against the Communist party. With the declaration of war on 3 September, the party, which conservatives had accused of dragging France into a war against Hitler, was now dissolved for opposing that war. During the war itself, the Communist left seems to have been more vigorously pursued than the pro-German fringe groups that were also proscribed when the war broke out. Certainly no other deputies were unseated.

Long before 1940, therefore, an important group of Frenchmen had come to regard revolution as the main threat to France and war with Hitler as a regrettable diversion from the main task of preventing that revolution. The antibolshevists of the 1930's formed a major ingredient of the Vichy notables. They extended all the way from traditional conservatives through disillusioned liberal participants in the Popular Front to socialist and trade union leaders whose positions had been threatened by Communist growth in 1936. Indeed, antibolshevism is the nearest thing to a Vichy common denominator.

The Revenge of the Minorities

THOSE EXCLUDED FROM POWER BY THE POPULAR FRONT were obvious candidates for its succession. Participants in the nationalist demonstrations of 6 February 1934 were a leading case. Jean Chiappe, whose removal as Paris prefect of police had helped provoke the demonstrations, reappeared as governor-general of the French Levant (only to have his plane shot down near Cyprus on his way to Beirut in December 1940). Louis Darquier de Pellepoix, president of the Association of the wounded of 6 February 1934, and perhaps the most virulent anti-Semite of the interwar years, earned unexpected power and influence as French commissioner for Jewish affairs (1942–44). Another member of the association, Charles Trochu, became president of the Paris city council in November 1941. Jean Ybarnégaray held the Ministry of Youth and Health in 1940, and Philippe Henriot became the regime's radio spokesman in 1944. Veterans of those demonstrations were a kind of fraternity, and one finds job-seekers during Vichy being recommended as "good 6 February men." [19]

There were also those who had lost power or influence after the elections of 1936 or who had been removed from office by the Popular Front. The year 1940 was a kind of homecoming

---

[19] See Frédéric-Dupont's recommendation of Lt. Col. Gaëtan de Villers for a job in the Commissariat-général pour les Questions Juives (*CDJC*, document no. XLII-109).

for men like Laval, frequent minister in the early 1930's and out in the cold after the elections of 1936. Laval reveled quite frankly in his revenge against the Popular Front. He told U.S. Chargé d'Affaires Freeman Matthews in November 1940 that the Popular Front had been a "vile and criminal demagogy" that had "turned Frenchmen against democracy." [20]

Former deputies who had been defeated in 1936, like Pierre Cathala, now returned to public life. So did others who had run for election and failed, like Raphaël Alibert and Joseph Barthélemy. A few top appointive officials returned to high office as well; prominent among these was Marcel Peyrouton, who had been removed in 1936 from his post as high commissioner in Morocco, and now became minister of interior in 1940.

There were the leaders of interwar veterans' organizations. Divided by personal rivalry and conflict of interest into a plethora of small pressure groups between the wars, the two major veterans' organizations (the UNC and the UFC) had managed only partially to compose their differences in a National Veterans' Confederation in the early 1930's. An inflated rhetoric according to which the "generation of the trenches" was supposed to run the country that it had saved clashed badly with the mediocre achievement of the veterans' movements. They could agree only to protest against the deflationary cuts in pensions of 1934 and 1935. They blamed their inefficacies on the Third Republic and assailed the republic bitterly for frittering away the fruits of their victory.

A number of interwar veterans' leaders stepped up to assume that role which the "generation of the trenches" had claimed to have been cheated of by the Third Republic. The single Légion Française des Combattants offered them an end to internal rivalries, unity under authority, and an official mission to "extend [the new order] to the remotest village and make the new order prevail." [21] While some interwar veterans' leaders like Jean Goy took a fascist stance in Paris and served on the Paris municipal council, and others like Georges Lebecque and Henri Pichot

---

[20] *FRUS*, 1940, II, 404. For other, similar remarks, see p. 28.
[21] *L'Almanach de la Légion française des combattants*, 1941, 46.

served quietly in legion posts, others—most notably Georges Scapini and Xavier Vallat—took leading positions at Vichy.

On the other side of the coin, many of Vichy's most prominent victims were the clearly marked enemies of the 1930's right. It was not merely the wartime leaders (Daladier, Reynaud, General Gamelin) who were imprisoned and then tried. Marx Dormoy, the Popular Front minister of the interior who had prosecuted the underground anticommunist terrorists known as the "Cagoule" in 1937 and had removed Jacques Doriot from his perpetual office as major of Saint-Denis, was first expelled from office as a member of the *conseil-général* of the Allier in July 1941 and then murdered by Cagoulards later the same month. Jean Zay, charged with subverting French youth as Popular Front minister of education, and Georges Mandel, the leading anti-armistice minister of 1940, were murdered by Milice in the summer of 1944. Stanley Hoffmann was right to call Vichy "the revenge of the minorities." [22]

On closer inspection, however, the prewar minorities did not all enjoy equal revenge. In particular, Vichy cannot be described as simply a takeover of France by the protofascist "Leagues" that had marched and demonstrated so noisily in the 1930's. Few of the 1930's league leaders got very far at Vichy. Colonel de La Rocque, whose Croix de Feu and its successor, the Parti Social Français, was by far the largest of the interwar leagues, expected a major role in any authoritarian successor to the Third Republic. There is a fascinating glimpse, in François Chasseigne's trial, of PSF efforts to obtain four places in the city council of Issoudun, for example. At the top, however, La Rocque complained about "total ostracism" by Vichy, whose new Veterans' Legion was controlled by "those most hostile to me and to our work." In September 1940 he urged his followers to display "formal discipline behind Marshal Pétain" but "absolute reserve" toward all members of the government, while attempting to keep his movement going (now rechristened Progrès Social Français) as an independent force. The PSF was banned in the Occupied Zone,

[22] Stanley Hoffmann, "Aspects du régime de Vichy," *Revue française de science politique* VI:1 (1955).

and La Rocque was arrested there briefly in January 1941, where the colonel's rivals from more militantly fascist prewar leagues persuaded the Germans that the PSF was "chauvinist" and under "Jewish influence." Eventually, La Rocque accepted a "fusion" with the Veterans' Legion in August 1941, at the high point of efforts to make veterans the main organized political support of the regime. This meant in practice that his approximately 350,000 members were swallowed up in the Legion. La Rocque himself was compensated with a post as *chargé de mission* attached to Pétain's cabinet, where, American diplomats learned, he kept telephoning for something to do. This essentially colorless figure had thus gravitated to his proper level. A few of La Rocque's followers enjoyed high office at Vichy. Jean Ybarnégaray had been leader of the party's parliamentary group after 1936. Paul Creyssel, a former Radical deputy who joined the PSF group in December 1936, became secretary-general for propaganda in 1943. Félix Olivier-Martin, professor of law at Poitiers and prewar PSF militant, replaced Lamirand as secretary-general for youth affairs in 1943. Other PSF leaders, however, were bitterly disillusioned by their failure to dominate the new regime. Barochin, who could still tell an American diplomat in March 1942 that the PSF was the only organized force capable of running France, was by then deeply disillusioned by "collaboration" and contemptuous of Vichy. Charles Vallin, former vice-president of the PSF, escaped to London in the summer of 1942 expecting a cabinet position, but accepted simple mobilization as an officer in the Free French Forces. The PSF's inconsequence at Vichy helped complete its dispersal as a political movement.[23]

[23] Colonel de la Rocque letter to presidents of PSF sections, Clermont-Ferrand, 16 September 1940 (Centre de documentation juive contemporaine, dossier XXXIII, which contains a whole file on La Rocque gathered by his enemy Xavier Vallat); *Ministère public c/Chasseigne*, 34; the 29 April 1941 ban on the PSF in the Occupied Zone is mentioned in T-77/OKW-1444/5,594,887 ff. Samples of German police information about "Jewish influence" in the PSF may be found in *CDJC*, documents no. XLVI-37 and LXXVIII-1. Information on La Rocque as a member of Pétain's cabinet and on the views of Barochin is contained in U.S. Dept. of State Serial File 851.00/2385,2698,2928. For Vallin, see Jacques Soustelle, *Envers et contre tous* (Paris, 1947), I, 407. There is much interesting

The other major 1930's league leaders gravitated to Paris, where they attacked Vichy for its old-fashioned clerical, patriotic air and its halfhearted association with the world fascist "revolution." The most able and successful of these was Jacques Doriot, whose Parti Populaire Français was believed to have 30,000 members, 4,000 of them active, in 1941. Doriot's personal magnetism permitted him to remain mayor of the Paris working-class suburb of Saint-Denis through his evolution from head of the young Communists in the 1920's to creator of the fascist Parti Populaire Français in the 1930's. He never held Vichy office, not even in 1944. He was remembered there with hostility as the organizer of resistance within the army to the French occupation of the Ruhr in 1923 and the Rif War in 1925. Laval and Darlan both went out of their way to block Doriotist influence in Vichy organizations and won Abetz' assistance in preventing Doriot from becoming an alternate German candidate for the office of prime minister. Laval tried, without success, to get the Germans to dissolve the PPF after the total occupation of France in November 1942. There were, nonetheless, active centers of PPF activity in the Vichy zone, especially in Tunisia and Marseille. Moreover, two major Vichy ministers and several high ministerial officials had spent time in the PPF in the late 1930's. Paul Marion, who like Doriot moved from the Communist party to fascism, served as editor in chief of Doriot's *Emancipation nationale* and as director of propaganda for the PPF until January 1939, when he broke with Doriot over "the Stalinist character of your relations with people" and "the weakness of your reactions in face of the pan-German surge since Munich and the recent Italian provocations." He served as Darlan's minister for information and, having helped undermine the Darlan government in March–April 1942, remained as head of propaganda

---

material in Philippe Machefer, "Sur quelques aspects de l'activité du Colonel de la Rocque et du 'Progrès social français' pendant la seconde guerre mondiale," *Revue d'histoire de la deuxième guerre mondiale,* no. 58 (April 1965). La Rocque's obscurity at Vichy and his arrest, along with so many other nationalist figures, by the Germans in 1943 allow such recent works as Edith de la Rocque, *La Rocque tel que je l'ai connu* (Paris, 1962), and Philippe Rudeaux, *La Croix de feu et le PSF* (Paris, 1967), to treat La Rocque as a member of the Resistance.

efforts under Laval. Pierre Pucheu, international sales director for the French steel industry, abandoned La Rocque for Doriot in 1936 because the former seemed too soft; he, too, left the PPF in January 1939 after Mussolini's public claims to Tunisia, Corsica, and Nice. He became Darlan's minister of industrial production and then of the interior in 1941. Similar evolutions were followed by Pucheu's friends Yves Paringaux, *directeur du cabinet* in the Ministry of the Interior under Darlan, and Robert Loustau, coal mining entrepreneur who held high positions under Pucheu in the Ministry of Industrial Production in 1941 and in Gibrat's Ministry of Communications, and by Emile Boyez, secretary-general in the Ministry of Labor in 1944. Those who remained with Doriot after the party split of 1939, however, circulated in the Paris world rather than the Vichy world. Doriot drew funds from Abetz, tried to get his followers lucrative places as provisional administrators of Jewish businesses, and occupied a leading role in the client journalistic and political life around the German presence. His main energies went into the Anti-Bolshevik Legion (Légion des Volontaires contre le Bolshevisme), the French volunteers who fought in German uniform on the Russian front after the summer of 1941. Doriot himself left for the Russian front on 4 September 1941. One could say that after April 1942 Doriot occupied the Damocles' sword position against Laval that Laval had occupied against Darlan after February 1941. Laval, however, with Abetz' support, was much more successful in shutting Doriot out than Darlan had been against Laval.[24]

[24] For Laval's efforts to keep Doriotists out of the Veterans' Legion and its later paramilitary force, the Service d'Ordre Légionnaire, see U.S. Dept. of State Serial File 851.00/2866,2919. Doriot tried to interest the Germans in supporting him in a bid for power in September–November 1942 and had the backing of people like Sicherheitsdienst head Walter Schellenberg. Abetz consistently supported Laval, however, as in Abetz (Paris) 5295 to Ribbentrop of 19 November 1942 (T-120/928/297509011), which warns against Doriot as too "active" and "nationalist." For Laval's efforts to take over the Anti-Bolshevik Legion for Vichy and christen it the Tricolor Legion, see General Bridoux, "Journal," and a German foreign office report by Strack, Ausw. Amt Pol., 11, 3074, 25 August 1942 (T-120/3837/E044122–24). Hitler ordered Abetz to deny rumors that he envisaged Doriot as Laval's eventual successor in Ribbentrop (Feldmark) 1158 to Abetz, 21 September 1942 (T-120/1832/418612). Laval, however, failed

In addition to Doriot, Paris swarmed with a rabble of marginal conspirators and journalists from the 1930's radical right who enjoyed the security of German embassy pensions and a cardboard world of fictitious power. These included such raffish figures as the naval engineer Eugène Deloncle, linked to the prewar terriorist group the "Cagoule," which had assassinated some of Mussolini's enemies for him and whose main achievement in occupied Paris was blowing up seven Paris synagogues in the night of 2–3 October 1941, thereby getting his accomplices in the German security police into trouble with the Militärbefehlshaber in Frankreich. Deloncle's Mouvement Socialiste Révolutionnaire was thought by German intelligence to have 1,385 members in 1941. He struggled for preeminence with Doriot and Déat within such Paris collaborationist organizations as the Anti-Bolshevik Legion and was executed by the Gestapo in November 1943. Alongside this edifying figure was a cloud of minor hate-mongering journalists for whom Abetz' payments and an assured paper ration guaranteed their first regular appearance in print, if not any readership. There was the Corsican pilot and Bonapartist Pierre Costantini, who founded a Ligue Française D'Epuration, d'Entr'aide Sociale et de Collaboration Européenne and published *L'Appel.* He was charitably admitted to an asylum after the war. There was Henry Coston, the self-styled continuator of Drumont's campaign against Jews and Freemasons. There were the young antibourgeois novelists of the 1930's, such as Pierre Drieu La Rochelle who took over the *Nouvelle revue française,* Robert Brasillach of *Je suis partout,* Lucien Rebatet, and Louis-Ferdinand Céline. Some prewar radical right journals (*Je suis partout, Gringoire*) now turned their muckraking style against the chauvinism and social reaction they decried at Vichy. Other prewar journals were put into the hands of Abetz clients: Claude Jeantet, former diplomatic correspondant of Doriot's *La Liberté,* became editor in

---

to get the Germans to dissolve the PPF in December 1942. See Ribbentrop (Sonderzug) 1614 to Abetz, 26 December 1942 (T-120/935/298684–87). The most useful scholarly works on Doriot are Gilbert Allardyce, "The Political Transition of Jacques Doriot," *Journal of Contemporary History* I (1966), and Dieter Wolf, *Die Doriotbewegung* (Stuttgart, 1967).

chief of Pierre Dupuy's *Petit Parisien,* which Pétain had hoped to make his own organ in Paris. Marcel Déat became director of the paper for which he had written "Mourir pour Dantzig?" in 1939, *L'Oeuvre,* with some of the old staff remaining. Finally the German embassy created some new journals out of whole cloth, such as *La Gerbe,* for such writers as Henry de Montherlant and Count Clément Serpeille de Gobineau, a genetic racist without the style of his distinguished ancestor; and *La France au travail,* for those labor leaders like Georges Dumoulin and Marcel Roy for whom anticommunism had become more important than the survival of trade unions.[25]

The main point to make here is that none of the Paris *Ligueurs* achieved office at Vichy except Marcel Déat. Déat began as the kind of socialist willing to march in his captain's uniform to Père Lachaise cemetery on 28 May 1917 in the annual demonstration for the dead of the Commune of 1871. By 1931 he had become national secretary of the socialist student organization, a *lycée* professor, co-editor with Henri Moysset of the complete works of Proudhon, and a prominent younger intellectual within the SFIO. In 1933, along with Adrien Marquet and Barthélemy Montagnon, Déat broke away from the SFIO's Dreyfus-generation leadership to found the Neosocialist movement, a post-depression antiliberal heresy of socialism that emphasized a planned, autarkic economy and centralized authority within the nation. Although Déat was minister of aviation in the Sarraut cabinet of 1936, he had become a leading pacifist by the time of Munich. After the defeat, he was expected to be a major figure in Laval's single party, and in that relationship with Laval

[25] The most complete source for the content of journalism in occupied Paris is Michèle Cotta, *La collaboration* (Paris, 1964). For control and staff members, see Ministère de l'information. Notes documentaires et études, no. 218, "La Presse authorisée sous l'occupation allemande (1940–44)" (Paris, 1946). Information on Abetz' subsidies may be found in T-120/364/20639–45 for *La France au travail,* T-120/3485H/E019445–48 for *La France au travail* and *La Gerbe,* and an entire folder on the German embassy and the Press, Pariser Botschaft, Ordner 1134, "S 8 Geheim, 1940–44," filmed as T-120/3112. See also an extensive report by the Armistice Commission on parties in the Occupied Zone, as of 28 August 1941 (T-77/OKW-1444/5,594,887 ff.). The trial of the *Je suis partout* writers is reported in *Le Monde,* 17–18 November 1946.

lies the reason for his participation in Vichy in 1944. Déat was the other person arrested in the 13 December 1940 move against Laval, and after Laval had joined him in Paris, Déat founded in January 1941 what Abetz no doubt thought was going to be the long-awaited single party: the Rassemblement National Populaire. Abetz thought it was going to be a "front of the 'left' and fascists" capable of bringing pressure upon the "reactionaries" at Vichy. In fact, it became merely one Paris splinter group among many. The RNP received Georges Mandel's apartment as a headquarters, enjoyed money and support from the German embassy, and campaigned for European unity under Germany in the crusade against bolshevism. Darlan, as the main target of Déat's attack upon Vichy's technocrats, clericals, and "defeated and decorated military men," told General Vogl in July 1941 that he would not sit at the same table with RNP leaders. After Laval returned to power in April 1942, Déat continued to receive his and Abetz' support as the most useful Paris rival to Doriot. Déat carefully excluded Doriotists from the new Front Révolutionnaire National he founded on 28 April 1943. By December 1943, therefore, after Pétain had proven Vichy's powerlessness by failing to remove Laval a second time, Abetz and Laval were able to introduce Déat into the government as minister of labor and national solidarity simultaneously with Joseph Darnand as secretary-general for the maintenance of order. By 1944, then, with the gradual using up and disappearance of the more regular notables who dominated Vichy's most autonomous years, it was possible for some of the Paris radical right to come to power at Vichy. But the only man to do so was a former Third Republic minister who had been Laval's key barrier to Doriot in Paris. Vichy was not the triumph of the prewar protofascist leagues.[26]

[26] The main published work on Déat, "Claude Varenne" [Georges Albertini], *Le Destin de Marcel Déat* (Paris, 1948), is a naïvely revealing apologia by the secretary-general of the RNP and later *directeur du cabinet* in Déat's Ministry of Labor and Social Solidarity. See also *Pétain et les allemands: Mémorandum d'Abetz* (Paris, 1948), 75. Darlan's remark to General Vogl is found in Wirtschafts- und Rüstungsstab, Frankreich, Abt. Ch. des Stabes, 352/41 of 16 July 1941 (T-77/OKW-1444/5,594,826). For Déat's support of Laval against Doriot in the Anti-Bolshevik Legion and in Doriot's autumn 1942 efforts to get German backing as Laval's successor, see Abetz memorandum to Ritter, 23 July 1942 (T-120/926/

Of course, it can be objected that the league leaders of the 1930's had triumphed in their ideas if not in their persons. There is no question that anti-Semitism, antiparliamentarism, and antiliberal reaction in all its forms were made easier by their long poisoning of public opinion. Charles Maurras, in particular, had already carried out "an intellectual and moral coup d'état." [27] By 1940, Maurras, always more interested in ideas than in action and now in his seventies, contented himself with an occasional lecture on Frédéric Mistral and the continued appearance until November 1942 in the Vichy zone of *Action française*. His damage had already been done. As Eugen Weber has said, many Frenchmen were Maurrassien without knowing it. The generation of 1940 was literally steeped in his ideas, from Pétain's speech writer René Gillouin and his *chef de cabinet* Henri Dumoulin de Labarthète to Charles de Gaulle. Maurrassiens were important in the army, the higher civil service, business, and in the Resistance as well as at Vichy. German intelligence was uncomfortable with the *Action française*'s longing for the days of Richelieu, and they even discussed arresting Maurras in 1943. The point remains: the 1930's league leaders did not move *en bloc* into Vichy office. [28]

Another minority failed to get equal "revenge" in 1940: conservative deputies. Even though the conservative minority in the parliament since 1936 had led the attack upon what they liked to call Blum's "Marxist experiment" in France, [29] and although they had voted almost unanimously for Pétain's full powers on 10 July 1940, they did not have the role under Vichy that they would have obtained in a lesser swing of the pendulum. One thinks of Jacques Bardoux, Laval's fellow senator from the Puy-de-Dôme and the author of numerous works in the 1930's

297241–50), Abetz (Paris) telegram 5295 to Ribbentrop of 19 November 1942 (T-120/928/297509–11), Schleier (Paris) 5640 to Ribbentrop of 3 December 1942 (T-120/935/298801). For the Front révolutionnaire national, see Schleier (Paris) 1359 of 1 May 1943 (T-120/1669H/394286).

[27] Stephen Wilson, "The *Action française* in French Intellectual Life," *The Historical Journal* XII:2 (1969).

[28] For a hostile German report on *Action française*'s preference for a divided Germany in the tradition of Richelieu, see T-120/434/220159–60.

[29] The phrase is from Jacques Bardoux, *L'Ordre nouveau: Face au communisme et racisme* (Paris, 1939).

on the need for a stronger state and for a middle way between communism and fascism. Or of Anatole de Monzie, a leader of the pro-Munich lobby of 1938, whose disappointment with Vichy is spelled out in his *La Saison des juges* (1943). Henri Lémery, Pétain's closest friend in the Senate, was minister of colonies briefly in the summer of 1940, along with seven other parliamentarians, including Ybarnégaray, Marquet, and other conservatives. Most of these went out on 12 July 1940. Pierre-Etienne Flandin, bringing in Senator Georges Portmann, gave a more parliamentary cast to things briefly in early 1941. But in general, Pierre Laval was the regime's exceptional parliamentarian; he helped justify his own survival by a frank animosity toward parliament. Of the thirty-five men who held posts of minister or Ministre-secrétaire d'état at Vichy between 25 June 1940 and August 1944, only eleven were parliamentarians, including six (Laval, Flandin, Chautemps, Marquet, Cathala, and Déat) who had been Third Republic ministers. Of the eleven, seven were already out by 12 July 1940, another (Marquet) in September, and Déat did not get office until 1944. Among the eighteen men who held posts of Secrétaire d'état between 1940 and 1944, with access to full cabinet meetings but not to ministerial meetings, only four were former Third Republic parliamentarians. The profound revulsion against deputies, even conservative ones, excluded from power at Vichy an important segment of the prewar conservative leadership.

Experts

"WE HAVE THE REPUBLIC ON TOP AND THE EMPIRE underneath," Paul Deschanel said around the turn of the century. In fact none of the successive French Republics has wanted to dismantle the centralized, professional bodies of public administration, rooted in enlightened despotism and systematized by the Jacobins and Napoleon, which form one of the proudest and most highly trained senior civil service leaderships in the world. The Second Republic used the prefects to impose the new regime on a reluctant countryside in the spring of 1848 and planned to create a loyal civil service through a single Ecole d'Administration. The Third Republic, born in counter-revolution, preferred to replace the personnel of Napoleon III's imperial bureaucracy rather than to abolish it. In the nineteenth century, while such British agencies as the Treasury and the India Office were establishing professionalism in the civil service, and while the Prussian civil service built upon a professionalism already well-established, the top French bodies of public administration also became professionalized, without interruption by revolutions or successions of regime. This meant creating special schools, entrance examinations, and strict regulations concerning advancement in such bodies as the Council of State, the Inspectorate of Finance, the Cour des Comptes, the prefectoral corps, the diplomatic corps, and the military officer corps. At the very period when universal manhood suffrage became applied to parliamentarians (1848) and to local government (1884), therefore, a less conspicuous parallel evolution created bodies of experts wielding increasing real powers in the state, beyond the reach of electoral control.[30]

It would be wrong to overlook the mutual interdependence of experts and elected officials in Third Republic public life, but toward the end of the Third Republic the dominant note was antagonism. Two common stereotypes in French literature reflect that antagonism. On the one hand, the deputy: a self-made man, provincial, often a garrulous southerner, raffish, eloquent, and not above backstairs deals and combinations. He was trained for no discipline or skill except getting elected, creating a clientele, and perhaps becoming ministerial material by knowing when to support a government and when to begin cultivating the opposition. One thinks of the politicians Romain Rolland's Jean Christophe met at the home of the deputy Achille Roussin: "brilliant talkers, mostly southerners, they were astonishingly

---

[30] For individual *grands corps de l'état,* see Pierre Lalumière, *L'Inspection générale des finances* (Paris, 1959); Charles E. Freedman, *The Conseil d'état* (New York, 1961).

dilletantish." On the other hand, the cool, superbly trained Parisian upper-class members of the *grands corps de l'état,* more likely to have lunch with the Duchess of Guermantes than with Achille Roussin. The hostile literary stereotype portrayed them as a permanent "wall of money" against ineffectual electoral representatives, men who had the real power to buy and sell France, like Ferral's brother in André Malraux' *La Condition humaine,* an official of the Finance Ministry who helped Ferral create a business empire in Indochina.

Behind these two literary stereotypes stood two social realities. On the one hand, the social origins of deputies grew markedly more modest over the course of the Third Republic. Country lawyers were the largest group, with teachers, country doctors, modest landowners, and store owners following along. This tendency was encouraged by the fact that the French parliament overrepresented small towns and rural France under the Third Republic. Many a deputy, even a prominent and successful one like Waldeck-Rousseau, could admit that he "never got used to Paris." Insofar as they had attended any of the *grandes écoles,* deputies were likely to have been trained in literature or philosophy at the Ecole Normale Supérieure, like Jaurès and Blum.[31] Recruitment to the *grands corps,* by contrast, grew more and more centered upon cultivated and wealthy Parisians. This mandarinate was the elite of an elite, selected through a daunting series of relentless examinations for which one prepared at expensive private schools. For the ultimate test, the written examination (concours) for entry into one of the *grands corps,* it became almost essential to attend the private Ecole Libre des Sciences Politiques in Paris. In 1934–35, 113 of the 117 successful candidates for the Council of State, 202 of the 211 who passed the exam for the Inspectorate of Finance, 82 of the 92 who passed the exam for the Cour des Comptes; and 240 of the 280

---

[31] Mattei Dogan, "Political Ascent in a Class Society: French Deputies, 1870–1958," in Marvick (ed.), *Political Decision-Makers* (New York, 1961). The fullest study of rural overrepresentation in the Third Republic is J. M. Cotteret *et al., Lois électorales et inégalités de représentation en France, 1936–60* (Paris, 1960). For Waldeck-Rousseau's remark, see Pierre Sorlin, *Waldeck-Rousseau* (Paris, 1967).

accepted into the diplomatic corps were graduates of *sciences po.*[32]

It is not surprising that these two social groups—deputies and experts—belonged to almost separate worlds under the Third Republic. The only prominent deputies who came from the *grands corps* in the later Third Republic were Joseph Caillaux and François Piétri (inspectors of finance) and Léon Blum (councillor of state), although one also finds a few backbenchers drawn from the *grands corps,* diplomacy, or the military. There were twenty-seven such "experts," for example, out of nearly a thousand deputies and senators in 1902.[33] Few graduates of the elite schools cared to risk their careers in the rough and tumble of politics. One finds only four deputies among some 2,500 members of the alumni association of the Ecole Libre des Sciences Politiques in 1938.[34] As for passage the other way, from deputy to high civil servant, schooling and professional rules of advancement virtually precluded it. At work, of course, local elected officials and prefectoral officials played each other off in a complicated symbiosis. At the top, experts worked for parliamentary committees and staffed the ministries. But the two types of career were remarkably separate in origins and attitudes as well as in literary stereotypes. The evolution was toward closed careers.[35]

Interwar stresses increased antagonisms between experts and deputies. As seen from the *grands corps,* the deputies seemed at best dilettantes, at worst ignorant bumpkins. Their decisions seemed to be made on the basis of political expediency rather than knowledge and efficiency. In contrast to this "jeu du forum," according to senior public administrators like Peyrouton and Bouthillier, trained experts had no reason to indulge in political intrigue. They saw public service as a "realistic"

[32] Pierre Rain, *L'Ecole libre des sciences politiques, 1871–1945* (Paris, 1963), 89 ff. In 1938 only 62 of the school's 2,000 students had financial support.

[33] *Annuaire du parlement,* 1902.

[34] Societé des anciens élèves de l'Ecole libre des sciences politiques, *Annuaire* (Paris, 1938). Two of the four deputies, René Dommange and Frédéric-Dupont, represented conservative Paris constituencies.

[35] Roger Grégoire, *La fonction publique* (Paris, 1954), 69.

process of "doing," rather than a "political" process of "making an impression." At his trial, Bouthillier boasted that "I never played politics, neither as student nor as public official. I never belonged to a political party or sought elective office. My activity was purely administrative." [36] Bouthillier's contempt for "politics" needs no further comment, but few deputies would have accepted his claim that administration was politically neutral. In particular, the Cartel des Gauches government of 1924 and the Popular Front of 1936 accused this closed elite world of erecting a "wall of money" against the economic reforms of Left governments, of quietly sabotaging economic policy by their permanent, uncontrollable influence in favor of an interlocking network of banks, corporations, and powerful families.

Each side in this underground tug-of-war thought the other side was gaining ground in the 1930's. Senior public administrators were discreet, but occasionally they spoke their minds. Henri Chardon, section president in the Council of State, could tell an audience of alumni of the Ecole Libre des Sciences Politiques in 1936 that France had been "out of political equilibrium" for fifty years: "She has given an excessive preponderance to political powers." [37] The left parties were much franker about their fears that permanent conservative administrators stood between parliament and the actual application of public policy. The Popular Front's education minister, Jean Zay, revived the 1848 idea of a single national school of public administration whose recruitment would produce a more democratic senior civil service. Nothing had been enacted, however, when the Popular Front ran out of steam.

Regarded more dispassionately, it was the experts who actually gained ground in the twentieth century. As elected legis-

---

[36] Marcel Peyrouton, *Du Service public à la prison commune* (Paris, 1950), 120; Yves Bouthillier, *Le Drame de l'armistice* (Paris, 1950), I, 13, 177; II, 256. *Ministère public c/Bouthillier*, 36.

[37] *La réforme de l'état,* Conférences organisées par la société des anciens élèves et élèves de l'Ecole libre des sciences politiques (Paris, 1936). Most of the conservative blueprints for constitutional reform provided a larger role for experts or functional representatives than in traditional French republican practice. See Jacques Bardoux, *La France de demain. Textes du comité technique pour la réforme de l'état* (Paris, 1936).

latures were confronted by more complex financial and technical matters, elected nonspecialists became less and less qualified to take well-informed decisions. The replacement of temporary legislative committees with permanent legislative committees in 1910 was already a major step away from the concept of all-competent elected representatives of a single national will. Not only did permanent committees encourage deputies and senators to specialize; they hired staffs from the *grands corps de l'état* who actually understood such matters as budget drafting, money management, and social insurance. A more ominous signal of legislative inadequacy between the wars was the new practice of voting full powers to a government to enact unpopular but necessary legislation by decree, without parliamentary vote, during economic crises. There was a tendency to appoint professional experts instead of members of parliament to ministerial posts, visible first in the military ministries, with Marshal Pétain as minister of war after the February riots of 1934 and General Maurin as minister in 1935–36. It was only a matter of degree, then, when Daladier and Reynaud named such nonelected experts to the war cabinets of 1939–40 as railroad engineer Raoul Dautry as minister of armaments (13 September 1939), playwright Jean Giraudoux and later newspaper magnate Jean Prouvost as ministers of information, Inspector of Finance Yves Bouthillier as minister of finance (5 January 1940), and Pétain again as minister without portfolio (18 May 1940).[38]

Pétain's first ministry (17 June–12 July 1940) could be considered a mere quantitative expansion of war government, about half deputies and half experts, many of them having already

[38] See Robert K. Gooch, *The French Parliamentary Committee System* (New York, 1935); Jacques Soubeyrol, *Les Décrets-lois sous la quatrième république* (Bordeaux, 1955). Denis Bichelonne, future Vichy minister of industrial production, appeared already as Dautry's *chef de cabinet*. Dautry himself, an apostle of the preeminence of expertise over representation between the wars, was excluded from office under Vichy and was thus available to continue this tradition as the Fourth Republic minister of reconstruction. See his *Organisation de la vie sociale* (Cahiers du redressement français, 1924), and his *Métier d'homme* (Paris, 1937), which calls for a "revolution of order," planning, and elite leadership, with admiring references to Lyautey and Rathenau.

served under Reynaud. The experts did not simply administer the state in an emergency, however. They entered public office like conquering heroes, with an alacrity and an explicit sense of vindication that shows how frustrated they had been behind the scenes in the later Third Republic. Even after the war, Marcel Peyrouton was willing to write that after the "bureaucratic revolution" of 1940, "the French administration had never been so useful, so respectable, so vigilant." [39]

The men who had exercised shadow control over Third Republic ministries, from senior administrative positions in the ministerial departments, now became ministers themselves. The professional senior public administrators, high civil servants, and members of the *grands corps de l'état* held major ministries: Alibert (former councillor of state) as minister of justice; two inspectors of finance, Baudouin and Bouthillier, as minister of foreign affairs and minister of finance. By the law of 15 July 1940, moreover, every ministry had a permanent secretary-general who was simultaneously a member of the council of state. The practice of detaching members of the *grands corps* to other prestigious posts continued at an even higher rate than under the Third Republic. For example, there were Inspectors of Finance François Piétri as ambassador to Spain in late 1940, Henri Dumoulin de Labarthète on Pétain's staff, Jacques Barnaud as chief economic negotiator for the regime (Délégue-général du gouvernement français pour les relations economiques franco-allemandes, February 1941–November 1942), Yves Bréart de Boisanger as head of the economic delegation to the Armistice Commission at Wiesbaden, Fournier as head of the French national railroads, and still others as prefects (Donati, Roger-Machar.), heads of Organization Committees (De Carmoy, Jacques Guérard), and secretaries-general of ministries (Henri Culmann). Councillors of state were even more frequently assigned to outside posts, such as the new permanent offices of secretary-general in each ministry. One thinks also of André Lavagne on Pétain's staff and a number of prefects (Chéneau de

[39] Peyrouton, 84.

Leyritz, Olivier de Sardan, François Ripert). Yves Bouthillier could well call the regime "the primacy of administration over politics." [40]

Experts included more than simply high civil servants, of course. Vichy conceptions of good governance meant not only that inspectors of finance should administer the economy and councillors of state manage ministerial departments, but that doctors should administer public health, farmers agricultural policy, engineers public works, and veterans and prolific fathers patriotism. Among Vichy ministers there were such other experts as six military officers in defense and colonial posts, a career colonial administrator (Peyrouton), engineers (Jean Berthelot, Denis Bichelonne, Robert Gibrat), executives of major corporations (Pucheu of the Comité des Forges' international sales branch, and Renault's nephew Lehideux), a judge (Frémicourt), law professors (Barthélemy, Georges Ripert), agricultural experts (Caziot, Achard), and academics (Carcopino, Chevalier). Broadly understood, experts and professionals in various fields made up eighteen of the thirty-five ministers of the Vichy regime as against eleven parliamentarians, and seven of the eighteen secretaries of state as against four parliamentarians.

The influx of experts and professionals brought impressive talents into the new regime. There was nothing marginal about the new expert ministers. They had been important men before 1940. In scholarly terms, at least, they were a much more impressive group than the ministers of the late Third Republic. Denis Bichelonne was the "gros major" of the Ecole Polytechnique, the man with the highest scholastic record in the school's history. Jean Berthelot had stood first in his class at both the Ecole Polytechnique and the Ecole des Mines. Robert Gibrat had stood first in his class at the Ecole des Mines and high at Polytechnique. The high civil servants were products of the most rigorous series of diplomas and examinations in any public ad-

---

[40] Bouthillier, I, 13. The number of *Conseillers d'Etat* detached for outside duty grew from two in 1937, four in 1939, seventeen in 1941, to nineteen in 1943. After a decrease to 11 in 1946, it continued to rise after the war: 15 in 1947, 26 in 1953. See Conseil d'Etat, *Annuaire*.

ministration in the world. In American terms, this was a brain trust; in British terms, a regime of double firsts.

The experts came into their own in the fall of 1940. The first Pétain government, with its substantial number of parliamentarians, gave way to the 12 July 1940 government with two parliamentarians, (Laval and Marquet) and the 6 September cabinet with one (Laval). December 13 was, at least in part, an attack upon the sole remaining Third Republic parliamentarian. Following the Flandin interlude (in which another parliamentarian, Georges Portmann, served briefly as minister of information), Darlan's regime was the experts' high noon. Such men as Lehideux, Pucheu, Barnaud, Berthelot, and Gibrat worked seriously for a united and modernized European planned economy. The experts' decline began with Laval's return in April 1942. More suspicious than ever and determined to keep tight control over the government, Laval surrounded himself instead with cronies, often former parliamentarians like himself. Pierre Cathala, a school friend, ex-Radical politician, and twice minister in Laval governments during the Third Republic (interior in 1931, agriculture in 1935), replaced the professional Bouthillier at the Ministry of Finance. René Bonnefoy, who had run Laval's newspaper *Le Moniteur du Puy-de-Dôme* since 1927, took over press affairs at the Ministry of Information. Cronies even replaced high civil servants in some posts of secretary-general of ministries, such as Georges Hilaire of the prefectoral corps, an old interwar friend of Laval, who became secretary-general of the Ministry of the Interior.[41] A further erosion of professionalism occurred with the total German occupation in November 1942. The two ministers who resigned at that point came from the expert contingent: Robert Gibrat and Admiral Auphan. By 1944 even technicians could see that the regime was finished and it was finally essential to call on strong-arm men like Darnand and Paris ligueurs like Déat. At its height, however, Vichy was more the creation of experts and professionals

[41] Hilaire wrote a defense of Laval, *L'Homme qu'il fallait tuer* (Paris, 1949), under the pseudonym of Julien Clermont. See also Pierre Cathala, *Face aux réalités* (Paris, 1948), and *Ministère public c/Bonnefoy*.

than of any other social group, and to judge Vichy is to judge the French elite.

Traditionalists

No WESTERN COUNTRY MOVED INTO THE URBAN AND industrial era without regretful backward looks. Since France moved only slowly and incompletely into this era, argument was still possible in 1940 about the place of cities and heavy industry in the national future. England, too, had her William Cobbetts and John Ruskins during the most optimistic period of industrial growth; the antimodernist rebellion was even stronger in France and still very vigorous in 1940.

It was only in the census of 1931 that the French population had been declared half "urban." [42] This was a stage passed by Britain early in the nineteenth century and by Germany, the United States, and Japan before the beginning of the twentieth. Thus France had known her greatest world role as a mercantilist and rural nation. Industrialization and urbanization had accompanied the long decline from the most powerful and populous state in the world under Louis XIV to the uneasy and doubting status of one major power among many in 1939. It was only natural that many Frenchmen attributed their past greatness to a balanced society and economy, the virtues of craftsmen and peasants, and essentially preindustrial values, and they attributed their decline to departures from these values. Even France's most recent great effort—holding Verdun in 1916—was credited by many more to peasant doggedness than to coal and steel. From this perspective, the defeat of 1940 was a punishment for whoring after modernity.

Modernity was, first of all, ugly. Daniel Halévy quoted with approval Michelet's remark that every age has its monuments

---

[42] *Urban,* in the categories of the French census, meant a commune whose chief town had more than 2,000 inhabitants.

and that those of the twentieth century would be barracks and factories. More to the point, modern economic structures were vulnerable. There exists a whole depression literature by economic observers later close to Marshal Pétain, such as Lucien Romier, who insisted that the French balanced society, with its large elements of self-sufficient small farmers, was much more resilient than the overspecialized British, American, and German economies. Those more highly industrialized economies, with their heavy reliance upon credit, advertising, and mass consumption, fell victim to speculative excesses and wild fluctuations. The depression, Romier thought, would be a healthy purge for overinflated luxury economies.[43]

Modernity was, finally, socially unstable. The city and the industrial division of labor eroded the national moral fiber. Urban and industrial populations were notoriously less fecund than rural populations. The decline in the French birthrate, the rot at the heartwood of French national life, seemed directly attributable to the modern abandonment of the countryside. The city and the industrial division of labor also produced the class struggle. By replacing organic communities of "whole" people with anonymous anthills of antagonistic proletarians and bourgeois, an industrializing country sowed unrest within its own walls.[44]

[43] Michelet, *Origines du XIXe siècle,* quoted in Daniel Halévy, *La Fin des notables* (Paris, 1937), 69. Lucien Romier, *Problèmes économiques de l'heure présente* (Montréal, n.d. [1932]). Romier was trained as a historian but worked as a publicist for businessmen's associations. He edited *La Journée industrielle* and was on the editorial board of *Le Figaro.* Although he believed in industrial rationalization [see the *Idées très simples pour les français* (1928), written for Ernest Mercier's "Redressement Français"], his dominant theme was fear and contempt for mass consumer society. See *Qui sera le maître: Europe ou Amérique* (1927). He was thought to be Pétain's closest adviser in 1941.

[44] The best example is probably Gustave Thibon, host of Simone Weil in 1941 and frequent guest of Marshal Pétain at Vichy. See Victor-Henry Debidour, "Un Défenseur des communautés organiques au XXe siècle, Gustave Thibon," in Claude Bernardin et al., *Libéralisme, Traditionalisme, Décentralisation: Contribution à l'histoire des idées politiques* (Paris, 1952), 125–27. Another example is René Gillouin, who wrote Pétain's most traditionalist policy statement, the speech of 13 August 1940. See his doctrinal articles in *Revue universelle,* 25 July and 10 August 1941. Barrès' novel *Les déracinés* (1897) and Proudhon were points of departure for this school.

Traditionalists worked from an equilibrium model of both economy and society. Like a healthy free economy, a healthy society should return to its natural stable balance after any shock. "Progress" was a will-o'-the-wisp, more likely to make a society sick and vulnerable, just as enticing people into debt for new consumer products made an economy vulnerable.[45]

To the traditionalists, the defeat of 1940 reflected France's divergence from the social patterns of her age of greatness. That diagnosis was itself a blueprint of reform. The very suffering of defeat could be portrayed as a first step toward moral regeneration. France had sinned by riches, class antagonism, and easy living. She would be healthier purged of debilitating urban and industrial excesses. "The French renaissance will be the fruit of that suffering," Pétain had already said on 13 June 1940 at Cangé.[46] Beyond that, the traditionalists talked seriously about reversing recent French social evolution. Pétain publicly declared "family agriculture" the "principal economic and social base of France" in his message of 11 October 1940. Agricultural, family, and regional proposals came wrapped in a language praising a simpler, more organic society. Vichy was to be the last stand of men who believed a nation could exert world influence without passing through the industrial revolution.

The traditionalists' critique of the division of labor led some of them to anticapitalism. Gustave Thibon argued that both capitalism and Marxism, for different reasons, rested upon fullest development of economic man, the division of labor carried to its furthest possibility, and the perpetuation of large structures. The genuinely revolutionary path, he felt, lay not through the industrial revolution but away from it. Thibon attempted to enlist French socialist tradition in his return to preindustrial values by drawing upon Proudhon, not the Proudhon of "Property is theft" but the Proudhon who wanted to replace state authority by free associations of independent artisans. The trouble, of course, was that replacing the state by self-regulating

[45] Romier, *Problèmes,* 162–63. See also Alfred Sauvy, *Histoire économique de la France entre les deux guerres* (Paris, 1967), II, 22, for others who rejoiced that France's old-fashioned economy was "timide et prospère."

[46] General Emile Laure, *Pétain* (Paris, 1941), 433.

economic associations led not to the guilds of printers or carpenters of 1840 but to the Organization Committees of giant corporations in 1940. Ironically, the very devotion of such traditionalists to the liberties of a simpler society left them defenseless against the craftier businessmen who quickly turned Vichy to privileged cartelization.[47]

This inner incoherence helps explain why the traditionalists made so little of their powerful position at Vichy. At first glance, they seem to have occupied the center of the stage. Pétain himself was a traditionalist. So was General Weygand, defense minister until 6 September 1940 and thereafter Vichy proconsul in French Africa, and a large proportion of the senior officer corps. *Secrétaires d'État* Lucien Romier and Henri Moysset, professor at the Centre d'Études Navales before the war and editor of the collected works of Proudhon, took major roles in preparing the labor charter, the regionalism plan, and the constitutional drafts of the National Council. Traditionalists were in charge of the Ministry of Education and the Vichy youth movement (Lyautey's disciple, Georges Lamirand). They predominated in Vichy mass organization: General de la Porte du Theil's Chantiers de la Jeunesse and the veterans' movement, the Légion Française des Combattants (Xavier Vallat, followed by another Lyautey disciple, François Valentin, conservative deputy representing Barrès' old constituency at Nancy). Traditionalists like Gillouin, Thibon, and Thierry-Maulnier filled the columns of *Le Temps* and *Le Figaro,* the main newspaper voices of the unoccupied zone. Traditionalists were the public face of Vichy.

Traditionalists helped reconcile several major overlapping social groups to the new regime. The officer corps remained almost entirely loyal to the regime through a combination of traditional obedience, professional rewards, and enthusiasm for a more hierarchical and authoritarian social order. French Catholics had every reason to be enthusiastic. Other traditional conservatives with misgivings about the break with England found the regime's religious policy reassuring. The Protestant

[47] Gustave Thibon, *Diagnostiques* (Paris, 1942). See also Léon Liebman, "Entre le mythe et la légende: 'L'Anti-capitalisme' de Vichy," *Revue de l'Institut de Sociologie* (Institut Solvay), 1964.

François Charles-Roux, for example, permanent secretary-general of the Foreign Office in the fall of 1940 and suspected of pro-Allied leanings, still talked with delight to the Nuncio, Monsignor Valerio Valeri, about the regime's return to religion.[48] Even the small but vocal Catholic left felt that it had more in common with the precapitalist and antisecular policies of Vichy than it had had with the individualist, secular republic. Emmanuel Mounier's *Esprit* continued to appear until late 1941 with a doctrinal position that overlapped with Vichy pretensions of ending the class struggle and finding a more organic replacement for political democracy.

The traditionalists' apparent power at Vichy was misleading, however, not only to contemporaries but to historians. They were conspicuous for their role in ceremony and their control over the written and spoken word at Vichy. The less visible and audible experts and professionals, however, actually set Vichy social policy, as I hope has been apparent in the chapter 2 discussions of agricultural and industrial affairs. Furthermore, the traditionalists' position eroded over time. They were most conspicuous in 1940, with Weygand at Defense, Baudouin as minister of foreign affairs, Xavier Vallat organizing the Veterans' Legion and General de la Porte du Theil the Chantiers de la Jeunesse, and Jacques Chevalier restoring religious instruction to public education. Even the experts of the early ministries—the monarchist Alibert as minister of justice, the paternalist colonial official Peyrouton as minister of the interior—belonged to the Vichy of hierarchy and authority more than to the Vichy of industrial rationalization and progress. Catholics began to give way to irreligious figures like Pucheu, even in propaganda functions (Paul Marion), in 1941. Radical Catholics broke with the regime over social policy in 1941 and a large cross section of Catholics over anti-Semitism when the deportations started in July 1942.

It is ironic, then, that the conspicuous but ineffectual tra-

---

[48] I have examined the officer corps more fully in *Parades and Politics at Vichy* (Princeton, N.J., 1966). For Charles-Roux, see *Actes et documents du Saint Siège relatifs à la seconde querre mondiale* (Vatican City, 1967), IV, 174–75.

ditionalists were so much more thoroughly purged at the Liberation than the experts, as we shall see. In a very real sense, their futility had already been abundantly demonstrated during the Vichy regime itself. Looking back from the France of the 1960's, the traditionalists of twenty years ago seem totally irrelevant. They had not seemed so in 1940. It was the Vichy experience itself that stripped the veil from French antimodernism by letting it come to power.

The Left at Vichy

THE VICHY ELITE CAME BY NO MEANS EXCLUSIVELY from the Right. The earthquake of 1940 also sprang open rifts and fissures within the Left. The vacuum of power opened opportunities for several sets of losers in 1930's quarrels within the non-Communist left. During the most active period of the National Revolution, a few leaders of the Socialist party (SFIO) and a number of leaders of the French trade union movement participated actively in the regime of Marshal Pétain.

Before looking at them, however, we must clear away a group of renegades from the Socialist and Radical parties who had already moved outside them before the war. In other words, we must deal with the ex-left first in order to avoid all confusion with the minority left of 1940. Evolution of politicians from youthful socialism to an opportunist parliamentary centrism, as in the case of Pierre Laval, was too frequent a Third Republic phenomenon to cause confusion here. In addition, however, there was a set of heresies of the Left in the 1930's that moved some Socialist and Radical politicians not into expedient centrism but into marginal new movements. Vichy offered opportunities to some of these. First, there was a kind of Jacobin concern for a "pure, hard" republic that alienated some younger Radicals from that party, the very personification of the "republic of pals." Gaston Bergery's "frontiste" movement of the late 1930's was an effort to escape party altogether in a new mass movement by which France could "catch up" and cease to be an "island of mediocrity" in the face of fascism and communism. By October

1938, he was calling for a "Government of Public Safety" capable of leaping beyond the sterile combinations of Popular Front and National Front to be both anticommunist and antitrust.

> To struggle against the trusts without struggling against the Stalinists is to lose the middle classes and peasants who represent nearly three-fourths of France. To struggle against the Stalinists without struggling against the trusts is to throw into opposition the working class, without whose cooperation social peace and any effort of reconstruction are myths.[49]

Bergery was active behind the scenes in the summer and fall of 1940, drafting Pétain's message of 11 October 1940 on controlling the excesses of capitalism, for example. He then became Vichy ambassador to the Soviet Union.

Another route away from the traditional left parties passed through economic planning and the attendant need for national authority. The Neosocialists of Marcel Déat broke with the SFIO at the annual congress of November 1933 on that ostensible point.

Some ex-left deputies passed directly into new authoritarian parties. It is remarkable how successfully La Rocque's Parti Social Français, in particular, drew upon disaffected Radicals as well as upon conservatives. Paul Creyssel, for example, passed from Radical in 1932 to "independent radical" (i.e., opposed to the Popular Front) in 1936 to PSF in December 1936. He was to be secretary of state for information at Vichy in 1943. As the more moderate PSF recruited among disillusioned Radicals, some renegade Communists passed directly from one militancy to another, as in the case of Doriot's Parti Populaire Français and the other former young Communists, such as Paul Marion, who joined it. Others, like François Chasseigne and L.-O. Frossard, who left the Communist party in 1929 and 1923 respectively, returned to the SFIO before becoming disillusioned with parliamentary solutions altogether.

Most of these ex-leftists were young, frustrated by the domination of the SFIO and the Radicals by elderly leadership that

[49] Gaston Bergery, "Conditions de la France nouvelle," *La Flèche,* no. 133, 26 August 1938; "Gouvernement de salut public," ibid., no. 141, 21 October 1938.

had emerged during the Dreyfus Affair. A final ex-leftist at Vichy was more a relic of an earlier form of left heresy. Hubert Lagardelle had been a leading spokesman of syndicalist hostility to parliamentary socialism before World War I as editor of *Le Mouvement socialiste*. He had published the works of leading European antiparliamentary revolutionaries and had introduced a leading syndicalist theorist to a leading practitioner: Georges Sorel to Benito Mussolini. Having then followed Mussolini's route from syndicalism to nationalist corporatism, Lagardelle had been called to Rome by Ambassador Henry de Jouvenel in January 1933 as "social councillor of the embassy," where he remained until 1940 without having, it seems, aided Franco-Italian relations by that remote and perhaps embarrassing acquaintance with Mussolini. When Lagardelle was made minister of labor in April 1942, replacing Belin, he had become a sixty-eight-year-old relic and the Labor Ministry largely an instrument of coercion.[50]

The ex-leftists at Vichy are perhaps less surprising than the minority leftists. From the trade union movement came a number of union officials ready to participate in the National Revolution. Although Léon Jouhaux, president of the CGT, was unwelcome at Vichy even if he had wanted a public role, his assistant director, René Belin, who had worked his way up through the ranks of the telephone union, felt released from a hostile majority. Belin's followers had set themselves apart in the 1930's around the review *Syndicats,* to defend a pure syndicalist conception of the CGT's role: its complete separation from party politics. Union hostility to middle-class parliamentary socialists was traditional in the CGT, but in 1936 syndicalism had become a code word for opposition to Communist power in the unions. When the CGT and the Communist unions (CGTU) were reunified in the spring of 1936 after fifteen years' separation, the Communist unions brought with them a tight subjection to the parliamentary party and its electoral tactics. A number of unionists resented this, on both traditional and ideological grounds. The *Syndicats* group also marked its distance from the Communist party after 1936 by opposing rearmament as a threat to

[50] *Ministère public c/Lagardelle.*

peace, by urging concessions to Hitler over Czechoslovakia, and by remaining skeptical of parliament as an avenue of social reform.

The men around *Syndicats* gathered some quite impressive force in French trade unionism in the late 1930's. One minority had become infatuated with economic planning, to which the syndicalist doctrine of replacing the state by workers' associations was theoretically adaptable. Georges Lefranc, for example, head of the CGT's night-school program in the 1930's and editor of the syndicalist planned-economy journal *Révolution constructive*, found himself in a minority as the SFIO parliamentary leadership in the 1930's rejected economic planning as a device to prop up capitalism.

A much larger minority reacted to the growing threat of war with more militant pacifism. The Left, remembering its role in 1914, had good reason to fear another "union sacrée" that, as Bergery said, would prevent continuing the struggle against "our own economic aristocracy" by diverting workers' energies into war. André Delmas' teachers' union (Syndicat National des Instituteurs) and Mathé's union of postal and telegraph workers were leaders in efforts to refuse war on behalf of Czechoslovakia in 1938 and to oppose rearmament. They organized the strike of 30 November 1938 and the "Immediate Peace" petition of the fall of 1939, signed by intellectuals as well as such labor leaders as Pierre Vigne, head of the mineworkers' federation. The French left was genuinely divided as to whether preparing for war against Hitler would deter war or encourage it. The two founders of the Comité des Intellectuels contre le Fascisme, ancestor of the Popular Front, reacted in opposite ways: Paul Rivet for pacifism, Paul Langevin for rearmament. André Delmas' pacifist motion received over a fourth of the votes at the November 1938 CGT congress. As the old syndicalist and pan-European Francis Delaisi said to Christian Pineau in June 1940, why should any more Frenchmen die for the City of London? [51]

[51] Gaston Bergery, "Le Pacte Franco-Russe" (Paris, 1935); André Delmas, *A Gauche de la barricade* (Paris, 1950). H. W. Ehrmann, *French Labor from Popular Front to Liberation* (New York, 1946). Christian Pineau, *La Simple vérité* (Paris, 1969), I, 67.

The largest left minority were the anti-Communists. As war against Hitler came to seem "Moscow's War," pacifism enhanced anticommunism. So did the ancient syndicalist tradition that rebelled at close union ties to a political party. There were also practical reasons for CGT disgruntlement with the Popular Front. When the Communist unions were reintegrated into the CGT in 1936, a number of union locals found themselves with a Communist majority and a number of CGT local leaders were voted out of office. Georges Dumoulin, for example, longtime CGT head for the Nord department, lost his place. Marcel Roy similarly lost his position as head of the metalworkers' federation. Raymond Froideval was forced out as head of the construction workers' federation. These displaced union officials, and more like them, gravitated to the *Syndicats* group. Even those who continued to control their unions after the Popular Front reunited them, such as André Delmas, were full of denunciations for Communist "colonization" since the "disaster" of 1936. These men formed the "Independence of Syndicalism" tendency at the CGT congress of November 1938, which received 7,221 votes against the 16,582 votes for the official position and 1,280 abstentions.[52]

The war itself completed the process by which some union officials arrived at Vichy. As Bergery had predicted, another "union sacrée" (with the Communists underground) led the CGT to accept wartime arbitration and cooperation with the regime, an infringement of peacetime syndical liberties that it seemed normal to continue in June 1940. The war also exposed the failure of traditional socialism, as seen by such figures as Georges Lefranc. His article in *Esprit* in June 1940 sums up all the disillusion of the left minorities of the 1930's. Traditional socialism had played its cards and lost in 1936. In 1936, the Left had passed from a minority to a mass, and Rousseau had been proven wrong. The mass was mentally inferior and morally weak. Efforts to convert them to economic planning went over their heads. It was a time to run socialism by an elite, authority, and faith. Communist betrayal further proved that workers'

[52] Delmas, 106, 154–55, 169; Ehrmann, 102.

liberties must be defended in a national rather than an international context. The old ideals were now "a pile of ruins." Quoting Belin, he said it was time to accept the integration of workers into the economy and cooperation with such state machinery as arbitration. Workers must bury what is dead and move forward.[53]

The elimination of communism followed by parliamentary socialism opened the way for these outsiders of the Left. René Belin became minister of industrial production and labor from 14 July 1940 to 23 February 1941 and remained minister of labor until 18 April 1942. Raymond Froideval and Georges Lefranc served on his staff. Some of the anti-Communist union officials had already gotten their pre-1936 jobs back with the suppression of the Communist party in September 1939. Antibolshevism carried Georges Dumoulin, Marcel Roy, and others as far as cooperation with Abetz' labor propaganda newspapers in Paris, *La France au travail* and *L'Atelier.* Dumoulin went on to serve as inspector-general of the Comités Sociaux, those stillborn local mixed committees of workers, administrators, and employers foreseen under the Charte du travail, when Henry Lagardelle became minister of labor in 1942. Marcel Roy was named a workers' delegate to the Organization Committee for the automobile industry. Even a number of more circumspect union leaders cooperated for a time with the new labor machinery, if Georges Lefranc's memory is correct.[54]

Naturally enough, the antiparty bias of Vichy made it easier for selected union officials than for SFIO leaders to participate. A few SFIO leaders had broken with Blum in 1936, however, over rearmament and pacifism. Paul Faure, secretary-general of the SFIO, was the most prominent of these. Paul Faure, son of a socialist and himself a Guesdist from his school days, re-

[53] Georges Lefranc, "Bilan de notre socialisme," *Esprit,* no. 92, June 1940. See also P.-A. Touchard, "L'Evolution du syndicalisme," *ibid.,* no. 89, February 1940.

[54] *Ministère public c/Belin;* Georges Lefranc, *Les Expériences syndicales en France de 1939 à 1950* (Paris, 1950); for Dumoulin, see *Figaro,* 25 June 1942, *Ministère public c/Marquet,* 78, and Ehrmann, 71, 103, 105, 203, 220, 247–48. For Marcel Roy, see *Le Temps,* 2–3 May 1941, Ehrmann, 102, and Lefranc, 24.

tained a virulent anticommunism from the split at Tours in 1920, which he continued between the wars with a brusque abruptness proper to a party functionary rather than to a deputy. He was also a leading proponent of pacifism in the party. Although the views he expressed in *Les Marchands de canon et la paix* (1924) were orthodox in the 1920's, only a minority followed Faure in continuing to oppose rearmament after 1936 in the face of Hitler. Although Paul Faure expected to become a minister in 1940, he served only as adviser to Laval. He reappears briefly in the German documents as an emissary between Vichy and the Germans after Laval's dismissal on 13 December 1940.[55] The other major SFIO renegade was Charles Spinasse, Blum's Minister of National Economy in 1936. He belonged less to Vichy than to the journalistic world of Paris, where he edited *Le Rouge et le bleu* in 1941–42.

The outsider-left at Vichy casts some light on quarrels in the CGT and the SFIO before the war. More importantly, it shows the breadth of Marshal Pétain's following, at least for the first year or two. Far from being new men, or leaders of the 1930's radical right, the collaborators were a selection of Third Republic notables from one end of the political spectrum to the other. It is now time to see how long this elite remained collaborators.

[55] T-120/221/119666, 199826; T-120/587/243422.

IV / Collaboration—1942–44:
Between Liberation and Revolution

IN RETROSPECT, THE WINTER OF 1942–43 WAS THE war's turning point. On 23 October 1942 the great tank battle began at El Alamein, hardly two hundred miles from the Suez Canal, which turned back Rommel's deepest advance in North Africa. During the night of November 7–8, Allied forces landed on the south shore of the Mediterranean in Morocco and Algeria. Rommel was now taken from behind, and the dream of some German strategists, particularly navy men like Admiral Raeder, of making that sea an Axis lake was at an end. Although the Germans quickly occupied the rest of France, fortress Europe was now vulnerable from the south. On the eastern front, General Paulus' Sixth Army—twenty-two divisions—was encircled and cut off by a Soviet counterattack at Stalingrad in the days after November 20. Paulus surrendered on 31 January 1943. Besieged Leningrad had finally been relieved early that same month. The German high tide on the eastern front had passed.

During the same weeks, Vichy France also lost its main elements of independence. Responding to the Allied landing in North Africa, German forces moved into the southern zone on

November 11. All of France was now directly occupied (the Italians occupied those areas east of the Rhône that they had previously inspected under the armistice terms; Germans occupied the rest). Although the armistice remained in effect and although Hitler carefully maintained the useful fiction of Vichy French sovereignty,[1] the practical conditions of life in the Vichy zone were now little different from those in the north. A German officer, General von Neubronn, resided at Vichy as the representative of the senior German commander in the west, General von Rundstedt (*Oberbefehlshaber West*). The Armistice Army's dissolution on November 28 freed French officers from direct military discipline but not from their oath to obey Marshal Pétain's orders of inaction. The two trump cards in Vichy's hand now vanished: the French fleet, scuttled on November 28 as the Germans prepared to seize it, and the empire, now largely in Allied hands. Of Vichy's bargaining counters (fleet, empire, and the threat of joining the Allies), the first two were gone, and by remaining in Vichy even after a total German occupation, Marshal Pétain had shown that he would never use the third.

Domestic conditions in France also grew much worse in 1942–43. Laval's old pleas for striking improvements in the conditions of life, concessions "die ins Auge fallen," seemed more fruitless than ever after the summer of 1942. This was the period, we now know, in which Germany finally began to subject its civilian population to the rigors of a war economy nearer the sort endured in England since 1940.[2] The occupied countries were explicitly intended to have it worse than the Germans. French food rations were reduced in July 1942. Massive Jewish deportations began in the same month. Volunteer labor from the west was replaced by Laval's "relève" system in September, whereby a prisoner of war was released for every three skilled

---

[1] This issue was settled on 22 December 1942. See German Foreign office account, Pol. 1 M. 3503 g.Rs., 23 December 1942 (T-120/4634H/E208777–84).

[2] Alan S. Milward, *The German Economy at War* (London, 1965); Albert Speer, *Inside the Third Reich* (New York, 1970), 222, 256. At the beginning of 1942, production of civilian consumer goods in Germany was still only 3 percent below peacetime levels. The Germans took real austerity measures only after Stalingrad.

French workers sent to Germany, and finally in February 1943 French workmen were drafted for German factories. By this point Vichy had irrevocably lost its mass base of acceptance.

A few highly placed figures began to join the Allied cause after November 1942. Most of these were simply overtaken by the Allied landing in North Africa. Admiral Darlan was the most eminent. Having served loyally as commander in chief of the armed forces after Laval replaced him as head of the government in April 1942, and having just finished an inspection tour of Vichy defenses against Allied invasion in Africa, he had been called back to Algiers on November 5 by the news that his son Alain had been hospitalized there with polio. Surprised and enraged by the Allied landing, Darlan commanded the Vichy defenses in North Africa and then accepted a cease-fire on November 11 only after the Germans had entered the unoccupied zone of France and there was nothing left to save by observing the armistice. He tried for the next week to get the Allies to accept a neutral Pétiniste regime in North Africa. Only after General Mark Clark had threatened to institute direct Allied military government, and after General Barré's Vichy forces in Tunisia had actually entered into combat on 17 November against German reinforcements arriving there, did Darlan agree to commit French resources in North Africa to the Allied side. There arose in North Africa a sort of "inverse Vichy" under Allied occupation. At the top, Darlan served as high commissioner of the "État français," claiming secret approval of Marshal Pétain whose public orders for continued resistance against the Allies were attributed to German pressure. "The Marshal is no longer free," said a Darlan proclamation of 21 November. Around him, Darlan formed an "Imperial Council" of the senior Vichy officials and officers present and willing to participate in the war against Germany: General Bergeret, Vichy aviation minister; General Noguès, high commissioner of Morocco; Governor-General Boisson of French West Africa, Governor-General Yves Châtel of Algeria, and General Henri Giraud, who had been brought off from occupied France in a British submarine in order to head pro-Allied French military forces in North Africa. Under this regime, the bulk of the

French Army and administration in North Africa, ardently Pétiniste, returned to war against the Axis. Vichy legislation remained on the statute books, including Jewish disabilities, even after Darlan's assassination on December 24. That courageous handful of French officers in North Africa who had conspired in advance to help the Allied landing instead of to repel it (General Mast, Colonel Béthouart, and others) were quietly penalized. In this fashion, a large number of loyal Vichy officers and civil servants switched to the Allied side in perfect legality and without abandoning the National Revolution. For example, the commander of French troops in Algeria, General Alphonse Juin, who had only eleven months earlier negotiated with Marshal Goering in Berlin about what the French would do if Rommel had to fall back into Tunisia, now set out to earn his Marshal's baton as commander of French forces in the Italian campaign in 1943.[3]

Other senior Vichy and ex-Vichy figures rallied to the Darlan-Giraud regime in North Africa. Pierre-Etienne Flandin had already gone to North Africa from his retirement in Cap St. Jean Ferrat in October 1942; Pierre Pucheu, who had been Darlan's minister of the interior up to April 1942, left for

[3] The complicated evolution of Admiral Darlan is most reliably followed in *FRUS*, II, 1940, in the absence of a trial. Although his aide Major Dorange made discreet contact with Robert Murphy in October 1942, he did not expect an Allied landing so early, and Major Dorange was instrumental in helping crush the pro-Allied coup at Algiers military headquarters in the early hours of November 8. See *FRUS*, II, 1942, and Yves-Maxime Danan, *La Vie politique à Alger de 1940 à 1944* (Paris, 1963), 103–6. Without citing any contemporary American sources, Danan claims that American authorities preferred to deal with Vichyite authorities in North Africa in November 1942 because the Resistance would have made the American "take-over" harder. The Vichy authorities were, of course, the only available force capable of controlling the French officer corps. I have analyzed the officers' evolution from defense to neutrality to association with the Allies against the Germans during the period November 8–17 in more detail in *Parades and Politics at Vichy* (Princeton, N.J., 1966), chap. 11. General Bergeret won acquittal in 1948 by an apparently fictitious claim that he knew in advance about the Allied landing and went to Algiers to join it. Haute Cour de justice, Arrêt de non-lieu: General Bergeret. The most useful accounts of November 1942 from the point of view of the few French officers who tried to facilitate the Allied landing by a simultaneous coup are an article by Colonel Jousse in *Esprit*, 1 January 1945, and the memoirs of General Béthouart, *Cinq années d'espérance* (Paris, 1968).

North Africa through Spain in February 1943 expecting to be mobilized as a reserve officer; Marcel Peyrouton, who had been returned after 13 December 1940 to his prewar post as ambassador to Argentina as a punishment for his role as minister of the interior, resigned in April 1942 when Laval came back to power. He went to Algiers in January 1943 and was made governor-general of Algeria. There were a few upper civil servants, like the director of the foreign exchange section of the Finance Ministry, Maurice Couve de Murville, who crossed to North Africa through Spain in May 1943. The Darlan-Giraud regime also drew a few general officers from France after November 1942, in contrast to the Free French. Jean de Lattre de Tassigny, who had been imprisoned in November 1942 for trying to move his unit of the Armistice Army into the mountains as the Germans entered the Vichy zone, escaped with the aid of his wife and son. He was to become marshal of France for commanding the French advance into Bavaria and Austria in 1945. General Alphonse Georges, former commander of the northeastern front in May–June 1940, arrived in Algeria in June 1943 but took little part in subsequent events. The Darlan-Giraud neo-Vichy regime in North Africa offered a way back to power for some Vichy outsiders. It offered a legitimate way back to the war for some genuine *attentistes* for whom the wait was now over.

What needs explaining is how few major Vichy figures left seats of power in November 1942. Only two men left the cabinet: Admiral Auphan, minister of the navy, and Robert Gibrat, secretary of state for communications, who had been in North Africa inspecting construction work on the Mediterranean-Niger Railway and who returned to Vichy before deciding to resign. Neither joined the Allied cause. Except for Couve de Murville, the high civil servants continued by and large to serve the state. Only the diplomatic corps, whose members were already overseas and open to another perspective, suffered substantial defections after November 1942. Some members of the public services, of course, were working secretly for the Resistance at their posts, including such celebrated Resistance figures as Jacques Chaban-Delmas, inspector of finance and future general in the Forces Françaises de l'Intérieur, and future prime minister in the

Fifth Republic. If the civil service resistance assumed the same proportions as that of the general population, however (and we have no evidence that it was either lower or higher), it ran around 2–3 percent. In the activist organizations, some militant patriots such as Biaggi shifted after November 1942 from the Veterans' Legion to such conservative resistance movements as the OCM (Organisation Civile et Militaire). The general impression at Vichy after November 1942 remained one of continuity. Secessions were the exception rather than the rule.

Even for those Frenchmen studying the course of the war for signs, the turn of the tide was not yet obvious. The very scope of the 1940 defeat nurtured a faith in German invincibility that was slow to weaken. Even in 1943 some signs still pointed to German progress. On the eastern front, they retook Kharkov in March 1943 and continued to hold vast tracts of Russian soil until the Soviet counterattacks of late 1943 pushed them back once more. It was in the spring of 1943 that Allied shipping in the North Atlantic suffered its heaviest casualties of the whole war. Even after the Allied landing of November 1942, it was tempting to believe that the Allies would be incapable of gathering a preponderance of force anywhere at the perimeter of fortress Europe. Even if one believed that Hitler could no longer defeat England, it was a vast leap from there to believing in 1943 that the Allies could defeat Hitler. Thus people like Gaston Bergery, now Vichy's ambassador to Turkey, told German Ambassador Franz von Papen in Istanbul in September 1943 that Pétain's position was growing stronger. Admiral Bléhaut, minister of colonies, could still write a sentence in August 1944 beginning with the words "whatever the outcome of the war." [4] Vichy leaders, not unintelligent men, could imagine a stalemate or a compromise peace far into 1944.

Some may have held on at Vichy because they felt they faced only execution from the other side. That burned-boats feeling took on some substance when Pierre Pucheu found himself arrested and put on trial in May 1943 instead of welcomed quietly into the army as a reserve officer as he anticipated. When

---

[4] Von Papen's report on conversation with Bergery, (T-120/6726H/ E510434); *Ministère public c/Bléhaut,* fascicule 2.

Pucheu crossed the Pyrenees into Spain in early 1943, he could suppose that his old colleagues like General Bergeret who were still influential in North Africa would make the transition easy. When he arrived in Casablanca on 9 May 1943, however, the climate in "liberated" North Africa was already switching from neo-Pétinisme to Gaullism. By the time General de Gaulle himself arrived from London to make Algiers his headquarters on May 30, Pucheu had already been consigned to forced residence on May 11 in an outpost at the edge of the Sahara. He was the first Vichy minister to be tried under the 3 September 1943 decree of the French Committee of National Liberation at Algiers charging all Vichy ministers with treason, promising them trials after the Liberation, and ordering public servants not to obey their orders. He was shot on 20 March 1944. Already, reported German intelligence, collaborators knew they had to win or die.[5]

At bottom, however, the decisive reason holding men to the Vichy solution was an instinctual commitment to public order as the highest good. Public servants continued to obey the state. Even more, as the state came under challenge by Resistance vigilantism, a commitment to the ongoing functioning of the state reinforced the weight of routine. Other members of the elite chose the known over the unknown: the possible future risks of discredit over the certain present risks of resistance. Resistance was not merely personally perilous. It was also a step toward social revolution.

Allied victory could seem an even greater threat to social order than continued German occupation after 1942. Personal considerations aside, the promise of violent liberation at Allied hands held more risks than advantages. For one thing, Allied invasion meant a return to war, perhaps another long bloodbath on French soil like the one that had led France to the brink of revolution in May–June 1917. Secondly, an Allied invasion threatened to trigger an internal rising by a Resistance movement that

---

[5] Deutscher General Vichy "Akte 7a: Stimmung; Akte 7b: Lage" (T-501/120/383-87, 397-402); Pierre Pucheu, *Ma Vie* (Paris, 1948); Paul Buttin, *Le procès Pucheu* (Paris, 1947); Gen. Schmitt, *Toute la vérité sur le procès Pucheu* (Paris, 1963).

in 1942-43 was assuming ever more clearly the dimensions of domestic social revolution. With its major Communist participation and its pronouncements about the new republic of the future, the Resistance could seem directed more at the French social status quo in 1942-43 than against the German Army. The priorities were clear for many Frenchmen of status and property. German occupation might be bad, but liberation by force would be worse. By late 1943, the prospects of Russian expansion in Europe were adding a further specter.

Even as Hitler seemed to lose the initiative in the winter of 1942-43, therefore, and even as the conditions of life in occupied France grew more unbearable, threats to order grew simultaneously more ominous. Those threats helped drown out other signals that might have made deliverance at Allied hands seem more feasible and more desirable by 1943. Conditions were growing worse in 1943, but that was not necessarily a signal to throw oneself into the cauldron of renewed war. The worse things became, the more precious was the French island of neutrality.

General de la Porte du Theil, who had been caught on an inspection trip in North Africa by the Allied landing, returned to preach duty and unity to his Chantiers de la Jeunesse in metropolitan France. The conflicting orders, confused loyalties, and incipient civil war he had seen among French authorities there during the painful evolution from opposition to association with the Allies between November 8 and November 17 tormented his straightforward soldier's heart. The "moral crisis" produced by the "American attack" could very well repeat itself soon in France, he warned the staff of the Youth Camps. When that day came, "the only way to maintain internal peace" would be to adhere to "the most absolute loyalty toward the marshal, the sole responsible figure . . . and sole guarantor of national unity. . . . He has received a mandate to lead us, and the enlightenment for that will never fail him." Since the authorities were the only source of accurate information, the only result of following individual promptings would be chaos. "The problem facing France," he wrote, "is essentially a problem of internal order." No disinterested help could be expected from outside. The Free French of London and Algiers were no "more free" than the marshal. "Unfortunately, they egg us on from outside, knowing that is the only way to reduce us to their will." France's only real salvation is to continue to work on her own salvation from within, "to save what we still have, which is not negligible: an administration and a university that express French thought and that carry on the education of French youth according to the traditional line."

Some dreamers might think, wrote General de la Porte du Theil, that France could be liberated "in a few months" by resolute action. Such hotheads "forget to what an extent the defeat has damaged us."

> There is no lack of doctors who offer violent prescriptions. Violence leads to nothing durable. No outsider will help us for our own reasons: a dangerous illusion fostered by softness and lethargy of too many Frenchmen. Only we can make some place for ourselves in the Europe which will have to be reconstructed some day. Whatever way you turn the problem, there are peoples of 30 to 80 millions who cannot simply be removed from the map or reduced to slavery without sowing the causes of future wars. On condition, of course, that they are really nations and not undisciplined masses divided into rival bands.[6]

In the period following November 1942, a return to war was no more palatable to many Frenchmen than before. Indeed, the values and priorities that had recommended the armistice in June 1940 seemed more compelling than ever. What had been called "Moscow's War" in 1939 now promised to become a *guerrilla* as well. Pétain and Laval advocated a compromise peace with mounting urgency in 1943. Their conversations with high-ranking Germans in 1943 returned over and over to two fixations: avoidance of any more fighting on French soil and French mediation of a compromise peace.

[6] *Sources, éléments de travail pour les chefs des Chantiers de la jeunesse,* no. 16, November 1942; Chantiers de la jeunesse, *Bulletin périodique officiel,* no. 112 (15 Nov. 1942), no. 113 (25 Nov. 1942), and no. 115 (15 Dec. 1942). I owe access to these publications to MM. Pierre Martin and Dominique Morin in Paris. General de la Porte du Theil's deportation by the Germans in May 1944, which won him acquittal after the war, followed a German decision to arrest all leaders capable of any role whatever in France. It was typical of German inability to distinguish between Vichy nationalists and the Resistance.

Pétain's "main goal," he had already told Prince Rohan on 20 October 1942, was to "keep France from becoming a battleground." He came back to the same words repeatedly in 1943. His "greatest worry," he said to General von Neubronn on 15 July 1943, was that France would again "become a battleground." All he wanted was peace for fear of Bolshevik expansion, he told the German Consul-General Roland Krug von Nidda, whom he encountered in the park in Vichy on 23 August.[7]

Pétain grasped at straws in his yearning for a compromise peace. In October 1942, talking with Prince Rohan, he expected the defeat of Russia and Britain that would lead the United States to a compromise peace. Then Hitler, he thought, could turn to making the New Europe in which Germany, Italy, Spain, and France could all play leading roles. With General von Neubronn in July 1943, he found it possible to hope that when Giraud and de Gaulle had worn each other out squabbling in North Africa, his many supporters there would help restore Vichy authority. The worst enemy was fanaticism. In August 1943 he held forth to Krug von Nidda on the virtues of a common German-Anglo-Saxon front against bolshevism. The virtues of such an alliance would be apparent to all Europeans, he thought, if only Britain were not led by the fanatical Churchill and the United States by the Jews. It would be far more preferable, for example, than "a renewed German-Bolshevik compromise." Nettled by this sly reference to the Hitler-Stalin Pact of 1939, Krug assured Pétain that "in spite of temporary reverses" Germany would accept only a "final solution" and no compromise settlements with either side. Krug must have deepened Pétain's despair by showing that the Germans were no less blindly "fanatical" than Churchill.

Despite such discouragements, Pétain and Laval kept trying to thrust France forward as the possible mediator of a compromise peace. On 9 February 1943 Pétain drew Krug von Nidda

[7] Pétain-Prince Rohan conversation, 20 October 1942, in German Foreign Office file, "Abwehr-Frankreich" (T-120/894/291479–83). The Pétain-von Neubronn conversation of 15 July 1943 and the Pétain-Krug von Nidda conversation of 23 August 1943 are found in Pariser Botschaft, Bdl. 1120, "Politische Beziehungen Frankreich-Deutschland, vol. 2" (T-120/3546H/E022140–41, 022155–56).

out on the Russian campaign, a subject in which he expressed great interest and considerable knowledge. Then he suggested that France would be a convenient go-between if Germany ever needed to come to an understanding with the western Allies in order to concentrate all her forces on the Communist enemy. In March Laval reminded Schleier that Germany was unlikely to be able to march simultaneously into Moscow, London, and Washington. A more ideal future, he suggested, was "cooperation between America and Europe in which France is to be the connecting link." France could play this role, he explained, if "the Axis powers declare their readiness to secure for her a future in the New Europe which corresponds to her continental and imperial past." The dream of neutral France stepping forward as the sole remaining arbiter among the exhausted giants must have been a very tempting one in the otherwise bleak and helpless position of 1943. Mediation was perhaps the only way back to French influence without war, and France could perhaps purchase more independence by proving her usefulness in that role. It was only a pipe dream, but some of the less skillful character witnesses in Pétain's trial were still talking about it in 1945. The ancient General Lannurien recalled that Pétain believed that only he would be "strong enough to talk to both the Germans and the Allies when the day of the green baize tables" had come. The only trouble was that the Allies were no more interested in green baize tables than the Germans.[8]

Marshal Pétain and his cabinet members whose 1943 language survives were not *attentistes*. They were not waiting for the moment to jump back into the war. They were dead set against an Allied landing that could only provoke total German occupation on the one hand or internal civil war on the other.

[8] Achenbach (Paris) 910 to Berlin of 9 February 1943 (T-120/1832/418619-20) reports Pétain's mediation suggestion to Krug von Nidda. Laval's mediation efforts in 1943-44 are given particular attention in Geoffrey Warner, *Laval*, 360, 365-67, 392-96. Also see below, p. 328. General Lannurien's testimony appears in *Procès Pétain*, 317 (*Journal officiel* edition). General de la Porte du Theil also recalled Pétain's arbitration hopes in *Tronçais*, the "alumni" bulletin of the Chantiers de la Jeunesse, special issue on Pétain's death, 1951. By then, 1943 ideas of an anti-British, pro-American, anti-Communist Europe had acquired a Cold War currency in which Pétain and Laval could appear as forerunners.

They wanted France to evolve back to continental and imperial power within the new European status quo, even in 1943. They still longed for the compromise peace they had hoped the United States would mediate in 1941. They chose the apparently lesser risks of continued collaboration over the risks of revolution that armed liberation seemed to entail.

Threats to the Social Order—1: Resistance

And now, set Europe ablaze!
—*Winston Churchill's instructions to the Special Operations*
Executive, 1940

The Marshal . . . agreed to sign the armistice and to preside over this government in order to save his country from revolution and ruin. . . .
—*General Huntziger to General von Stülpnagel, 7 August*
1940 [9]

THE VICHY REGIME CAME INTO EXISTENCE MASTERING a movement of resistance to the armistice in the colonies. Its very credibility as a legitimate regime depended on its continuing ability to neutralize anti-German activists. From the moment it persuaded Generals Noguès and Mittelhauser in North Africa and the Middle East to accept the armistice on 25 June 1940 up through its first year of existence, Marshal Pétain's regime had been quite successful. Although the internal Resistance had begun to trouble public order after the summer of 1941, the Gaullist movement was probably weaker in France after the loss of Syria to Britain in July 1941 than before.

Active opposition to an authoritarian and widely supported regime is a minority business at best. Resistance requires a clear target, and in the unoccupied part of France it was not altogether clear to a lot of anti-German Frenchmen whether Vichy was

[9] M. R. D. Foot, *SOE in France* (London, 1966); *DFCAA*, I, 108.

an enemy too. Resistance also requires some hope, and until late in the war, throwing the Germans back across the Rhine seemed beyond mortal strength. Resistance, finally, means accepting lawlessness on behalf of a higher good and the replacement of routine by a life of relentless improvisation. Only the young and the already outcast can adapt easily to a life of extended rebellion, and that is why the Resistance in France contained a disproportionate share of the young, Communists, and old street-fighters from the prewar protofascist leagues. The active resistance's outlaw status, in turn, magnified the fears it aroused in solid citizens.

It was with an act of assassination that active resistance first thrust itself upon French public consciousness. The shooting of the naval cadet Moser on the subway platform of Barbès-Rochechouart in Paris on 21 August 1941 has already been described, as has the sickening toll of hostages whom the Germans shot following the subsequent assassinations of that autumn. The point is that active resistance to the German occupation stepped upon the stage firmly linked to the Bolshevik menace. Marshal Pétain's speech of August 11, 1941, and the extensive security legislation of that week cemented that identification, as did the German propaganda label of "Communist" attached to the hostages they shot. Pétain, Darlan, and Goebbels tacitly agreed to link all active resistance to bolshevism.

While direct action by the Resistance subsided after the fall of 1941—1942 was the time at which the Gaullists and the internal Resistance began to coordinate their organizations—resistance took on a more militant and alarming cast again after November 1942. It was Hitler who did most to mobilize young people for the Resistance by trying to mobilize them for work in German factories. Laval's efforts to placate Gauleiter Sauckel with volunteers having failed, the Service du Travail Obligatoire began summoning whole age classes of young Frenchmen in draft contingents to go to work in German factories in February 1943. Young men faced the choice of taking the train to Germany or the path to the mountains. Thousands who could get to remote areas chose the mountains, and encampments of young men, the *maquis,* sprang up in the Alps, the Massif central, and the Pyrenees. The camps had, of course, to eat and to defend themselves. They supported themselves at least in part by raids on sources of money and supplies. They raided offices of the STO and burned draft files. It is not inconceivable that a few more sinister renegades joined them. The *guerrilla,* which Pétain and others had feared in 1940 would destroy France, had begun.

The issue of premature violence divided even the active Resistance. General de Gaulle publicly deplored the assassinations of 1941 for their waste of life for the sake of no immediate gain. The Resistance was always torn between those preparing for action on some still-distant D-day and those taking action at once. Deeper there lay the division between those who wanted only to chase the Germans out and those who wanted also to change French society root and branch. There was a muted civil war within the armed Resistance in 1943 and 1944 between those Resistance groups solidly staffed by army officers and the *francs-tireurs* partisans. Some of the postwar trials turned up the edge of the rug under which these distressing clashes have been swept, suggesting that the military resistance, the Secret Army, actually executed some of the "anarchical" *francs-tireurs* as "bandits." A report by Joseph Darnand, secretary of state for the maintenance of order in 1944, indicated that it was not rare to see notices posted in the *Haute-Savoie* declaring that

> We, members of the Secret Army, have this morning executed such-and-such, belonging to the *francs-tireurs* partisans, who committed acts of brigandage contrary to the mission which we imposed upon ourselves: to serve France honestly.[10]

Small wonder, then, that the solid citizens of France reacted no less vigorously than the military Resistance against the "anarchy" and "brigandage" that threatened their property and called down German reprisals. Already in 1941 General Laure called the assassinations "gangsterism" and General Weygand deplored them to American diplomats. By 1943 the identifica-

---

[10] *Les Procès de la collaboration* (Paris, 1948), 263, 314. See also the charges of "brigandage" by Prince Xavier de Bourbon, who had sheltered units of the military Resistance and who survived deportation to Dachau, *Ministère publique c/Chevalier,* 154. He admitted his group killed some "faux maquis."

tion of resistance with anarchy had become much more shrill. Jacques Chevalier, former minister of education and Pétain's godson, wrote the marshal panicky letters from Grenoble, where the alpine *maquis* were a major force. In late 1943 and early 1944 Chevalier was proposing the establishment of armed groups of "sure men" to form a kind of anticommunist counter-*maquis*. It had taken no more than a couple of hundred men to hold Seville until Franco's arrival in 1936, he pointed out to Georges Hilaire in a letter of 2 August 1943. "It is in that way, and not in any other way, that order can be saved in France as it was on 19 July 1936 in all the regions of Spain where such a solid secret organization existed." Even after the war, before juries of Resistance veterans, some Vichy officials continued to maintain that they had known of no Resistance in 1943 except "brigands." [11]

The prospect of liberation by the sword, under the auspices of "brigands," was anything but alluring to many Frenchmen. Some 45,000 volunteered for the infamous Milice in 1944, partly, perhaps, to escape from labor service, partly for fanaticism, but at least in part to help defend "law and order." Counting police and military guard units as well, it is likely that as many Frenchmen participated in 1943-44 in putting down "disorder" as participated in active Resistance. Almost every Frenchman wanted to be out from under Germany, but not at the price of revolution.

Under these conditions, the number of active Résistants was never very great, even at the climactic moment of the Liberation. After the war, some 300,000 Frenchmen received official veterans' status for active Resistance service: 130,000 as deportees and another 170,000 as "Resistance volunteers." Another 100,000 had lost their lives in Resistance activity. This brings the total of active Resistance participation at its peak, at least as officially recog-

[11] General Laure, "Journal," 26 August 1941. It should be noted that this manuscript was edited in 1947 for publication. For Weygand, see *FRUS*, 1941, II, 449. Jacques Chevalier's letters are found in *Ministère public c/Chevalier*, 39–63. The *francs-tireurs* seem to have raided a chateau in 1944 where Chevalier had stored the "cartridges of our chosen sharpshooters." It is not impossible that some so-called Resistance units of conservative social composition were in fact more active against the *maquis* than against the Germans. See also trials of General Delmotte, 71; Jean Ybarnégaray, 91; Admiral Bléhaut, fascicule 2, 18–22.

nized after the war, to about 2 percent of the adult French population.[12] There were no doubt wider complicities. But even if one adds those willing to read underground newspapers, some two million persons, or around ten percent of the adult population, seem to have been willing to take even that lesser risk. Let nothing said here detract from the moral significance of those who knew what they had to do. But the overwhelming majority of Frenchmen, however they longed to lift the German yoke, did not want to lift it by fire and sword.

Perceiving the Resistance as a minority of outlaws, the Vichy regime was drawn ever closer into complicity with the German occupation authorities' effort to crush it. The very logic of Vichy's existence required it to keep order. The Vichy strategy of seeking to replace the Germans and restore French sovereignty in the police and military fields drew the strings of complicity even tighter. From the beginning, the Vichy regime had found German concessions easier to obtain in those areas that permitted a stronger Armistice Army and French police to help keep order. The security legislation of August 1941 and Interior Minister Pucheu's efforts to restore French police initiative in the Occupied Zone, though not very successful, pushed the regime further down the same road. When German security in France was shifted from the army to the SS in the spring of 1942, Laval concluded a police agreement that by giving French police more autonomy in the Occupied Zone actually associated them even more closely with German security measures. SS General Karl Albrecht Oberg was named head of security in France on 11 March 1942, to take effect on June 1. Heydrich, who came in person on 7 May to install the new arrangements, had apparently been convinced by his experience in Czechoslovakia that local police cooperated more willingly when given some measure of independence (Heydrich's faith in indigenous police control was misplaced, for he was assassinated by Czech patriots a few weeks later). By an exchange of letters in July 1942 between General

---

[12] Gordon Wright, "Reflections on the French Resistance," *Political Science Quarterly* LXXVII: 3 (September 1962), 336–49, summarizes this information usefully in English. Other estimates put the total active Resistance at 45,000.

Oberg and René Bousquet, a prefect before the war and an old friend whom Laval had made secretary-general to the head of government for police affairs, the sovereignty of French administration and the independence of French police in the Occupied Zone were explicitly recognized, in "contrast to the preceding period." German police were limited to combating "enemies of the Reich." French police were given full independence in matters of internal order "against anarchism, terrorism, and communism, and generally against all foreign actions susceptible of troubling order within France." All French citizens charged with crimes, even political crimes, would be dealt with exclusively by French authorities. The French police would not be required to take any role in designating hostages or to take part in any actions that went beyond the armistice.

René Bousquet seems at the time to have regarded this agreement as at least a partial victory: the end to direct German orders to French police in the Occupied Zone and the explicit recognition of French administrative sovereignty there in police matters.[13] In fact, greater independence for the French police in the Occupied Zone meant a larger role in measures against the Resistance and an entering wedge for German police measures in the unoccupied zone. The fall of 1942 was, of course, the period when French police rounded up some 8,000–10,000 foreign Jews in the unoccupied zone for deportation. Laval could report to the Council of Ministers on 23 October 1942 that recent French police actions had rounded up 400 leading terrorists, arrested 5,460 Communists, and seized 40 tons of illegal arms. General Heinrich von Stülpnagel received Bousquet to congratulate him and sent his congratulations to Laval via Fernand de Brinon. In the unoccupied zone, a joint French-German radio detection team equipped with fake French ID cards uncovered nine clandestine radio transmitters in the fall of 1942 and arrested 29 persons, including Major Faye and his accomplices at Marseilles who had provided the radio link between General Giraud and

[13] Tribunal militaire de Paris, "Procès Oberg-Knochen," 13 September–9 October 1954 (Centre de Documentation Juive Contemporaine, dossier LXIV-1) fascicule 1, 49 ff., fascicule 9, 23 ff.; *Ministère public c/Bousquet*, 107–34.

the Allies. The price of limited "independence" for the French police was vigorous action against "dissidence."[14]

After the total occupation of France on 11 November 1942, the decision to continue the Vichy regime meant that French officials would continue to struggle for autonomy. René Bousquet engaged in new conversations on police powers in November with a "firm will to maintain and safeguard the principle of French government sovereignty." An agreement on 2 April 1943 between Bousquet and General Oberg allocated police responsibilities in the formerly unoccupied zone along the same lines as the agreement of July 1942 in the Occupied Zone. The French police were solely responsible for French citizens charged with all crimes except direct actions against the German forces; German police, however, could intervene wherever they felt their security was threatened. That security indeed became perilous during 1943, and while the French police arrested some 9,000 persons in the course of that year for "Gaullism, Marxism, or hostility to the regime," the German police arrested 35,000.[15] Bousquet's efforts now seemed too lukewarm to the German authorities, and after Pétain had made one more effort in December 1943 to get rid of Laval,[16] they forced the Vichy government to accept Joseph Darnand as secretary-general for the maintenance of order on 15 December 1943.

Darnand's period as Vichy police boss, on the very eve of D-Day, marked a turn from professionalism to vigilantism in police work, the final paroxysm of a moribund dictatorship. Darnand, a much-decorated World War I commando hero who had vegetated between the wars as a veterans' militant and garage owner in Nice, came into his own again under Vichy as head of the Nice branch of the Légion Française des Combattants. His

---

[14] General Bridoux, "Journal," 23 October 1942; Tribunal Militaire de Paris, Procès Oberg-Knochen, 59. The "Desloges" radio detection mission into the unoccupied zone is discussed in Procès Oberg-Knochen, 53 ff., *Ministère public c/General Delmotte,* and *Ministère public c/Bousquet,* fascicule 2, 28.

[15] René Bousquet note of 24 November 1942, quoted in *Ministère public c/Bousquet,* 6–15; Procès Oberg-Knochen, fascicule 2, 69; Abetz report to Ribbentrop, 7 January 1944, quoted in Procès Oberg-Knochen, fascicule 3, 99.

[16] See below, pp. 322 ff.

strong-arm tactics there were something of an embarrassment to the early leadership of the Legion. In 1942 and 1943 Darnand was active in the Anti-Bolshevik Legion in Paris, and made a tour of the French volunteer units on the eastern front with Doriot. "Everything had gone soft around the Marshal" by 1943, he said at his trial, and "I was a revolutionary." When Darnand was forced upon Vichy as secretary-general for the maintenance of order in December 1943, he raised the old paramilitary arm of the Veterans' Legion, the Service d'Ordre Légionnaire, known since January 1943 as the Milice, into a national parapolice force of volunteers against the Resistance. This body recruited some 45,000 toughs and fascist fanatics ready to shoot it out with the *maquis*. Under Darnand, Franco-German collaboration against the Resistance reached its climax with the campaign against the *maquis* of the Glières plateau, in the Haute-Savoie south of Geneva, in March 1944. There the most powerful of the *maquis,* strongly fortified in a natural alpine citadel and in close contact with London, launched a premature movement in anticipation, either by confusion or deception, of a massive Allied airdrop. The Milice assisted a full German division in reducing the Glières *maquis*, producing some 400 casualties on the Resistance side. The main anti-Resistance effort was now decisively German: some 80,000 Frenchmen were deported by the German police in the summer of 1944. But the Vichy regime had followed the path of maintaining a French police in fictitious autonomy, and down that path lay not merely collaboration between French and German professional police but also the worse excesses of an officially encouraged anti-Resistance vigilantism. In May 1942 René Bousquet had warned Heydrich against filling a "moat of blood" between France and Germany by the continued execution of hostages. By 1944 another "moat of blood" had been filled between two Frances by the Vichy regime's equation of Resistance with disorder.[17]

---

[17] *Ministère public c/Darnand;* Pierre Cluzel, *Le Drame héroïque des Glières* (Paris, 1945); Procès Oberg-Knochen, fascicule 2, 79 ff., for Darnand and for details of other French auxiliary groups such as the "Bande Bonny-Lafont" or the Gestapo de la rue Lauriston, which aided the German

Threats to the Social Order—2: Second Front

> [*Vichy leaders*] *are convinced that a British military victory
> on the continent is impossible, but, admitting its possibility
> for the sake of argument, they say it can only be accom-
> plished at the cost of a complete social breakdown in
> Germany which would soon spread over the rest of the
> continent. The horrors forecast are reminiscent of similar
> nightmares depicted in 1918. These dangers inestimably be-
> come more acute, they say, as the duration of the war is
> extended and destruction increases; an early peace and a
> drawn peace are therefore what France must strive and wish
> for, a peace in which the French will have a certain arbitral
> role.*
>
> —H. Freeman Matthews, 27 December 1940 [18]

> *The Allies want to reawaken Gaullist zeal and stimulate
> incidents which would appear to reveal breaches in French
> unity. They want to unleash an insurrectionary war in France.*
>
> —Robert Havard de la Montagne, 25 August 1942 [19]

THE BEST WAY TO AVOID REVOLUTION WAS TO KEEP
France out of the war. The relation of war to revolution had
been at the heart of revolutionary and counterrevolutionary strat-
egies since the nineteenth century. Marx's view of war as a social
catalyst had been given clearer focus by Lenin, who argued that
intensifying capitalist competition would lead inevitably to imperialist wars that signaled the last stage of capitalism. The im-
plication was that war was socialism's opportunity, though it
was a rare left revolutionary who went as far as the early Mussolini or Jules Guesde and actually rejoiced in that fact. The

---

police. The fullest account of the Milice is Delperrie de Bayac, *La Milice,
1918–45* (Paris, 1969). Pétain sent Laval a long report on 6 August 1944
on excesses committed by the Milice. See *Procès Pétain,* 290–91.

[18] *FRUS,* 1940, II, 430.

[19] "Second Front," *La Revue universelle,* 25 August 1942.

standard establishment view was the opposite: a healthy little victorious war was supposed to divert domestic discontent and tighten patriotic sinews.[20]

World War I and the Russian Revolution changed all that. For people like Pétain, who had been named commander in chief of the French Armies in May 1917 in order to halt the runaway military mutinies in that spring and early summer, there could be no further doubt that in the present state of technology war had become an engine of social dissolution rather than of social solidarity. They agreed with Stalin's assertions in the early 1930's that the next war, however deplorable the suffering it would bring, would spread the revolution. Only segments of the French left clung to the pre-1914 notion that war would solidify the French population and submerge French revolutionaries in a new "sacred union" as in 1914. Neither French conservatives nor revolutionaries had found any reason to rejoice in their World War I experience.[21]

All the arguments that had made Frenchmen dread war in 1939 and grasp hopefully at a way out in June 1940 were reinforced by 1942. The earlier resentment about the "brutal selfishness" of Churchill's obstinacy was sharpened as the continued war tipped one French colony after another into British hands and as the first British bombings of French cities began with the 3 March 1942 air raid on the Boulogne-Billancourt Renault works. Early hopes that the neutral United States would step in and mediate an end to the conflict were not completely dashed by Pearl Harbor. As late as August 1942, Vichy spokesmen were

---

[20] Jules Guesde is supposed to have remarked to his fellow French Socialists in July 1914, "I don't understand your fear of war. War is the mother of revolution." Harvey Goldberg, *Life of Jaurès* (Madison, Wisconsin, 1962), 480. For the young Mussolini, see Stuart J. Woolf, "Mussolini as Revolutionary," Journal of Contemporary History, II, 190. For the establishment, see Arno Mayer, "Domestic Causes of the First World War," in Leonard Krieger and Fritz Stern (eds.), *The Responsibility of Power* (New York, 1968).

[21] Robert C. Tucker, *The Marxian Revolutionary Idea* (New York, 1969), 140; for the French left's fear of another "sacred union," see Gaston Bergery, "Le Pacte Franco-Russe" [Paris, n.d. (1935)], 9. For French officers' reactions to the 1917 mutinies, see Guy Pedroncini, *Les mutineries de 1917* (Paris, 1967).

still urging the United States to be an arbitrator rather than a liberator in Europe.[22]

By that time the fear of returning to war had taken on an urgent new actuality. The second front was on everyone's lips. Laval first raised the subject of an "Allied attack" on French Africa with Abetz on 23 May 1942, expressing his fears about French public opinion if there were no German concessions improving the quality of daily life. Pétain faced the prospect of a second front, Rudolf Rahn reported after talking with him at the end of May, "with an extraordinary display of apprehension." The controlled Vichy press argued that since Allied difficulties with supply and transport against the submarine-infested North Atlantic would keep any Allied landing down to commando level, the Allies were restricted to operations on the level of the Dakar fiasco of September 1940. As at Dakar, the Allies would have to rely upon internal complicities to compensate for inadequate force. The Allies would attempt some operation on the continent only as a result of Russian pressures rather than tactical readiness. Under such conditions, an Allied operation on the coasts of Europe would be more likely to divide France and turn her into a stalemated battleground than liberate her. If an Allied commando failed, it would prompt the German occupation of the rest of France; if it succeeded, it would bring war and revolution home. Either prospect filled Frenchmen with foreboding. Roger Martin du Gard, writing to André Gide on 30 August 1942, couldn't agree with those who thought peace was close. He foresaw two or three years ahead of "massacres, social insurrection, and material shortages," followed by years more of disorders and readjustments. He was not far wrong.[23]

---

[22] Admiral Platon's speech at the funeral for the victims of the air raid on Boulogne-Billancourt accused the British of renouncing victory in favor of "murders without any military significance." He wished the British had shown similar zeal at Dunkirk in May–June 1940 "when we asked for RAF help in vain " (Centre de Documentation Juive Contemporaine, document no. CLXXXIII-50). Examples from 1941 of Vichy efforts to persuade the United States to mediate a compromise peace are found in *FRUS*, 1941, II, 396, 457, 461. For August 1942, see U.S. Dept. of State Serial File 851.00/2933.

[23] Abetz (Paris) to Berlin No. 2145 of 23 May 1942 (T-120/422/ 217099 ff, also printed in *Mémorandum d'Abetz*, 159, 177); Geoffrey

For Frenchmen in North and West Africa, a prime target for an Allied landing especially after the United States had moved into Iceland in 1941, fears of an Allied landing had an added incentive. The arrival of a foreign army would increase native unrest and eclipse French prestige in native eyes, already deeply shaken by the defeat of 1940. An interesting evolution along these lines of thought was that of General Noguès, Delcassé's son-in-law and a Popular Front appointee as governor-general of Morocco in 1936. In 1940, as commander in chief of French forces in North Africa, he had vigorously opposed the armistice until it was made clear to him that the navy would not come to North Africa to support continued war. Once again governor-general of Morocco, he helped keep German inspectors under close surveillance and control, partly to keep the victors out of the eyesight of Moroccans. Increasingly in 1941 and 1942, he warned Americans that he would oppose an Allied military presence in Morocco with equal adamancy. Under the impress of the need for colonial stability, he evolved from belligerent in 1940 to firm neutralist by 1942. It was only one example among many of colonial officials' fears that liberation meant native risings.[24]

These twin arguments for social order—domestic and colonial—together with reluctance to see France once more a battleground explains why so many Vichy officials with access to American ears warned in the summer of 1942 that an Allied landing would meet French resistance.[25] Even pro-Allied French officers, deeply involved with U.S. representative Robert Murphy in planning a return of French North African forces to war

---

Warner, *Pierre Laval and the Eclipse of France* (London, 1968) 311–12. For press analysis of the coming second front, see *La Revue universelle*, 25 August 1942. André Gide-Roger Martin du Gard, *Correspondance* (Paris, 1968), II, 262.

[24] *FRUS*, 1942, II, 254, 256, 308, 319, for Noguès' fears in 1942 that an Allied landing would trigger a native rising and draw the Germans into North Africa. For similar views expressed by Governor-General Pierre Boisson of French West Africa, *ibid.*, 341.

[25] For Laval and Rochat, see *FRUS*, 1942, II, 181–83, 187–89. For views attributed to Pétain, 190.

against the Axis, grew nervous about a "premature" landing as the summer of 1942 brought its rumors.[26]

Vichy authorities went beyond warnings in 1942. The small Armistice Army's vigorous preparations to resist an Allied landing were a sign that they meant business. On July 31 the cabinet at Vichy decided that in case of an Allied invasion, Marshal Pétain would appeal to French citizens to remain loyal to their armistice obligations.[27] In Africa, Moroccan defenses were reorganized and troops were sent to advanced coastal positions for the summer invasion season. The Vichy government asked Germany to permit more modern equipment in West Africa, including armor and aviation, and obtained partial satisfaction finally on August 27 in exchange for making the neutral ships in French Mediterranean ports available to the Axis for charter. In early October women and children of the French community were evacuated from Dakar. In mainland France, defense measures were studied and an exercise held at Hyères in September. Prefects in the Mediterranean departments instructed police to exert special vigilance against parachutists. In July British subjects still living along the Mediterranean coast were moved inland. In the French officer corps, age limits were lowered in order to force into retirement several division commanders (notably General Frère) who were not considered reliable for action against an Allied landing. On August 12 Abetz reported to Berlin that Pétain wanted to discuss joint Franco-German defense measures for the coast of the Bay of Biscay. As that coast lay in the Occupied Zone, it is apparent that the Vichy regime wanted to reassert its military role, as it was simultaneously trying to reassert its police role, across the Demarcation Line.[28]

[26] *FRUS*, 1942, II. For Col. Van Hecke, 299. For unnamed "friendly officers," 319, 362. Giraudist officers were alarmed at the possibility of a landing before their target date of spring 1943 and offended at the British seizure of Madagascar in May 1942.

[27] Abetz to Ribbentrop, Paris 3331 of 4 August 1942, in Botschafter Ritter, op. cit. (T-120/926/297252). This is in fact what Pétain did in June 1944.

[28] Oberkommando der Wehrmacht, Abteilung für Wehrmacht Propaganda, "Geheim-Akten über Fremde Staaten: Frankreich" (T-77/OKW-1605/2,488,982; 6,500,019 ff; 6,500,0411 ff; and 6,500,052 ff); General Bri-

In the midst of these preparations came a warning signal that seemed to confirm all the Vichy preconceptions about an Allied landing. On 19 August 1942 an Allied amphibious force consisting mostly of Canadians came ashore at Dieppe and on the highlands north and south of the town. After a few hours, tl Germans destroyed this force and took most of the survivor. prisoner. The artillery and tanks put ashore helped German and Vichy propaganda claim that this was the Allies' maximum effort, designed to secure a foothold through local complicity and to expand through insurrection. Vichy's relief at the Allies' failure was not feigned.

In addition to congratulating the German Army publicly for "cleansing" French soil of the invader, Pétain seized the occasion to make a new bid for French military autonomy. He wrote to Hitler on August 21 proposing that, in view of "the most recent British aggression, which took place this time on our soil, . . . France participate in her own defense" and demonstrate "my wish that France make a contribution to the safeguard of Europe." In other words, he was renewing more urgently his proposal of nine days earlier for joint Franco-German coastal defense planning. As Fernand de Brinon recalled, the current phrase around Vichy was "to open a French crenellation in the Atlantic Wall." It was the long-sought opportunity to reimplant the French Army in the Occupied Zone.[29]

---

doux, "Journal"; Abetz (Paris) to Ribbentrop 3478 of 12 August 1942 (T-120/434/220263). See also Robert O. Paxton, *Parades and Politics at Vichy* (Princeton, N.J., 1966), chap. 10.

[29] The defense at Marshal Pétain's trial succeeded in casting doubt on the very existence of Pétain's 21 August letter to Hitler. German archives show, however, that the letter did reach Berlin, where the various officers of the Foreign Ministry who commented upon it took it to be genuine. Abetz (Paris) 3627 to Ribbentrop of 22 August 1942 transmitted the letter (T-120/434/220294 and T-120/929/297221), and the Political Branch (Pol. 11) commented upon it (T-120/4634H/E208594–602). Since the Vichy communique using the offensive word *cleanse* was published only in the Occupied Zone, it cannot be definitely traced to Pétain or Laval, but Pétain poured out his bitterness against the "enemy" and his relief at their failure to German Consul-General Roland Krug von Nidda on August 20 (T-120/434/220287–91). U.S. Chargé d'Affaires S. Pinckney Tuck had already reported in early August that Pétain was determined to resist Allied "aggression" (*FRUS*, 1942, II, 190). Fernand de Brinon in *Procès Pétain*, 287–89, and in *Mémoires* (Paris, n.d.), 125–26.

High-ranking Germans were no more eager for autonomous French help in August 1942 than they had been since the end of the "new policy" of 1940 and of May–June 1941, however. "France declared war on us," Hitler had said in a war conference on 5 May 1942, "so she must bear the consequences." Only the ever-enthusiastic Otto Abetz showed some interest in Pétain's proposal. He suggested on September 4 that the French be permitted to build Atlantic coastal fortifications instead of paying occupation costs. Berlin's only gestures were to liberate all the citizens of Dieppe (some 750 strong) in German prisoner-of-war camps, in recognition of their city's failure to rise in support of the Canadians, and to agree finally on August 27 to permit an armored unit to be set up in West Africa to repel possible Allied action there, in exchange for the German right to charter neutral merchant ships interned in French ports since 1940. Hitler doesn't seem to have bothered to answer Pétain's letter.[30] Once again, it was German indifference and suspicion rather than French reluctance that blocked a striking step toward Franco-German military cooperation. Pétain talked with Prince Rohan on October 20 about the kind of deal he wanted to make in the face of threatened Allied landings: "If they give us our sovereignty, we will be a defensive barrage. 'Ihr gebt Souveränität, wir machen Barrage.' "[31]

It was in this mood that the Vichy government learned in the night of 7–8 November 1942 that Allied forces were coming ashore in Morocco and Algeria. In view of what we know now about widespread Vichy attitudes toward an Allied landing in 1942, the vigor of the French defense should not be surprising. Although the French army command in North Africa, which had drawn Armistice Army units back from the coast in the fall of 1942 in the belief that the invasion season was over for another

[30] Hitler's 5 May 1942 remark is found in T-73/192/405497, quoted in Edward L. Homze, *Foreign Labor in Nazi Germany* (Princeton, N.J., 1967), 135. Abetz (Paris) 3869 to Ribbentrop of 4 September 1942 (T-120/926/297200–2). The negotiations over neutral shipping and the persistent French requests for armor in West Africa may be followed in T-120/434/*passim,* in T-120/926/297207–11, and in the unpublished diary of General Bridoux.

[31] T-120/894/291479–83.

year, was taken completely by surprise, the French fought back as vigorously as they could. In Morocco and the *Oranais* area of Algeria, there was far more than a mere token resistance for German eyes. The official Allied death toll was 663. The few middle-ranking French officers who had conspired in advance to aid the Allies and who had been notified at the last minute did not succeed in taking over command in any locality for more than a few hours.[32]

After the war considerable mystification was created around claims by Pétain's defense that the marshal had sent two telegrams of "secret accord" to Darlan, on November 10 and 13. This is supposed to reflect Pétain's real approval of switching to the Allied side, as distinct from his public exhortations to fight on against the "aggressors." Everything is wrong with that now well-rooted tale. Although Darlan publicly claimed Pétain's secret support in November and December 1942, there is, in the nature of the case, no contemporary evidence. Even if Pétain approved of Darlan's actions on November 10 and 13, the policy being approved at that point was neutrality and not support for the Allies. And it is altogether out of character. The Allied landing was a disaster to Pétain's hopes for a compromise peace. Only the threat of even tougher French defense of the mainland might deter the Allies from the next, even more disastrous move.[33]

---

[32] Information about French troop movements to the Atlantic coast of Morocco in the spring of 1942 and their retirement in the fall may be found in T-77/OKW-2285/5, 596,253, and *passim*. Some French troops were also sent to the Rif mountains at the same time.

[33] The November 10 message was first described at Pétain's trial from shorthand notes taken by Dr. Ménétrel, Pétain's physician and confidant. See Louis Noguères, *Le Véritable procès du maréchal Pétain* (Paris, 1955), 448. The message concerned is probably the same expression of "entire confidence" in Darlan published in *Le Figaro* on 10 November 1942, although neither prosecution nor defense was aware of that. Darlan at that point was declaring himself Clark's prisoner and refusing to take responsibility for a general cease-fire. The Nov. 13 alleged message was added to the story in Admiral Auphan's trial in July 1955, fascicule 2, 58, 110. See also Auphan and Mordal, *La Marine française pendant la seconde guerre mondiale* (Paris, 1958), 294, 304, and Marshal Alphonse Juin, *Mémoires 1: Alger, Tunis, Rome* (Paris, 1959), 96, 108. The problem with that story is that on November 13 Laval was trying to get the Germans to acquiesce in a neutrality arrangement between Noguès, Darlan, and the Allies that would exclude Giraud and preserve "the present organization . . . intact." See below, footnote 50. Darlan did in fact write to Admiral Leahy on 27 No-

Vichy authorities rushed to prepare defenses against anticipated further landings on the Mediterranean coast of France itself. Although the Germans occupied the rest of France on
November 11, the Armistice Army, which had followed orders
of calm almost without exception, was not dissolved. The Germans authorized the creation of an autonomous French defense zone around the great naval base at Toulon and the main
units of the French fleet. French Army units were moved in and
prepared for coastal defense. As in Syria and during the Allied
landings in Morocco and Algeria, Vichy rejected the notion of
French and German troops fighting shoulder to shoulder. Their
weapons pointed in the same direction, however, and it seems
likely that if Allied forces had attempted to land near Toulon in
mid-November 1942 they would have been greeted by no less
French gunfire than in North Africa ten days earlier. It was the
kind of defensive autonomy within the Occupied Zone that
Pétain had been seeking since Dieppe.[34] As it happened, Hitler
decided to dissolve the Armistice Army, citing the "betrayal"
of those French officers now fighting alongside the Allies in
Tunisia, and attempted to seize the French fleet on November
27. The fleet was scuttled in Toulon harbor in Vichy's most determined act of neutrality.

Not even the disasters of November 1942 ended Vichy's efforts to negotiate some area of defensive autonomy. As we shall

---

vember 1942 that "confidential messages passed to me by someone at the
French Admiralty" informed him that "the Marshal was, in the bottom of
his heart, of the same opinion" as Darlan. See William D. Leahy, *I Was
There* (New York, 1950), 485. That claim was, of course, the basis for the
new legitimacy in North Africa and very much in Darlan's interest to assert.
For the view that the marshal's "accord" covered only Noguès' and Darlan's
efforts to get rid of Giraud, see the occasionally inaccurate article of General
Schmitt, "Le général Juin et le débarquement en AFN," *Revue d'histoire
de la deuxième guerre mondiale,* no. 44 (December 1961).

[34] The Toulon agreement, negotiated on November 11 by Admirals
Marquis and de Laborde and Commander von Ruault-Frappart, Admiral
Raeder's representative, may be found in *Ministère public c/Marquis et
Abrial.* See also *Documents on International Affairs, 1939–46,* II, "Hitler's
Europe," ed. Margaret Carlyle (London, 1954), 148. I have covered these
questions more fully in *Parades and Politics at Vichy* (Princeton, 1966),
chap. 11. The most complete German account is in the papers of General
von Neubronn, Deutscher General Vichy, "Akte 7a - Stimmung, Akte 7b -
Lage" (T-501, DGV 70/23588).

see, the revival of a French armed force was a major element in the last efforts by Pétain and Laval for a sweeping settlement with the Germans at the beginning of 1943. The very attempt shows the persistence at Vichy of two ideas: hope for a compromise peace and expectation that France, neutral in an increasingly fanatical world, could be an effective mediator. As against these dreams, an Allied landing in Europe seemed an "aggression." It was a damaging Freudian slip when Laval referred at Pétain's postwar trial to the Allied "aggression" of June 1944, but it had been by no means an unusual point of view at Vichy.[35]

The suffering caused by Allied bombing in France in 1943 and 1944 helped make even anti-Germans prefer a compromise peace to armed liberation. It may shock Americans, who have inflicted aerial bombardments on many peoples but have never endured one, to learn that their approach seemed more a menace than a promise of liberation to many staunchly anti-German Frenchmen. General Bridoux' reports from the postal censor in May 1943 reported "indignation" over Allied bombings in the industrial suburbs of Paris even in a population with a "general belief in Allied victory." Resistance journals such as *Témoignage chrétien* had to spend precious space countering hostility to Allied bombers. André Gide, who was overtaken by the war in Tunis in the spring of 1943, saw from the ground the "absurd results" of high-altitude bombing that cost thousands of civilian casualties while doing apparently the least damage to Germans. "What sense do these idiotic destructions make?" Some Frenchmen in Tunis even thought that the Germans were raiding in camouflaged planes to bring discredit on the United States. Gide also foresaw that armed liberation meant civil war:

> That liberation of France which the Anglo-Saxons promise us, that liberty will prove for us, I fear, the occasion of serious upsets and of lasting internal dissensions of which I shall presumably never see the end.[36]

[35] *Procès Pétain* (Paris, 1945), 499 ff.
[36] General Bridoux, "Journal," 11 May 1943; Monique Luirard, "Le Courrier français du Témoignage chrétien," *Cahiers d'histoire* XIV:2 (1969), 181–209; *The Journals of André Gide,* translated and edited by Justin O'Brien, vol. IV (New York, 1951), 182, 186, 189, 192. Gide found

The joyful delirium of the Liberation of Paris in August 1944 has overlaid the earlier dread at that prospect. Part of that joy no doubt was relief at a *fait vite accompli*. In anticipation, however, the prospect of Allied landings could not have been a happy one. The World War I experience and the fact of extremely heavy Allied shipping losses in the North Atlantic suggested that the Liberation would bog down into years of slogging on French soil. The Americans, those masters of the technology of destruction, were getting around the problem by raining high explosives from five miles up. Beyond the remaining handful of Vichy partisans in 1943 and 1944 was a mass of Frenchmen who wanted the Germans out but not at the price of such slaughter. There was still an acquiescent mass upon whom Pétain and Laval could build their last efforts to negotiate a sweeping agreement with Hitler in 1942 and 1943.

Last French Bids for Collaboration: 1942–43

LAVAL'S RETURN TO POWER IN APRIL 1942 WAS A TACIT acceptance of the old strategy's validity. Although he never repeated Darlan's July 1941 proposal for replacing the armistice with normal diplomatic relations, he continued to offer voluntary French association in exchange for more normal living conditions for Frenchmen. He still worked far into 1943 for that elusive "broad settlement" that would set France free to evolve back to some reasonably significant role within the new European power system.

Laval was unlucky in his moment of triumph, however. His revenge for 13 December coincided with a sharp increase in pressures from all sides upon France. It was in the summer of 1942 that the implications of a long war were finally borne in upon the German civilian population. Germany's first really total economic organization for war, organized now by the

the British bomber pilots more daring and therefore more accurate than the Americans.

young architect Albert Speer who became minister of armaments production in the spring of 1942 and eventually replaced
that sybaritic dilettante Goering as head of the national economic
planning organization, visited its austerities upon the German
people. The belts of occupied peoples were expected to tighten
even more narrowly than the belts of Germans. Food rations
having been reduced in Germany on 6 April 1942, for example,
quotas of food delivery to Germany from the occupied areas—
including France—were sharply raised in July. At a conference
on food supplies in Berlin on 6 August 1942, Goering said that
questions of inflation or scarcity in the occupied countries were
of no interest to him, even though the French food delivery
quotas were described as "extraordinarily high." Abetz, who had
telephoned nervously about the impact on French domestic stability, admitted that as a matter of policy Frenchmen should eat
less than Germans and accepted a plan to draw the new quotas
from the Occupied Zone, leaving the Vichy zone free to help
feed the rest of France as it chose.[37]

More ominously, Polish and Russian laborers having been literally worked to death by 1942, Germany began to turn to the
west for foreign labor. Fritz Sauckel, a former merchant seaman
and early Nazi who had proven his narrow-minded toughness
as gauleiter of Thuringia, was given the job in March 1942 of
coordinating all use of foreign labor in the Reich. On April 25,
1942, Rudolf Schleier, Abetz' deputy in the German embassy in Paris, warned Laval informally that the voluntary re-

---

[37] For Germany's late adoption of a war economy, see Burton H. Klein,
Germany's Economic Preparation for War (Cambridge, Mass., 1959), and
Alan H. Milward, *The German Economy at War* (London 1965). The
Vichy cabinet accepted the new quotas in July as, in Brinon's words, "a
French contribution to the feeding of Europe in the battle against bolshe-
vism." Laval then attempted in a meeting with Dr. Michel on 3 August to
obtain more authority over price-fixing in the Occupied Zone, to get the
Germans to publish the exact figures of the food quotas, and to stop illicit
food-buying by German soldiers on the black market. See Abetz (Paris)
2941 to Berlin of 11 July 1942 (T-120/5618H/E402844) and Schoene
(Paris) Del. Wirt. 276 of 10 August 1942 (T-120/434/220253–54). For the
views of Goering and Abetz, see Wiehl memorandum (unnumbered) of 11
August 1942 and Wiehl memorandum Ha Pol 812/42 of 24 August 1942
(T-120/434/220255–57, 220310–11). "I dream of edibles," wrote André
Gide on 7 May 1943. *The Journals of André Gide*, IV, 186.

cruitment of labor for Germany in France had been insufficient and that far more was going to be expected. Fritz Sauckel's Order No. 4 of 7 May 1942 authorized the use of force to obtain labor in all occupied countries, and on June 15 Sauckel came to Paris to give Laval an unpalatable alternative: either increase French labor volunteers or accept labor conscription. It was at this June meeting that Laval wriggled off the horns of the dilemma by proposing the notorious *relève* scheme: a French prisoner of war would be paroled for each three French skilled laborers recruited to work in German factories. The full propaganda resources of the regime could not meet Sauckel's quotas under the *relève* system, however, and a Vichy law of 4 September 1942, directly imposed by Abetz, permitted the conscription of workers for Germany in individual cases. Finally, in February 1943 conscription of whole age groups began under the Service de Travail Obligatoire. Beginning with Laval's return to power, therefore, France was becoming, after Poland, Germany's largest source of foreign labor and the largest source of skilled labor in all occupied Europe.[38]

That was not all the bad news for France in the summer of 1942. The German military staffs were reluctant to permit any increase in French armaments in West Africa or the recruitment of more French soldiers at home. Police affairs in the Occupied Zone were shifted from the Militärbefehlshaber in Frankreich to the SS in May. General Henri Giraud's daring escape in May from a German fortress gave the Germans an excuse for refusing any further discussion of early release of prisoners of war. In July began the most bestial of the German depredations, the massive deportation of foreign refugee Jews from France to the

---

[38] For general German labor policy and for comparative figures by nationality, see Edward L. Homze, *Foreign Labor in Nazi Germany* (Princeton, N.J., 1967). Homze's details on negotiating the French labor supply for Germany, drawn mostly from the Nuremberg trial documents, need to be supplemented with other unpublished German material. I have used primarily Deutsche Botschaft, Paris, Pol. 3 Nr. 46, "Franz. Gewerkschaftswesen, franz. sozialpolitik. Einsatz franz. und anderer ausl. Arbeiter in Deutschland" (T-120/5636H-5637H). See also Alan H. Milward, "French Labour and the German Economy, 1942–45: An Essay on the Nature of the Fascist New Order," *Economic History Review* XXIII: 2 (August 1970).

extermination camps in Poland and eastern Germany. Laval had reason to complain to Abetz on May 17 and May 23 that Germany was being harder on him than it had been on his predecessors.[39]

The United States was also growing much tougher on Vichy France. Laval had always been more personally identified in Washington with outright military collaboration than his colleagues, and Admiral Leahy was summoned home when Laval assumed the prime ministry, leaving only a chargé d'affaires to represent the United States at Vichy. The United States was now a belligerent, and although she was not at war with France, the earlier American policy of helping keep France neutral was no longer enough. In particular, the way in which French facilities and equipment in the Caribbean were put to use became a vital factor in the struggle against German submarines in American waters. After Laval returned to power, Secretary of State Hull would no longer accept the assurances Darlan had made after the German submarine visit to Martinique in February 1942. On 9 May 1942 the United States government demanded that all French ships in the Caribbean be totally immobilized with their ordinance removed, that the United States oversee communications with the French islands, and that the Allies use the merchant ships and gold there. In return for Admiral Robert's agreement to these measures, obtained finally in October, the United States government recognized Robert as the ultimate governing authority of these French possessions. The German authorities, believing that the United States was preparing to seize French possessions in the Caribbean, tried to get Laval to forbid any agreement between Admiral Robert and the Americans and to order immediate scuttling of French ships there in the event of an Allied effort to seize them. Laval seems to have conducted a genuine "double game" in this instance, assuring Abetz on 16 May that Admiral Robert had been ordered

---

[39] Abetz (Paris) telegrams no. 2051 and 2145, 17 and 23 May 1942 (T-120/422/217051-54, 217099-101), also reprinted in *Mémorandum d'Abetz,* 159, 177. Laval's story that Goering warned him not to return to the government in April 1942 since things were going to become tougher for France is probably a postwar invention.

to enter into no agreement with the United States. The narrow-ing French freedom of action in the empire, caught between ever more determined belligerents, was made clear by these Caribbean pressures.[40]

In July and August 1942, as the seesaw battle in the Libyan desert brought Rommel deep into Egypt again, the United States tried to force Laval to move the French naval squadron of Ad-miral Godefroy, which had been immobilized at Alexandria since the armistice, to some more secure Allied base. The Ger-mans, in turn, threatened to hold France accountable for a vio-lation of the armistice if the ships were moved to another Allied base or fell into Allied hands. Only Rommel's failure to overrun the Suez Canal spared Laval an impossible choice and left the Godefroy squadron to rust on at Alexandria. The narrowing field for neutral maneuver in a widening war was once more ap-parent.[41]

The United States decision to accredit an official representa-tive to the Gaullist Committee of National Liberation in July 1942, the first serious breach in Roosevelt's policy of aloofness from the Free French, was a further ominous blow at Vichy's claim of legitimacy.

Vichy's authority in the Indian Ocean and Asia also suffered serious blows as Laval returned to power. In Indochina the Japanese violated their agreement of 1940 and seized the en-tire merchant fleet. Following rumors that Laval planned to per-mit Japanese forces to use Madagascar, the British invaded Mada-gascar in May 1942.[42] Wherever Laval turned, the French empire

[40] These complicated maneuvers may be followed best in *FRUS*, II, 1942, and in T-120/422, 434.

[41] See the same sources as in footnote 39 and T-120/1450. Both the Caribbean units and the Godefroy squadron remained neutral after No-vember 1942. The Godefroy squadron's crews eventually rallied to the Allies after the fall of Tunisia in May 1943.

[42] Laval suggested to the Germans in April 1942 that France, whose relations with the Japanese were now much better than they had been under Darlan, could be useful to Germany in Asia. He proposed to discuss Japanese naval use of Madagascar with Ambassador Mitami. Governor-General Annet in Madagascar seems to have received orders to accept the presence of Japanese submarines but to resist any British force. Woermann memorandum Nr. 1807 of 29 April 1942 (T-120/4639H/209091–92) and *Ministère public c/Brévié et Annet.*

of 1940 was being eroded away by the efforts of both sides to use French wealth for their own war interests. In retrospect Laval returned to power at the moment when a neutral was becoming ever less a possible arbiter and ever more a pawn of the more determined belligerents.

Like Darlan before him, however, Laval chose to regard increased German needs as an opportunity rather than a danger. All the themes of 1940 were revived in Laval's first meeting with a prominent German. He wanted a "lasting settlement" rather than mere piecemeal adjustment, he told Albert Speer on 19 June 1942. France would provide "intensive economic aid" and even a military alliance to assist in "the heroic struggle in the east" if only collaboration would produce striking results visible to every Frenchman. Although German demands now went beyond the armistice, Laval could fulfill them if the French people gained some hope about their nation's fate. French interests, for example, required freedom to develop toward the south—the imperial theme again. Laval mentioned a whole series of issues on which concessions would do no damage to German political or military interests: return of the northern departments to administration from Paris; return of French peasants to their lands in the northeastern "forbidden zone"; leave for prisoners of war in spite of Giraud's escape. Finally Laval asked Speer to help arrange a high-level meeting with Ribbentrop—that summit meeting which had been anticipated by both sides in December 1940 and which still eluded Laval.[43]

Through the summer and fall of 1942, however, Laval saw only lesser German functionaries. He used every piecemeal German demand as an occasion for renewing his larger aim of a broad general settlement. Confronted with higher food quotas in July 1942, for example, he tried to bargain for better conditions for French prisoners of war. Faced with the issue of providing French labor for Germany, Laval asked Sauckel on a number of occasions to place these negotiations within the framework of a larger political settlement. Sauckel always replied that he was

[43] T-120/5636H/E407349-52.

a mere technician without competence in these broader matters.[44]

The best Laval could do was reestablish some fragments of French administrative sovereignty within the Occupied Zone in the summer of 1942. The police agreements between René Bousquet and SS General Oberg have already been discussed. In April 1942 the Vichy press agency, Office Français d'Information, was finally permitted to function in the Occupied Zone. Vichy's attempts to "open a French crenellation" in the German West Wall, however, and to extend the Armistice Army's defense preparations to the Occupied Zone had gotten nowhere by the fall of 1942. Neither had his plan, along with Defense Minister Bridoux, to transform the Paris-based Anti-Bolshevik Legion from a warren of agitators and conspirators into the Tricolor Legion, an official unit of the French Army ready to impose a French presence "in all theaters where French interests are at stake." [45]

In the light of these mostly frustrated efforts through the summer and fall of 1942, the Allied landings in North Africa in November offered Laval opportunity as well as danger. The main danger was the risk of empire and mainland now being swallowed up by both belligerent sides. The opportunity was the renewed possibility of summit meetings, the third and last major effort at a sweeping settlement by Vichy leaders.

The arrival of Allied forces in Morocco and Algiers made it impossible for Vichy to keep German forces out of French North Africa any longer. Heretofore, successive German demands for bases had been rejected or postponed, and the Armistice Commission inspection teams were delayed and then restricted in their movements in Morocco. When the OKW offered German air support around midnight on November 7, the

[44] Schoene (Paris) Del. Wirt. 265 of 21 June 1942 (T-120/434/220168–70; Abetz (Paris) No. 2517 of 16 June 1942 (T-120/588/243943–47).

[45] Ministère de l'Information, *La Presse autorisée sous l'occupation allemande* (Paris, 1946). André Lavagne of Pétain's cabinet recalled after the war that improving contact with the Occupied Zone was the "constant obsession, the preoccupation" of the regime. *Procès Pétain*, 307. For the *Tricolor Legion* experiment, see my *Parades and Politics at Vichy*, 273–77.

French delegation to the Armistice Commission attempted to impose the condition that German planes not use airfields in French North Africa. Unlike the Syrian case of July 1941, however, the OKW insisted late on November 8 that the French open airfields to them in North Africa within an hour. At 1:15 A.M. on November 9, Laval accepted by telephone, and a massive German airlift and sea lift of forces into Tunisia began. Thus the Germans got Bizerte without concessions, fifteen months after the Protocols of Paris had been blocked. There still remained the unoccupied zone, however, and French officials such as Secretary-General Charles Rochat briefed German Consul-General Roland Krug von Nidda repeatedly on the vigor of French defenses in North Africa in hopes of persuading the Germans they were not needed. Hitler was no more willing to rely on French arms in November 1942 than he had been in earlier lesser crises, however, and he appears to have ordered the total occupation of France as early as November 8. Early on November 11, German troops moved across the Demarcation Line without opposition and proceded to occupy the French Mediterranean coast. All of France and the empire was now occupied either by Axis or Allied armies.[46]

On the other hand, Hitler had been forced to take an interest in France again. As long as an anti-Allied French force remained a possible bargaining agent, Laval had a chance to raise the subject of a broad general settlement once more. In November and December 1942 and in early 1943, Laval received the high-level attention from Germany that no Frenchman had received since the Darlan-Hitler meeting of May 1941 and the Pétain-Goering meeting of December 1941. On November 8, in response to a series of precise questions from Hitler whose exact text we no longer have, Laval replied that while he, personally, favored a declaration of war against England and the United States, Pétain could not be brought to such a decision.

[46] The German air support issue is fully documented in *DFCAA,* V, 423, and in T-120/926/297022-23-54. For French efforts to persuade the Germans that French defense in North Africa was genuine, see Roland Krug von Nidda's reports in T-120/443, 110. I have discussed the military details much more fully in *Parades and Politics at Vichy* (Princeton, N.J., 1966), chap. 10.

Laval then asked to come to Germany to discuss the questions of war and the "development of Franco-German relations" directly with Hitler.[47] After a harrowing drive through the foggy mountains, Laval arrived at Munich at 4 in the morning on November 10 and spent two days trying to bargain an "active French role in the war against the British and the United States at the side of the Axis" in exchange for a "German declaration of the independence" of France within her 1914 frontiers (i.e., without Alsace-Lorraine) and a colonial empire equivalent to her 1939 holdings. A draft memorandum in French dated 11 November 1942 at Munich survives to attest to the kind of autonomous association Laval was working for. Hitler, however, cut him off when the conversation turned to political matters. He said he wanted only practical talk. When Laval said he had hoped to see Hitler earlier, Hitler said he had hoped to have Bizerte sooner. In the end the only concrete result of Laval's trip was his pressure upon Vichy to keep up resistance in North Africa. Laval spent hours on the telephone with Vichy and it was at this point that Admiral Darlan, who had ordered a cease-fire, was removed from command in Algiers and replaced between November 11 and 13 by General Noguès. Defense to the end in North Africa was essential to Laval's offer of collaboration.[48] But Hitler went ahead and occupied the rest of France anyway.

Hitler still cared enough about Vichy's existence to send Pétain a letter in the night of November 10–11 explaining why the total occupation had been necessary and offering the old man the return to Paris that he had so coveted in 1940. Marshal von Rundstedt came personally to Vichy the morning of the 11th to explain things. Pétain told Rundstedt that while his public protest was necessary to satisfy public opinion, his main hope was that there would be no incidents. He asked that Nice not be oc-

---

[47] Abetz (Paris) 5057 of 8 November 1942 (T-120/926/297067).

[48] The fullest accounts of the Laval-Hitler-Ciano meetings of 10–11 November 1942 are interpreter Paul Otto Schmidt's notes, found in T-120/F1/0126–55. See also Schmidt, *Statist auf diplomatischer Bühne* (Bonn, 1949), 564. The 11 November 1942 memorandum is found in T-120/F9/0006–7. Geoffrey Warner, *Pierre Laval and the Eclipse of France,* attributes this document to the German side, erroneously in my opinion. Laval's postwar claim that he rejected a German offer of alliance "through thick and thin" (*Laval parle,* 135; *Procès Pétain,* 201–7) is diametrically wrong.

cupied by Italians and that Toulon be left unoccupied to show the neutrality of the French Navy. He sadly declined the offer to return to Versailles in view of public opinion. If anyone thought that Pétain would take the total occupation as a signal to jettison the now-defunct armistice strategy, his fear of disorder and his clinging grasp upon the status quo must soon have disabused them.[49]

By contrast, Laval got back from Munich in the afternoon of November 11 boiling with projects to regain some Vichy autonomy. General Noguès had now replaced Darlan briefly as commander in chief in North Africa, and Laval tried to get the Germans to acquiesce in a cease-fire there with Giraud excluded and the "present organization" (i.e., Vichy personnel and institutions) left "intact." The next day, with Darlan once more the supreme Vichy commander in North Africa, Laval tried to get the Germans to allow Vichy to accept another compromise by which the Americans would hold the coast and Darlan would retain French sovereignty over the interior as a neutral. The Germans saw the whole business as an attempt to cover up for inadequate French defense against the Allies.[50] Tunisia was the nub of the German efforts to counterattack, and Laval sent Admiral Platon there to reassert an active French role in holding the Allies at bay. Platon told Roland Krug von Nidda on 15 November that although his orders had been phrased as a mere fact-finding mission in order to mollify dubious members of the cabinet, he expected to take military command in Tunisia and to "drive the Anglo-Saxons from Algeria and Morocco."[51] This was the moment, also, when the independent French defensive

[49] There is no contemporary evidence for a plan to fly Pétain out to North Africa on November 11, 1942, as mentioned in such reminiscences as Jules Roy, *Le Grand naufrage* (Paris, 1966).

[50] Abetz (Paris) 5150 and 5155 of 13 November 1942 (T-120/928/297616-17); Ribbentrop (Sonderzug) 1413 of 14 November 1942 to Abetz (T-120/928/587-88). These efforts to neutralize North Africa during the period November 11-14 were no doubt the subject of any "secret accord" telegrams Pétain may have sent to Darlan during that period.

[51] Abetz (Paris) 5202 of 15 November 1942 to Ribbentrop (T-120/974/302947-50 or T-120/928/297558-61). Platon's aide, Commandant Brunet, who had spent six months in a British prison after Dunkirk, was said to "hate Britain like the plague."

enclave was being set up around the Toulon naval base. The same day, November 15, Laval told Krug von Nidda that he had got the cabinet to disavow Giraud publicly and to accept his proposal of a "clear course" for Germany "through thick and thin." [52] Finally, Laval got Pétain on November 17 to grant him full powers to issue laws and decrees. Laval told the Germans he intended to use his "dictatorial powers" to regularize and normalize Franco-German relations around a "reconciliation" and an "entente." He held out the possibility of a French declaration of war and suggested that a French "Imperial Legion" be created to help reconquer North Africa. He asked to visit Hitler again in order to agree upon the "practical solutions" to Franco-German collaboration. [53]

The astonishing features of Laval's efforts during the week after his meeting with Hitler at Munich were the Germans' disinterest and Laval's persistence. By this time, no one on the German side had much interest in French collaboration. The German diplomatic troubleshooter Rudolf Rahn, who had arranged the passage of German aircraft through Syria in May 1941, was now sent to oversee the German buildup of forces in Tunisia. "It is not your task to act on a basis of Franco-German collaboration," he was instructed by Ribbentrop on November 17, for the Germans assumed "that all French forces in Tunisia had more or less gone over to the Americans." Rahn was ordered to treat all French officials with "the greatest distrust" and to be as reserved as possible on all questions "until our forces in Tunisia are so strong that they preclude further movement of Tunisian forces into dissidence." He was to black out all news to Vichy in order to keep the Allies from getting information about Axis troop movements. [54] Nor did any of Laval's efforts deter Hitler from abolishing the Toulon enclave on November 23, dissolving the Armistice Army on the 27th and attempting the same day to seize the

[52] Abetz (Paris) 5214 of 15 November 1942 (T-120/928/297554–56). Thus Laval himself seems to be the proposer of the alliance "through thick and thin" that he claimed after the war the Germans offered him. See footnote 48 above.

[53] Abetz (Paris) 5252 of 17 November 1942 (T-120/974/302941–43).

[54] Ribbentrop (Fuschl) 1441 of 17 November to Rahn (T-120/974/302939–40).

French fleet. Hitler wrote that the French Army in North Africa had violated the armistice and so its counterpart in the metropole must cease to exist.[55]

Laval, supported by Pétain, persisted anyway in the effort he had outlined in Munich on November 10 and in Vichy on November 15 to purchase a broad Franco-German settlement with the offer of full alliance. Pétain's answer to Hitler's November 26 letter begged permission to reestablish the French Army, without which Vichy's autonomy was a sham. Laval wrote more concretely to Ribbentrop on December 5 offering to use his new powers to "share in the fight against communism" and the reconquest of the empire if a meeting with Hitler produced the kind of "visible results" likely to reconcile French opinion. Pétain assured Marshal von Rundstedt on December 10 of his readiness for a "positive French contribution to the war against bolshevism," provided that France had "unimpaired sovereignty" and an army to keep internal order. Up to now, he said, French hopes had not been fulfilled. But he still hoped that France could take part "with honor and dignity" in the new European order.[56]

Laval was allowed to plead his case with Ribbentrop on December 19—the meeting with the foreign minister that he had been seeking since November 1940. The Germans acceded to only one substantial French request: the creation of new Vichy military forces for internal order and action in the empire. In particular, a volunteer Phalange Africaine authorized at this meeting eventually provided one company of Frenchmen within the German 334th Infantry Division in the Tunisian campaign of the spring of 1943. Beyond that, all Laval's requests for "visible results" were rejected. There was no longer anything for the Demarcation Line to demarcate, but occupation costs were higher than ever since the total occupation of France in No-

[55] Hitler's letter of 26 November 1942 to Pétain is found in Ambassador Ritter's files (T-120/935/298859–71). See also the dossier on French "guilt" in November 1942 assembled by the OKW (T-77/OKW-133).
[56] Pétain letters to Hitler and Marshal von Rundstedt of December 5 and 7 (T-120/935/298782–88, 298763–64); Laval letter of 5 December (T-120/935/298782–88); Schleier (Paris) 5827 to Ribbentrop, 10 December 1942 (T-120/110/115452–55).

vember; the prisoners of war remained in Germany; the departments of the Nord and the Pas-de-Calais remained under administration from Brussels; the Ostland company continued to settle
German farmers in the closed zone of northeastern France. If
the Germans ever really wanted France as an associated belligerent, they were never willing to pay the rather modest price
Laval asked in November–December 1942. Hitler clearly preferred direct occupation to collaboration in any real sense.[57]

It would be tiresome to describe in much detail Laval's continued efforts in 1943 to breathe some life into the Vichy system,
deprived now of whatever elements of independence it once
possessed in the unoccupied zone, the Armistice Army, the fleet,
and large imperial possessions. His efforts reveal that unshaken
conviction of the New Europe's permanence and that single-
minded antibolshevism that make it impossible to merely dismiss
this last part of his career as rank opportunism. In May 1943 he
was still telling Sauckel, come for more French workmen, that
he wanted to fit such discussions into the negotiation of a
larger agreement—an "Ausgleich." On May 12, he actually
saw Hitler once more to obtain authorization of the symbolic
military unit, the "First Regiment of France" that was finally
created in July 1943, and to ask for a similar symbolic navy
unit. In July 1943 he was hoping that French contractors could
play a major share in fortification work on the Mediterranean
coast. On 4 October he implored Rudolf Schleier, Abetz' assistant, to arrange another meeting with Hitler to work for building
the New Europe and to settle the authority question in France.[58]

There were a few straws to grasp at in 1943. One was the increasing role of Albert Speer in German economic planning. As
Germany's war needs increased, France became her single richest supplier. Two conceptions of how best to tap French wealth

[57] The results of the Laval-Ribbentrop meeting of 19 December 1942 are
found in Ribbentrop (Sonderzug) 1614 to Abetz, 26 December 1942
(T-120/935/298684–87), and in T-77/OKW-999/5,632,984–90. For the
Phalange Africaine, see Louis Noguères, *Le Véritable procès du maréchal
Pétain* (Paris, 1955), 363; T-77/OKW-1443; and *Ministère public c/Del-
motte*.
[58] T-120/3546H/E022126–32; Schleier (Paris), unnumbered telegram
of 4 October 1943 (T-120/4120/071186–90).

for the German war effort competed at Berlin. On the one hand, a pillaging school, led by foreign labor tsar Sauckel, attempted to move as many French workmen as possible to the Reich, without regard for the overall impact of piecemeal requisitions on the French economy. On the other hand, Albert Speer's more sophisticated and technocratic approach proposed to stimulate French industry and agriculture and fit them into a larger European Common Producing Unit. By December 1943, Laval's Minister of Industrial Production Denis Bichelonne had been able to negotiate with Speer the exemption of some 3,301 plants, with a total labor force of 723,124, from the Service du Travail Obligatoire. Production of consumer goods was actually increasing in France in 1944. The number of French laborers drafted to work in Germany declined accordingly.[59] In the last analysis, however, the Germans maintained the fiction of Vichy autonomy only because it helped keep internal order. But they refused to allow Vichy the reality of associated status into which Laval, Bichelonne, busy French industrialists in such favored industries as automobiles and aluminum, and those terrified of the Resistance could still have led many Frenchmen. Laval himself summed up his experience of Vichy offers and German tightfistedness in a reproachful remark to General von Neubronn, Marshal von Rundstedt's representative in Vichy, in June 1943. "Why have you never supported us? You even hindered the fortification and supply of our colonies."[60]

Pétain's two desultory efforts to get rid of Laval during 1943 should not suggest that the marshal was swinging with the pro-Allied tide. He was simply trying to reassert his neutralism and his traditionalist social philosophy more vigorously. The first

[59] See Alan S. Milward, "German Economic Policy Towards France, 1942–44," in K. Bourne and D. C. Watt, Studies in International History (London, 1967), and Alan S. Milward, "French Labour and German Economy, 1942–45: An Essay on the Nature of the Fascist New Order," Economic History Review XXIII: 2 (August 1970).

[60] Deutscher General Vichy, Nr. 152/43 of 10 June 1943 (T-501/DGV 70–23588/412–16). Many prominent Frenchmen would have been reconciled to the regime as late as 1943 if it had won more German concessions. Georges Bonnet, for example, still expected a diplomatic post in August 1943 (T-120/4120/071159–60).

crisis boiled up in April. Pétain seems to have sent his old friend, the World War I fighter ace Colonel René Fonck, to sound out German intelligence officials in Paris about a change of government. Three major Pétain grievances recur in the rather fragmentary contemporary material. Diplomatically, Pétain did not think Laval had a foreign policy adequate to the world ideological struggle of 1943. According to Himmler's aid Walter Shellenberg, on advice from Salazar, Pétain wanted to recover office as prime minister (he had been only head of state since April 1942) in order to pursue an active mediating role designed to bring the United States and Germany together in a compromise alliance against their real mutual danger, communism. Laval, however, talked less of mediation than of alliance with Germany. On the domestic side, as in April 1942, Pétain longed for a more actively traditionalist internal policy. Dr. Ménétrel had complained as early as January 1943 that Laval wanted to restore a "pre-1939 capitalist republic." Lucien Romier complained to General von Neubronn that Laval was "too much an old-style politician," insufficiently energetic against Freemasons and Jews, who tried to run everything himself. Pétain wanted to summon the National Council. He was also said to resent Laval's large role in the efforts to re-create a new French Army. And Laval had succeeded neither in defending the empire nor keeping internal order. Running through it all was Pétain's bitterness at having been kicked upstairs. He complained of not being kept informed and of not attending all cabinet meetings.

Hitler, irrevocably interpreting Laval's removal in December 1940 as a personal affront to himself, wrote Pétain on 29 April 1943 that he would "not permit another 13 December 1940" and that Laval "alone was capable of assuring to France the place she deserves in the New Europe." Pétain replied that he remained faithful to the "policy of entente" but that it would work only if built upon "sound bases." Nothing could be done unless France was restored to order and broke definitively with the political errors of prewar France. "I will not tolerate that anyone in France keep me from pursuing internal revival according to the national and social program defined in my messages, in harmony with a foreign policy which is the only reasonable one, but which will not be crowned with success without the help of a new internal order." [61]

Pétain tried again in the late fall of 1943. Internal disorder had increased, and even the Germans recognized that Laval was "universally detested." Vichy's mass following had vanished, and the Paris collaborators waited in the wings for power. On 12 October 1943, while Pétain and General von Neubronn were talking about the need for increased police forces, Pétain burst out on a new tack. The trouble was, Pétain said, that Laval had no popular appeal. The prefects didn't listen to him. He was trying to do everything himself, which was beyond his power. Pétain suggested he should reassume the prime ministry himself, as before April 1942. "I will lead domestic policy energetically, and we will align foreign policy with Germany without him." As Pétain's plan ripened, he proposed to make a public address on 13 November 1943 in which he would announce that Laval was dismissed, that succession would be settled in case of his death by the Council of Ministers, but that the constitutional authority voted Pétain by the Third Republic's National Assembly on 10 July 1940 should go back to that body. This attempt to root the regime more deeply in constitutionality was an acknowledged effort to compete with de Gaulle's step toward parliamentarism with the convening on November 3 of a Consultative Assembly in Algiers. But in addition, there remained Pétain's old personal antipathy toward Laval, Pétain's military scorn for the old republican politician, and a growing concern that the domestic changes since 1940 might be endangered unless someone less unpopular than Laval managed the country's internal affairs.

Hitler was determined that both Pétain and Laval should remain in their present offices "under all conditions." Not only

[61] Walter Schellenberg, Memorandum, RSHA Amt VI, 24 April 1943 (T-120/1832H/418671–73); handwritten memorandum, probably by General von Neubronn, 30 April 1943 (T-120/2318/485224–37); Ménétrel's remark is found in T-120/4120/071040. For the Romier-Neubronn conversation, May ? 1943, see T-120/2318/485222–23. The Hitler-Pétain letters of 29 April 1943 are found in T-120/2318/485209–20. Ribbentrop ordered the Gestapo to guard Laval at this point.

was Pétain forbidden to go through with the constitutional changes in his regime, but he was assigned a German shadow in the person of the diplomat von Renthe-Fink. It was from this point on—December 1943—that all French legislation had to be submitted to German scrutiny. Pétain was required under direct German pressure to take Marcel Déat and Joseph Darnand into his government to answer his own complaint that internal disorder was increasing. Although Pétain went on "strike" for a few days in mid-November, refusing to exercise the prerogatives of his office as head of state, he went no further into opposition. His threat to make the French government a purely administrative regime like Belgium—the proper solution in June 1940— was self-defeating in November 1943. Having grasped for sovereignty in 1940, and always having put domestic order above all else, Pétain was condemned to exercise that wisp of sovereignty under German surveillance to the bitter end.[62]

Let no one imagine that these two feeble attempts to replace Laval in 1943 betrayed any secret sympathy on Pétain's part for the coming Allied Liberation. Every contemporary evidence of his views in 1943 reinforces an impression of an old man clutching at order, neutrality, and a compromise peace as a way around the approaching invasion. By late 1943 he was laying plans for keeping internal order if the Allies landed, as expected, in mainland France. On 27 August 1943, Pétain and Laval together met with Marshal von Rundstedt at the Château de Charmes, near Vichy, for this purpose. It was agreed that Pétain would issue orders in the event of an enemy landing that would keep the French population "quiet and orderly."[63]

[62] The best contemporary sources for the November–December 1943 crisis are the papers of General von Neubronn (T-501, Deutscher General Vichy 70/23588) and Auswärtiges Amt, Richtl. Pol. 11, Bundle 17/2, "Material, Allg.: Ausgehende Telegramme" (T-120/6726H). See also Louis Noguères, *Le Véritable procès*, 567–98.

[63] Pétain-Rundstedt meeting, 27 August 1943 (T-120/3546H/ E022159 ff.). Other conversations may be found in Pariser Botschaft, Bundle 1120, "Politische Beziehungen Frankreich-Deutschland, vol. 2, Apr. 24, 1943–Aug. 20, 1943," (T-120/3546H). See also Pétain's letter of 20 January 1944 to von Rundstedt confirming his intention to issue orders of neutrality in case the "menace" of an Allied landing should be realized. Noguères, *Véritable procès*, 615.

That was indeed the policy followed when the long-dreaded landing took place in Normandy on 6 June 1944. Pétain issued a proclamation calling upon all Frenchmen to remain neutral. French blood was too precious to waste, he said. By the Liberation, regular French forces had never fought the Allies side-by-side with German forces. Vichy France had never declared war on the Allies. Pétain's neutralism had prevailed over Laval's more aggressive proposals. In the last analysis, however, it was Hitler rather than the French government who had rejected the voluntary association of France in a German-dominated Europe.

1944: The Dream of Peaceful Transition, the Nightmare of Civil War

BY EARLY 1944 EVERYONE BUT A FEW FANATICS KNEW the end was at hand. Vichy had become a shadow regime. The marshal himself, still standing for some fixed point in the turmoil, did remain disassociated in the public mind from his ministers. He could still be cheered in Nancy, Rouen, and even in Paris in the spring of 1944. But he was surrounded now by a German guard, and after the Paris visit on 26 April, he spent most of May 1944 in the Occupied Zone, at the Chateau of Voisins near Rambouillet, a few miles west of Paris. That was Pétain's return to Paris, at long last, when it was meaningless. At the administrative level, government officials quietly prepared for a change of regime. Some areas of government—food rationing, for example—hardly functioned at all. Most of the history of that Merovingian court in 1944 is without real significance.[64]

Vichy could still influence the transition to a postwar regime, however, and its efforts to do so show once more where its priorities lay. The dreaded civil war was at hand. There remained one chance to evade it, however, if the activist Resistance could be prevented from becoming a de facto civil power and if

[64] The best-informed account is the later chapters of Warner, *Laval*. See also André Brissaud, *La Dernière année: Vichy 1943-44* (Paris, 1967).

a peaceful transition could be arranged between anticommunist "moderates" on both sides. The approaching German evacuation presented the same frightening void of administration as the proposed French evacuation overseas had done in June 1940. The permanence of an orderly state had to be assured at all costs.

The interesting feature of Vichy in 1944, therefore, is the effort to effect an orderly transfer of state authority. Those hopes, and the bitterness aroused by de Gaulle's refusal to accept the mantle from Pétain, are the lasting value of memoirs of 1944, such as Jean Tracou's *Le Maréchal aux liens,* a book otherwise tendentious and unreliable.[65]

In Algiers, General de Gaulle's circle was also grappling with the problem of orderly transition. When the Vichyite local authorities were dispossessed or vanished, de Gaulle wanted them replaced neither by anarchy, Communist *francs-tireurs* partisans from the hills, nor an American military government. His plan, worked out in detail by Michel Debré, was to designate loyal and able administrators in advance who were prepared to step into place immediately as Gaullist super-prefects, Commissaires de la république, similar in regional scope and in police powers to Darlan's regional prefects of 1941. In retrospect a certain harmony of interest in an orderly transition appears in both Algiers and Vichy, a harmony drowned out at the time by more conspicuous discords.[66]

There were groups on both sides eager in 1944 to arrange a peaceful transition between Vichy and the non-Gaullist opposition. One such effort was made by followers of General Giraud, the conservative anti-Germans who had wanted to bring the regular French Army back into the war legitimately, who had agreed secretly in advance to help the American landing in North Africa in November 1942, and who had run liberated North Africa along National Revolution lines from November 1942 until mid-1943. A leader of this group, the wealthy vegetable-oil producer Jean Lemaigre-Dubreuil, a leader of the

---

[65] Jean Tracou, *Le Maréchal aux liens* (Paris, 1948).
[66] The chapter in de Gaulle's memoirs on the first winter after the Liberation is entitled "L'Ordre."

pro-Allied conspiracy in Algiers in November 1942, tried to establish contact between Laval and Washington in July 1944, through Vichy Ambassador François Piétri at Madrid. Lemaigre-Dubreuil, along with Jules Sauerwein, a French journalist in touch with German intelligence in Lisbon, thought that a compromise peace might be acceptable to the United States as the Russians seemed about to sweep into Europe. Ribbentrop found out about it on 14 July 1944 and ordered German officials to break off all contacts with these men.[67]

As the Allied armies moved toward Paris, Laval made a better-documented attempt to set up a constitutional alternative to the Free French. On 12 August 1944 he appeared suddenly at the asylum near Nancy where Edouard Herriot was being held in forced residence and took the former Chamber president and Radical party leader back with him to Paris. Laval wanted Herriot to reconvene the National Assembly, a proposal reminiscent of Pétain's plan of the previous November. It is not clear whether Herriot took the idea seriously or not, and in any event, on August 16 the Germans rearrested him.[68]

Pétain was making a parallel effort on his own to ensure some kind of orderly transfer of authority. It seems likely that he never ceased to believe in the virtues of the National Revolution, for in his one statement at the trial in 1945 he declared that France could build only upon the lines which he had laid down. On 11 August 1944, he empowered Admiral Auphan to contact de Gaulle in order to negotiate whatever "political solution" would "prevent civil war" and safeguard "the principle of legitimacy which I embody." No doubt he thought that Auphan, who had left the government in November 1942 without joining the Resistance, would be acceptable to both sides. Auphan also carried sealed instructions ordering him, in case Pétain himself

---

[67] See Geoffrey Warner, *Pierre Laval and the Eclipse of France* (New York, 1968), 393–96, and Auswärtiges Amt, Referat D 11 (Inland), "Akten betreffend Auslandsmeldungen des SD betr. Frankreich," (T-120/4120/071205–31). Lemaigre-Dubreuil had left the new regime in North Africa after General Giraud publicly denounced the National Revolution in a speech on 14 April 1943.

[68] The best-informed accounts are Michel Soulié, *La Vie politique d'Edouard Herriot* (Paris, 1962), 518–21, and Geoffrey Warner, *Pierre Laval,* 401–3.

were prevented from exercising office, to summon the regency council foreseen in Pétain's plans of November 1943.[69] De Gaulle, whose claim to legitimacy was based on quite different grounds, naturally refused to see anyone offering to anoint him in Pétain's name.

All of these plans for an orderly continuity were so much writing on the water. Determined to keep the Vichy loyalties alive, the Germans removed both Laval and Pétain eastward under protest, ahead of the liberating armies. Laval refused to serve as prime minister after being taken to Belfort on the night of 17 August. Pétain wound up with a shadow court in the old Hohenzollern castle of Sigmaringen. He too refused to exercise his office of head of state. Only Doriot, on top at last, tried to give orders as a French government in exile. The Liberation advanced in a climate very like civil war. Direct executions by the Resistance, mingled with all sorts of obscure settling of scores, produced at least 4,500 deaths. During the more formal purge processes that followed, 124,750 persons were tried, 767 were executed under sentence of treason or contact with the enemy in time of war, and over 38,000 were sentenced to some form of prison term. Thousands were expelled or demoted in the public service.[70] It will not do, of course, to blame de Gaulle's intransigence for the passions and breakage of the Liberation. Pétain's followers had elected to use the occupation not merely for day-to-day administration but for a domestic revolution directed against their internal enemies. They had grasped for the full exercise of French sovereignty under German occupation. In the name of order, they had put all the resources of the state to work upholding an obsolete armistice. In the end, they reaped the divisions they sowed and the disorder they had compromised everything to avoid.

[69] Admiral Auphan later enjoyed presenting facsimile copies of his *ordre de mission* to visitors, including this author. See also Warner, *Laval*, 402.
[70] Peter Novick, *The Resistance Versus Vichy: The Purge of Collaborators in Liberated France* (New York, 1968).

V | A Balance Sheet: The Legacy of Vichy

Breaks and Continuities

OFFICIALLY, THE VICHY REGIME AND ALL ITS WORKS were simply expunged from history when France was liberated. The acts of the "de facto authority," as the Comité Français de Libération Nationale called Vichy, were declared null and void by an ordinance issued in Algiers on 9 August 1944. The purge of collaborationist officials had already been announced with the formation by the CFLN of a purge committee on 18 August 1943. The ministers of all successive governments since 16 June 1940 were arraigned before a specially created High Court of Justice by a decree of 18 November 1944. The first Vichy minister to be prosecuted, Pierre Pucheu, had already been condemned to death by a military court in Algiers and shot in March 1944.[1]

In law, things were supposed to go back to the moment just

[1] Peter Novick, *The Resistance Versus Vichy* (New York, 1968); Robert Aron, *Histoire de l'épuration* (Paris, 1967–69).

before midnight on 16 June 1940, when President Albert Lebrun had summoned Marshal Pétain to form a government replacing that of Paul Reynaud. In practice, the clock would not turn back, nor did the liberators of France really want it to. In fact, the architects of postwar innovation could not always avoid building upon Vichy legislation or legislating in parallel directions. For good or evil, the Vichy regime had made indelible marks on French life.

Long after the Liberation, the ruptures and breaks of that passionate time were far more apparent than the continuities. Liberation writers talked about "four years to strike from our history." Former Vichy ministers reflected bitterly upon the "revolution of 1944." Highly exaggerated figures placed the toll of Frenchmen killed by Frenchmen during the Liberation as high as 120,000, though the total was probably closer to 4,500. Over 100,000 Frenchmen were jailed, facing trial, confiscation of property, or loss of jobs, if not death. The creators of the Fourth Republic set out to make all things new. No wonder change and discontinuity seemed the dominant mode of late-1940's France.[2]

It is now time to correct the balance with more attention to the continuities that link Vichy to postwar regimes. The breaks were real enough, and anyone who spends much time in France has met outcasts like the embittered Chantiers de Jeunesse veteran Roland Oyarzun in Jean-Louis Curtis' novel *Les justes causes,* flotsam and jetsam of a shipwrecked cause. In a long view, and in social rather than personal terms, however, continuities probably prevail over breaks between Vichy and subsequent regimes.

For one thing, the Resisters' new parties, newspapers, leaders, and programs turned out to be far more ephemeral after the war than anyone would have predicted in 1944. The resisters expected to govern. What Sartre called "the Republic of silence," however, did not survive its transformation into an everyday

---

[2] André Mornet, *Quatre années à rayer de notre histoire* (Paris, 1949). Yves Bouthillier, *Le Drame de l'armistice* (Paris, 1950), talks in his preface about the "revolution of 1944." Conflicting figures on the summary executions of the Liberation are admirably reviewed and assessed by Novick, Appendix C, 202–8.

administration. The coalition of the three great Liberation parties —left Catholic MRP, Socialists, and Communists—was exploded by the beginnings of the Cold War (the Communists were excluded by Ramadier in May 1947 after they had refused to continue to support wage austerity) and by the revival of the issue of state aid to Catholic schools in 1951. By then the new parties derived from Resistance movements—MRP, UDSR— were losing their electorate to reviving conservative parties or surviving Third Republic parties. Although a few Resistance newspapers—e.g., *Combat*—and weeklies—e.g., *Témoignage chrétien*—hung on, the vast majority succumbed to mass circulation dailies built upon prewar establishments, like *France-Soir* and *Le Figaro*. Only *Le Monde,* the great daily that received the confiscated presses and offices of *Le Temps,* was a lasting innovation in the postwar press. It was the work of Hubert Beuve-Méry, whose Resistance days had been preceded by ardent service in the Ecole de Cadres at Uriage. The elaborate innovations expected in the Fourth Republic constitution boiled down to compromises in the text and a revival of Third Republic practices in the application. The Resistance proved ephemeral as government.[3]

At the same time, important elements of the Vichy regime survived. On the surface, there were striking reappearances. Three associates of Pétain, including his lawyer Jacques Isorni and former staff member Roger de Saivre, were elected to the Chamber in 1951. The conspicuous diminution of purging zeal after 1950 was followed by a general amnesty in 1953, allowing others to return to public life. Fourteen former Vichy officials sat in the French parliament by 1958. René Coty, elected president of the republic in 1953, had voted "yes" in July 1940. During that same year two former Vichy officials became ministers: André Boutemy, former Vichy prefect, became minister of health, and Camille Laurent, former official of the Peasant Corporation, became minister of agriculture. The Académie Française, which had expelled Abel Hermant and Abel Bonnard in 1945 and left the seats of Pétain and Maurras unfilled until their deaths, elected Vichy intellectuals Jacques Chardonne

[3] Philip M. Williams, *Crisis and Compromise: Politics in the Fourth Republic* (London, 1958), remains the best account of this evolution.

(1950), Thierry-Maulnier (1955), and Henri Massis (1960) in the following decade. Jean-Louis Tixier-Vignancourt, director of the Vichy radio in 1940, received over a million votes as a presidential candidate in December 1965. The important survivals lay under that more conspicuous surface, however. With much less fanfare, whole sectors of Vichy personnel and policies continued to function after the Liberation.

In the most elementary human terms, many Frenchmen who had served Vichy continued to do their jobs under the new regime. It would have been both unjust and impractical to punish those average Frenchmen who had merely gone on filling some job, obeying the instructions of an apparently legitimate regime, and whose skills were just as essential as before to the orderly functioning of society: postmen, clerks, engineers. Like other Liberation regimes and like the Allies at Nuremberg, the French CFLN and provisional government punished the makers and shapers rather than the executors of policy except where underlings had sinned by excess of zeal for the occupying power. Indeed, liberated France punished a smaller proportion of its total population with prison terms than any other occupied Western European country and executed a smaller proportion than Belgium.[4]

The postwar trials and purges did not visit all sectors of the Vichy leadership with the same severity, moreover. Some portions of the French elite survived almost intact across the entire war, occupation, and Liberation, while others suffered extensive turnover of personnel or even permanent loss of power or prestige. The patterns of leadership survival and discontinuity are in themselves a revealing lineament. Experts, businessmen, and bureaucrats survived almost intact; intellectuals and propagandists were much more heavily purged; Third Republic deputies were rejected nearly as totally by the Liberation as they had been by Vichy.

The Liberation's pretended administrative revolution had

[4] Novick, 159 n., 186–87. A law of 14 September 1944 held that civil servants were liable to prosecution only if they had gone beyond orders to aid the Germans or if they had had the power to ignore Vichy orders. *Ministère public c/Dayras*, 78.

relatively little impact upon personnel in the long run. Reviving proposals from the Second Republic of 1848 and from the Popular Front, Liberation leaders proposed to democratize recruitment and advancement in an upper civil service alleged to have undermined the Third Republic and to have participated eagerly in the authoritarian system of Vichy. They meant to make the purge permanent from below by nationalizing the old elite Ecole Libre des Sciences Politiques and by setting up a single Ecole Nationale d'Administration to train a new breed of republican experts. On its twentieth anniversary, however, the ENA was clearly just another rung in the traditional elitist educational ladder up which advanced the most favored and hardest-working of future top public administrators, more homogeneous than ever. The Liberation set out to destroy the "chapels" of the upper bureaucracy, commented *Le Monde,* and it created a cathedral.

Even in the short run, the high civil servants came through a hostile Liberation remarkably intact. No doubt, those senior civil servants who lost seniority or rank or were retired early after screening by purge commissions in each government branch would find that remark ludicrous. At the very top, notably, those high civil servants who had accepted ministries or secretaryships of state at Vichy were automatically charged before the High Court of Justice with crimes against the state. Their vacancies, however, were filled from below by promotion from within the *grands corps*. Professionalism resisted dismantling of the bureaucratic system and encroachment by nonprofessionals with almost total success.

The survival of bureaucracy in modern states hardly needs explaining, but there were special reasons in liberated France for that survival. The enemies of professionalism were divided. The proponents of a return to amateur public administration, the replacement of central authorities by Tocquevillian local notables, were mostly Pétiniste social nostalgics who were themselves more discredited at the Liberation than even the high civil servants. The proponents of a total replacement of high civil servants with Resistance cadres, mostly Communists, were opposed in this endeavor by the non-Communist Resistance parties. With the enemies of professionalism canceling each other out, the *grands corps de l'état* survived one more change of regime virtually intact. It was no moment, of course, for amateurs, however heroic. The economy of penury, that feature of Vichy life which had required the most total economic control in French history, continued without much relief into the late 1940's. Indeed, the bread ration of the winter of 1947 was lower than it had been under Vichy. The Resistance itself was as strongly marked by a preference for *dirigisme* over the chaotic "liberal" economy of the 1930's as Vichy had been. And finally, all French parties, including the Communist party, chose order over revolution in 1944. Like Vichy, the Liberation wanted to control the administration, not abolish it.[5] The *grands corps* carried their enhanced influence and their new experience from Vichy planning forward into the postwar regimes' experiments in *dirigisme* and rule by experts.

A look at the yearbook (*annuaire*) of each *grands corps de l'état* gives an impressive display of continuity across the tormented years between 1939 and 1946. Most stable of all was the most purely technical body, the Cour des Comptes, which audits public accounts. No less than 98 percent of the active 1942 personnel still figure in the 1946 yearbook, and indeed 99 percent in the 1949 yearbook, two of the wartime presidents, MM. Amet and Brin, having been restored to the rolls as presidents emeritus.

What is more, new men brought into the Cour des Comptes by the Vichy regime remained after the war, with the same apparent seniority. The Cour des Comptes enlarged during the war as the public sector expanded. In particular, a law of 16 May 1941 submitted the accounts of all public funds, including organizations subsidized by the state, to the Cour des Comptes' scrutiny automatically and not case by case as before. Thus the total membership of the Cour des Comptes grew by 4 percent,

---

[5] For apparent Communist orders to work within the system between 1944 and May 1947, see Alfred J. Rieber, *Stalin and the French Communist Party* (New York, 1962). There is much information on the Resistance leaders' rejection of the liberal economy and adoption of planning in Henri Michel and Boris Mirkine-Guetzévitch, *Les Idées politiques et sociales de la résistance* (Paris, 1954), and Henri Michel, *Les Courants de Pensée de la résistance* (Paris, 1962).

from 201 to 209, between 1938 and 1942, then by 2 percent to 214 in 1946, again by 4 percent to 223 in 1949, and by 8 percent to 242 in 1952.[6] Under these conditions of rapid expansion, the Cour des Comptes could fill its highly expert ranks only by rapid promotion of junior men and by adding outside experts at the top. The largest number of outside experts was added in 1941 (four *conseillers-maitres* and three *conseillers-référendaires de 2e classe*), in 1943 (three and two), 1945 (three *conseillers-maitres*), and in 1950 (seven *conseillers-référendaires de 2e classe*). All the men recruited during Vichy continued after the war at the same level. Thus the shape of the hierarchical pyramid of the Cour des Comptes changed from the broadly based structure with many junior men of the prewar years to the postwar structure top-heavy with many senior men. Only by the early 1950's does a look at the yearbook show that the Cour des Comptes' younger ranks were filling up to match the scale of the upper ranks. Not only continuity, then, but a certain professional ascent and fulfillment is apparent in the Cour des Comptes through the Vichy period, whatever the members' individual griefs and sufferings as French citizens and consumers. They not only endured, they prospered professionally.[7]

Next come two *grands corps* whose continuity is slightly less than that of the Cour des Comptes, for their professionalism was tainted by the service of many members in ministries: the Council of State and the Inspectorate of Finance. In the prestigious Inspectorate of Finance, some 97 percent of inspectors-general active in 1948 had also been serving in 1942, along with 75 percent of the inspectors-second class (some of these were too young to have served in 1942).[8]

---

[6] The Cour des Comptes' sphere of competence was further enlarged on 31 December 1949 to include social security and family allowances. For the membership of the Cour des Comptes, see *Bottin administratif,* 1938, 59–60; 1946, 21–22; 1949, 63–64; 1952, 75–76; Ministère des Finances, *Annuaire,* 1942.

[7] Note the rather satisfied tone with which the president of the Cour des Comptes reported how "effective" the court had been under Vichy. Cour des Comptes, *Rapport au président de la république. Années 1940–45* (Paris, 1947), 6.

[8] Ministère des Finances, *Annuaire,* 1942; *Adresses des membres de l'IGF* (1948).

The Inspectorate of Finance also expanded during the war to keep up with increased tasks. To its traditional responsibility of reviewing state financial accounts was added a mission of financial information for the growing planning and *dirigiste* functions of the Ministry of National Economy.[9] Recruitment classes nearly doubled, a reflection of both the increased prestige and the increased responsibilities of the inspectorate. In place of the five or six new members that had been normal before the war, the class of 1941 contained ten and the class of 1942 nine. Thus after the purge of 1940, the inspectorate remained about constant, having had 202 members in 1938 and 200 in 1942, and then grew to 214 by 1948. Furthermore, every one of the 32 recruits of the Vichy years, including two postwar prime ministers, Félix Gaillard (1957) and Jacques Chaban-Delmas (1969), continued after the war. Some of these young members of the *grands corps,* of course, had brilliant Resistance records. Chaban-Delmas, who was already active in the Resistance before passing the entrance examination for the Inspectorate of Finance in 1943, became a military delegate of Free France shortly afterwards, and eventually brigadier general in the Liberation army. In general, however, professional continuity counted for more than Resistance activity in the postwar survival of the Vichy recruits to the *grands corps.*

It was inevitable that the purge should affect the Inspectorate of Finance more than the Cour des Comptes, for more than a third of the inspectors normally spent some time lending their expertise to the ministries, in policy-making jobs. This makes the essential continuity of this distinguished group of experts even more remarkable. The Vichy purge removed four men from the Inspectorate of Finance: Leca and Devaux, who had been caught at the Spanish border in June 1940 with the papers and secret funds of Paul Reynaud; André Diethelm, who joined de Gaulle; and Hervé Alphand, who was Jewish (later Ambassador to the U.S., 1956–65); four others "resigned." The postwar purge was little larger. Some nine inspectors of finance who had served the Vichy regime in capacities more political than technical were

[9] Inspection des Finances, *Rapport sur l'activité de l'Inspection générale des finances en 1941* (Paris, 1942), 4–5.

expelled: ministers like Bouthillier and Baudouin, secretaries-general of ministries like Barnaud and Guérard, diplomats like François Piétri. In addition, both purges interrupted the normal promotions of some men or placed them on inactive duty without expelling them from the inspectorate. These included Joseph Avenol, shunted aside by Vichy because he had been secretary-general of the League of Nations, or Henri Culmann, who lost seniority after the war for having served as a leading figure in creating Vichy corporative institutions. But the dominant impression, as one leafs through the yearbooks, is still that of continuity.

The same holds for the Council of State, another prestigious agency whose talented members continue to be much in demand for sensitive posts in government and industry. Indeed so many of the councillors of state were placed on leave after 1940 to take important posts in the new regime that the total number of active members of the council dropped from 113 in 1938 to 105 in 1942.[10]

At the same time, the Council of State, like the other *grands corps,* saw its functions expanding. The council's juridical function as a court of law for private persons seeking redress of administrative grievances went on as before. Its consultative function in lawmaking, preeminent under Bonapartist regimes but attenuated under the Third Republic, was revived by Vichy. The law of 18 December 1940 reestablished a fifth section (legislation) that examined all legislation in the drafting process and that even gave legislative initiative to the Council of State. The secretary-general of each ministry was automatically attached to the council. The Council of State rose to these new demands by more rapid promotions of its younger members, which enlarged the upper ranks and provided a kind of professional fulfillment, as in the Cour des Comptes.

Only those who left the Council of State to serve as prefects, ministers, or secretaries-general of ministries after 1940 were removed from the corps in the postwar purge, however. Even in

[10] Some of this drop also was the result of Vichy removal of Jewish members. The total was up to 134 by 1952. This figure does not include the secretaries-general of ministries, all of whom were *conseillers d'état en service extraordinaire.*

this somewhat more politicized *grand corps,* 80 percent of the section presidents, 76 percent of the conseillers d'état en service ordinaire, and 70 percent of the maîtres des requêtes serving in 1942 are still found in the 1946 yearbook (two more reappear in the 1949 yearbook, having been reinstated).[11]

What is striking in all these *grands corps* was their resistance to replacement of professionals by amateurs forced upon them for political reasons. The yearbooks show that vacancies created in senior posts by either Vichy or the Liberation were filled largely by promotion from within.

We come now to *grands corps* which have a stronger political coloration. The judiciary, the diplomatic corps, and particularly the Prefectoral Corps carry out a regime's policy in such conspicuous ways that one would expect substantial turnover of personnel here through the years of war, occupation, and Liberation.

The judiciary performed the extraordinary feat of enforcing the law of successive regimes virtually without personnel change. Judges were given prominent roles in the regime, like all experts: judges like Frémicourt and law professors like Joseph Barthélemy, dean of the Paris law faculty, replaced politicians in the office of minister of justice. In return, judges were required like other public officials to take an oath of allegiance to Marshal Pétain, and a circular of Minister of Justice Barthélemy in 1942 warned that career advancement in the magistracy depended upon "devotion to the new order and to the person of the Head of State." The fact that special courts had done the dirtiest work of the regime helped the regular magistracy to retain some vestige of independence. The judges of the Section Spéciale of the Paris Cour d'Appel, set up in August 1941 to mete out swift punishments after the assassination of a German serviceman in Paris on August 14, were sentenced on 8 June 1945 to terms ranging from a few years in prison to hard labor for life (Judge Benon, president of the section). Not all the members of the Tribunal d'Etat were career magistrates. De Gaulle himself and other leading Resistance figures had been sentenced in

[11] *Bottin administratif,* 1938, 54–56; 1946, 18–19; 1949, 58–60; 1952, 69–71. Ministère de l'Intérieur, *Annuaire* (1942).

absentia by courts-martial. The regular judges, therefore, had been spared the most sensitive cases. Having applied Vichy's law for four years, the magistracy went on applying the Fourth Republic's law from the august heights of a bench that seemed to have preserved its Olympian purity. This state of affairs produced not a few ironies during the postwar trials. There was, for example, old André Mornet, who had prosecuted Mata Hari and who came out of retirement to prosecute Laval and Pétain with evangelical fervor, shouting "there are too many Germans in this room" when the audience muttered during Laval's travesty of a trial. Mornet's righteous wrath was tempered somewhat when Pétain's trial was reminded that Mornet had taken the oath to Pétain like all judges, that he had been named to the Riom court that had tried the Third Republic leaders (he had apparently not served), and that he had served on the denaturalization commission which revoked the citizenship of many recent immigrants. No wonder Mornet called his book about Vichy *Four Years to Strike from Our History.*[12]

The diplomatic corps was more stable than might be imagined, considering the pitfalls awaiting ambassadors at changes of regime. The legal forms by which the Vichy regime was installed in July 1940, its recognition by other governments ranging from the Vatican to Moscow, maintained the existing diplomatic corps virtually intact up through 1942, with the exception of a few Jews and Masons purged by Vichy and a handful of dissidents. A large part of the embassy staff in Washington resigned when Laval returned to power in April 1942. There was a genuine wave of resignations in November 1942. Moreover, the diplomatic corps, with its highly political function of representation, could not resist outside amateur appointments. Vichy named more politicians (Senator Henry-Haye as ambassador to Washington, Senator Léon Berard as ambassa-

---

[12] *Ministère public c/Dayras,* 61, has information regarding the postwar sentences of the Section spéciale judges. The judges' oath was required by a law of 12 August 1941. Barthélemy circular of 25 March 1942, Ministère de la justice, *Bulletin officiel,* 1942, 26–29. The magistrate Guy Raïssac has particularly accurate information on the Vichy judicial system in *Combat sans merci* (Paris, 1966). For Mornet, see Raïssac 211, 363 n., *Ministère public c/Brinon,* 119, and *New York Times,* 23 July 1955.

dor to the Holy See, Deputy François Piétri to Madrid, Deputy Gaston Bergery to Moscow and then to Ankara) and military men (Admiral Bard to Switzerland) as ambassadors than the Third Republic had done.

Even with these elements of discontinuity, more than half the diplomatic corps survived the years of turmoil. The 1947 yearbook of the diplomatic corps contains some 1,100 names. Approximately 450 of these are older career men who were already present in 1939 and who had served at least some time under Vichy. Another 200 had entered the diplomatic service under Vichy. A final group of about 450 are new men, mostly recruited by the traditional examination, but some apparently brought in more irregularly from the Free French forces and Resistance groups. In these rather summary terms, nearly two-thirds of the diplomatic corps served both Vichy and the Fourth Republic. The impression of continuity is enhanced when one remembers that even in peaceful times there is a substantial turnover in any eight-year period by retirement, death, and resignations.[13]

The Prefectoral Corps had the closest political identification and the least highly developed professional structure of all the *grands corps de l'état*. A prefect is, in the words of the law of 23 December 1940, "the sole representative of the government in the department."[14] As the chief executive official in each district (*département*), a prefect was an essential link in the application of government policies at the local level. New regimes usually found old prefects too closely identified with the policies of predecessors and insisted upon naming new ones. French practice still recognized a government's right to a free choice of prefects, even though the Prefectoral Corps had become a professional body with its own system of recruitment and advancement from within which, increasingly, a minister of the interior was expected to choose his prefects. The Second Republic's

---

[13] Ministère des Affaires Etrangères, *Annuaire diplomatique et consulaire*, 1939 and 1947. Personnel changes may be followed in detail in Ministère des Affaires Etrangères, *Bulletin officiel*, 1ʳᵉ année, no. 1 (Jan.–Mar. 1942) *et seq.*

[14] Ministère de la Justice, *Bulletin officiel*, 1941, 24.

minister of the interior in 1848, Ledru-Rollin, changed all the prefects; all the Second Empire's prefects were removed in 1871. After the 16 May 1877 constitutional showdown had been won by republicans, 87 prefects and 267 subprefects were changed. Against this background, the Vichy purge of Third Republic prefects was relatively modest. Interior Minister Adrien Marquet, the Neosocialist mayor of Bordeaux, retired 35 prefects under the law of 17 July 1940 permitting more or less arbitrary removal of civil servants and named 67 new ones in Vichy's grandest prefectoral reshuffle. Eventually some 40 men were made prefects from outside the service (mostly military officers and councillors of state), but only 9 of those were still there in 1944. Thus professionalism continued to gain ground. Vichy seems to have had less trouble finding sympathetic men in the prefectoral corps than did the Liberation, representing, as it did, the continuity of administration. The liberation purge was as sweeping as those of the nineteenth century. The French Committee of National Liberation in Algiers named new prefects in advance to all 87 mainland departments, only 20 of whom were drawn from the Prefectoral Corps. Another 67 were outsiders "delegated" to their functions by governmental authority ("préfets délégués"). Over time, however, these new men of the Liberation period drifted back to their original jobs, so that by 1947 the Prefectoral Corps had become an amalgam, about half from the old Prefectoral Corps, many of whom had come up through the ranks holding junior posts under Vichy, and about half Liberation prefects "integrated" into the corps. The postwar prefects were also younger men, as is normal in a time of rapid personnel turnover; the same was true of the Vichy prefects.[15] Here is a genuine breach of professionalism and an array of new faces that comes closer to matching the reputation of the period 1939–46 as one of massive personnel change.

The overall impression created by a look at the personnel of the *grands corps* is one of basic stability. Continuity varied according to the political and professional functions of each *corps,* but even at the unstable end of the spectrum, nearly half the

[15] Pierre Doueil, *L'Administration locale à l'épreuve de la guerre* (Paris, 1950), 41, 283 ff.

professionals in the Prefectoral Corps survived the years 1939–46.

Outside the professional corps of senior administrators of the upper civil service lie the more general forms of expertise. Businessmen and engineers, for example, probably experienced very little personnel change during this period. No businessman was tried for collaboration after the war, although there were actions against illicit war profits or tax evasion, the extent of which is still privileged information. Louis Renault, whose automobile works built tanks for the Germans, died in prison before he could be tried. Renault was the only manufacturer whose plants were confiscated permanently by the state, and indeed the Renault works, like the Berliet truck factory at Lyon, might have been returned to private hands had M. Renault lived as long as M. Marius Berliet, who built 2,330 trucks for the Germans but who stubbornly refused to recognize legal actions against him after the war. He died in 1949, and his firm remained in family hands.[16] It is difficult to study personnel changes among leading businessmen, for they are not members of a closed professional corps like upper civil servants with their names and ranks in a promotion list. But just as the prewar leaders of business and trade associations tended to become the heads of Vichy's Organization Committees, so the leading industrialists of the Vichy period retained control of their sources of social power through the Liberation. Nationalization touched some of them: in addition to M. Louis Renault, there were the executives of the insurance companies, banks, coal mines, and gas and electric works that were taken over by the state in 1945–46. But one would find far more continuity than change in the upper industrial, commercial, and engineering ranks, swelled further by Vichy figures who found postwar careers in business. Officials of the Peasant Corporation, too, were the backbone of postwar agriculture pressure groups.[17]

By contrast, other sections of the French elite were perma-

---

[16] Michel Laferrière, *Lyon: Ville industrielle* (Paris, 1960), 386.

[17] For business, see Henry W. Ehrmann, *Organized Business in France* (Princeton, 1957). For agriculture, see Pierre Barral, *Les Agrariens* (Paris, 1966), 296, and Gordon Wright, *Rural Revolution in France* (Stanford, Calif., 1964).

nently changed by the catastrophes of 1939–46. Significantly, it was the traditionalists, who had had less influence at Vichy in the long run than the experts, who were much more vigorously uprooted at the Liberation than the experts. Although they had exerted a diminishing effect on Vichy policies, they had been men of the word. They had commanded newspaper pages, radio hours, and public platforms. When innovations like regionalism were discussed, it was the traditionalists who had done all the talking about provinces and tradition, while the experts had quietly gone ahead and established regional prefectures in a way repugnant to them. But the traditionalists had provided the words and voices of Vichy, and they were marked men.

Those traditionalists who had occupied policy-making positions came before the High Court of Justice: some, like Raphael Alibert, Jacques Chevalier, and Pierre Caziot, went to prison and lost their property and civic rights (the vote). Henry Moysset died in 1949 before he was to come up for trial. Those traditionalists whose duties involved mostly youth work, like Georges Lamirand and General de la Porte du Theil, were acquitted. Jean Borotra, who had been deported by the Germans later in the war, like General de la Porte du Theil, was a member of the Haut Comité des Sports in the 1960's without having lost any of his fervor for Marshal Pétain's efforts to save French youth through athletics. Gustave Thibon remained isolated and ignored in a country retreat despite the publication of an occasional book. Some Pétiniste traditionalists made a form of comeback by being elected to the French Academy: notably Thierry Maulnier in 1955 and Henri Massis in 1960. By that time, however, few Frenchmen knew even the names of France's forty immortals. A more serious revival crystallized around the campaign for Algérie française in the late 1950's and the early 1960's. General Weygand and René Gillouin, who had been together in 1937 in the Rassemblement National pour la Reconstruction de la France, found themselves together in a new authoritarian nationalist movement to defend the empire from the world Communist conspiracy in the 1960's, the CEPEC (Centre d'Etudes Civiques et Politiques) of Georges Sauge. The high point of that revival around the Algerian issue, abetted by fears of the burgeoning new youth culture of the 1960's, was the presidential candidacy of Jean-Louis Tixier-Vignancourt in December 1965. Tixier had been commissioner of press and radio briefly in late 1940 and an official of Pétain's Rassemblement pour la Révolution Nationale in 1941. He received 1,250,000 votes in December 1965. An outpouring of sympathetic Pétain biographies beginning in 1966 argued that the marshal would have known how to deal with dissident youth. By and large, however, the traditionalists were condemned to obscurity along with the whole social nostalgic attitude. The vision of old France, surviving her flashier neighbors through balance and thrift, was almost totally replaced by the more dynamic vision of a new France competing in growth, vigor, and material power with her neighbors. Postwar conservatives, whether growth-conscious businessmen or Mao-reading colonels fresh from Indochina or Algeria, had little in common with the social traditionalists of the 1930's and 1940's. Vichy was the traditionalists' last stand.[18]

The fate of the overtly fascist intellectuals and party leaders in occupied Paris was even more final. Men of public platforms, their words condemned them to suffer at the Liberation. The lucky ones escaped into exile, like Déat to an Italian monastery and Céline to Denmark. Drieu la Rochelle managed to commit suicide. Robert Brasillach, Georges Suarez, and Jean Luchaire were executed. Philippe Henriot, Minister of Information and the voice of Radio Vichy, had been assassinated on 28 June 1944. Jacques Doriot had been killed when Allied aircraft strafed his car on a German highway in 1945. Darnand, who had entered the government at the last, as Secretary-General for the Maintenance of Order in December 1943, had the blood of the Resistance on his hands as commander of the Milice. He was executed on 10 October 1945. Officers and members of the Milice, as the most conspicuous collaborators in the battle against the Resistance, were dealt with very severely by Liberation courts.[19]

[18] For an example of the new biographies' suggestion that Pétain would have known how to handle the "blousons noirs," see Georges Blond, *Pétain* (Paris, 1966), 309.

[19] For Darnand, Luchaire, and Brinon, see *Les Procès de la collaboration* (Paris, 1948). For the Milice, see Jacques Delperrie de Bayac, *Histoire de la milice, 1918–45* (Paris, 1969).

That the intellectuals, propagandists, and anti-Resistance militants of Paris and of Vichy's last stage in 1944 should have come to violent ends at the Liberation is not surprising. What is curious is how fully the parliamentarians of the Third Republic were also eliminated from the postwar world, not by violence but by scorn. Frenchmen of the Liberation were as hostile to the deputies of 1940 as Vichy had been. Of all sections of the prewar French elite, deputies display the least continuity across the period 1939–1946.

It was the deputies of the Third Republic, after all, who had voted exceptional powers to Marshal Pétain on 10 July 1940. They bore a heavy responsibility for giving Vichy far more than mere caretaker powers. The decree of April 1944 that made ineligible for reelection the 569 deputies and senators who had voted "yes" on 10 July 1940 was to be expected.[20]

It was the whole Third Republic parliamentary system, however, and not merely the 569, that Frenchmen wanted to punish at the Liberation. Some resistance groups, such as the heavily bureaucratic and military OCM (Organisation Civile et Militaire), wanted to exclude all Third Republic leaders without exception from postwar roles and to continue Vichy's Riom trials.[21]

In this climate, even the 80 who had voted "no" in July 1940 found no automatic return to public life after 1944. The survival rate of the 80 across the war years is far lower than that of any of the *grand corps*. Of 623 members of the Assemblée Nationale (the new lower house) in 1949, only 88 (14 percent) had been members of either house in 1938. Communist parliamentarians, who had been expelled from Parliament by Daladier in January 1940, survived the war better than their colleagues: there were 31 Communist deputies in 1949 who were veterans of 1938. The other veterans were divided among some who had been taken to

---

[20] See, for the efforts of these men to return to political life, the Association des Représentants du Peuple de la IIIe République, esp. no. 4, January 1947, "Lettre aux adhérents." (BDIC: O Pièce 24975).

[21] Cahier of the OCM, 1942, quoted in Maxime Blocq-Mascart, *Chronique de la résistance* (Paris, 1945), 168–70.

North Africa aboard the *Massilia* and therefore missed the vote of 10 July 1940, 7 who had voted "yes" and whose ineligibility had been lifted, and some 30 who had been among the 80 "no's" of July 1940. In the Conseil de la République (Senate) of 1949, only 23 of 318 (7 percent) were veterans of either house in 1938, and since 8 of these were former senators who had voted "yes" (only one senator had voted "no" in July 1940), one finds few of the 80 here either. In all, less than half of the 80 returned to public life after the war, a far lower survival rate than any of the *grands corps,* even allowing for the greater age of parliamentarians.

The postwar rejection of Third Republic political figures, indeed, was nearly as vigorous as Vichy's had been. Frenchmen voted twenty-five to one in the referendum of 21 October 1945 to consider the Third Republic dead and to empower the new National Assembly to draft a new constitution.[22] Indeed, considering the major steps taken outside parliament by Fourth Republic governments (the establishment of the Commissariat au Plan, for example) and the enhanced role of executive and experts intended in the Fourth Republic and achieved in the Fifth, one sees that the postwar French rejected more than the personnel of the Third Republic. They rejected its style and decision-making techniques as well. On the single issue of satisfaction with the Third Republic, postwar French voters felt closer to the "yes" men of 9–10 July 1940 than to the "no's."

In terms of personnel, therefore, Vichy experts and technicians survived into liberated France more widely than did the less influential social nostalgics or the Paris fascists or even the Third Republic deputies.

The same holds for the survival of Vichy legislation, programs, doctrines, and attitudes. Upon closer inspection, the Liberation did not actually abolish all Vichy legislation. Although the ordinance of 9 August 1944 began by declaring null all acts of the "de facto authority," it actually nullified only a list

[22] Philip Williams, *Politics in Postwar France,* 2d ed. (London, 1958), 14–16. Some of the 80 were dead by 1944, of course; Mandel and Zay had been murdered by the Milice.

of acts appended to the ordinance. The rest of Vichy legislation remained, at least for "a period of transition" required, for example, by the practical working of economic agencies. Furthermore, declared the ordinance, some advancements in career during Vichy might prove to have been merited, business transactions were presumed valid, and indeed some Vichy acts were inspired only by "the interest properly understood of the good functioning of services." [23] One can scan the criminal, civil, and commercial codes, for example, and find a scattering of legislation from the early 1940's. The statute books were not swept clean at the Liberation.

Vichy left some mark in the areas where traditionalists had been most active: family law and public morals. The old-age pensions law of 1941 was incorporated bodily in postwar social security legislation, and indeed it had been, in Pétain's own words, a "promise made by others," unfinished business from the 1930's. Family allowances, subsidies for large families, remained the policy of postwar governments as it had been the policy of both Daladier and Pétain. Although Vichy's "exceptional and involuntary experiment in alcoholic disintoxication" vanished with the end of scarcity, one still sees in bars posters proclaiming the age limit set in 1940. [24]

In a curiously roundabout way, the work of Vichy traditionalists survived most conspicuously in church-state relations. Although the church hierarchy was so discredited by its support of Vichy that General de Gaulle refused to permit Cardinal Suhard of Paris to attend the Te Deum at Notre Dame when Paris was liberated, the church as a whole was less subject to attack by the Fourth Republic than it had been by the Third. Traditional radical republican anticlericalism of the Gambetta-Clemenceau-Combes persuasion was going the way of the Masonic "republic of pals." The Catholic left, marginal in the 1930's, found that

---

[23] *Journal officiel de la république française* (Algiers), 10 August 1944, 689–94.

[24] Sully Lederman, *Alcool, Alcoolisme, Alcoolisation*, Institut National d'Etudes Démographiques, Travaux et documents, Cahier #41 (Paris, 1964), 139.

the same anticapitalism and rejection of the atheist radical republic that had made it Pétiniste in 1940 put it in harmony with the Resistance in 1944. Many priests and Catholic laymen had, of course, served actively in the Resistance, where the fusion of Communists and priests in the *maquis* became one of the clichés of Resistance history. Social experiments such as the worker priest movement grew not only from this Resistance amalgam but from the Catholic anticapitalism of early Pétain supporters like Father Godin and from the selfless volunteers who went under Vichy auspices to minister to French laborers working in German war plants. Into the vacuum left by a discredited conservative hierarchy stepped a vigorous Catholic left ready to take predominance in the postwar French church. Postwar political developments also helped make the church less controversial after the Liberation than it might have been. Communist leader Maurice Thorez' "hand extended to the Catholics" in the early Popular Front days of May 1934 was extended again in the period of Communist participation within the system between 1944 and May 1947. A Catholic left party, the Mouvement Républicain Populaire, found itself splitting the electorate three ways with the other two major parties of the Resistance, the Communists and the Socialists. Under these conditions, a quiet shift of power within the French Catholic church took the place of a purge, and it was politically impossible to undo all the church's Vichy gains. Seven bishops were quietly retired. By 1951 state aid could be voted again to Catholic schools in France.

By contrast, the traditionalists' social policy came to seem less wrong than simply irrelevant. Labor unions returned stronger than ever at the Liberation, of course, and although the principle of a labor statute for the civil service, battled for between the wars and obtained under Vichy, was retained, the postwar statute was totally devoid of Vichy's prohibitions upon unions and strikes in the civil service. As for the vision of a harmonious balanced society with a large role for artisans and peasants, Vichy itself had long departed from that course.

It is in the areas of public administration, economic modernization, and planning that the survival of Vichy measures—like personnel—is most marked. The descent was not always lineal, of course, but the evolution we have seen at Vichy, away from traditionalist values toward administration by experts and planned modernization, conformed with the longer-term trend in French politics and society.

The links are closest, naturally, in the most technical realms, such as rationing and price controls. Here the basic problem of penury imposed its own logic upon Vichy and Fourth Republic administrators alike, until the beginning of the 1950's. Here technical considerations had a certain neutrality, the flower of the French civil service had put its expertise to work, and abrupt new starts would have been paid for in chaos. Vichy war economy structures survived for some time, sometimes under different names. Even the Organization Committees, the corporative regulatory structures within the business world, survived until April 1946 under another name (*offices profession-nelles*). At least one chairman of an Organization Committee entered a postwar government. Aimé Lepercq, head of the Organization Committee for the coal industry, became minister of finance in the provisional government following the Liberation of Paris in August 1944.[25]

Even when the need for wartime economic management had ended, it was clear that the ground gained by experts over elected representatives at Vichy would never be lost. Such significant measures as the Monnet Plan for managed economic growth under sustained government control were created by executive decree rather than by parliamentary statute. Although the Fourth Republic gravitated in this as in so many ways back toward the practices of the Third, subjecting some of the later Five-Year Plans to greater parliamentary scrutiny, the role of public administrators in the national economy remained nearer to Vichy practice than to traditional republican practice. The vital process

---

[25] Pierre Doueil, *L'Administration locale à l'épreuve de la querre* (Paris, 1950); J.-M. Jeanneney and M. Perrot, *Textes de droit social et économique français* (Paris, 1957), 455–56. Lepercq was also a leader of the most technocratic Resistance movement, the Organisation Civile et Militaire. He was killed in an automobile accident on 9 November 1944.

of budget-drafting under the Fourth Republic, in which the old parliamentary haggle over each item gave way to professional drafting in the Finance Ministry's Direction du Budget that neither minister nor deputies could fully evaluate, resembled Vichy practice more closely than Third Republic practice.[26] The total number of civil servants maintained the steep climb begun in the late 1930's and continued under Vichy. And the brief and disastrous renaissance of parliamentary supremacy in the Fourth Republic eventually gave way to the Fifth Republic's administrative state. De Gaulle and his former mentor and adversary Pétain resembled each other in many respects, but in none so closely as when they talked contemptuously of the "regime of parties."

Vichy had also broken the ice for regional reorganization. Unless one counts the comparatively unimportant economic regions set up shortly after World War I, Vichy made the first significant departure from the department as the unit of local administration since the Napoleonic "Year VIII" (1799). The super-prefects of 1941, with their special authority over police and supply problems for a whole region, were an innovation whose practical merits outweighed a tainted origin. The ordinance of 10 January 1944 by which the French Committee of National Liberation appointed *commissaires de la république* to assume local authority in each region as it was liberated matched their circumscriptions to the Vichy super-prefectures. It was essential, after all, for Liberation forces to have administrators ready for each existing level of local government. Beyond that pragmatic necessity, however, lay a clear choice by the CFLN of regions as a more effective level for maintaining order than departments in the automobile age. The *commissaires de la république* functioned only until March 1946. In March 1948, however, Minister of the Interior Jules Moch revived the super-

[26] J. E. S. Hayward, *Private Interests and Public Policy* (London, 1966), 76–80, on the approval of the Fifth Plan. For budget procedures, see Christian Chavanon, "Les Hauts fonctionnaires," *Aspects de la société française* (Paris, 1954), 175: "If you want to have some influence in this domaine, become a *rédacteur* in the Direction du Budget and not a deputy."

prefect concept in the I.G.A.M.E. (inspecteurs-généraux administratifs en mission extraordinaire), created to deal with the strike wave of 1947–48.[27]

Like Vichy regionalism, postwar regionalism was administrative rather than federal. The best measure of central authority is financial. Vichy had further tightened the "tutelle," the control exercised by the central government over local spending. The central budget grew much more rapidly than local budgets, further reducing the ability of the latter to take local initiative. Whereas the budgets of departments and communes had reached about 33 percent of the national budget between the wars, they amounted to only 17 percent of the national budget in 1946. Despite some intentions to the contrary, postwar regionalism, like its Vichy predecessor, has meant a net increase of central authority where it has functioned at all.[28]

Vichy and French Society

Although social traditionalists occupied conspicuous positions, enjoyed the preference of Marshal Pétain, and influenced the rhetoric and style of the Vichy regime, the occupation years moved France decisively away from their vision of France: balanced, rural, personal. For a variety of reasons, conscious and unconscious, Vichy moved France significantly toward the technicians' vision: urban, efficient, productive, planned, and impersonal.

This social trend was partly the unintended effect of a war economy, which was partly, in turn, the result of increasingly urgent German pressures for greater French war production, accompanied by favors for the most concentrated sectors of French industry. The trend resulted, too, from the technicians' ability to survive the purge and to find common ground with

[27] Doueil, 20–69. The regional inspectors of economy and police also survived.
[28] Doueil, 259–76.

Resistance ideas of innovation. The technicians had shared with Vichy traditionalists the ideal of social order. Now they shared with many Resistance veterans the ideals of a managed economy, a strong paternalist state, and planned economic expansion. Allied with the Vichy traditionalists, they had been unable to protect France from German encroachment. Now allied with the modernizing wing of the Resistance, they confronted a new threat in the postwar world: American and Russian hegemony. This they tried to meet by planning a new industrial revolution in France.

There is hardly an aspect of social structure that did not move during Vichy toward the modernizers' model. The "return to the soil" campaign, for example, did not stop the flow of Frenchmen away from agriculture. In the short term, of course, French cities were hungrier, more policed, and more often bombed than farms or small towns. The census of March 1946 showed that, since 1936, 16 of the 54 French cities over 50,000 had lost population, some of them (like Paris) continuing a longer trend of movement to the suburbs, while others reflected an abandonment of the northern and eastern areas for the relative security of southern towns or farms. But the census-taker's conclusion that agriculture had stopped losing labor was premature.[29]

This rural reflux was more precautionary than preferential. Much of it consisted of wives and children staying with in-laws for the duration, rather than families remaining on the farm or returning to it permanently. The long, slow decline in cultivated land in France continued during the occupation labor shortages, while the only wartime increases were in the "kind of agriculture that can be left to itself": pastures, woodlots, etc.[30] Once the temporary advantages of rural life had ended after the Liberation, the course of Frenchmen to the cities took up again more vigorously than ever. France had ceased to be predominately rural with the census of 1931. Vichy's nostalgic social

[29] République française, Institut National de la Statistique et des Etudes Économiques, *Recensement général de la population effectué le 10 Mars 1946* (Paris, 1949), vii–ix; see also *ibid., Annuaire statistique de la France*, vol. 57—1946 (Paris, 1947), 19.

[30] France, Ministère de l'Agriculture, *Statistique agricole annuelle, 1942.* (Paris, 1944).

pronouncements and even assistance to new farmers did not reverse a trend that lay deep in French social development.

Industrial rationalization and concentration into larger plants seems to have actually increased during the Vichy period, although good figures are harder to come by here.[31] It is clear enough that German policy toward France favored concentrating war production in the most efficient plants and closing the less efficient plants to release labor for Germany.[32] Furthermore, one surmises that Albert Speer's protected plants, "S-betriebe," from which no workers could be deported to Germany, were chosen for high productivity. The efforts of Pierre Laval to extend this system in France worked in the same direction. While small businessmen fumed about Vichy's favoritism toward "trusts," [33] big businessmen and technicians in government at Vichy also promoted industrial rationalization and concentration. Europe must organize against the growing economic challenge of the United States, François Lehideux, Darlan's minister of national equipment and Louis Renault's nephew, told an elite audience of students at the Ecole Libre des Sciences Politiques at Paris in February 1941.[34] It was under Lehideux's auspices that a Ten-Year Plan for developing French productivity was enacted in May 1941 and that the law of 17 December 1941 empowered the state to close inefficient plants.[35] The state's authority to allocate raw materials was also used in the direction of rationalization, to judge from the protests of those who were left out.

[31] The French census' survey of business firms ceased with the 1936 census and began again with different categories in 1958. No comparison of firm size between 1936 and 1946 is possible. See also David Landes, *The Unbound Prometheus* (Cambridge, 1968), 225: "The historical experience of concentration is almost terra incognita."

[32] Individual cases of German authorities closing inefficient plants in the Occupied Zone in 1941 are reported in U.S. Dept. of State Serial File 851.5018, documents 126, 137, 139.

[33] See examples in German intelligence reports, T-77/1444/5,594,874 ff. See also Pierre Nicolle, *Cinquante Mois d'armistice* (Paris, 1947), for the frequent disgruntlement of this lobbyist for small business.

[34] Ecole Libre des Sciences Politiques, *Conférences d'information*, no. 1 (7 February 1941).

[35] *Le Temps,* 5 May 1941, 15 May 1941. Jean-Michel Jeanneney and Marguerite Perrot, *Textes de droit économique et social français* (Paris, 1957), 474; *Ministère public c/François Lehideux*, 10; *Ministère public c/Berthelot.*

Although there exist no good wartime or immediate postwar figures on the size of French firms, there is some statistical evidence of the move toward concentration. Production figures for the occupation years remained highest in those industries that were already the most concentrated before the war: coal mining, metallurgy, transformation of metals, glass-making. Indeed, aluminum production was higher under Vichy than it had ever been before. By contrast, wartime production in the most dispersed industries (textiles, leather, chemicals) limped along at even less than average production figures. It was the concentrated industries that continued at nearly prewar pitch until the end.[36] Vichy practice (as distinct from Vichy rhetoric) encouraged industrial concentration.

Vichy also afforded French businessmen and administrators the most substantial lesson in planning and state management of the economy up to that time. The management of an economy of penury, under German occupation, had to be far more thorough and more stringent than the World War I experience had been. The World War I experience of planning had been gradual, empirical, and temporary. The occupation experience was intentional, total, and designed to apply to an economy of abundance as well as to an economy of want. With Germany taking over half of French national revenues in occupation costs and with French and German consumers competing with ready cash for few goods, total market management was inevitable.[37] What was not inevitable was a new climate of opinion that held planning and management to be the only permanent solution to French postwar revival.

An ethic of planned growth and productivity had moved to the fore. Before the war, the apostles of growth in the French

[36] France, Institut National de la Statistique et des Etudes Economiques. *Annuaire statistique de la France,* vol. 57—1946 (Paris, 1947), 100, 107. See also "Population active, production, et productivité dans 21 branches de l'économie française," *Etudes et conjonctures* (February 1965), 73–108. Charles P. Kindleberger makes a similar case from postwar figures in Stanley Hoffmann, ed., *In Search of France* (Cambridge, Mass., 1963).

[37] E.g., coal production in France stayed close to 1938 levels, but coal consumption in France dropped below 1890 figures. See *Annuaire statistique,* 1946.

economy were minority voices. They were found mostly on the Right, as in such technocratic businessmen as Ernest Mercier of the electricity business and Auguste Detoeuf. Most of the Left was more interested in distribution than in growth. Most businessmen were interested mainly in preservation. It was during Vichy that the apostles of growth moved from oddity to commonplace. Vichy ministers of industrial production had more in common with the expansionist 1960's than the protectionist 1930's. The word "productivity" has become a new religious exhortation, wrote the director of the French census bureau in 1946. "Pilgrimages are organized to those sacred shores [i.e., the United States] where productivity was first revealed to men." [38]

At the deepest levels of mass social consciousness, Frenchmen decided to have more children. After the interruptions of 1939–40, French family size began to climb, although the continued separations of the occupation kept that new affirmation of French national vigor from showing up in statistics. It was in 1945 that the postwar baby boom became perceptible, and for the first time in a century France's population figures turned sharply upward. It is hard to overestimate the importance of this change of mood, and it is hard to explain it. It meant that with Vichy the period when the French population contained more and more old people began to close. Indeed Vichy was the climax of that process. During Vichy, the number of Frenchmen over sixty kept climbing from 14.7 percent of the total population at the beginning of the war to 16 percent at the end, and it would have mounted still higher if the death rate of the elderly had not risen in that period of cold, undernourishment, and grief. Vichy stands as the triumph of gerontocracy in France and the beginning of its end. [39]

Nowadays everyone talks about the "new France" of the 1950's and 1960's. Statisticians' figures are less vivid than the astonishing physical changes that any tourist can see: the old

---

[38] F.-Louis Closon, in preface to 1946 French census. For the technocratic left before 1940, see Georges Lefranc's journal *Révolution Constructive* and Jules Moch, *Confrontations* (Paris, 1952).

[39] See age distribution figures in the 1946 census.

villages in which a few crones in black shawls were replaced in a decade with crowds of brightly dressed children. The shift to farm machinery and tractors, not to mention television and washing machines, was equally rapid. The middle 1950's were the point at which the changes began to show in consumption, production, and population figures.

Some of the roots, though, go back to the shock of 1940 and to the experiences of Vichy. It was then that the nostalgic vision of France was finally discredited; not eliminated, but reduced to enclaves. It was then that a new generation of technicians and businessmen acquired new experience and new power. It was then that the baby boom began. Only one part of the Vichy leadership worked consciously for that kind of France. Many of them abhorred it. In retrospect, however, Vichy's surface struggles will perhaps be less significant in the end than the beginnings here of one current, which was to merge with one current of the Resistance to make the New France. François Lehideux could have written the first chapter of that all-time best-seller of the 1960's in France, *Le défi américain.*

Was Vichy a Lesser Evil?

IN THE END, ONE MUST MAKE SOME OVERALL JUDG-ment of the immediate results of collaboration for Frenchmen. With all its one-sided social favors and with all its complicity in the brutal last stages of nazism's paroxysm, did it not save many Frenchmen from still worse direct German administration? Was it not better to have Frenchmen administering Frenchmen than the tender ministrations of a gauleiter? Did not the Vichy regime save France from "Polandization"? Did it not "éviter le pire"?

Marshal Pétain elected to base his defense in 1945 on pragmatic material grounds, and most of the Vichy ministers followed his example. This defensive terrain was marked out for Pétain by Henri Massis, the old Action Française pamphleteer, in the declaration drafted for Pétain when the retreating German armies carried him off to Germany in August 1944:

> For more than four years, resolved to remain in your midst, I tried every day to serve the permanent interests of France. Loyally, but without compromise, I had only one goal: to protect you from the worst. . . . If I could not be your sword, I tried to be your shield. Sometimes my words or acts must have surprised you. Know that they hurt me more than you yourselves realized. But . . . I held off from you some certain dangers; there were others, alas, which I could not spare you.[40]

In his one statement before the High Court of Justice, Marshal Pétain developed the shield theory further:

> I used my power as a shield to protect the French people. . . . Every day, a dagger at my throat, I struggled against the enemy's demands. History will tell all that I spared you, though my adversaries think only of reproaching me for the inevitable. . . . While General de Gaulle carried on the struggle outside our frontiers, I prepared the way for Liberation by preserving France, suffering but alive.[41]

Pierre Laval, in his turn before the High Court, claimed that his government had managed to "éviter le pire," to act as a "screen" between the conqueror and the French population. The refrain was taken up by succeeding defendants before the High Court and by a stream of self-exculpating memoirs.[42]

Despite these partisan origins, the material advantage theory has been quite widely accepted. Robert Aron, trying to strike a reasonable balance on the basis of the trial records, the only sources available in 1954, argued that life was easier, statistically speaking, for Frenchmen than for others in occupied

---

[40] Georges Blond, *Pétain* (Paris, 1966), 468–69, attributes this text to Henri Massis.

[41] République française. Haute Cour de Justice. *Procès du Maréchal Pétain* (Paris, 1945), 9.

[42] *Le Procès Laval;* Guy Raïssac, *Combat sans merci* (Paris, 1966), 403. Among memoirs, see, e.g., Yves Bouthillier, *Le Drame de Vichy* (Paris, 1950), I, 138, on "la politique du bouclier," and II, 280; Pierre Pucheu, *Ma Vie* (Paris, 1948), 287; Pierre Cathala, *Face aux réalités* (Paris, 1948), 102–5; Raïssac, *Combat,* 370.

Europe. The reproaches against Vichy, he said, are moral rather than material.[43]

In its most widespread form, the material advantage thesis argues that Vichy kept France from "Polandization," and everyone knows that the Poles suffered more in World War II than the French. Nazi contempt for Slavic Untermenschen makes Poland an invalid comparison with France, however. Nazi purists might well cast aspersions upon French "mongrelization" and lack of racial self-consciousness, but they did not contemplate French extinction. The shield theory must be understood in terms of actual German demands, rather than in terms of vaguely infinite possibilities of evil. It can be validly tested only in comparison with fully occupied Western countries like Belgium, Holland, or Denmark, or other collaborating regimes like Quisling's Norway. If incomplete occupation or the existence of a quasiautonomous indigenous administration spared France any of the rigors of direct German rule, those favors should show up in comparison with fully occupied Western countries without an indigenous collaborationist regime.

One can suppose two ways in which Vichy France could have suffered less than France under a gauleiter. The German occupation authorities might have asked for less in order to reward and solidify a useful collaborationist regime. Or if the German occupation authorities asked no less of France than of fully occupied Western nations, the Vichy regime might have been better able or more willing to refuse excessive demands than would a gauleiter. A hard comparative look at the material conditions of life in Western occupied countries fails to show any important advantage for France, either granted by or extorted from Berlin.

Frenchmen were no better nourished than other Western occupied countries. Comparison of caloric intakes in France and fully occupied Western nations is, of course, treacherous ground, for access to food depended greatly on one's location, ready cash for the black market, or connections—and a cousin on the farm

---

[43] Robert Aron, *Histoire de Vichy* (Paris, 1954), 736. See also Guy Raïssac, *Combat*, 23, 348, on Vichy leaders' "louable desseins de tempérer les épreuves."

might be more useful in that respect than a cabinet minister. Average figures mean even less in this case than in most, and agricultural statistics are certainly less reliable for French *paysans* than for Danish dairy farmers. Nevertheless, it appears that French caloric intake was the lowest in Western Europe, with the exception of Italy, which is astonishing for so rich an agricultural country. Furthermore, in Eastern Europe, Rumania, Bulgaria, Hungary, and the Protectorate of Bohemia-Moravia seem to have eaten better than France. French caloric intake is estimated to have descended under the occupation as low as 1,500 calories a day where there was access to black market supplies and even lower for city populations where there was not.[44]

Not all the French hunger can be attributed directly to German occupation policy, of course. With much food production in the hands of a notoriously small, independent, and secretive peasantry, France suffered as much from maldistribution as from genuine shortages. Moreover, France had depended before the war upon imports of some staples, such as vegetable oils, so that Allied blockade and shipping shortages made matters worse.

There is no sign, however, that Vichy managed to win significant concessions in those areas where German policy added to French hunger. The armistice provision (copied from that of 1918) that French prisoners of war should not be repatriated until the peace produced a serious labor shortage in agriculture, keeping French agricultural production from ever returning to prewar figures. The petroleum shortage prevented the replacement of farm laborers with machines. Moreover, the gigantic German requisitions of French foodstuffs, for the occupying army and for export to the Reich, were among Germany's most important single sources of nourishment. France supplied more foodstuffs to Germany, both absolutely and relatively, than did even Poland.[45]

[44] I have accepted the figures of Karl Brandt, *Management of Agriculture and Food in the German-Occupied and Other Areas of Fortress Europe* (Stanford, Calif., 1953), passim; League of Nations Economic, Financial, and Transit Dept., *Food, Famine, and Relief, 1940–46* (Geneva, 1946), 4.

[45] Brandt, 33, 564.

It was indeed explicit German policy that the French should have a lower standard of living than the Germans. Both Goering and Abetz, as we have seen, thought that Frenchmen should have less to eat than Germans. Abetz stated early in July 1942 that French wages must remain lower than those in Germany (which had been the lowest in industrial Europe in the 1930's) so that French workmen would go to work in Germany.[46]

It begins to look as if material conditions of life in occupied Europe depended less upon avoiding total occupation and having an indigenous regime than upon Germany's ethnic feelings about the occupied power and upon simple opportunity. Bargaining by Vichy was quite incapable of preventing increases in Germany's food delivery quotas in France in the summer of 1942 and in early 1943 or of preventing France, the richest agricultural producer of the occupied nations, from experiencing localized malnutrition.[47]

The same pattern prevails in other material conditions of life—inflation, for example. Pierre Cathala claimed after the war that if Germany had collected taxes directly, as in Belgium, inflation would have been worse. In reality, the franc depreciated more rapidly in 1940–44 than the currency of any other Western European country except Italy.[48] All the Western occupied countries faced roughly comparable inflationary pressures: drastic shortages of goods coupled with high public expenditures. All of them, whether quasi-autonomous regimes as at Vichy or not, retained their local currency. All of them tried to defend it by controlling the market. The Vichy regime, however, was unsuccessful in trying to remove the special inflationary pressures contained in the armistice arrangements. Under the armistice provisions for French payment of occupation costs, support costs, and clearing deficits in Franco-German international accounts, the German occupation authorities were getting 58 percent of the French annual budget. Much of this was being pumped

[46] See above, p. 310. Abetz (Paris 2857) to Berlin of 7 July 1942 (T-120/434/220101–5).

[47] For the food delivery negotiations of July–August 1942, see T-120/434.

[48] Pierre Cathala, *Face aux réalités* (Paris, 1948), 84. A. J. Brown, *The Great Inflation* (Oxford, 1955), 304–5.

back into the economy, further inflated by the German use of scrip (Kreditkassenscheinen). Although the Vichy authorities managed to reduce German use of scrip in the Occupied Zone, their attempts to reduce occupation costs are an eloquent example of their inability to negotiate a favored position.

Occupation costs were levied at 20 million marks a day, and the exchange rate set at 20:1 by *diktat* in August 1940. Vichy declared a unilateral cessation of occupation costs on December 1940, in an evident attempt to cash in on the German "new policy" that had been expected at Vichy to lead to conspicuous concessions. The German occupation authorities insisted that the issue was nonnegotiable, and during the German "cold shoulder" of early 1941, Vichy was unable to broach the issue. When Darlan was received at Berchtesgaden in May 1941, Vichy believed it had won a reduction in occupation costs and even announced the fact. The reduction was agreed upon only months later, however, and the French had to agree to pay 10 million marks a day in francs and another 5 million in gold and foreign exchange. Then, after the total occupation of November 1942, occupation costs were raised to 25 million marks a day. Vichy was never able to negotiate a less inflationary armistice arrangement.[49] France remained most subject to inflation of the Western occupied nations, second only to Italy.

Nor can it be claimed that Vichy won any territorial immunities by collaborating. With the exception of Belgium, shorn of the few square miles of Eupen and Malmédy-Moresnet that she had gained from Germany in 1919, none of the other Western occupation nations suffered the de facto territorial annexations and amputations that France did. Alsace and Lorraine were placed under Nazi gauleiters and administered as part of the Reich. The rest of northeastern France was also sealed off from returning refugees and from French officials in a "Sperrzone," and farms "abandoned" there during the campaign were re-

---

[49] Alfred Munz, *Die Auswirkungen der deutscher Besetzung auf Währung und Finanzen Frankreichs*. Studien des Instituts für Besatzungsfragen in Tübingen zu den deutschen Besetzungen im 2. Weltkrieg, 9 (Tübingen, 1947), 76; Cour des comptes, *Rapport au président de la République, 1940–45*, 25; *Ministère public c/Bouthillier*, fasc. 2, 74 ff.; Weizsäcker files, *passim*.

settled with German settlers by an agency of the German Ministry of Agriculture called the Ostland Company.[50] Finally, the two northwestern channel coast departments of the Nord and Pas-de-Calais were placed under the German military government in Brussels rather than the Militärbefehlshaber in Frankreich.

It is, of course not possible to know what the territorial disposition of Western Europe would have been in the event of eventual German victory. Holland and Belgium might have been swallowed up entirely. France, it appears from the German Foreign Office's preparations for an eventual peace treaty, would have survived as an independent if truncated nation, probably excluded from the *Grosswirtschaftsraum,* or German-centered European free-trade zone.[51] Vichy cannot claim to have saved the very existence of France, for that existence was not at stake. As for saving France from partition, it is not clear to what extent German sympathy for Breton, Flemish, and Burgundian autonomists (the last virtually fictitious) was ever meant to turn France into some kind of "Confederation of the Seine." The local German support for such movements never reflected a settled Berlin policy of partition, and that support was quietly withdrawn in the fall of 1940. The most one can claim for Vichy in this respect is that an amenable united France had been proven more useful to Hitler than a series of provinces; even a gauleiter would have hesitated to drive a population to desperate resistance by threatening to carve up the country.[52]

[50] The Ostland Company settled German farmers on some 166,000 hectares in the departments of the Ardennes, Meuse, Meurthe-et-Moselle, Vosges, Haute-Saône, Doubs, and parts of the Aisne, Somme, and Jura. Cour des Comptes, *Rapport au président de la république, 1940–45.* See map in Brandt, 486.

[51] For economic and political draft peace terms, see the Foreign Office "Friedensverhandlungen mit Frankreich" files: T-120/365, 368. See also Ribbentrop's "Grosswirtschaftsraum" file, T-120/830.

[52] Various German proposals and opinions about the future of France (there was no settled policy for the eventual peace settlement) are ably summarized in Eberhard Jäckel, *La France dans l'Europe de Hitler* (Paris, 1968). See also the work of the army officer who drafted the armistice terms, [Colonel] Hermann Böhme, *Entstehung und Grundlagen des Waffenstillstandes von 1940* (Stuttgart, 1960), for Hitler's intentions in the summer of 1940.

Moreover, Vichy efforts to halt the de facto annexations of Alsace, Lorraine, and the northeastern "Sperrzone," mentioned above, were utterly unsuccessful. In the very honeymoon of the "new policy" of November 1940, trainloads of dispossesed Frenchmen from the two provinces were dumped into France with little more than the clothes on their backs. Laval's stratagem of acquiescing in the loss of Alsace while suggesting plebiscites in Lorraine received no flicker of response from Germans. Darlan reopened the question of both provinces in Berlin in May 1941, but the only concession he obtained was permission for French soldiers on leave to visit their homes in the northeastern forbidden zone. Vichy did manage, by and large, to avoid direct German occupation of the empire until the battle for North Africa began in November 1942, with the major exceptions of German inspection teams in Morocco and Dakar and German use of French airfields and equipment in Syria for support of the Iraqi rising of May 1941. Berlin simply ignored the efforts of both Laval and Darlan to obtain a German guarantee of French frontiers and an equivalent imperial territory in an eventual peace settlement. Collaboration won no territorial favors for France.[53]

Vichy's effectiveness as a "shield" has been most persistently claimed in the areas of forced labor for German factories and the Jewish Final Solution. Laval claimed after the war that while the Germans took 80 percent of Belgian workers to Germany, they took only 16 percent of French workers.[54] As for Jews,

[53] Vichy protested more vigorously over German measures in Alsace-Lorraine than over any other issue except the execution of hostages. See *DFCAA*, II, 383–86; *DGFP*, Series D, XI, documents no. 271, 331, 354, 526; T-77/OKW-1444/5,594,611; T-120/4634/E208639 ff; and T-120/368/passim. For Laval's acceptance of the loss of Alsace, see his conversation with Grimm on 28 August 1940 (T-120/2624H/D525934–37), his United Press interview of May 1941 (*Le Temps*, 28 May 1941), and his proposals of November 1942 for a German territorial guarantee (T-120/926/297075–76). For Darlan, see the Paris Protocol negotiations of May–July 1941. Vichy even had the support of Otto Abetz, who feared the repercussions of German policy in Alsace-Lorraine upon improved Franco-German relations in late 1940. See Abetz (Paris) 1049 of 31 October 1940 (T-120/121/120107–8). The Militärbefehlshaber and the Armistice Commission were opposed to possible further expulsions in August 1941 (T-120/855/285106; T-77/OKW-1444/5,594,613–14).

[54] Laval testimony in *Procès Pétain*, 206. Less absurd but erroneous figures were published later in *Laval parle*, 130, and Pierre Cathala, *Face*

Xavier Vallat, who had been Commissaire aux Questions
Juives in the Vichy government from 29 March 1941 to 6 May
1942, claimed in his trial that Jews were better off under Vichy
than under a gauleiter.

> So, the basic question is this: was it better that the French govern-
> ment concern itself with the Jewish problem or leave the entire
> material and moral responsibility for it to the occupation authori-
> ties?
> As for me, I think it was better that the French Government got
> into it. . . .
> At a time when out of 4,343,000 native Jews who lived in Austria,
> Belgium, Czechoslovakia, Germany, Greece, Holland, Luxemburg,
> in Poland, and in Yugoslavia only 337,500 survived—that is to say
> that 92% of the Jews disappeared, the figures given for France [by
> the Anglo-American Commission of Enquiry on the Palestine Ques-
> tion, 1946] . . . prove that if, alas, most of the foreign Jews died
> in deportation, 95% of the Jews of French nationality are fortu-
> nately still living. That is my answer.[55]

Unfortunately the shield was less successful in either case than
the Vichy defense claimed.

If few French workers went to Germany in the earlier stages
of the war, it was because Polish and then Russian prisoners of
war and women were the mainstay of German forced labor. Only
when those sources were exhausted by the very brutality of their
treatment was volunteer labor replaced by forced labor in the
Western occupied countries. In April 1942, Hitler appointed
Fritz Sauckel, former gauleiter of Thuringia, to the office of
plenipotentiary for foreign labor and authorized him to impose
conscription of labor on occupied Belgium, Holland, and France.

It would be a striking justification for the Vichy shield theory
if at this point the Germans had asked less of collaborationist

---

aux réalités (Paris, 1948), 102, where it is claimed that while 50 to 80
per 1,000 of the total population of Belgium, Holland, and Poland were
sent to work in German factories, only 13 per 1,000 of the French population were forced to work in Germany. Cathala, 105, then repeats Laval's
claim to have "saved ⅘ of the French."

[55] *Le Procès de Xavier Vallat présenté par ses amis* (Paris, 1948),
117–18.

France or if Laval had proven able to win concessions for his new ministry.

The Germans asked no less of the Occupied Zone of collaborationist France than of totally occupied Belgium and Holland, and much more of France than of collaborationist Norway and Denmark (who contributed little to foreign labor working in the Reich).[56] Only the Paris embassy, among German agencies, seems to have been worried about the political cost to Vichy of forced labor in 1942. Rudolf Schleier, Abetz' second-in-command at the Paris embassy, warned Laval on 24 April 1942, through Consul-General Krug von Nidda, of what was coming and urged Vichy to counter the blow by making the volunteer system much more effective. At first Laval took this advice, permitting the establishment on May 1, 1942, of permanent German recruitment offices in Lyon, Marseilles, and Toulouse, enjoying the full support of French labor offices.[57] These efforts to increase French volunteer labor for Germany did not prevent the eventual introduction of forced labor in France, however. In fact, France became the largest single supplier to Germany of foreign male labor in all occupied Europe in 1943, east or west. Sauckel's Anordnung Nr. 4 of 7 May 1942, instituting forced labor in the west, makes no distinction between the French Occupied Zone and other occupied areas. And after November 1942, all of France was occupied. By November 1943, 1,344,000 French males were working in German factories, slightly ahead of the Russian and Polish male contingents. French women workers, at 44,000, came in third place, well behind the Russian and Polish women. Moreover, on January 5, 1944, Sauckel said he planned to draft an additional million Frenchmen to work in Germany. The German government spared Frenchmen none of the agonies of forced labor.[58]

[56] Edward L. Homze, *Foreign Labor in Nazi Germany* (Princeton, N.J., 1966), 148, 200.

[57] Schleier (Paris) 449 to Krug von Nidda (Vichy), 24 April 1942; Schleier (Paris) 526 to Krug von Nidda (Vichy), 5 May 1942. Centre de Documentation Juive Contemporaine, Paris, document nos. CLXXXIV-23, 24.

[58] Homze, 195. Sauckel's Anordung Nr. 4 is found in T-120/5636/ E407359–68.

There remains the possibility that Pierre Laval, working within the quasi-autonomy of Vichy, delayed or mitigated the application of forced labor to the unoccupied zone. His old associate Pierre Cathala tried to prove after the war that Laval had managed to "éviter le pire" with his famous Auvergnat peasant horse-trading: "Sauckel wants men, I will give him legal texts," Laval is supposed to have said.[59]

Cathala's claims don't stand. Sauckel got legal texts and men too.

Never a man to leave the initiative to others, Laval was ready with a counterproposal when Sauckel came to Paris in mid-June 1942 to apply the new German labor policy to France. France enjoyed a unique tactical position in occupied Europe with respect to manpower. Two million able-bodied young Frenchmen were already in Germany as prisoners of war, and Laval now threw them into the bargaining scales with the notorious *relève* scheme: the release of one prisoner of war for every three French workers who volunteered to work in Germany. Hitler accepted this plan after a telephone conference with Sauckel on 15 June, and Laval worked out the details with Sauckel on the spot.

Laval clearly thought he had gained something, as the volume of French propaganda shows. The return of war prisoners, however few, touched the deepest emotions of both the French public and Pétain himself. Laval marked the political importance of the *relève* by going in person to greet the first trainload of returning prisoners at Compiègne on August 11, with maximum publicity. The other thing Laval thought he had gained was French sovereign control over one more area of threatened German direct administration.

And so the French government worked frantically to meet the quota of French volunteer workers. It supplied the names and addresses of specialists, arranged the closing of inefficient shops, and extended the work week, all measures designed to release a skilled labor pool for the *relève*. More strikingly, Laval asked German authorities secretly for a letter threatening direct

[59] Pierre Cathala, *Face aux réalités* (Paris, 1948), 97 ff.

German forced labor if the *relève* did not work. He and Pétain thought this would help convince the reluctant.[60] Although the *relève* got off to a slow start, with only 19,000 skilled workers signed up by 7 October, Vichy's strenuous efforts had recruited 181,000 workers by 21 November, of whom 90,000 were specialists.[61]

Even if Laval had managed to stave off direct forced labor until 1944 by means of the *relève,* it would have been a questionable bargain. In concrete terms, it was not really the three-for-one exchange which propaganda claimed. Laval and Sauckel agreed on 15 June that France would supply 400,000 workers, including 150,000 with special skills. The *relève* applied only to skilled workers; i.e., a maximum of 50,000 prisoners would be freed in return for eight times that many volunteer workers. Moreover, the exchange returned mostly farm boys to France at the expense of men with such vital industrial skills as lathe-turning, a short-term gain perhaps for French food production but a bad bet for the French future in Europe. The Germans, in turn, merely lowered the expense of keeping French war prisoners. The net result was that Vichy wound up doing Sauckel's job about as well as Sauckel could have done it himself. Most damning of all, the *relève* didn't buy any French exemption from forced labor in the long run anyway.

None of these Vichy efforts prevented Sauckel's general labor draft decree from being promulgated in occupied France on 20 August 1942 anyway, along with the rest of occupied Western Europe (a violation of Article III of the armistice, which attributed administration of both zones to the French.) Furthermore, in the effort to forestall the extension of the August 20 decree to the rest of France, Laval chose to exercise the shadow of remaining French sovereignty by issuing a French law "in the

[60] Schleier (Vichy) 1842 to Paris, 6 October 1942 (T-120/5367/ E407490–91). Schleier talked to Pétain too.

[61] The whole labor question is best followed in the files of the German embassy in Paris: Deutscher Botschaft, Paris—T-120/5635H, 5636H, 5637H, and in Edward L. Homze, *Foreign Labor in Nazi Germany* (Princeton, 1966), chap. 9. Homze's data, drawn mostly from Berlin materials, needs to be supplemented with the local perspective of the Paris embassy.

same sense" on 4 September 1942. This act established machinery in the unoccupied zone for drafting individual French skilled workmen, prevented French workmen from changing jobs freely, and made it more difficult to escape German recruitment. Thus the basic statutes for forced labor were already on the books when the rest of France was occupied in November 1942. When Sauckel came up with a new quota of 500,000 more workers from all France in January 1943, the Service du Travail Obligatoire was set up in February to draft whole age groups. Thereafter, all Frenchmen were subject to forced labor.[62]

How much time had been won? The Sauckel decrees had gone into operation in Holland on 6 April 1942, and the largest Dutch annual contingent went that year. In Belgium an *arrêté* of 6 October 1942 established obligatory work in Germany for Belgian men and women, although it was not until September 1943 that individual conscription was replaced by the kind of call-up by year-classes that had been instituted in France in the preceding February. Thus France had a forced labor draft a bit after Holland and a bit before Belgium. Since Frenchmen were being more or less coerced to go to Germany under the *relève* anyway, the few months gained over Holland in unoccupied France before the STO of February 1943 does not seem a very good bargain.

A little calculation establishes that in the long run, French people suffered proportionally about as much as Belgium, and a little more than Holland, from forced labor. Total French labor figures in Germany, including prisoners of war who were set to work, amount to about 3.3 percent of the total population, as compared with about 3.4 percent of Belgian and 3.0 percent of Dutch total populations. Vichy France failed to win real respite from forced labor for the French in either zone.[63]

Two forces finally did save a number of Frenchmen from the STO. In fact, of the million men Sauckel asked for in January 1944, only 38,000 French workers actually went to Germany in the remaining months before the Liberation. Vichy can take credit for neither of these effective barriers. One was Albert

---

[62] For the 4 Sept. 1942 law, see T-120/4634/E208594–602.
[63] Figures from Homze, 195; the calculations are mine.

Speer, who struggled for influence against Sauckel in 1943–44. Speer, whose approach was technocratic rather than punitive, believed that it was more efficient for workers to produce for Germany in their own countries than to be brought to Germany where they had to be fed, supplied, and protected from Allied bombardment. Since plants were earmarked as "Speerbetriebe" or "S-betriebe" all over Western Europe, no special favors were being shown in France. No doubt a number of young French workers owed their lives to Albert Speer, however.

The other real barrier to the STO was the *maquis*. It became very difficult to compel young French skilled workers to go to Germany after the beginning of 1944 and virtually impossible after the Allied invasion of Normandy in June 1944. Vichy can take no credit for either of these shields, of course. They would have developed and worked as well, all other things being equal, under a gauleiter.[64]

There remains the somber business of the Jewish Final Solution. It is true, as Xavier Vallat claimed, that a larger proportion of the Jewish populations of totally occupied Holland, Belgium, Norway, and Italy (totally occupied after 1943) perished than that of France, even taking refugees and citizens together.[65] The real question, however, is not whether fewer Jews were deported from France than from the totally occupied countries, but whether more Jews were deported from France because of Vichy

---

[64] For Speer, see footnote 59, page 322. Homze, 224–25, estimates that 14–20 percent of factories in Italy and France were earmarked "Speerbetriebe." Laval and Cathala, *Face aux réalités,* tried to claim credit for Speer's policy, and that no doubt would also have been a defense of Bichelonne had he not died in Germany in 1945 before standing trial. STO figures used here for 1944 are taken from Jacques Desmarest, *La Politique de la main-d'oeuvre en France* (Paris, 1946), 176 ff. They do not include the number of prisoners of war also working in the Reich.

[65] I have accepted the figures in R. Hilberg, *The Destruction of the European Jews* (Chicago, 1961), 670, which show that the prewar Jewish population of Holland had declined at the Liberation by 86 percent, Belgium by 55 percent, Norway by 50 percent, Italy by 35 percent, France by 26 percent and Denmark by 15.4 percent (my percentages). Concentrated in Amsterdam, the Dutch Jews were the most vulnerable; 105,000 out of 140,000 perished. Werner Warmbrunn, *The Dutch under German Occupation* (Stanford, California 1963), 12, 35, 61 ff., 165 ff. There seem to be no figures in German archives distinguishing between French citizens and refugees in France among the victims of the Final Solution.

preparations and assistance than would have been the case if the Germans had had to do it all alone. Vichy bears a heavy burden of responsibility, seen in these terms.

It is true that the unoccupied zone of France provided a refuge of sorts for tens of thousands of Jewish refugees from Germany and Eastern Europe for the first two years. Republican France having taken over from England the role of Europe's refugee haven in the late nineteenth century, German Jews and then, after September 1939, Polish Jews, followed a well-worn path to the west. The fact that the armistice and the division of France into two zones kept many of these refugees one jump ahead of the German armies was not the result of any Vichy sentimentality about the refugees. In fact, Vichy objected vigorously when the Germans delivered more expatriate Jews into the unoccupied zone in the fall of 1940. After protest, Vichy acquiesced in Article 19 of the armistice, which empowered Germany to demand the extradition of German citizens who had sought refuge in France. Under this provision, such prominent figures as Herschel Grynspan (who had assassinated a German diplomat in Paris in 1938) and the socialist economist and Weimar minister Rudolf Hilferding were delivered back into German hands—an ominous first warning about the precariousness of asylum in Vichy France. Moreover, Vichy did everything possible to encourage the further emigration of Jewish refugees. At a time when French Jews were being uprooted from the economy, there was no possibility of foreigners settling. Vichy also revoked some recent citizenships, enlarging the number of Jews in France without the protection of citizenship. Finally, Vichy gathered destitute Jewish refugees into work camps. Although Pétain spared them the yellow star, thousands were waiting behind barbed wire when the Germans came into the unoccupied zone in November 1942. Only those with money had managed to use southern France as a springboard for safer havens. For the rest, the French tradition of refuge made the unoccupied zone a trap.

The possibilities of sheltering Jews in southern France were far greater, say, than in the ghetto of Amsterdam. Furthermore, by the time the Germans actually arrived in southern France, in

November 1942, there had been ample time for emergency arrangements. The final irony is that Italian-occupied Alpine France provided the cover in 1943 that Vichy refused. Many French citizens did the same, but the Vichy authorities deserve none of their credit. Vichy bears the guilt for not having used its opportunity for the kind of escape operation that the totally occupied Danes managed to carry out by moving almost the entire Jewish population by small boat to Sweden in September 1943.

This survey suggests that the shield theory hardly bears close examination. The armistice and the unoccupied zone seemed at first a cheap way out, but they could have bought some material ease for the French population only if the war had soon ended. As the war dragged on, German authorities asked no less of France than of the totally occupied countries. In the long run, Hitler's victims suffered in proportion to his need for their goods or his ethnic feelings about them, not in proportion to their eagerness to please. Vichy managed to win only paltry concessions: a few months of the *relève* instead of a labor draft, exemption from the yellow star for Jews in the unoccupied zone, slightly lower occupation costs between May 1941 and November 1942, more weapons in exchange for keeping the Allies out of the empire. Judged by its fruits, Vichy negotiation was barren.

In the last analysis, fruitful negotiation depends upon some comparable capacity of each party to threaten the other with damage if acceptable compromises are not made and to withhold that damage if acceptable compromises are made. Vichy's one serious threat—to take fleet and empire over to the Allied side—lacked credibility. Vichy leaders could not exercise it without suffering more than the Germans. To be sure, the Germans did not want the effort and expense of a total occupation of France. Vichy leaders could delude themselves for the first months that France had found a cheap way out of the war. Even after the sufferings increased, however, they could not flee abroad without sacrificing the National Revolution, their commitment to internal order, and, after the Gaullists took over the empire from the Giraudists, their personal liberty and even life.

Early in the occupation, the Vichy leaders did not want to threaten to renounce the armistice; later on, they couldn't. In all of Laval's dealings with German officials, I have found only one threat even to resign. On 27 August 1942 Laval threatened to quit office if Sauckel's forced labor decree, applied to the Occupied Zone on 20 August, were extended to the unoccupied zone. Laval agreed, however, to issue a French law "in the same sense" for the unoccupied zone on 4 September, suggesting that he was much more interested in retaining the outward show of Vichy sovereignty than in blocking the policy of forced labor itself by exercising his ultimate weapon of breaking the armistice. No other threats to resign by Laval, and none by Darlan, turn up in the voluminous German records of their many conversations. Instead, the characteristic Vichy technique was to warn the Germans against creating a hostile public opinion, beyond Vichy capacity to control, by excessive severity. In other words, as long as the armistice and Vichy sovereignty was something they wanted more than the Germans, Vichy leaders were limited to the same sort of threat that lower civil servants could make in totally occupied countries. "Don't push our population too hard," they said in effect, "or it will become unmanageable." [66]

Pétain made no more forceful threats than the others. There remains the curious plan for Pétain to present himself at the Demarcation Line as a hostage in September 1941 when the Germans began their reprisal executions, but we know about it only because Pucheu, perhaps to add negotiating pressure, told Abetz about it. The gesture was of course never carried out. The fact that Pétain did not renounce the armistice in November 1942, upon the total occupation of France—and there is no contemporary evidence that it was ever considered—proved to the Germans that he would never resign. They did not have to take very seriously his brief "strike" as head of state during his

---

[66] For Laval's threat to resign on 27 August 1942, see Schleier (Paris) 928 to Krug von Nidda (Vichy), 4 September 1942 (T-120/5637H/ E407374-76). For a more typical Laval technique, warning the Germans that public opinion might become so hostile that he would be imprisoned and hence unable to help serve Germany further, see Schleier (Paris) 6280 to Berlin, 31 December 1942 (T-120/935/298646-48).

last effort to get rid of Laval in November–December 1943, and indeed Pétain soon gave in. Pétain ceased exercising the powers of head of state in earnest only when the Germans took him by force off French soil, to the castle of Sigmaringen in August 1944. No one at Vichy ever seriously made the threat that Thiers claimed he issued to Bismarck as they began negotiations at Versailles in February 1871:

> You mean to ruin France in her finances, ruin her on her frontiers. Well, take her. Administer the country. Levy the taxes. We shall retire and you shall be left to govern her.[67]

In the last analysis, the sovereignty of Vichy was a negotiating liability rather than a negotiating asset. The Vichy leaders had asked for an armistice in the summer of 1940 to prevent revolution and to remake France along different lines. The continued existence of the Vichy regime had to be defended, as the price of fulfilling those aims. It was something for which Vichy leaders made concessions, rather than something for which Germany made concessions. A gauleiter would have made many Frenchmen suffer; in the end he might have gotten less.

Profits and Losses

THE VICHY REGIME DID NOT SAVE THE FRENCH PEOPLE from suffering, perhaps even more suffering than that endured by totally occupied countries in Western Europe. That suffering was not endured evenly, moreover, on all shoulders alike. Not even the most conscientious war economy of penury can spread the burdens and equalize sacrifices with a perfectly even hand. The Vichy war economy was colored by ideological favoritism and distorted by the pressures of interest groups. It would be misleading to speak of beneficiaries of the regime, for the occupation was a bitter experience for all Frenchmen. Nevertheless, some

[67] Louis Adolphe Thiers, *Notes et souvenirs* (*1870–73*) (Paris, 1904), 113.

Frenchmen found themselves in a less exposed position under Vichy than others, better able to shelter from the blows of a tormenting epoch. A few even enjoyed, for a time, the fruits of power or the economic favors of war production. In that sense, we can ask upon whom the regime smiled more and less, who benefited more and less from the Vichy regime.

Some of the particular victims would have suffered regardless of the existence of an armistice or a quasi-sovereign French regime: the farmers of the northeastern "Sperrzone" whose lands were colonized with Germans by the Ostland corporation; prisoners of war; the victims of bombings, first by the Axis and then by the Allies; refugees under direct German occupation north of the Demarcation Line. To their number were added the particular victims of the Vichy regime itself: Jews, luminaries of the former regime, Communists, workmen recruited to work in Germany. All of these conspicuous victims have their memorial. Other groups were victimized more subtly by Vichy economic policies and interest groups.

Urban wage earners were the unannounced pariahs of the regime. Real wages went down. The inflationary pressures incidental to any great war were enormously magnified in France by the gigantic hemorrhage of occupation costs, which turned about half the national revenue into purchasing power for the German armed forces in France. Even granting that Vichy finance ministers were somewhat more successful in keeping inflation in check than the early Fourth Republic was to be, the official cost of living went up by slightly over half between June 1940 and December 1942 and then doubled again by August 1945.[68] The official cost of living, however, was not what it actually cost a city dweller to procure the necessities of life. The extreme scarcity of goods, magnified by the uncontrollable nature of small peasants and merchants, helped divert goods into the black market and hoarding. The money for the official price and the correct number of ration tickets might simply not purchase any food at all, if the stores were empty. Cash or a cousin

---

[68] A. J. Brown, *The Great Inflation* (Oxford, 1955), 304–5. It increased far more rapidly during 1945–48 than it had during the war, although Yves Bouthillier exaggerates his success in *Le Drame de l'armistice*.

on the farm was sometimes the only way to get anything to eat. Because of the black market, the fragmentation of the French distribution system, and the business orientation of the regime, price controls were less effective than wage controls. Wages fell far behind prices. When Laval was planning a wage increase in July 1942, for example, Ambassador Abetz had figures showing that while prices had increased by 70 percent since the beginning of the war, wages had risen only 30 percent. The gap was even greater by 1944.[69]

Added to this cruel wage-price pinch, labor was made more helpless by the abolition of national trade unions and the outlawry of strikes. The few strikes of which we have knowledge, such as a miners' strike in the Nord in May 1941, were brutally repressed. The "functional" representatives of workers in the corporative organization, the Comités sociaux, were formed very slowly where they were formed at all, and workers were placed there in a position of permanent minority by dividing membership three ways among employers, technical staff, and workers. By their very nature, the corporative structures, even those in which some workingmen were included, were intended to dismantle the workers' side of the previous adversary system of labor relations. Although unemployment was soon replaced by a labor shortage in the unoccupied zone, working people were subjected almost without redress to long hours and lagging wages, political discrimination in employment, and the threat of forced labor in Germany. Immense ground had been lost since 1936.[70]

On the other hand, it was a time of opportunity for those

[69] Abetz (Paris) 2857 to Berlin, 7 July 1942 (T-120/434/220101-5). Abetz was torn between his orders to keep French wages lower than German, to encourage volunteers to work in Germany, and his efforts to prove to France that national socialism was "not reactionary."

[70] Although the Vichy regime did not repeal the forty-hour law or the paid-vacation law of the Popular Front, it used decree power (as the Reynaud and Daladier governments had done) to authorize longer hours. The best source for unemployment statistics under Vichy is Jacques Desmarest, La politique de la main-d'oeuvre (Paris, 1945), 126 ff. The work week grew from an average 35.6 hours in December 1940 to 46.2 hours in March 1944. Institut national de la statistique et des études économiques, Mouvement économique en France de 1938 à 1948 (Paris, 1950), 62–63.

with scarce commodities to sell. The most obvious new power, for housewives dealt with it twice a day, was the "grocers' dictatorship." Not even the scheming butter-and-egg lady of Jean Dutourd's *Au bon beurre,* of course, had unlimited privileges in a world where even the most commonplace articles were scarce. She had a newfound power to lord it over her former arrogant customers, however, and she reveled in it. And her euphoria colored the regime and the marshal himself in the rosiest hues.

Small, self-supporting farmers enjoyed the shelter afforded by primitiveness. The peasant plot on the *massif central,* with no tractor to lie idle and no more than one horse to attract the German army purchasing agent, could probably still turn out the mediocre living it had produced in 1939, provided the sons were not in a German prisoner-of-war camp. By 1942 that mediocre living was worth a king's ransom. Moreover, the chances for lucrative sales in a world with nothing to buy probably improved the cash position of many small farmers. The main enemy was the age-old one, the predatory and inquisitive state.[71]

Industrialists can hardly be described as flourishing in an economy whose total production ranged from a half to a third of the mediocre prewar level of 1938. All business sectors, however, enjoyed the benefits of Vichy corporatist self-regulation, the limiting of competition through universal cartels, and the dismantling of organized labor. Some businesses were "more equal than others," of course. Scarce raw materials were allocated by the state (the Offices de Répartition in the Vichy zone, the German military government economic branch at the Hotel Majestic in the Occupied Zone) according to clear priorities. Firms engaged in war production for Germany boomed, while nonessential industries were starved for materials, stripped of machinery, drained of workmen. A look at production figures for the occupation years in the *Annuaire statistique* shows where the favors lay. The new aluminum industry was producing more than

---

[71] For the wartime position of French farmers, see Pierre Barral, *Les Agrariens de Méline à Pisani* (Paris, 1966), Gordon Wright, *Rural Revolution in France* (Stanford, Calif., 1964), and Michel Cépède, *Agriculture et alimentation en France pendant la IIe guerre mondiale* (Paris, 1961). Thirty-six percent of prisoners of war were from the agricultural sector. *Mouvement économique 1938–46,* 63.

before the war, as were the energy industries—electricity, gas, petroleum. Wood and building materials worked at 70–90 percent of prewar levels. Next, at levels below prewar figures, but still above average, came metallurgy and the transformation of metals. By contrast, textiles, leather goods, chemicals, and paper limped along at barely a third of 1938 business levels. The rubber industry was simply unable to get raw materials. By and large, the most concentrated and rationalized sectors, those dominated by a handful of major firms—automobiles, aircraft, aluminum, steel—were in the forefront of this forced-draft boom. The most dispersed, fragmented, and antiquated sectors of industry, by and large, were among those further discriminated against.[72]

The stock and bond markets were also up after the bad years of the 1930's. State bonds were all up over par during the occupation for the first time since World War I. Many issues were at their highest level since 1931. The stock market also moved upward. Since these gains for investors and *rentiers* seem to have run ahead of losses due to inflation, at least at first, they help explain how Finance Minister Yves Bouthillier could take pride in the "relative financial stability" that he claimed the armistice had permitted him to assure.[73]

There were even some illicit fortunes founded. It was open season on Jewish properties that were sold off cheaply. Better still, one might become *administrateur provisoire* of the property of Jews who had fled to the unoccupied zone or abroad and milk it for quick profits. Restitution could not always be made after the war if, for example, there was no one left to repay. There was also the black market and even the possibilities of exploiting the Resistance. We are now in the murky underworld of Vichy profiteering, where documentation is totally lacking. Although there were some prosecutions for illicit wartime fortunes after the war, nothing concrete has been made public.

---

[72] Production figures for the occupation period, organized by industry, appear in Institut National de la Statistique et des Etudes Economiques, *Annuaire statistique,* vol. 57 (1946), Résumé rétrospectif, 100–7.

[73] State bond quotations appear in the *Annuaire statistique, 1946,* 149–57, along with selected stock prices. Yves Bouthillier, *Le Drame l'armistice* (Paris, 1950), 12.

At the top, Vichy's elite lived well. Laval had amassed his fortune between the wars. The High Court of Justice, with all its unseemly courtroom vituperation of the man, could find no blatant graft in his wealth. As owner of the chateau of the village of Châteldon, where he had grown up as the innkeeper's son, a few miles from Vichy, Laval enjoyed showing visitors about his acres, mud on boots, pointing out depredations made by the British in the Hundred Years War. His great pleasure was the table, and the country restaurants along the Allier River near Vichy seem to have been able to oblige.

Darlan enjoyed more conspicuous ostentation. An impressive villa near Toulon bought from a Jewish family by the Oeuvres Sociales de la Marine as a rest home for Navy personnel, was actually fitted out at a cost of eight million francs for Darlan's private use. Its sumptuous furniture made the Cour des Comptes doubt the Navy's postwar story that the villa was meant to be a clandestine Mediterranean command post.[74]

Marshal Pétain lived in personal austerity at the Hotel du Parc in Vichy. He was paid, however, in the coin of adulation. Delegations of scouts, veterans, artisans, and peasants crowded his anterooms. Enthusiastic crowds greeted his travels. He indulged his taste for fatherly aphorism in radio and newspaper messages. Despite some attempts to limit the practice, his name was attached to streets, squares, and most of the major public works commenced during Vichy: the one steamship launched during the occupation, the great suspension bridge begun across the Seine at Tancarville. Admirers bought him a fine Burgundy vineyard and renamed it the Clos du maréchal.[75] Above all, his cabinet and press reminded him daily that he was his country's savior.

Large sums in secret funds and subsidies went to favored officials and editors. Most of these were the Paris embassy's hangers-on, however, rather than Vichy personnel. Of all the ministers and secretaries of state brought before the High Court

[74] Cour des Comptes, *Rapport au président de la république pour les années 1940–44* (Paris, 1945), 8.
[75] Cour des Comptes, *Rapport au président de la république pour les années 1940–44,* (Paris, 1945), 22.

of Justice after the Liberation, only Fernand de Brinon, the journalist and founder of the Comité France-Allemagne who became Laval's agent in Paris in 1940 and then the official Vichy government delegate in Paris, seems to have benefited from large-scale corruption. He was arrested at Nancy with his Jewish wife in 1944 with nearly 5,000,000 francs in cash and jewelry valued at 850,000 francs. M. Caujolle, the court's financial expert, established that the de Brinons had lived far beyond their income before and after 1940, with country homes, servants, and thoroughbred horses, without finding exactly where it had all come from. Joseph Darnand, too, was rumored to have profited from the legendary "treasure of the Milice." [76] The conspicuous high-livers of occupied Paris, such as the actress Corinne Luchaire, daughter of Jean Luchaire, *Nouveaux temps* editor and president of the Paris press association, were major recipients of Otto Abetz' press funds.

Vichy's favoritism was nothing as simple and vulgar as graft, however. By and large, the Vichy elite was highly professional and financially correct. The Vichy regime spread its favors by the subtler play of economic and social policy. The regime is hierarchical, Marshal Pétain never tired of saying. It was hierarchical in its profits and losses as well as in the allocation of power. Vichy spoiled the rich.

A Moral Balance Sheet

THERE IS, FINALLY, A GRAVE MORAL CASE TO BE MADE against the Vichy elite. There is, first of all, the charge of using the defeat of 1940 for narrowly sectarian purposes, to seek revenge upon the Popular Front and to remake France along new lines, no less partisan than the old and in the service of narrower interests. This does not mean that they had plotted the defeat of France in advance. But their domestic enmities were so

[76] For Brinon, *Les Procès de la collaboration* (Paris, 1948), 81–87; for Darnand, ibid., 279, 317, 319.

all-consuming, after four years of the Popular Front and its successors, that they committed the most elementary of political errors. They wrote new laws under an armed foreign occupation.

There is also the charge of abetting the further internal division of France. No other major occupied country entered the war so torn; no other major occupied country used the occupation as the occasion for such a substantial restructuring of domestic institutions. When biographies of Marshal Pétain began to appear in 1966, it became regular practice to blame the poisons of division attending the Liberation upon de Gaulle's rigorous sectarianism and the upwelling of revenge encouraged by Resistance lawlessness.[77] A will to healing reconciliation co-existed within the Liberation forces alongside a well-justified determination to purge and punish the collaborators, however. It was most visible in the Liberation army, a successful amalgam of Armistice Army, Free French, and Forces Françaises Libres under two ex-Pétiniste officers (Marshals de Lattre de Tassigny and Juin) and one Gaullist officer (Marshal Leclerc de Hauteclocque). If that will to reconciliation did not prevail over the will to revenge in 1944, it was very largely because the Vichy regime had not been the mere caretaker regime in 1940–44 that its defenders claim. Vichy waged another round in the virtual French civil war of the 1930's. Then, its geopolitical gamble having failed and war having ended neither in German victory nor in a French-mediated compromise but in total Allied victory, Vichy reaped the winds of sectarian passion that it had sown.

There is, finally, the issue of complicity. Continually repurchasing its shadow sovereignty at a higher and higher price, the Vichy regime made many Frenchmen accomplices in acts and policies that they would not normally have condoned. Marshal Pétain, in particular, was a figure to whom millions of Frenchmen looked with more than usual confidence. After the total occupation of France in November 1942, or at least after the constitutional crisis of November–December 1943, it was time to cease lending the stamp of one's approval to an enterprise that

[77] See, for example, Georges Blond, *Pétain* (Paris, 1966); Jean Tournoux, *Pétain et De Gaulle* (Paris, 1966); Guy Raïssac, *Un Combat sans Merci* (Paris, 1966).

no longer worked. "Old age is a shipwreck," as de Gaulle observed, but Germans who met Petain in 1943 still found him fresh and alert.[78] Moreover, he was surrounded by men whose brilliance of preparation and of administrative career made them superior to the Third Republic leadership of the late 1930's. These able and intelligent men led other Frenchmen deeper into complicity with the besieged Third Reich's last desperate paroxysms: the Final Solution, forced labor, reprisals against a growing resistance. What can explain such egregious choices?

Tactical motives, the hope of saving France from worse, can not explain that complicity after November 1942. Of the four elements composing the Vichy bargaining position—military defeat, continuation of others in the war, the stranglehold of German occupation upon the richest two-thirds of France, and the exclusion from German grasp of the French fleet and empire—only the last one was ever within Vichy's control. After the total occupation of France, the scuttling of the French fleet, and the return of French North Africa to war in November 1942, Vichy no longer had even that leverage. Life was clearly no easier for Frenchmen by then than for the totally occupied Western European countries.

Clearly other motives led Frenchmen deeper into that final complicity. Bureaucratic inertia and blindness to considerations beyond the efficiency of the state were among them. Beyond that was the attraction of the National Revolution for its partisans.

At bottom, however, lay a more subtle intellectual culprit: fear of social disorder as the highest evil. Some of France's best skill and talent went into a formidable effort to keep the French state afloat under increasingly questionable circumstances. Who would keep order, they asked, if the state lost authority? By saving the state, however, they were losing the nation. Those who cling to the social order above all may do so by self-interest or merely by inertia. In either case, they know more clearly what they are against than what they are for. So blinded, they perform jobs that may be admirable in themselves but are tinc-

[78] See the Krug-Pétain meetings of 9 February 1943 (T-120/1832 H/ 418618–20) and 22 August 1943 (T-120/3546 H/E022155–56).

tured with evil by the overall effects of the system. Even Frenchmen of the best intentions, faced with the harsh alternative of doing one's job, whose risks were moral and abstract, or practicing civil disobedience, whose risks were material and immediate, went on doing the job. The same may be said of the German occupiers. Many of them were "good Germans," men of cultivation, confident that their country's success outweighed a few moral blemishes, dutifully fulfilling some minor blameless function in a regime whose cumulative effect was brutish.

Readers will prefer, like the writer, to recognize themselves in neither of these types. It is tempting to identify with Resistance and to say, "That is what I would have done." Alas, we are far more likely to act, in parallel situations, like the Vichy majority. Indeed, it may be the German occupiers rather than the Vichy majority whom Americans, as residents of the most powerful state on earth, should scrutinize most unblinkingly. The deeds of occupier and occupied alike suggest that there come cruel times when to save a nation's deepest values one must disobey the state. France after 1940 was one of those times.

APPENDICES,
BIBLIOGRAPHICAL NOTE,
AND INDEX

Appendix A
The War Question of January 1942

No Vichy controversy better illustrates the pitfalls of seizing a few documents out of context than the war question of January 1942. Otto Abetz' July 1943 memoir, published as *Pétain et les allemands: Mémorandum d'Abetz sur les relations franco-allemandes* (Paris, 1945), claimed that Vichy had wanted to declare war on the Allies following Pearl Harbor, in exchange for political concessions, but that Hitler had missed that opportunity. The prosecution before the High Court of Justice, following up this lead, got French military justice officials in Germany to look for corroboration. They unearthed Abetz' telegram no. 126 to Ribbentrop of 13 January 1942 (now microfilmed as T-120/405/214258–60 and T-120/898/291966–68) reporting that a rump session of the Vichy cabinet (Pétain, Darlan, Moysset, Romier, Bouthillier, Pucheu, with Benoist-Méchin also present) voted on January 11 in favor of declaring war on the Allies. In November 1945 a sealed dossier of thirty-eight documents that Benoist-Méchin had given Darlan, probably in April 1942, turned up at the Quai d' Orsay. It contained, among other papers about Franco-German relations in 1941 and 1942, two letters by Benoist-Méchin to Darlan, dated 9 and 12 January 1942, concerning French readiness to declare war on the Allies in exchange for a "profound modification" of the current Franco-German relationship. These documents figured prominently in the later trials, such as those of Jacques Benoist-Méchin and Yves Bouthillier. Pétain was also interrograted in his prison on the Ile d'Yeu in January 1947, revealing that the old man was by now genuinely senile (see the report in *Le Monde,* 19 January 1947).

The full sequence of Franco-German government relations (best followed in Ernst von Weizsäcker's "Frankreich" file, vol. 6, T-120/405) for this period puts the whole affair into perspective. It is true that Hitler began to reopen the French question in December 1941–January 1942, with Rommel being pressed toward the frontiers of Tunisia, as he always did when he needed something from France. It is also true that Darlan and Pétain, as always, were no less eager than in the fall of 1941 for a sweeping Franco-German settlement. The entry of the United States into the war on 7 December 1941 introduced the new issue of whether France would break relations or not, but the January 1942 negotiation should be seen as the last gasp of the Protocols of Paris maneuvers rather than merely as a response to the American entry into the war. The final essential point is that the January 1942 negotiation was the work of subordinates, Abetz and Benoist-Méchin, who were disavowed by superiors on both sides.

Otto Abetz found his fortunes at a low ebb following the final failure of the postprotocol negotiations at the end of 1941 and the misunderstanding of the Pétain-Goering meeting on December 1 at Saint-Florentin. Back in Germany for consultations, he had a rare meeting with Hitler on January 5, 1942. This heady experience seems to have prompted him to mount a major diplomatic scheme of his own. Hitler, who wanted the use of Bizerte for aid to Rommel, seems to have mused about the possibilities of meeting Darlan and of negotiating a peace settlement with France in the event of a French entry into war against the Allies. For the moment, however, even a French rupture of diplomatic relations was put off for further consideration. (See Abetz' report to Ribbentrop of this meeting, T-120/405/214238–39, and *Mémorandum d'Abetz,* 128–39.) Hitler may have been tempted by the idea of shifting occupation forces from France to the Russian front.

Back in Paris on January 9, Abetz sought out Jacques Benoist-Méchin, the prewar propagandist for a French understanding with Hitler who was now Secretaire-général à la vice-présidence du conseil and Darlan's roving negotiator with the Germans. Hitler's rather hypothetical musings now blossomed into a firm four-point offer. If France was ready to "march with us to the end of the conflict," there could be a "profound modification" of the current Franco-German status, preliminary accord over a peace treaty, study of material and economic means France would need to meet her new responsibilities and of the best way to present the matter to French public opinion. If the French were agreed in principle (and Hitler did not want an immediate French declaration of war), Hitler, Abetz said, was "ready to grant a Treaty of Peace which will astonish the French." Benoist-Méchin reported this proposal, perhaps further inflated, in his letter of 9 January to Darlan [see text in *Procès Benoist-Méchin* (Paris, 1948), 340–46]. He asked for a reply by the following Monday.

There is no reason to doubt that these issues were indeed discussed at Vichy. A sweeping settlement was just what Darlan had been working for since February 1941. General Juin had just been in Berlin working out what would happen if Rommel had to withdraw into Tunisia, thus bringing the North African desert war onto French soil. Pétain had just seen Goering, with a fat dossier of concessions the French wanted in exchange for their cooperation in such matters. The reply that Benoist-Méchin brought back on 12 January (see text in *Procès Benoist-Méchin,* 347–49) was affirmative in general principles but surrounded by all sorts of qualifications. Benoist-Méchin pointed out to Abetz that in no case could France be drawn into operations that would require total or partial mobilization. Vichy was apprehensive about too quick action. A solution must move by stages, with clear material and psychological preparation in advance. Benoist-Méchin talked mostly about African operations, to which he said Vichy was already committed by Pétain's agreement about Rommel. In other words, the same Vichy plea for caution and for concessions that would strike public opinion in the eye, coupled with an interest in an overall settlement. There was no mention of immediate French war on the Allies.

The French were interested in what they were told was Hitler's new mood; Abetz now had to get Ribbentrop interested. In his telegram of 13 January (T-120/405/214258–60), Abetz reported having given Benoist-Méchin "his own" opinion of overall Franco-German relations —i.e., he recognized his own initiative in what had been presented to the French as an offer from Hitler. Then he said that France was "ripe for a discussion of fundamental questions." Unlike the case in 1941, he said, the French were ready for negotiations without political preconditions. Abetz said he had never mentioned a preliminary peace to the French. But the French had "unanimously" decided to declare war on Britain and the United States in return for "satisfactory status" after the war.

Abetz had consistently misrepresented the terms of his conversation, first to the French, then to his own superiors. Neither government went any further with it. Hitler's thoughts about some possible French solution to both his North African and Russian front problems, if they were anything more than figments of Abetz' imagination, were fleeting. Rommel had begun to advance again in early January. Darlan, on his side, made it clear to Schleier on 29 January that he could see no German interest in a French declaration of war upon the Allies. France, he said, would declare war on the Allies only if the Allies invaded the empire. See Schleier (Paris) 423 to Abetz (Berlin) 30 January 1942 (T-120/405/214294–95). Hitler still rejected cooperation with France that would purchase a soft peace. See the Goebbels Diaries, 7 March 1942.

Benoist-Méchin was left high and dry. He kept asking Abetz what had happened to the "constructive" French answer, which he understood had been relayed to the German military high command (Benoist-Méchin note to Abetz, 25 March 1942, *Procès,* 351). Abetz' influence continued to diminish with Ribbentrop, who finally told him on 25 November 1942 to "cease all activity in the domain of political developments and Franco-German relations, and take no personal initiatives." (Ribbentrop 1475 of 25 November 1942, T-120/928/297469–71; also text of telephone message in *Ministère public c/Bouthillier,* fascicule 4, 116).

Appendix B
Glossary of French and German Abbreviations

CDJC	Centre de documentation juive contemporaine, Paris
CFLN	Comité français de libération nationale
CFTC	Confédération française des travailleurs chrétiens
CGT	Confédération générale du travail
CGTU	Confédération générale du travail unitaire
CO	Comité d'organisation
DFCAA	Délégation française auprès de la commission allemande d'armistice
DGFP	Documents on German Foreign Policy
ENA	Ecole nationale d'administration
FRUS	Foreign Relations of the United States
LFC	Légion française des combattants
OKH	Oberkommando des Heeres
OKW	Oberkommando der Wehrmacht
SFIO	Section française de l'internationale ouvrière
SD	Sicherheitsdienst
SNI	Syndicat national des instituteurs
STO	Service du travail obligatoire
UNC	Union nationale des combattants
UFC	Union fédérale des combattants

Bibliographical Note

I shall not make a tedious list of all the materials used in the preparation of this book. Readers interested in the specialized bibliography of particular questions should consult the footnotes at appropriate passages. Even the general reader, however, needs to know that authentic sources of information about Vichy France are both abundant and uneven. They are abundant because the subject is nearly contemporary; they are uneven because the French government still, at this writing, closes official Vichy papers to research.

That is a revealing fact in itself. When a regime is defeated and discredited, its innermost secrets are likely to be pawed over sacrilegiously by the victors. It is a mark of the essential administrative continuity of France through war, occupation, and Liberation that Vichy's public records passed in uninterrupted confidentiality from one regime to its enemy and successor. In many cases the custodians were the same person. The full record of how policy was made, upon what grounds and after what dissensions, is no more accessible for Vichy than for the later Third Republic.

That seemed to me insufficient reason to renounce scholarly interest in a period as much in need of demythologizing as Vichy France. At best, a historian must pit his ingenuity against imperfect sources, and there is already more authentic Vichy material available than one man can cover in a lifetime. The results of Vichy domestic policies are clearly visible, for the regime made no secret of most of them. As for foreign policy, French officials can be followed virtually hour by hour as they dealt with officials of Germany and the United States.

Even the inner workings of the Vichy official world are not altogether closed. One government agency, the Commissariat aux Questions Juives, had no successor to take custody of its archives. Integral runs of a substantial part of its working papers can be followed at the Bibliothèque de Documentation Juive Contemporaine in Paris. Since the Commissariat received all sorts of ministerial memoranda, this archive's interest extends well beyond the question of Vichy Jewish policy.

The papers of the French delegation to the German Armistice Commission at Wiesbaden have also been published: Délégation française auprès de la Commission Allemande d'armistice, *Recueil de documents publié par le gouvernement français,* 5 vols. (Paris, 1947–59). The Armistice Commission was entrusted with applying the armistice to France at the beginning, when everyone expected a brief interim period of purely technical negotiation. Its deliberations are the essential source for Vichy high policy in the early months, though less so after spring 1941. The editors omitted some major pieces from the first volumes, but fortunately the later volumes, edited in more serene days, went back and picked up some very interesting 1940 material. The gaps can be filled from the German archives and from a typed set of minutes kept by the French delegation's economic branch: Délégation Française auprès de la Commission Allemande pour l'Economie, "Comptes-rendus des réunions du 1er juillet 1940 au 5 août," 10 vols. A set of these minutes is found in the Bibliothèque de Documentation Internationale et Contemporaine, in Paris.

The curtain has been further lifted by the postwar trials of Vichy leaders. These have been the main source for such standard works as Robert Aron, *Histoire de Vichy* (Paris, 1954), translated as *The Vichy Regime*. In principle, all Vichy cabinet members came before a special High Court of Justice set up in 1944, 108 cases in all. Lesser figures were tried in regional Courts of Justice and Chambres civiques, 124,751 cases in all.[1] Transcripts of the public sessions of some of the major trials have been published: Pétain, Laval, Benoist-Méchin, Brinon, Darnand, Pucheu, and Vallat (excerpts) before the High Court of Justice; Marras before the regional Court of Justice at Lyon. Notes on

---

[1] Peter Novick, *The Resistance Versus Vichy* (New York, 1968). See also the work of the High Court's second-presiding judge, Louis Noguères, *La Haute Cour de la Libération* (Paris, 1965).

some of the other public sessions are deposited in the Bibliothèque de Documentation Internationale et Contemporaine. The original trial records are held at the National Archives in Paris.

No doubt these trial records are the richest single source for the regime's inner workings, but they must be used with great care. They contain isolated nuggets rather than whole veins of contemporary letters and papers, placed in artificial contexts by the trial proceedings. For the prosecution wanted only to prove that the accused's acts fit the penal code definition of the crime of which he was accused, such as "transactions with the enemy." He was likely to bring forward in public session only those fragments of documents that strengthened his case. The defense, by contrast, presented character testimony more than documents and minimized his client's role in decision-making. Neither party addressed himself to historians' questions: a sustained analysis of the defendant's thoughts and actions.

So far we have talked only about the final hearings of these trials, the public sessions. Far more valuable to a historian would be the preliminary arraignment sessions (*instructions*) during which the accused was confronted for the first time with a far wider range of documents. Of course, the whole dossier prepared for the prosecution would be the most valuable source of all. It will be a long time before these most sensitive materials are opened to research. In the meantime, President Louis Noguères of the High Court of Justice has published an extremely important selection of materials from Pétain's prosecution dossier: *Le Véritable procès du maréchal Pétain* (Paris, 1955).

The publications of the regime also provide a great wealth of completely unclassified material. Used with elementary attention to the rules of evidence, the Vichy press is very revealing. The regime and its supporters went to great pains to say what they wanted the public to think. The Vichy press was dominated by traditionalists, who wrote without inhibition in their long-awaited triumph. Researchers using the Vichy press must remember that other interests and other attitudes were actually more quietly decisive, especially in economic and social matters. The Vichy press was subject to guidance rather than prior censorship, with penalties for those who ignored the guidance. An important record of press guidance is the collection of daily instructions to editors published after the war by Pierre Limagne of the Catholic daily *La Croix—Ephémérides de quatres années tragiques,* 4 vols. (Paris, 1945–48). These instructions applied, of course, to the Vichy zone. The press of Paris and the Occupied Zone were more directly under German command. A survey of the Paris press, with excerpts, is conveniently published in Michèle Cotta, *La Collaboration* (Paris, 1964). There is unfortunately no companion volume in this excellent "Kiosque" series on the Vichy press.

Vichy government publications reveal a great deal about the motives and aims of internal policy. Decrees and laws continued to appear in the *Journal officiel,* even though there were no longer parliamentary debates. Each major ministry published its circulars and instructions in a *Bulletin officiel.* Personnel and policy changes may be followed in the *annuaires* of the main high civil service organs such as prefectoral corps, Council of State, and Inspectorate of Finance. Law professors commented upon current legislation exhaustively in the bulletins of the main legal publishing houses, Dalloz and Sirey. All these official and semiofficial publications reveal more about Vichy domestic policy than one might think, for the bureaucracy was applying reforms that it was convinced were both legitimate and permanent. The Cour des Comptes' postwar review of Vichy finances, *Rapport au président de la république, années 1940–45* (Paris, 1947), is another rich source.

Vichy can not really be seriously studied without attention to the German archives captured by the Allies at the end of the war. Only here can high policy be followed from day to day with every decision imbedded in its full context. Only here can Vichy initiative be disentangled from German *diktat.* Most of the papers were microfilmed before the originals were returned to Bonn in the early 1960's. Sets of these microfilms are available in the United States National Archives in Washington and the Public Record Office in London.

The essential starting point for work in the German Foreign Office papers is George O. Kent, *A Catalog of Files and Microfilms of the German Foreign Ministry Archives, 1920–45* (Stanford, Calif., 1962). The files entitled "Akten betreffend Frankreich" or "Beziehungen Frankreich-Deutschland, 1938–44" kept by Staatssekretär Ernst von Weizsäcker, the top career official in the German Foreign Office throughout the war years, contain the heart of the matter: Abetz's telegrams from Paris, records of every important discussion between Vichy and German officials, memoranda on Foreign Office policy decisions. There is important additional information here and there in the files of Unterstaatssekretär Woermann, Ambassador Ritter, and the Foreign Office economic experts Clodius and Wiehl. The files of the German embassy in Paris add rich details on daily relations between Abetz and his French contacts as well as German reports on what they thought was going on at Vichy. The files of the German Armistice Commission at Wiesbaden, the Waffenstillstandskommission, should also be used to supplement the published French delegation papers.

The German military papers are equally essential. Here one can find his way with the aid of mimeographed "Guides to German Records Microfilmed at Alexandria, Virginia," available from the U.S. National Archives in Washington. German military records concerning France are indexed principally in no. 12 (Records of Headquarters, the German Army High Command, Part I), nos. 17–19 (Records of Headquarters, German Armed Forces High Command, Parts II, III, IV), and no. 30 (Records of Headquarters, German Army High Command, Part III).

Such archival riches mean that German policy toward France has been studied in Germany with a thoroughness little reflected in French works. The most recent work of synthesis is Eberhard Jäckel, *Frankreich in Hitlers Europa* (Stuttgart, 1966), translated as *La France dans l'Europe de Hitler* (Paris, 1968). Its comprehensive bibliography is the best current guide to other German works.

The United States Department of State also kept a close watch on French affairs. A very full selection of reports to Washington from the embassy at Vichy, together with conversations in Washington with Ambassador Henry-Haye and departmental memoranda concerning France, are published in the series *Foreign Relations of the United States* for the years 1940–43. Those who examine the State Department's raw files for those years will find nothing of importance omitted. William L. Langer, *Our Vichy Gamble* (New York, 1947), is still the most lucid statement of the State Department's perspectives at that time.

The British Foreign Office papers for the wartime period are now opening for research. In the meantime, one may consult Sir Ernest Llewellyn Woodward's semiofficial *British Foreign Policy in the Second World War,* volumes in progress, London, 1970–

The United States National Archives also has microfilms of some captured Italian documents: reports of the Ministero della Cultura Populare and reports on the work of the Franco-Italian Armistice Commission (U.S. National Archives Microcopy No. T-586). These deal mainly with matters of everyday detail.

Published works on Vichy run heavily to participants' memoirs or rely largely upon them. The historian of Vichy France should read these tendentious memoirs only after a thorough steeping in authentic contemporary materials. They were written under the pressure of threats to liberty, property, and even life. Without exception, their main historical value today is the light they cast upon their authors' efforts at rehabilitation and the kinds of alibis used. Their sheer bulk and their entrenched legends are a serious barrier to comprehension.

Some scholarly work is beginning to appear, however. This highly selective account will mention only recent serious works. The best-informed general French account is Henri Michel, *Vichy: Année 40* (Paris, 1966), which begins to reflect work done in the German archives. The works of Stanley Hoffmann are essential to understanding the significance of Vichy for French society. See his contribution to *In Search of France* (Cambridge, Mass., 1963); "Aspects du régime de Vichy," *Revue française de science politique* (January–March 1956); "Collaborationism in Vichy France," *Journal of Modern History* 40:3 (September 1968).

None of the spate of Pétain biographies of the late 1960's (Georges Blond, Pierre Bourget, J.-R. Tournoux) seems to have made any attempt to test its assumptions about collaboration against the German archives. The one Vichy biography that has gotten down to archival bedrock is Geoffrey Warner, *Pierre Laval and the Eclipse of France* (London, 1968). General Weygand has received sympathetic and thorough treatment from a lawyer with access to the papers of the High Court of Justice, Guy Raïssac, *Un Soldat dans la tourmente* (Paris, 1964), and a more balanced assessment by Philip C. F. Bankwitz, *General Weygand and French Civil-Military Relations* (Cambridge, Mass., 1967). Some other scholarly biographies are awaited.

The Vichy economy has now been placed on a firm basis of research by Alan Milward, *The New Order and the French Economy* (Oxford, 1970).

Much light has been cast on agricultural policies by Gordon Wright, *The Rural Revolution in France* (Stanford, Calif., 1964), and Pierre Barral, *Les Agrariens français de Méline à Pisani* (Paris, 1968). Henry W. Ehrmann, *Organized Business in France* (Princeton, New Jersey, 1957), has not been superseded. Neither has his early *French Labor from the Popular Front to the Liberation* (New York, 1946). It can be supplemented by Georges Lefranc, *Les Expériences syndicales en France de 1939 à 1950* (Paris, 1950), whose author drew upon experience in the Labor Ministry at Vichy under René Belin, and the work of a well-informed official, Jacques Desmarest, *La Politique de la main-d'oeuvre en France* (Paris, 1946).

The most useful recent account of the church is Jacques Duquesne, *Les Catholiques français sous l'occupation* (Paris, 1966). See also Emile Poulat, *Naissance des prêtres-ouvriers* (Paris, 1969).

A valuable collection of primary material on Vichy policy toward Jews has been published in a somewhat undigested fashion by Joseph

Billig, *Le Commissariat français aux questions juives,* 3 vols. (Paris, 1955–60). The most widely used general works—Gerald Reitlinger, *The Final Solution,* 2d ed. (London, 1968), and Raul Hilberg, *The Destruction of the European Jews* (Chicago, 1961)—make the unwarranted assumption that German pressure coerced Vichy into action.

Local government under Vichy is a potentially rich vein for study. A useful institutional manual is the work of a prefectoral official, Pierre Doueil, *L'Administration locale à l'épreuve de la guerre* (Paris, 1950). Michel Baudot, *L'Opinion publique sous l'occupation* (Paris, 1955), is limited, despite its title, to the Eure department. Aimé Autrand, president of the prefects' professional association, had access to some police files for *Le Département de Vaucluse de la défaite à la libération* (Avignon, n.d. [1965]). A model local social history, William A. Christian, Jr., *Divided Island: Faction and Unity on Saint-Pierre* (Cambridge, Mass., 1969), shows how the Pétain–de Gaulle split on a small French island off Newfoundland reopened old cleavages between a declining traditional society and a modern economic sector.

The Vichy forces of order have hardly been examined. There is no work on the police, but the more sensational Milice has been treated by the free-lance author J. Delperrie de Bayac, *La Milice, 1918–45* (Paris, 1969). My own *Parades and Politics at Vichy* (Princeton, N.J., 1966) assesses the social and political role of army officers in the regime.

Education at Vichy still awaits serious attention. Political and social attitudes are suggestively discussed in the aforementioned works of Stanley Hoffmann, while H. Stuart Hughes, *The Obstructed Path* (New York, 1968), examines some of the major intellectual figures active during these years. For the 1930's intellectual background, one should consult Jean Touchard, "L'Esprit des années 30," in *Tendances politiques de la vie française depuis 1789* (Paris, 1960); Pierre Andreu, "Les Idées politiques de la jeunesse intellectuelle de 1927 à la guerre," in Académie des sciences morales et politiques, *Comptes-rendus* (1957), 17–35; and Jean-Louis Loubet del Bayle, *Les Non-conformistes des années 30* (Paris, 1969).

Other neglected Vichy subjects include the bureaucracy, many aspects of business activity and economic policy, and colonial relations.

Finally, the atmosphere of those dreadful years grows more and more elusive for the young and the foreign. Here fiction is more helpful than memoirs. In my opinion, no one has matched the sardonic *A Bon beurre,* translated as *The Best Butter,* of Jean Dutourd, the moving *Les Forêts de la Nuit* of Jean-Louis Curtis, or the same author's novel of postwar divisions, *Les Justes causes.* And at this writing, Paris crowds are standing in line to see an extraordinary film evocation of life in Clermont-Ferrand during the Vichy period, Maurice Ophuls' *Le Chagrin et la pitié*.

Vichy has always aroused passion. Now, as it recedes in time, it should arouse hard thought.

Index

ABOUT THE AUTHOR

Robert O. Paxton was born in Lexington, Virginia, in 1932. He received his B.A. from Washington and Lee University, an M.A. from Oxford University, where he was a Rhodes Scholar, and his Ph.D. from Harvard University. From 1961 to 1967 he taught at Berkeley, and after two years at the State University of New York at Stony Brook is now Professor and Chairman of the History Department at Columbia University. He is the author of *Parades and Politics at Vichy: The French Officer Corps under Marshal Pétain* (Princeton, 1966), *Europe in the Twentieth-Century* (Harcourt, Brace, Jovanovich, 1975), and *Vichy France and the Jews,* with Michael R. Marris (Basic Books, 1981).